FILMMAKERS SERIES

edited by
ANTHONY SLIDE

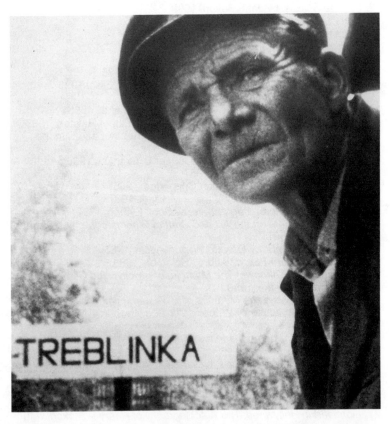

TREBLINKA

Shoah (1985) Museum of Modern Art/Film Stills Archive

THE HOLOCAUST IN FRENCH FILM

by

ANDRÉ PIERRE COLOMBAT

Filmmakers, No. 33

The Scarecrow Press, Inc.
Metuchen, N.J., & London
1993

British Library Cataloguing-in-Publication data available

Library of Congress Cataloging-in-Publication Data

Colombat, André, 1958-
    The Holocaust in French film / by André Pierre Colombat.
        p.   cm. -- (Filmmakers ; no. 33)
    Filmography: p.
    Includes bibliographical references and index.
  ⊍⁄ ISBN 0-8108-2668-2 (alk. paper)
        1. Holocaust, Jewish (1939-1945), in motion pictures. 2.
    Motion pictures--France--History. I. Title. II. Series:
    Filmmakers series ; no. 33.
    PN1995.9.H53C66 1993
    791.43'658--dc20   93-17016

To Pierre-Nicolas, Alban, Stéphanie and Julie

Acknowledgments

I wish to thank Frédéric Bonnaud and Alain Marchand at the Cinémathèque Française, Paris; Nicole Schmitt at the Centre National de la Cinématographie, Bois d'Arcy; and staff at the Motion Picture Library, Washington, D.C., for their help in locating and viewing films both in France and in the United States. I would like to acknowledge the Stills Library at the Museum of Modern Art, New York City, for their willingness to provide me with stills to illustrate this study. I am also very thankful to the "Friends of Le Chambon" and Pierre Sauvage for providing me with stills from the documentary *Weapons of the Spirit*.

Let me express my deep appreciation for the continued support I received from Harry James Cargas, Ilona Klein, and film director Pierre Sauvage. In Baltimore, I thank Ellen Jensen for her close and critical reading of the manuscript, and my colleagues at Loyola College for their inestimable encouragement. Thanks also to Marion Wielgosz and the Word Processing Center at Loyola College for their most valuable assistance.

Finally, I am most grateful to my wife and my family for their unrelenting support and endurance during the composition of this study.

Contents

INTRODUCTION

At the moment I speak to you, the icy water of the
ponds and ruins is filling up the hollows of the charnel
house. A water as cold and murky as our own bad
memories. War is napping, but with one eye always
open.

J. Cayrol and A. Resnais, *Night and Fog*[1]

Each time a national debate about French anti-Semitism or
the responsibility of Vichy France in the extermination of the
European Jews during World War II is fomented by current
events, two opposite reactions arise among those willing to
actively fight bigotry and intolerance. This opposition could be
noticed, for example, after the desecration of the oldest Jewish
graveyard in France, at Carpentras, on May 8, 1990. On one
hand, many feel that anti-Semitism is still alive because France
never really dealt with its past and its anti-Semitic heritage.[2] On
the other hand, many others feel that too much attention has been
paid to this controversy, in particular by the media, allowing on
many occasions various anti-Semites to create a false debate in
order to find publicity for their "theses." Consequently, French
anti-Semitism and its responsibilities in the Holocaust appear
paradoxically to be one of the taboo subjects about which the
French have continually argued at least since the early seventies.

Depending on their focus, French historians insist either on
the lack of academic consideration for this subject (like Pierre
Vidal-Naquet) or on its obsessive aspect in French debates and
public opinion (like Henry Rousso or Michel Winock). Marc
Ferro has also recalled that, except in 1914, France "fought no
war that was not sooner or later cross-bred into civil-war. The
second World War is an obvious case in point." (Ferro, 1984:

105) Consequently, French officials have always seemed to fear open national debates about history in general and French history in particular. In a very recent example, just before the Gulf War started, the French Minister of Culture asked the media to use their "good taste," their "common sense" and the "sense of balance" in their broadcasts. Consequently, lists of "chansons à risque," "hazardous songs" to avoid playing were made by various radios and local authorities—i.e. songs alluding to war, the Arabs or the Jews, songs by popular Arab singers, etc.[3] The airing of the eight episode mini-series *Au nom de tous les miens*, based on the story of the survival of the Polish-American Jew Martin Gray in the Warsaw Ghetto and in Treblinka, was interrupted.

It is to be recalled that, regarding the difficulties in dealing openly with history, anti-Semitism, and the Holocaust in particular, France is not an exception. As Michaël Marrus noted, the specificity of the extermination of the Jews was largely neglected worldwide by historians themselves until the trial of Adolf Eichmann in Jerusalem in 1961. It is only after that date that the word Holocaust started being widely used to differentiate the Shoah from other genocides (Marrus, 12-13). Of course, this is not to say that the general public in France was ignorant of Vichy's persecution of the Jews nor of the so-called "Final Solution." They were generally seen as a chapter in the general history of the deportations, a series of atrocities worse than many others but they were also considered somewhat as an anomaly or an abnormality outside European history itself and specific to a sort of Nazi madness. Consequently, until recently, the Holocaust was paid very little attention in history textbooks. In contrast, the history of the Résistance developed at a much faster pace, mostly under the path opened by the "Comité d'Histoire de la Deuxième Guerre Mondiale"[4] that also ordered the making of Resnais' *Night and Fog* in 1955.

Many survivors witnessed the horrors of the camps and published their testimonies right after the war.[5] Sometimes they described explicitly the French camps as Georges Wellers did, for example, in *De Drancy à Auschwitz* (1946). The most praised of these books on the literary scene was David Rousset's *L'Univers concentrationnaire* (*The Concentrationary Universe*) as it was given the Théophraste Renaudot prize in 1946. At the same time, the Centre de Documentation Juive Contemporaine (CDJC was created clandestinely in 1943) kept on gathering meticulous information about the persecution of the Jews in France.

As Simone Veil recalled on French TV in 1990, survivors like herself told what had happened and what they had seen on their return from the camps, but no one really seemed to be interested in their stories. The vast majority, including many survivors, just wanted to get on with their lives and to put their past behind them as much as possible. Many returning death camp prisoners also felt that one could not really understand or even believe the horror they had witnessed unless one had seen it with his or her own eyes.

Others looked suspiciously at the survivors suggesting that if they had survived either their horrifying stories were not completely true or there might be some "good reasons" why these few were still alive. Then, as was the case with Simone Veil, many survivors felt discouraged and stopped talking about the camps for many years. For most of them, the time for recollections would come much later. It would most often be an extremely painful task conducted mostly for the sake of saving the memory for future generations.

Léon Poliakov's *Le Bréviaire de la haine* and Robert Aron's *Histoire de Vichy* were respectively published in 1951 and 1954 and it was only in the late fifties that major literary works insisted on the specificity of the extermination of the Jews such as Elie Wiesel's *La Nuit* (*The Night*, 1958) and André Schwartz-Bart's *Le Dernier des Justes* (*The Last of the Just*), which received the Goncourt, the most prestigious literary prize in France, in 1959. Creating an often violent controversy, the first scholarly synthesis of the deportations was published only in 1968 with a clear distinction between the concentration camps and the death camps (Olga Wormser's *Le Système concentrationnaire nazi 1933-1945*). Robert O. Paxton's *Vichy France* was finally printed in Paris in 1973. It still is today the most widely praised study of the Occupation and includes a clear evaluation of Vichy's responsibilities in the persecution of the Jews. These dates offer some schematic and very revealing landmarks in the thousands of books published in France about the Second World War. As of now, Robert O. Paxton's and Michaël Marrus' *Vichy et les Juifs* (1981) as well as the seminal work of Serge Klarsfeld gather the most complete description and analysis of the persecution of the Jews in France and the responsibilities of Vichy in the Holocaust.

The representation of the Holocaust in French cinema followed an almost perfectly parallel evolution. In an incomplete and very schematic overview, one could remark that the first films made about the Holocaust in France after the war insisted on depicting what had happened in the camps. These first years could thus be considered a period of documentation in which the Jews were seen as victims among many others. Progressively however, while insisting more and more on the heroic actions of the Résistance, films started reminding audiences that there had been French Collaborators and traitors presented as evil but isolated or abnormal individuals. In this regard, Jean Cayrol's *Le Coup de grâce* (1965) is one of the most significant.

It was not until the early seventies that a real tide of films was made confronting the darkest and most controversial aspects of the Occupation of France by the Nazis. Finally, beginning in the mid-eighties, after the making of *Shoah*, any French film can refer to the Holocaust assuming that most of its audience will be exactly aware of both the specificity of the extermination of the Jews as well as the responsibility of French anti-Semitism in its realization. This does not mean that oblivion, hatred and lies are no longer threatening the memory of the Holocaust. It seems however that since 1989, another trend has started. It will be analyzed at the very end of this study.

It is now well known that, in 1971, Ophüls' film *The Sorrow and the Pity* created an enormous scandal because until then the French had refused to face the wide popularity of Pétain, the responsibilities of Vichy France in the persecution of the Jews and its collaboration with the Nazis. Two more French documentaries, while very different from each other, are often quoted at the same time among the best films ever made on the Holocaust itself or what made it possible: Resnais' *Night and Fog* (1955), and Lanzmann's *Shoah* (1985).

Because of its direct and violent impact on very large audiences at one time, the evolving representation of the Holocaust in French cinema is extremely revealing of the evolution of the various conceptions of French responsibility in the permanence of hatred and anti-Semitism. In consequence, the study of the representation of the Holocaust in French cinema can play a central role in understanding how any society deals or refuses to deal with the darkest and most threatening aspects of its collective psyche.

Although the American and French group of scholars denying the reality of the Holocaust—the so-called "Révisionnistes"—provoked a vast and violent movement of public and official outrage throughout France immediately after its formation in 1978, its very existence verified the fact that certain ideas obviously had not died with the end of the war. Although the actual number of militia men (about 28,500 men at its peak, in 1943), French men in the Waffen SS (7,000 fought in the Charlemagne Division after Sept. 1944), French Legion Volunteers (3,000 men), and official collaborators in France during the war represented a minority, their ghosts still seemed to haunt the contemporary French collective unconscious.

More than forty-five years later, at the end of the eighties, in parallel with the development of the fundamentalist church of Mgr. Lefèbvre (the "intégristes"), the French extreme right had become progressively stronger and the scandals linked to the anti-Semitic declaration of its leaders had multiplied. It is clear that such reawakening is always possible. The war in the Persian Gulf, and recent anti-Semitic actions in the Soviet Union, in Eastern Europe or even in the United States, especially in 1990, have demonstrated that the resurgence of anti-Semitism is far from being limited to the French political theater. In such a context, it seems urgent to remember, re-present and analyze the ideology and the propaganda that gave Fascism and Nazism their formidable power in the past. In this regard also, the necessity to remember and analyze what made possible the extermination of the European Jews by the Nazis plays a key role in the understanding of our own present and the use of racial hatred for political purposes.

In dealing with such questions, French cinema seems to have given a preeminent role to three major questions answered mainly by Resnais', Ophüls' and Lanzmann's films: "What exactly happened?" "How could we allow the Holocaust to take place?" and "What memory of these horrifying events should be kept alive for future generations?" While each one of these questions was asked simultaneously with the two others, their successive dominance seems to characterize rather well the evolution of the general representation of the Holocaust in French cinema from the tragedy of the deportations (1945-1961), to the Holocaust (1961-85), and the Shoah (beginning in the mid-eighties).

Since the time of the Lumière brothers, French cinema has commonly stressed attachment to the individual, inter-personal relationships in a well delimited space, general realism and its analysis of the "effet de réel," reality effect (Martin, 115-116). Because of these characteristics, French cinema seemed to be particularly able to analyze the complexity of the permanence of anti-Semitism as well as the complicities that enable it to develop in a given society. However, until the seventies, French films only alluded to the persecution of the Jews in France. Even the acclaimed "retour au réel," return to the real, and the aesthetic revolution in French cinema provoked by the New Wave did not change this general attitude. It would take the political turmoil of the sixties, the fall of De Gaulle, the total reevaluation of the values of French society and history, before anti-Semitism could be seriously analyzed in French cinema by some marginal and young directors.

It is also to be remembered that when Ophüls' *The Sorrow and the Pity* was shown in Paris in 1971, it was violently attacked mostly by the former Résistants and by the bourgeoisie but also, for opposite reasons, by the fashionably ultra marxist *Cahiers du Cinéma* of the seventies. Michel Foucault admitted that he "sort of liked *The Sorrow and the Pity*," almost excusing himself to his interviewers from the *Cahiers du Cinéma*. He did not think it was "a bad action to make it" (July-August 1974, 8). All of these critics concentrated on the representation of French society presented in the film but not on its consideration of the persecution of the Jews. I will analyze such critics in my chapter on the detailed analysis of this film.

Followed by and sometimes held responsible for the "mode rétro," retro fashion, of the liberal years of President Giscard d'Estaing, Ophüls' film has now become a recognized and much admired classic of French cinema. Fifteen years after this decisive step, French cinema was then confronted with opposite problems as the subject of the Collaboration and the Holocaust were no longer taboo but risked becoming banal or were wrongly assumed to be well-known and therefore ignored. In reaction to what happened in the seventies, Claude Lanzmann explained in the eighties that he felt the need to make his film partly because everyone mistakenly assumed that they already knew enough about the Holocaust and that, in consequence, it was useless to keep on talking about it. Two opposite reasons were alternatively used as excuses not to deal with the same subject: the controlled ignorance in the seventies or a supposed excess of knowledge in the eighties. It is during the same period that the Révisionnistes were put in the lime light by the media.

For these reasons, and despite frequent productions, films about the Holocaust or the Collaboration still appear as controversial exceptions to French cinematographic production in general. The violent conflicts that surrounded the review and the "thesis" of Faurisson, Guillaume, Roques, Notin et al. underlined two enduring problems of recent French history: the French people's difficulties in coming to terms with the responsibilities of Vichy France in the Final Solution and the challenge of representing the reality of the Holocaust and the specificity of the Shoah to any audience.

Indeed it has taken many years before France started investigating French responsibilities in the persecution of the Jews during World War II. In July 1989, in an article of the

French magazine *L'Express*, E. Conan and J.-M. Caradec'h recalled that:

> The trials of Pétain, Laval and Darnan, oriented around the theme of national treason, barely alluded to anti-Semitism and the notion of "crime against humanity" did not exist yet. No French citizen has ever been condemned for his participation in the Final Solution and France has never seriously looked into analyzing these old disgraces (33).

Similar remarks are also developed throughout Henry Rousso's *Le Syndrome de Vichy* (1989). Paul Touvier was arrested on May 24, 1989, forty-five years after the Liberation, after hiding for many years in various convents and, more recently, in Nice under the protection of the French "intégristes," Fundamentalists, of Mgr. Lefèbvre. His trial was still being documented while the continued installation of the Carmelites in Auschwitz and the anti-Semitic declarations of Cardinal Glemp were bringing to its peak a new crisis between the Church and the international Jewish community (Summer 1989). Touvier was the head of the Militia of Lyon, and under this title he was accused of several crimes against humanity. He was tried, acquitted and released from jail in the Spring of 1992, creating a general outrage among the French. His judges found him innocent because the Vichy Regime had never engaged in an open extermination program. In July of the same year, while participating in the official ceremonies for the anniversary of the *Velodrome d'hiver* roundup, French President F. Mitterrand refused to officially apologize for the crimes committed by Vichy because that government never represented the French Republic.[6]

In October of the same year, Doctor Garreta was found responsible for knowingly distributing HIV-infected blood to more than 1,250 hemophiliacs. Thanks to the complexity of French administration and the "understanding" French system of justice, he was condemned to... four years in jail. His deputy Jean-Pierre Allain was sentenced to two years in prison. Professor Jacques Roux, also found guilty, was given a four-year suspended sentence and former public health laboratory director

Dr. Robert Netter was acquitted. No one else was found guilty. When the sentencing was read, Garreta was living and working in Massachusetts. He said he would surrender to the French authorities. He is now in jail in France. This case bears a discouraging resemblance to the Touvier affair in which the French administration and justice systems also proved unable to punish "conscientious officials" and government administrators responsible for murdering hundreds of people, including dozens of children.

In another recent case, the former delegate of the Vichy police in the Occupied Zone, Jean Leguay, to be tried for, among other crimes, the deportation of four thousand fifty-one children to Auschwitz, died at the age of eighty-nine, just before his trial could even start. By comparison, the trial of the German Klaus Barbie was much faster to obtain and document: three years of instruction as opposed to the ten years for Leguay. Three years of instruction were also announced in 1989 for the trial of Touvier. It was precisely through Leguay's trial that Serge Klarsfeld and his wife, the famous Nazi hunters, expected to finally bring to public consideration the role played by the Vichy regime in the Final Solution.[7] Serge Klarsfeld and Richard Liebmann announced in September 1989 that they would also bring to trial René Bousquet, chief of the Vichy police and Leguay's boss. Bousquet was finally indicted during the Spring of 1991.

For the individual, being aware of the degree of guilt of the Nazis and the collaborating police officials remains a relatively simple and necessary task. It is much more complex, however, to define and evaluate the various degrees of responsibility of the French population as a whole. One could argue like Marcel Ophüls that only individual and not collective responsibility exists and that one can only proceed case by case. What complicates matters is the fact that, the same French population widely supported both directly and indirectly a government of collaboration which took a very active part in the persecution and the deportation of the Jews.

The unending debates about the significance of the widespread popular support Pétain and the Vichy government enjoyed constitute only part of the difficulties surrounding the representation of this specific period of French history. Away from these controversies, Claude Lanzmann's *Shoah* (1985) chose to reach the heart of the Holocaust, the extermination process itself, and to analyze how best to communicate or "transmit" the memory of the Shoah in its specificity. However before such a film could be made, French cinema had to overcome many obstacles in order to insist on the necessity of remembering a dreadful past that constantly threatens to be revived from its ashes in France and all over the world.

In this regard, both as a work of art and as the first major documentary made on the Holocaust, *Night and Fog* constitutes a necessary first step. Its primary purpose was to recall what exactly had happened and to protect from total oblivion a crucial but commonly repressed period of our recent history. It can be considered a necessary beginning in the representation of the Holocaust as it analyzes in detail how the Holocaust directly addresses our collective memory as well as the inevitable confrontation of our own individual conscience with "the concentrationary universe" (David Rousset). For this very reason this film had to create its own processes of representation and it is organized as an open work.

At this point, the representation of the Holocaust in French cinema benefitted greatly from the formal research of the avant-garde cinema in France—the New Wave Cinema—during the late fifties and early sixties. Since then, the making of a film or a documentary about the Holocaust should not only be linked to a reflection on cinema as a means of "re-presentation" but also to a study of the "effet de réel," reality effect, that, according to Christian Metz, characterizes it. Consequently, the masterpieces of French cinema dealing with the Holocaust, as opposed to Hollywood productions, are best characterized by their constant and specific efforts in their search for a cinematographic form that would allow them to best communicate the most distinctive aspects of the systematic murder of the European Jews by the Nazis.

Such remarks introduce crucial problems such as the role of the director and the attitude of the audience within the process of representing the Holocaust. The mere act of having seen one of these documentaries makes every spectator responsible for a part of the memory to be saved for future generations. A film about the Holocaust must never constitute just "another good show." It must indicate clearly how the memory of our collective past influences and structures constantly our present and our future. Such a reflection must be at the source of the structure of the film itself, the filming of every shot and the editing itself.

Besides these formal or structural problems, films about the Holocaust are faced with the difficult problem of representing the various attitudes and degrees of guilt of the bystanders. In analyzing the past, one must be careful not to attenuate the responsibilities of the criminals thanks to a historical study indicating that no nation openly tried to stop the Holocaust and that therefore everyone is more or less guilty. For the present and future, it is also essential to try to comprehend how and why entire populations could not or did not want to know more about what was happening to the thousands of Jews being deported for many years from all over Europe. In this respect, cinema can and has only recently started to play a key role, mainly since Ophüls' *The Sorrow and the Pity* (1971). This role is essential considering that, since 1945, the world community has been unable to prevent many other genocides and war crimes throughout the world. For this reason, the purpose of this essay is also to examine how the controversial subjects of the Collaboration and the extermination of the Jews have remained taboo for so many years in what is probably the most popular form of artistic expression.

The persecution and deportation of the Jews in France is of course at the heart of the enduring embarrassment of the French regarding the period of the Occupation. In this respect, the recent history of French cinema provides us not only with a unique key to the study of the progressive exclusion of the Jews from French political and economic life during the war but it also enables us to understand the formation and the persistence of many long lasting taboos.

The organization of the French Collaboration with the occupying army constitutes undoubtedly an extreme example which is central to the analysis of the various attitudes of civilian and military populations towards the persecution of the Jews from World War II to the present. The study of the silence caused by the ignorance, indifference, blindness, terror and different degrees of complicity that made the Holocaust possible is both a collective and very individual problem often consciously and unconsciously repressed. The same is true of the study of the function of remembering the Holocaust for future generations.

PART I

THE EVOLUTION OF THE
REPRESENTATION
OF THE HOLOCAUST

1. Persecution in the "Golden Age" of French Cinema, *1940-1945*

The Holocaust was in great part made possible by the terror, the silence, the indifference, the blindness or the various degrees of complicity surrounding its perpetration as they were imposed or facilitated by the Nazi regime. Because the essence of cinema is to produce images to be shown and sounds and words to be heard, films and documentaries, in general, can be considered as extraordinary tools to ultimately defeat the secret project of the Nazis and the silent serenity of many accomplices. For this reason, the manner in which films represent or avoid representing the Holocaust is of major importance for the protection of the memory of this event itself. Created by fear, indifference and a very efficient self-censorship, the taboos concerning the destiny of the Jews and anti-Semitism reveal an important characteristic that critics often forget to write about when they analyze the continuity of French cinema before, during and after the Occupation.

Most certainly, French cinema did not vanish during the war. However its Jews did while the industry prospered like never before. Key institutions were created like the Comité d'Organisation de l'Industrie Cinématographique (COIC, November 2, 1940), replaced after the Liberation by the "Office Professionnel du Cinéma" (OPC, August 1945) which finally became the Centre National de la Cinématographie (CNC, October 26, 1946) still in existence today. Advance payments to producers were instituted during the war as well as the Legal Deposit of films. The creation of such institutions enabled some excellent films to be made during the Occupation, often in continuation of the so-called "cinema of quality" of the thirties.

Only a few pure propaganda films were made in France and they remained unsuccessful. Pierre Ramelot's *Les Corrupteurs* (1942), a short fiction film, explained how Jews involved in show business took advantage of young, innocent French girls. It was to be shown before the movie feature *Les Inconnus dans la maison* which includes an ambiguous final speech with accents of national socialism and a criminal bearing a Jewish name.[8] Pierre Mamy's (alias Paul Riche) *Forces occultes* (1943) shows a young Representative ("député") finally "realizing" how Freemasons and Jews with their secret rituals progressively "ruined" his homeland. Dr. Tauber's *Le Péril juif* (1942), a German and French propagandist documentary, justified the official anti-Semitic campaigns by explaining how Jews were threatening the whole Western civilization (Polish Jews, wealthy Jews, Jewish politicians, socialist leaders and intellectuals, the Jewish traditions and their influence on culture and the arts, etc.).[9]

The distress and outcry of the population against the occupation of France was also subtly expressed in a few films like *Les Visiteurs du soir* by Marcel Carné (1942), and more directly, *Pontcarral, colonel d'Empire* by Jean Delannoy (1942). Jean Grémillon's *Lumière d'été* and *Le Ciel est à vous* can be interpreted either as reviving French nationalism against the invader or as being merely pro-Vichy films. Critics continue to disagree on the real meaning of these four movies.[10]

Some professionals were and still are indeed very proud of the fact that the politics of collaboration enabled French cinema not only to survive but to prosper. Many thought in 1940 that the defeat of the French army had been so total and so swift that there was no doubt England would soon lose the war and a peace treaty would be signed with Germany. In consequence, the French industry had to be saved to be given a chance in the new European order to come. Others just wished to survive protecting their jobs and waiting for what would come next. Whatever their interpretation of current events, no one seems to question the fact that the continuity of French cinema psychologically helped the French population live through the war by providing a very popular imaginary escape.

These interpretations however overlook the high price that had to be paid for such a continuity. Such arguments often forget that during this period of "getting by" with the politics of

Collaboration, Jewish actors, actresses, directors and producers were constantly persecuted. Many went into exile in the United States or in hiding in the south of France, mainly in Nice which was occupied by the Italians. In these two groups, including Jews and non-Jews, we find the names of Jean Renoir, René Clair, Julien Duvivier, Jacques Feyder, Max Ophüls, Jean Gabin, Charles Boyer, Louis Jouvet, Michèle Morgan, Françoise Rosay, Fritz Lang, Anatole Litvak, Billy Wilder, Marcel Dalio, Robert Stodmak, composer Joseph Kosma, designer Alexander Trauner, Jean Wiéner, director Roger Richebé and many others. Among the greatest directors, only Marcel Carné remained in France.

In a much needed study, Evelyn Ehlirch listed and analyzed most of the main dates marking the evolution of persecution of the Jews in the French cinema industry. With the additional help of Michaël Marrus, Robert O. Paxton, Philippe Bourdrel, Paul Leglise and Raul Hilberg, they can be summarized as such:

1940:

June 15:	First government formed by Pétain (The first of four from June 1940-August 1944)
July:	3,000 French Jews from Alsace are deported to the "Free Zone."
July 22:	Reconsideration of the naturalization of all foreigners since 1927 (6,307 French Jews lose their citizenship)
August 7:	Reopening of the German Embassy in Paris (Ambassador Otto Abetz).
August 16:	Law stating that one has to have had a French father in order to become a medical doctor.
August 27:	Cancellation of the Marchandeau Law prohibiting hate campaigns in the press.
September 27:	First German Ordinance about the Jews in France. The Jews that had fled to the unoccupied zone cannot return. The remaining Jews of the Occupied Zone must be registered (Hilberg, 393).

October 3: The "Status of the Jews" defines who is Jewish for the French state and excludes the Jews from public service and any profession influencing public opinion (teaching, working for the media, cinema, theater, etc.)

October 4: The "Préfets" have the right to put any foreign Jews in "special camps."

October 7: The Jews from Algeria lose their French citizenship.

October 18: Second German Ordinance about the Jews in France. All Jewish businesses must be registered.

October 22: 6,504 Jews are deported from Germany to Lyon. They will arrive in the French camp of Gurs on October 25.

October 26: First law by Pétain regulating French Cinema. Creation of the *carte d'identité professionelle*.

December: The Germans demand that the word *Juif* be put on the identification of every Jew in France.

1941:

February: Film production resumes in France with *L'Assassinat du Père Noël* by Christian Jacque.

April 26: Jews are banned from all professions "involving public contact or authority over Aryan employees."

July-September: New series of anti-Jewish decrees (Paxton *La France de Vichy*, 176)

November 29: Many Jewish businesses are confiscated. The rest are placed under the supervision of an assigned provisional administrator (a total of 41,900 businesses were seized). Creation of the Union Générale des Israelites de France (UGIF) in charge of managing part of the confiscated properties.

1942:

January 1:	Wannsee Conference. Final organization of the systematic extermination of the European Jews.
April:	New government under the direction of Pierre Laval (April 1942-August 1944).
May 5:	Heydrich arrives in Paris for the final organization of mass deportation of the Jews from France. The massive deportations from France to Germany begin.
May 28:	Jews of the occupied zone are required to wear a yellow star.
June 5.	Jews can no longer be members of the film industry.
July:	Systematic arrests of non-French Jews begin.
July 13:	The first deportation train leaves Bordeaux.
July 16-17:	Roundup of the Vélodrome d'Hiver (rafle du Vél' d'Hiv.): 12,884 stateless Jews are arrested with the participation of 9,000 French policemen divided into 888 teams under the direction of Jean Leguay (Bourdrel, 431-438).
November 11:	The German army invades the Unoccupied Zone, including Nice where many had found refuge.

1943:

September:	Jews in hiding in Nice are persecuted as Italy is occupied by the German army. Many Jews working in the cinema industry had until then found refuge in Nice where *Les Enfants du Paradis* was to be shot (Hilberg, 426).

1944:

August 19:	The "Comité de Libération du Cinéma Français" gives the members of the profession the signal to start the insurrection against the occupying armies.

(A minimum of 75,521 Jews were deported
from France to the concentration camps
including 2,000 children below the age of
six, 6,000 below the age of thirteen and
8,700 adults above the age of sixty. Less
than 3,000 returned. Twenty-two percent of
the deported Résistants survived the camps.
Three percent of the Jews did.)

In his monumental work, *The Destruction of the European
Jews*, Raul Hilberg has underlined the fact that the extermination
of the Jews is inscribed in a very old history of persecutions in
which the Roman Catholic church played a major role (Hilberg,
1-17). As the "oldest daughter of the Church," "la fille aînée de
l'Eglise," the country of the infamous Affaire Dreyfus (1898-
1902) and the land that had made a best seller of René
Drumont's anti-Semitic work *La France juive* (1886), France was
no exception to the increase of worldwide anti-Semitism.
However French anti-Semitism is not uniquely linked to the
history of the extreme Right, the Catholic Church, or the
conservative parties. Although not as often as the extreme right,
the left, and especially the Communist party of Maurice Thorez,
had also shown a violent anti-Semitism on many occasions
(Michel Winock, 186-217)

Nine years before the beginning of World War II, the
scandal of Luis Buñuel's *L'Age d'or* provides us with a clear
reminder of what the "real French cinema" ought to be for the
French extreme right of the thirties. In his book on Buñuel, Ado
Kyrou related the event as such:

On the evening of the third (December 1930), some
characters who were not customers came to see the
representation, waiting for the right moment to express
their 'high intellectuality.' On the screen, a character
placed a monstrance in the gutter. Then [in the
audience] screams started: 'We'll see if there are still
Christians left in France!' and 'Death to the Jews!'
smoke bombs exploded, spectators were beaten up, the

screen was stained with violet ink, the furniture was destroyed and paintings by Dali, Max Ernst, Man Ray, Miro and Tanguy shown at the entrance of the theater were torn up. After having interrupted the representation in this way and cutting the telephone wires, demonstrators, the 'commissaires' of the League of Patriots and the representatives of the Anti-Jewish League ran away.[11]

The film was officially prohibited seven days later following a campaign led by two newspapers, Le Figaro and L'Ami du Peuple.

The armistice of 1940 offered the extreme right a clear revenge over the Popular Front of the mid-thirties and the France of the Socialist Jew Léon Blum. The propaganda of the extreme right held the left, the Jews and the Freemasons responsible for the defeat and the decay of French society. Behind Pétain, many conservatives were able to insure the triumph of their idea of French grandeur and moral dignity condensed in the logo of the National Revolution: "Travail, Famille, Patrie" ("Work, Family, Homeland").

Although the elements of nationalistic propaganda and the return to traditional values were evident in varying degrees in French cinema, one constant remained throughout the Occupation: the lack of any even ambiguous allusion to the persecution of the thousands of Jews parked in camps such as Drancy, Pithiviers, Compiègne or Beaune la Rolande. It appears however that, during the Occupation itself, it was possible to make nationalistic films filled with more or less subtle anti-German implications (Les Visiteurs du soir, Pontcarral Colonel d'Empire, Lumières d'été, Le Ciel est à vous).

Whether they were working for the Continental, thanks to the politics of Collaboration, or for French producers, the attitude of French directors making films during the Occupation of France can be characterized by the following remarks of Evelyn Ehlrich:

> Both groups chose to ignore the banning and arrests of their Jewish colleagues, and both groups preferred not to understand the reasons for the occupier's liberality

toward the French film industry. For it was not only
those who worked at the Continental who unwittingly
provided propaganda for the New Europe and an
economic wedge for the German film industry. All of
the filmmakers who worked through the Occupation did
so with the express permission and encouragement of
the occupiers, and, by working, they legitimized the
occupier's presence. Yet, neither group can be blamed,
for they both believed that by making films they were
helping France (187).

Indeed, the high statistics of attendance to movie theaters during
the war show that the continuity of French cinema in a certain
way did help the French population to live through the years of
occupation.

As Henri Rousso noted: "In June 1940, while German tanks
were surging through France, more than 800,000 people found
time to go to the movies" (Rousso, 259). Some two hundred
films were made during the four years of the Occupation and
while the film industry made only 452 million francs in 1938, it
made 915 million in 1943. According to Siclier, the most
successful movies of the time can be organized in three groups:
first, "melodramas, comedies, psychological dramas, historical
films, musicals, films of adventures or mysteries" (Siclier, 20)
featuring stars of the time; second, films situated in fictional
settings often combined with the first group and, finally,
productions more or less discreetly inspiring a revival of
nationalism most often supporting but sometimes against the
Vichy government.

In the footsteps of Claude Autant-Lara, many did not
hesitate to characterize the Occupation as a golden era, "the
best," for French cinema during which *all the French were
working for the French*: the result was the apparition of *a true
school of French cinema*" (my emphasis)[12]. Such an enthusiastic
judgement deserves a closer analysis in order to understand its
patent anti-Semitism, its consequences and the distortions of
reality on which it is based. It is one thing to say, as René
Régent did, that a certain "French style" developed during the

Vichy regime because of a growing solidarity among certain groups of the society. It is another to see this period as the golden age of "French cinema" made by "all the French" and "for the French" at a time when both French and foreign Jews were being persecuted, totally excluded from the French cinema industry, rounded up and exterminated. As Paxton recalled, the expression "France to the French" was created by the anti-Semite Drumont, used by Charles Maurras and popularized by the review *Temps* on July 25, 1940 (Paxton, 185).

Most critics would indeed agree with Jean Siclier when he writes: "the so-called cinema 'of Vichy,' in its ideological and political sense, does not exist. Under the Vichy regime and under the German Occupation, French cinema, in a 'closely watched freedom,' was a cinema of industrial and economic survival, of artistic expansion whenever possible."[13] Many testimonies confirm that even under the supervision of the Germans, Dr. Alfred Greven, the head of the Continental Society of production, never asked his directors to make propaganda films. Propaganda films were indeed exceptions. As Marcel Martin noted, the Jewish consonance of the names of such negative heroes as the murderer in *Les Inconnus dans la maison* (Henri Decoin, based on G. Simenon's novel, 1941) can eventually be considered as "imprudent" or as an "unfortunate mistake" (Martin, 11). Nonetheless such "mistakes" undoubtedly fed the rampant anti-Semitism in Vichy France therefore assuring the film with a certain success. It is now common knowledge that, in 1921, Georges Simenon wrote a series of seventeen anti-Semitic articles entitled "The Jewish Peril." Simenon also benefited greatly from the Continental as he sold them the film rights to the adventures of his popular detective "Commissaire Maigret" for a considerable price (500,000 francs).

Some of the very best films produced in France were made during the Occupation (i.e. Carné and Prévert *Les Visiteurs du soir*, 1942; *Les Enfants du Paradis*, 1944; Clouzot's *L'Assassin habite au 21*, 1942; and *Le Corbeau*, 1943). However, claiming that the Occupation was the best era of French cinema "by the French for the French," refers directly to the fact that the

Germans did not impose an overwhelmingly strict control on French productions, that the competition of both American and British cinema was totally suppressed and also to the fact that both French and foreign Jews were totally excluded from the profession. More than forty-five years after the war, anti-Americanism and "France for the French" still remain two major themes of the racist right wing French Party, the PFN, to which Claude Autant-Lara belonged in 1989.

It is also to be remembered that the Germans, and Goebbels in particular, were very well aware of the negative effects of direct propaganda films on occupied populations and of the financial profits of such a promising industry. It was therefore infinitely more effective to select some French professionals and to give them the responsibility of making their own fiction films as long as the values they transmitted could be at least partially controlled.

In the cracks of such a system however, some films could be made that would enhance nationalism as well as reactions of revolt against the oppressor. These were made possible only by the will of a few individuals and the ability of the director of the Continental, Dr. Greven, to play with the new regulations. Such films were produced thanks to the faults of the system rather than by the system itself and they very quickly provoked anger among those in charge of German propaganda. Consequently, the anti-Semitic background and consequences of Autant-Lara's statement ("All the French were working for the French"), are quite clear even if, at the time of the war and perhaps because of his deep anti-bourgeois convictions, this director was not a supporter of the Vichy regime.

It is therefore necessary to recall that, in 1989, Autant-Lara made the opening speech at the European Assembly in Strasbourg as a representative of the extreme right French National Front also called the PFN ("Parti du Front National"). A few weeks later, in an interview with the French magazine *Globe*, he was to regret that Simone Veil, a survivor of the Holocaust and former president of the European Assembly, had not been exterminated at Auschwitz. In recent years, the head of the PFN, Jean-Marie Le Pen, also became famous for his statements declaring the Holocaust as a "minor event of World War II" (September 1987) and for making a play on words with the name of the politician Michel Durafour calling him "Durafour-crématoire" (September 1988; the French for "crematorium" is "four crématoire"). As Le Pen and Autant-Lara's party wanted "to return France to the French" (a slogan directed against the Jews, the Arabs and the Americans), the director's admiration for a time when French cinema belonged to "the French," under the protection of the Nazis, is not surprising.

Finally, the last implication of Autant-Lara's statement deals with a typical, ambiguous and very complex distrust of the final goals of American help that, during the Cold War, also brought together actors, directors and intellectuals from the left and right wings of the French political spectrum. More recently, the anti-American thesis of Autant-Lara's opening speech at the European Assembly in August 1989 seemed to be directly borrowed from the late forties and the early fifties, when the French cinematographic industry was being rebuilt.

The history of French cinema during and after the Liberation shows a very similar lack of concern, embarrassment, ignorance or rejection about the destiny of the Jews. It is clear that such attitudes do not only concern the period during the war. They are not merely a matter of past history. They indicate a profound difficulty in dealing with past events because they stress tendencies very active many years before and after the war and often dismissed with the excuse of the need to unify or rebuild a country.

With respect to the deportation and the extermination of the Jews, French cinema of the Liberation suffered profoundly from an auto-censorship, ignoring a subject which was seen as going against the need to unify a nation first occupied and then just liberated. Directors of the underground, organized in a Comité de Libération du Cinéma, filmed Paris under the Occupation and its Liberation (Robert Godin and Albert Mahuzier's *La Caméra sous la botte*, 1945; the collective work *La Libération de Paris*, 1944). They also filmed Normandy after the landing of the Allies, the

Vercors Resistance groups (Jean Grémillon's *Le 6 juin à l'aube*, 1945; Félix Forestier's *Au Coeur de l'orage*, made in 1944), camps of prisoners of war (Maurice Reynaud and Jean Faurez's *Offlag XVII A*, 1946), some concentration camps in Poland and Germany, and the return of the prisoners to France (Cartier-Bresson's *Le Retour*, 1945).

Today, as if by accident, only a very few photographs remain to bear testimony of the persecution of the Jews in France. In French film, the "Actualités Françaises" of 1945 were probably the very first to show images from the concentration camps in movie-theatres. *Les Camps de la mort* (1945) was a one-hour picture filmed by French and Allied war correspondents in the just liberated camps of Colditz, Langestein, Ohrdrus, Dachau, Buchenwald, Tehkla, Belsen and Mittelgladsbach. Some survivors are first seen in the cold and starving next to an abandoned train in Colditz. Langestein is described as a camp where everyone was to be killed and put in mass graves. In Ohrdrus, former inmates explain to the American officials how they were tortured.

In Dachau, the film explains how the inmates were used for "scientific" experiments and it shows the ovens of the crematorium, hanging clothes of the victims and wagons filled with six hundred corpses. It is only when showing images of Buchenwald that the film mentions that fifty thousand *Jews* received lethal shots as soon as they arrived in this camp. This final section insists on the methodic and systematic annihilation of the inmates: mention of tortures, crematoria working night and day, burned bones, ferocious dogs, flamethrowers, tattoos, tattooed skins used as lamp shades, corpses burned before the arrival of the Allies. The film however never mentions the specificity of the persecution of the Jews, i.e. that all Jews, and Gypsies, men and women, babies, children, adolescents, adults and elders, were to be exterminated through this process, just because they were born Jews or Gypsies. A general tone was set from these very first films about the death camps. Jews were to be presented as victims of the Nazis among others.

This tendency became even more obvious when such films were made by special interest groups. Between 1950 and 1954, for example, the Amicale Française des Déportés Résistants Patriotes et Familles de Disparus made a film showing its organized visit of the site of Buchenwald. This eighteen minute film, entitled *Buchenwald* shows some of the "twenty five thousand *patriots* that were turned in to the Gestapo by *traitors*" (my emphasis). These former members of the Résistance go to the site of the camp "to make sure that it really does not exist anymore."

While showing various commemorative ceremonies as well as the destroyed and empty camp sites of Buchenwald, Nordhaussen and Ravensbruck, the film insists on the presence and solidarity of a (Communist) Chinese delegation. In West Berlin, German police are shown arresting the guest speaker of the group while, in contrast, Wilhelm Pieck, the first President of the brand new East German Republic is shown supporting the commemoration for "the construction of a new and peaceful world."

This film seems to have had various simultaneous purposes. While it claims to be made uniquely to show the survivors that their nightmare is really over and that the memory of the victims is well preserved, its final goal seems quite different. In showing that the camps are no longer in use, *Buchenwald* tries to prove that the new Communist East Germany is the best ally to save the memory of the victims. Contrary to what some famous French survivors were proclaiming at that time—e.g. David Rousset, the author of *L'Univers concentrationnaire* (1945)—the film wants to show that concentration camps do not exist under Stalinist Communism. Stalinists and Chinese Communists are shown as "comrades" of the survivors. Of course, this more or less subtle recuperation of the Holocaust through Stalinist propaganda never even alludes to the extermination of the Jews.

Such a film directly reinforces the propaganda of the Stalinist French Communist party of the fifties according to which Stalinist camps never existed, the principal victims of the Nazis were the Communists because they were the first French

Résistants ("the Party of the 75,000 executed") and the reconstruction of the world can be based only on the new Communist Stalinist order. It will take a few more years and millions of victims of Stalin's dictatorship, to completely get rid of such lies and distortions of reality.

Another way to avoid the controversy about the various degrees of responsibility of Vichy France regarding the Holocaust is the familiar pretext which claims that there is no need to bring old wounds to the surface because it will not change anything anyway. For this reason, I cannot accept what Robin Buss calls "the almost prurient delight some take in reopening the sores" (Buss, 39), as sufficient grounds to reject such a debate. These "sores" still hurt precisely because the problems that caused them are still very much present, in great part because they were dealt with too late. Obviously the dark episode of the so-called *épurations*, the purges, following the Liberation could not answer any of those questions (see Ehlrich, 173-177 and Lottman's work *The Purge*).

Regarding the dangerous consequences of these common pretexts for radical rejection, the successive and contradictory interpretations given to Chavance and Clouzot's film *Le Corbeau* (1943) are extremely significant even if this movie does not deal in a direct and explicit way with the Holocaust. This film narrates the inevitable ascension of hatred and incrimination in a French village following a mysterious wave of anonymous letters. In the French press of the early forties, it was violently attacked as being a German tool for the anti-French propaganda at a time when the Vichy government was trying to unify the population behind the ideals of work, family and homeland.

Nonetheless, after the Liberation, Clouzot and Chavance were forbidden to work for two years because their film had gone against the myth of national unity and general resistance of the population against the invader.[14] However, to a much larger but non-official audience, this film embodied a violent denunciation of the rampant incrimination and of the anonymous letters against the Jews, the Résistants or any personal enemy during the Vichy régime.[15]

This example is significant for at least three reasons. First, it is indicative of the incapacity or the refusal of French cinema, for fourteen years after the war, to analyze in depth the dark sides of French history during the Occupation as well as during the "purges" of the Liberation. *Hiroshima mon amour* with its criticism of the so-called *épurations*, purges, was to be made fourteen years after the end of the war. *The Sorrow and the Pity* had its première in 1971 and it was not shown on national French TV until 1981.

Second, these two official condemnations of Clouzot's film by opposite parties show that any movie alluding to the situation of the Jews in France during the Occupation was for a long time not acceptable because it would involve a necessary and even more profound auto-criticism. Finally, this example indicates that the rebirth of the French cinema after the war would be very closely regulated according to a general and partly official consensus about what "real" and "good" French values were to be. In this sense, it can certainly be said that there was a continuity in French cinema before and after the Liberation, even if the themes it dealt with were to change in a radical manner.

2. Deportation, Resistance and Betrayal, 1946-1961

On May 28, 1946, after a long year of negotiating, the Blum-Byrnes Agreement concerning the reorganization of French cinema was signed. In short, this agreement cancelled the French cinema debt ($1,800 million) and offered a new loan ($500 million) in exchange for a wide opening of the French market to American productions. In order to protect French productions, four weeks per trimester were to be reserved for the showing of French films. During the following two years this period was to be reduced to two weeks and then to one week for the fifth and sixth years. After that time, free competition was to be restored. In exchange, the French were to impose no barriers to American exports.

This agreement was immediately viewed as scandalous and unacceptable by most members of the French cinematographic profession. It meant that after the first four years, the market was to be flooded by thousands of American productions made in great numbers in the United States during the war years and already made profitable. For this very reason there would never be any real competition possible between French and American productions on the French market. For many, the four week concession was too short and they opposed any quota system. In this context, French cinema had little chance to become profitable and survive unless it was to be put under an ever stronger tutelage of American producers.

Last but not least, many feared the ideological conditioning of French audiences that might be imposed by the domination of American productions. The merit of great American films such as *Gone with the Wind* was widely recognized. However, through the block booking system, the French cinema industry was also obligated to show hundreds of very low range productions whose main objective was often seen as promoting "the American way" in Europe. The opposition to this agreement signed paradoxically by the socialist Léon Blum was immediate and violent. It was partly led by the C.G.T. (Confédération Générale du Travail), the Communist oriented union. However, the agitated debates that followed at the French National Assembly led to the ratification of the Agreement on August 1. It was finally to be revised in the Accord de Paris, signed on September 16, 1948, and was more favorable to French interests.

Later, as the Cold War, the Korean War and the Vietnam War developed, different waves of anti-Americanism were to develop among French intellectuals and particularly in the cinematographic profession. In this respect, Autant-Lara's statement about the greatness of French cinema during the Occupation can be interpreted not only with regard to the persecution of the Jews but also as a well founded reaction of defense to the threat of the American domination of cinema in France (On this last interpretation see Martin, 15; Courtade, 222). However, after Autant-Lara's anti-Semitic declarations of the summer of 1989, such an interpretation appears to be insufficient.

In the context of the post-war years, French political and intellectual life were totally oriented towards the reconstruction of the nation as well as all of Europe. Major decisions were to be made considering the violent opposition of the two super-powers on the international scene. Once again, the necessity to unify and rebuild the French nation was to retain in oblivion or at least to postpone for many years, the study of the Holocaust, of the Collaboration and their consequences.

In that period of time, roughly from 1946 to 1961 (until the trial of Adolf Eichmann) the vast majority of French films dealing with the Second World War reinforced the myth of a unified country resisting the invader. The Resistance was to be depicted as active and generalized (*La Bataille du rail* René Clément, 1946), passive and isolated (*Le Silence de la mer* Jean-Pierre Melville, 1949) or simply as a matter of common sense, of an anonymous and quiet heroism rather than as a passionate commitment (*Le Père tranquille* René Clément, 1946). No mention of the persecution of the Jews by the French administration disturbed this reassuring representation.

Progressively however, a few cracks appeared in this silent consensus as some films started depicting the cowardice of sections of the bourgeoisie making deals with the occupying forces (*Boule de suif* Henri Jeanson and Christian Jaque, 1945, *Patrie* Louis Daquin, 1946), showing people profiting from the chaos of the Liberation or openly criticizing the bourgeoisie in general (*Manon* H-G Clouzot, 1948; *Le Diable au corps* C. Autant Lara, 1946). However, as Raymond Borde indicated:

> One sees what sort of trap was closing itself on French productions as most of these films were assassinated by the critics of the left because they presented a negative and depressing image of France and of the French. I wonder if, until 1950, one should not talk about a post-Vichy French cinema. To the bitter surprise of the clandestine militants, since the Liberation, the French Communist party had borrowed for its own use Marshal Pétain's motto: "Work, Family, Homeland."[16]

One exception, Claude Autant-Lara's dreary tale *La Traversée de Paris* (1956), violently criticizes greedy individuals of the lower class such as black marketeers trying to profit from the lack of food and from the suffering of the population in general. In many respects, this film is a cinematographic masterpiece that is a precursor to many works of the early seventies. Contrary to many other pictures of the Fourth Republic, Autant-Lara's work does not represent committed and exceptional traitors or collaborators but the people themselves and their darkest aspects. Only the popularity and acting of the two stars playing the main roles—Jean Gabin and Bourvil—make the main characters bearable at all.

The two protagonists must cross Paris at night in order to bring a pig cut into pieces from the Left Bank to Montmartre. One main character is presented as a typical French man (Bourvil as Martin) and the other (Jean Gabin as Grandgil) as an artist accompanying Martin for the experience of the trip. He is

disgusted by what he sees and constantly tries to make his
companion aware of the low life he has fallen into.

At the beginning of their many encounters and adventures,
Martin and Grandgil meet a young Jewish girl who is forced to
work as a maid and prostitute by an abject couple of bar owners.
As a very successful tragi-comedy, the film violently and bitterly
denounces the actual cowardice hidden behind a purely verbal
courage, the perverted opportunism, and the hideous world of a
people submitting to fear and trying to take advantage of
abjection itself. The encounter with the Jewish girl is just a step
among many others in this slow and unstoppable fall into the
sewers of Paris under the Occupation.

As the café owner threatens to denounce the two black marketeers to the police, Grandgil protects himself by threatening the
owner to turn him in because he employs a Jew. In saying so,
Grandgil proves that the café owner is not any more respectful of
the law than he and Martin are. The point of the scene is not the
denunciation of the persecution of the Jews but the characterization of the bar owner as a rat. At the end of the sequence,
Grandgil spits his most famous line: "Salauds de pauvres!" "You
filthy scum!" (literally: "You poor, you are nothing but
scum!"[17])

The only positive character in the film is Grandgil presented
as an exception, as a disgusted, revolted but isolated and powerless artist. Martin stands clearly as the average Frenchman, as a
coward doomed by fear and totally submissive to his sinister
boss, the black marketeer grocer Jambier (played by Louis de
Funès). This film was and still is very popular in France as
Martin was played by the renowned French comedian Bourvil
who French audiences were used to seeing as the typical "other"
French man. The artist Grandgil was played by the even more
popular Jean Gabin traditionally associated with the force and the
spirit of the French people itself.

Over all, Martin is a funny, arrogant and weak idiot and
Grandgil represents the powerless but deep revolt of the artist like
Autant-Lara that will have to wait for better times to reveal the
real French spirit. Both of them feel for the Jewish prostitute

even if they do not do anything to help her. Through this film the audience can still assimilate the night world of the black marketeers to the world of the "others" while each spectator can identify at the same time with the revolt of the artist. The character of Grandgil provides the spectator with a convenient distanciation and escape from the general abjection described in the film. Moreover, as the extremely brief allusion to the persecution of the Jews is exclusively used to underline the repelling opportunism of the café owners, it does not constitute in itself a condemnation of anti-Semitism.

Henry Rousso has noted that a few films of the Fourth Republic feature not only all kinds of dealers but also some Collaborators and traitors (*Les Maudits* R. Clément, 1947; *Manon* H.G. Clouzot, 1948; *Les Amants de Vérone* A. Cayatte, 1949; *Le Bon Dieu sans confession* C. Autant-Lara, 1954; and as a grotesque comedy: *Le Bal des pompiers* A. Berthomieu, 1948). During that time, according to Rousso: "If the Collaboration, Vichy or Fascism have no political status whatsoever and are rarely alluded to, the Collaborator, on the contrary, becomes a familiar or frequent protagonist" (Rousso, 262). One film deals with the return of the prisoners of war, not Jewish but in general, under the form of a series of amusing or serious sketches (*Retour à la vie* J. Dréville, H.G. Clouzot, A. Cayatte and Lampin; Rousso 262). Some deal with the Occupation and the Liberation through transposing famous literary works (*Boule de suif* Christian-Jaque, 1945; *Manon* Clouzot, 1948; *Patrie* Louis Daquin, 1945). The persecution of the Jews is only vaguely alluded to or missing altogether.

Even the very best and most admired films of that time only mention the persecution of the Jews in France. In Robert Bresson's *Un Condamné à mort s'est échappé* (1956; *A Man Escaped*), for example, the old man in the cell next to the hero's mentions that he has been arrested because he was found with dollars that a Jewish woman gave him. Even if the persecution of the Jews is briefly mentioned here, the victim portrayed in the film is this old country man who was arrested for dealing in some way with Jews, either helping them or selling his services to them. Nothing is said in the film of what happened to this woman while it is clear that this man will die because of "helping" her. At the same time, the film ends well thanks to the reconciliation of the main character, a hero of the Résistance, with a teenager wearing a "half French half German" uniform. Both are presented as two opposite French victims of the confusion produced by the War. In the end both help each other to escape and run away as free men with no other allusion to the Jews.

It was in this atmosphere that *Night and Fog* (1955) was to be made. Ordered by the very official Comité d'Histoire de la Deuxième Guerre Mondiale (the Second World War History Committee) it is not specifically a film about the extermination of the Jews but rather a documentary about the victims of the concentration camps in general including, among others, the political prisoners, the Résistants, the Gypsies and the Jews. At that time, it was easy for any French audience to identify with these victims without being forced to consider the still taboo subjects of French anti-Semitism and the deportation of Jews from France. I will argue that this shattering masterpiece served indirectly this purpose even if it was not at all the original goal of Alain Resnais who had included in his documentary the picture of a French policeman watching the camp of Pithiviers. Of course, in 1956, this image was to be censored.

By a curious historical coincidence, Alain Resnais's *Night and Fog* was shown for the first time in France (Cannes Festival, May 8, 1956), almost eleven years to the day after the unconditional surrender of the German army to General Eisenhower, in the French city of Reims (May 7, 1945), and two years after the fall of Dien Bien Phu (May 7, 1954), which was shortly followed by the beginning of the Algerian War of Independence (November 1st, 1954). In order to analyze a work such as Alain Resnais' *Night and Fog*, we must keep in mind the historical facts surrounding the Holocaust as well as the evolution of Resnais' art. We must also remember the local and international contexts in which this documentary was made.

As Resnais' work is often characterized as that of an *artiste engagé*, a politically committed artist, even against his own will,[18] we must consider this film both as the creation of an artist as well as one created by a politically involved individual. Consequently, *Night and Fog* must be studied at the same time as a work of art, an historical documentary and an interpretation of the Holocaust produced in the France of the mid-fifties. Such a point of view should enable us to analyze more precisely not only how this work was made but also why it was ordered by an official historical society in 1955 (not before or after), and why it has enjoyed such success with general audiences ever since its off competition première at the Cannes Festival in 1956.

Since the end of World War II and the capitulation of the German army (May 7, 1945), it became more and more impossible to ignore or to pretend to ignore what had happened to the Jews, the Gypsies, the Résistants, the Communists or the homosexuals sent from all over Europe to Nazi Germany. Survivors had come back to tell the horror of the extermination of ten million people. Soldiers of the liberation armies and thousands of war prisoners told what they had heard or seen. In France, the radio and the news of the movie theaters allowed no more doubt or denial about the terrifying reality of the extermination of six million European Jews.

Moreover, since the loss of Dien Pien Phu (Indochina; May 7, 1954) by the French Army and the beginning of the Algerian War of Independence, it was also very clear that the emergence of Third World countries on the international political scene directly posed the problem of the relationship between military and civilian power within a democracy. How far was France ready to go in order to keep its decaying colonial empire? Was the recently liberated France ready to deal with the liberation movements of its colonies? Should thousands of French soldiers die in order to restore a conservative image of French grandeur? Were the politicians of the Fourth Republic too confused, too divided or too weak to lead the country? Was the French army given too much or not enough power? Was the French army using or going to use torture in Algeria? All these questions were in the mind of every committed French intellectual in 1955, especially when Alain Resnais was asked to film his first major masterpiece, *Night and Fog*.

On the other hand, ten years after the end of World War II, many notorious Nazi war criminals and French Collaborators had already been released from jail. Xavier Vallat, the anti-Jewish commissioner of France, was released in 1950. The Alsacian SS men found guilty for their participation in the total destruction of the village of Oradour-sur-Glane were tried, condemned and then pardoned by the French National Assembly in 1953. Heinrich Wulff and Otto Hoff, found guilty for the hanging of 99 young men in June 1944 in Tulle, France, were released in 1955. Otto Abetz, former head of the German occupation of France, charged with the deportation of the French Jews, hostage taking, torture and killing of thousands of people, was released in 1954[19]. Some important Collaborators were still working for the French administration or French businesses, like Bousquet and Papon, while others, like Touvier, were to remain in hiding for a long time to come. And, since 1950, old supporters of the Vichy regime were campaigning very actively to rehabilitate the memory of Marshal Pétain (Rousso, 48-71). Did this mean that the time had come to forgive or to forget what was a few years earlier the unforgivable and the unforgettable? Was forgiving and forgetting even possible? Finally the mid-fifties also marked, especially in France, the beginning of the realization of a unified European Community whose dream started as early as 1949 with the creation of the "Mouvement Européen." To a few pioneers like Maurice Schuman, Pierre Mendès-France and, above all, Jean Monnet, achieving such a goal required a total reorganization of Europe freed of the traditional hatred and distrust that history had often slowly built up between many of its peoples. In any case, if the past could not been forgotten, it was obviously necessary to reanalyze recent history in the most impartial way possible in order to be able to build the European Community.

It was therefore indispensable for the France of the mid-fifties to either totally forget or to try to understand how, as in the first sequence of *Night and Fog*, a peaceful European landscape could hide in its depths the dreadful setting of a concentration camp. For many, it was necessary to finally face the most horrifying chapter of recent European history. If this could still be done in 1955 by Resnais and Cayrol's *Night and*

Fog in a rather general and poetic manner, the political turmoil of the late sixties would soon require that such questions be considered in relationship with the deep changes that were affecting French society as a whole.

In postwar France, the need to rebuild and modernize the nation was often used as a reason to overlook past divisions in order to unify the population. In a similar way, Charles de Gaulle had denied a key role to local Résistance members in his 1946 government and he had called for the rebirth of a very abstract "Eternal France." The Collaboration and French anti-Semitism were to be neglected for many years in part to protect the unity of the nation and the foundations of the European Community. For these two reasons, *Night and Fog* could be shown in 1956 only after an image showing a French gendarme watching the French camp of Pithiviers had been censored. The film was also withdrawn from the Cannes Film Festival for "diplomatic reasons." In that period, only one major film, Autant-Lara's *La Traversée de Paris* (1956), clearly described the underworld of black-marketeers taking advantage of the Occupation and, very briefly, the persecution of the Jews.

Today *Night and Fog* remains undeniably a poignant and powerful masterpiece. However, as many critics have noticed, this film, in its final version, never refers to the specificity of the extermination of the Jews nor that of the Gypsies. Although some images show stars of David and Jean Cayrol's text does include some Jewish names, neither the noun "Jew" nor the adjective "Jewish" are ever mentioned. Jews are presented as victims of the death camps among others as the film addresses mankind as a whole. Such an approach facilitated the identification of the victims of the Holocaust to all the victims of the Nazis in general. If it could still offend some German officials in Cannes, it was to create no serious controversy with French audiences. All these points will have to be considered in the detailed analysis of this film.

3. Nazis, Collaborators and the Holocaust, *1961-1970*

In his essay, *Le Syndrome de Vichy*, Henry Rousso studied the violent debates surrounding the well accepted myth according to which the whole French population was united against the invader and, consequently, actively supportive of the Résistance (Rousso, 42-55). This myth is called by the French the *résistantialisme*, Resistancialism. "Resistancialism" was reactivated with De Gaulle's return to power and the beginning of the Fifth Republic in 1958. Whether they show recently defeated yet free soldiers (*Un Taxi pour Tobrouk* D. de la Patelière, 1961) or French prisoners (*La Vache et le prisonnier* H. Verneuil, 1959), war films of this period clearly show individuals who refuse to consider that the war is over and who keep on fighting in their own particular ways.[20] Even if one of the escaping men of *Un Taxi pour Tobrouk* is a Jewish doctor, these films present no clear analysis of Jewish resistance or of the persecution of the Jews in France.

In 1961 however, while Eichmann's trial was taking place in Jerusalem, two French films were made that were directly based on the persecutions of the Jews. These two works are Armand Gatti's *L'Enclos* and Frédéric Rossif's *Le Temps du Ghetto*. Gatti is himself a former member of the Résistance, a reporter and a man of theater. His film can be characterized as a minute psychological analysis of an extremely tense relationship in a camp. It depicts a French Jew and a German Communist who have been told by the Nazis that the one who kills the other will be allowed to survive. In comparison to *Night and Fog*, as Freddy Buache noted, this "intense and modest fable" tries to describe the terror of the victims "from the inside" (Buache, 58).

Whereas it is clear that these men were arrested because they are a Communist and a Jew, the film is entirely centered around the psychology of the two characters. They become two victims of a perverted dilemma imposed by their executioners. References to the Holocaust and even the political deportations become secondary as the resolution of this dilemma between two human beings engulfs the film. A large variety of characters are introduced, including a gypsy, and the film makes it clear that although these men are of different backgrounds, they become comrades through their common suffering, their fight for dignity and their love of freedom. David, the Jew, is a somewhat privileged inmate because he is able to fix the Commandant's watches. The film makes it clear that his survival is extraordinary and David himself refers briefly to the persecution of the Jews by the French police. In the end, both David and the German Communist, Karl, try to escape and die. What matters, however, is that they never gave in to the monstrous game invented by their executioners. Although they never regain their freedom, they have recovered their human dignity and discovered a basic solidarity that defeats their executioners' project to turn them into vicious animals. Much influenced by Gatti's collaboration with Chris Marker, this film was a commercial failure.

With Frédéric Rossif, the case is entirely different. His documentary *Le Temps du Ghetto* is a long film dedicated to the depiction of the Warsaw Ghetto, the history of its organization, and its extermination. It is in black and white and made almost exclusively from footage shot by the Nazis themselves. It also includes a few sequences showing only the faces of a handful of survivors describing their personal experiences. Frédéric Rossif was a man of television, known for his long films about history, art and animals. His clear passion for historical footage led him to the making of many so-called *films de montage* and as such, *Le Temps du Ghetto* raises key questions about the use of historical footage filmed by the murderers themselves.[21] At the time of his death, in 1990, he was celebrated by many as the best French documentary director of his time. It is also during the same year that *De Nuremberg à Nuremberg*, his last documentary, was to be shown on French TV.

Le Temps du Ghetto starts and ends by showing staggering images of endless mounds of rubble from the ruins of the Ghetto after its uprising and its total destruction by the Germans. Almost the entire film is made of extremely rare footage showing many unbearable images of emaciated corpses lying in the streets of the Ghetto or pictures of men, women and mostly children trying to survive while dying of starvation. It could be made only because of Rossif's astounding research that enabled him to locate the footage shown in this film. This investigation succeeded in great part thanks to the director's experience as the founder and director of foreign acquisitions at the ORTF (French TV) in the early fifties.

The first part of this documentary explains and shows how the Ghetto got started, its organization, the division of Warsaw into German, Polish and Jewish zones and the construction of the wall that was to surround the Jewish Zone. Rossif explains that, at first, many Jews thought that the Ghetto and its wall would offer some kind of protection from the persecutions of the outside world. Very quickly, however, it became overcrowded. Everyone had to invent his own means of survival.

The film also represents the Judenrat as a group of elder Jewish bourgeois collaborating with the Nazis to organize life inside the walls. The commentary explains that:

> Very often, in order to save one's people, one becomes the executioner of one's people. The Jewish Council, the Judenrat, was the Ghetto's ambiguity. Presided over by the engineer Czerniakow, it was to represent law in a free society of slaves.

> In order to govern, one needs a police. The Jewish Council organized a police of one thousand men, most of them recruited among the sons of bourgeois families. Dressed like the German masters, in the Ghetto they were an instrument of evil and were accused of being just like the Gestapo.

However, a few minutes later, the commentary becomes much more temperate judging both the Jewish police and the Judenrat:

> Forced day after day to play the role of the oppressor, these men were caught in a trap. A time came when they had only one choice to make, between martyrdom

and ignominy. Like the economic collaboration, the administrative collaboration was a tragic necessity. In a short but astonishing sequence we see Czerniakow himself, the head of the Judenrat, in a meeting with other sages of his council. Later, the commentary indicates clearly that Czerniakow committed suicide when he realized that the massive deportations were about to start and he was asked to choose who should go first. Although the Judenrat was able to somewhat better the survival conditions of the Jews in the ghetto, it is mainly presented as a group that organized the Jewish police and collaborated with the Nazis. This rather critical and negative representation of the Judenrat and its leaders is the opposite of the one Claude Lanzmann would offer twenty-four years later in *Shoah* (see the detailed analysis of this film).

In contrast to Lanzmann's film, the most positive hero of the ghetto, according to Rossif's work, is not Czerniakow but the world renowned writer, doctor and educator Janusz Korczak. *Le Temps du Ghetto* portrays Korczak as "the symbol of dignity in the ghetto" and it presents the famous pedagogue in a manner that is very similar to its depiction in Wajda's 1991 film *Korczak*. A survivor of the ghetto is heard saying that when Korczak and the two hundred orphans were deported, Korczak comforted them, telling them that they were going "to a beautiful country, a country where there is no suffering." He chose to stay with the orphans until the end, and the children were singing on their way to the train that was to deport them to their death in the gas chambers of Treblinka. A very similar representation of Korczak in Wajda's 1991 film will be the source of violent attacks from Lanzmann against the Polish director. It is to be underlined here that in Rossif's film the event is described by an eyewitness, a survivor of the ghetto.

Rossif's film also assimilates the Jewish police into a clique of young members of the bourgeoisie collaborating actively in the persecution of the Ghetto's population. Various images show the Jewish police dressed by the Gestapo, carrying clubs and wearing boots. They are seen beating and hurrying dozens of Jews out of a building, including women, children and the elderly. These images raise some key questions as Rossif uses them only to demonstrate that the Jewish police engaged in some very violent actions. Even though the film starts with a short text warning the audience that all the images shown were filmed by the Nazis, in this particular sequence, the director lets the spectator forget that the Nazis were filming and supervising such scenes.

This is not to deny the fact that the Jewish police took an active part in such actions. However the very images used by Rossif were filmed for Nazi propaganda and documentation. All of them were intended to degrade and humiliate the Jewish people as well as to show that the Jews were successfully being exterminated, including the images showing Jews persecuting other Jews. When dying Jews are shown staring at the camera, dancing in front of it, or avoiding any eye contact, they are confronting not only Nazi officers but an unknown, indifferent or perverted audience as well.

For this reason, Rossif's commentary is sometimes impaired by its lack of clues reminding the audience of the origin of these images during the film itself. The most powerful and unbearable sequences of this documentary show dying, emaciated children, their corpses lying on the sidewalks or being picked up. Such images are insufferable by themselves and need no explanation in order to invert the purpose they were suppose to serve according to the Nazis. However, Rossif also uses images of Jews persecuting the Jews to characterize the Jewish police as such. In this case the director uses Nazi images to serve the purpose intended by the Nazis, to show that the Jews were persecuting their own. In this specific case, Rossif seems to forget that the Jewish police were indeed acting upon the orders of the executioners. The images showing them rounding up other Jews cannot be considered as mere documents and must be interpreted as a staged event. The whole film however insists on the fact that *all* the Jews of the Ghetto, including the Jewish police and the Judenrat, were to be systematically exterminated. In the end, it is made clear that the purpose of the uprising was not the inconceivable liberation of the Ghetto but the last opportunity to have a dignified or at least humane death.

Throughout the film, many survivors are interviewed as they tell various episodes from their life in the Ghetto. Only their faces are shown, surrounded by a dark black haze. Some speak in the past, others in the present. All of them seem to hallucinate, staring into the vacuum that surrounds them, speaking with quiet and regular tones. In consequence, these testimonies provoke no rupture with the footage. In these specific occurrences, no difference is being made between images filmed by the Germans and interviews filmed by Rossif himself. In both cases the presence of the cameraman is deleted and *Le Temps du Ghetto* remains a powerful and truly terrifying but distant nightmare. In contrast, the obliteration of this historical distance will constitute one of the key differences between the effects produced in Lanzmann's *Shoah* and this film.

Rossif's film insists clearly on a very specific chapter of the Shoah and on the systematic and total extermination of the Jews. It is sometimes questionable because of its direct use of German footage and because of its purely informative utilization of the commentary that contrasts violently, for example, with the poetic text of *Night and Fog*. It remains a petrifying testimony and a rigorous masterpiece of the so-called *film de montage*. Because it motivates almost uniquely historical knowledge and emotions giving a secondary role to critical thinking and contemporary analysis, it is a key work in the representation of the Holocaust in French cinema that remains however less influential than the "documentaries" of Ophüls and Lanzmann. In that respect, Rossif's last documentary, *De Nuremberg à Nuremberg* (1990), will not be any different.

Because he concentrates on the Warsaw Ghetto, Rossif never mentions the persecution of the Jews in France. During the same years, however, other French films do show some militia men, Collaborators and traitors (*Marie Octobre* Julien Duvivier, 1959; *Vacances en enfer* J. Kerchbron, 1961). Here again, Jews and French anti-Semitism are alluded to within a plot in which the unity of the French people prevails in spite of the evil of some French "enemies of France."

Henri and Francine Torrent's *La Mémoire courte* (1962)
provides a sarcastic comparison of life in France, England, the
Soviet Union and the United States during World War II. With
a derisory tone, the *film de montage* parallels the nonchalant
lifestyle of the French middle and upper class in Vichy and in
occupied Paris with the struggle of the British, Soviet and
American peoples against the Nazis. While the film follows the
chronology of the war, it insists clearly on the fight of "the
people" in every country including in France. Collaborators are
presented as traitors or opportunists seduced by Pétain and Laval.
The film makes no allusion to the wide popular support Pétain
benefited from.

La Mémoire courte makes four brief allusions to the
deportations and the extermination of the Jews. While describing
the invasion of the Soviet Union, the commentator explains that
"the Gestapo hounds the political executives and the Jews, while
the SS deport entire villages." The second allusion refers to "the
anti-Semitism of the Nazis and their servants" in France. The
film then mentions the roundup of the Vélodrome d'Hiver, the
deportation of 150,00 Jews from France, and concludes showing
a group of Jews who found refuge in Switzerland, dancing
happily. We are also shown images from the Warsaw ghetto
after the evocation of the "desperate patriotism" of Poland. The
commentary mentions the famine, the revolt and the extermination of the ghetto. Then we see the barracks of Auschwitz and
a naked child dying slowly on a pile of hay. The commentator
remarks that "no one will feel responsible for that."

Finally, while the film depicts the end of the war in Europe,
we are shown some images of a camp for women that has just
been liberated. The commentary states that only then "horrified
people discover what the Allies' propaganda had already talked
about but no one wanted to believe." In brief, *La Mémoire
courte* offers a sarcastic account of everyday life in France during
the war. It clearly portrays the persecution of the Jews but it
fails to allude even briefly to anti-Semitism among the French
people, Pétain's popularity or the responsibility of the French in
the persecution of the Jews which began in the very first months

of the Occupation. Following the leftist indoctrination of its time, the film tries too hard to prove that, throughout the world, "the people" was unified against fascism.

One of the best examples of this treatment of the Occupation is provided by Jean Cayrol's and Claude Durand's feature film *Le Coup de grâce* (1965). It tells the story of a former collaborator (Michel Piccoli as Capri) trying to live under a fake name (Bruno) in Bordeaux, the town where he turned in four hundred people to the Gestapo. He is also responsible for the deportation and death of Gérard, a Résistant and Yolande's husband (Danielle Darieux).

Bruno is first attracted to Yolande and then to her younger friend Sophie who he intends to marry. As Jean-Baptiste, a playwright and Sophie's friend, starts having doubts about Bruno's real identity, Bruno becomes more and more nervous and defensive. As Sophie presses him with questions about his past, Capri finally breaks down, reveals his identity and runs into hiding like a mad dog. At that point Yolande and all the former members of the Résistance gather the families of Capri's victims to organize a chase. After hiding terrified in a basement and a gigantic underground submarine factory, Capri will die on a mound of litter, like a rat, stabbed by the man who provided him the fake papers for his escape.

The two main characters of the film are Bruno (alias Capri) and Sophie. In the middle of the film Sophie tells him that as a young girl during the war she was in hiding because her mother was Jewish. It is the only allusion in the film to the persecution of the Jews. The spectator is never told what happened to the mother nor whether or not Sophie considers herself a Jew. What matters for the film is that she is in love with Bruno and that during the war she was also in love with Gérard. In the end, she is the only one who refuses to chase Capri even though she is the one who forced him to reveal his identity.

Like the other films of this period dealing with the same subject, *Le Coup de grâce* is mainly a psychological study that mentions the Holocaust in its background. What matters the most is the fact that Capri is unable to live with his double identity. He is constantly tortured by others' memories of his past crimes and the impossibility of justifying them to others or even to himself. He is forced to live and die like a rat, unable to know or share any love. In the end, *Le Coup de grâce* appears to have an unrealistic happy ending as the evil Collaborator is tortured by his past and punished by the friends of his victims. If the film offers some excellent sequences due in great part to the acting of Michel Piccoli, its depiction of interiorized struggle and final castigation of a criminal are too far from reality to make this story really convincing. The title itself indicates that the victims' families gave Capri the necessary last and fatal stroke that ended his misery.

In 1965, Philippe Arthuys' *La Cage de verre* was directly in response to the recent trial of Adolf Eichmann held four years earlier in Jerusalem. As the trial was used by Israel to recall the world of the Holocaust, this film shows the other side of the coin as the trial also forced many survivors to face once again the horror of vivid memories some of them had tried to overcome for so many years. Arthuys' film is a beautiful one and summarizing its "plot" can in no way do it justice. It indicates, however, the main tensions from which the film develops its strength.

Pierre, the main character of this film is a Jew, a survivor of the extermination camps. As Eichmann's trial is going on, Pierre is working for the future of Israel, on an irrigation project in the Negev desert. This job puts him in contact with Sonia, another survivor. In the meantime Helen, Pierre's wife, hosts Claude, a foreign journalist who's coming to cover the trial. Claude and Helen were in love as teenagers. As Pierre is asked to testify at the trial his memories become more and more obsessive and he feels more and more isolated and distant from his wife. For Pierre: "Love masks solitude. It does not fill it up." He believes that only Sonia can understand what he is going through. It is indeed Sonia that convinces him to testify.

At the same time, Helen realizes that a distance is growing between her and her husband, and she gets closer to Claude. As she discovers that Claude does not comprehend what Israel and the trial mean to the Jews, she understands that nothing is left of the love she once felt for him. In the end, Pierre and Helen get closer again, "not as a couple but as an association." The film ends on a positive note showing Antoine and Tamar, a journalist and an Israeli woman, in love. In the last image, Tamar is happy "defying all the Eichmanns of the world."

The first images show children playing on ruins while Pierre's voice explains: "I was a child like any other. At least I believed so. Sometimes the other children would call me 'Yid,' 'dirty Jew' and I would fight." In spite of all the suffering, Pierre's will to survive originated in his father's admonition: "Someone has to tell what happened."

The first sequences of the film make clear that the *cage de verre*, the glass cage, is indeed the cage made out of glass in which Eichmann was kept during his hearing. It is also a very rich metaphor continued in various forms throughout the film. As many images show Eichmann calm, even imperturbable, taking notes during his trial, it is clear that the murderer has no remorse whatsoever. His heart itself appears as an empty, hard, cold glass cage that is absolutely not touched by the outside world.

In contrast, Pierre and Helen live in a spacious apartment with large bay windows. As it becomes evident that Pierre is prisoner to his memories of the camp that might destroy his relationship with Helen, the couple's apartment turns into a glass cage. Throughout the film, shop windows and mirrors reinforce this metaphor, recalling to Pierre his past, the other man he was and unsuccessfully tried to forget. In a similar vein, Pierre is often reminded of the camps in a very obsessive manner by many different images: the gate and the guard protecting his irrigation project; the water sprinkler in the ceiling of a building or an overcrowded elevator.

For this reason, Pierre expresses some uncertain opposition to the trial as it seems that it makes many survivors suffer deeply from their recollection while at the same time Eichmann himself is totally at peace with himself. Then Pierre is heard admitting: "We were crazy to believe that we were done with this." Pierre also criticizes Claude's attitude and the attitude of the press in general as most of the journalists came to Jerusalem attracted by the extraordinary event the process constitutes in itself: "The world has its trial." Finally, Pierre is afraid that the trial will allow other executioners to feel good about themselves just because they will be able to say that they were not as bad as the Nazis: "As long as they do a little less than what the Germans did with the Jews, everybody will have a clear conscious."

In the end however, Claude begins to understand what Pierre is going through. After Helen told him how she lived for thirteen years with her husband without ever hearing about his years in the camps, Claude harshly replies: "I am interested in Pierre's anguish, not in the anguishes of a little bourgeois woman." At the same time another journalist, Antoine, forgets about the trial and falls in love with an Israeli woman, Tamar, as he understands more and more what the trial means to her in particular. It is only after remembering atrocities committed by the French army in Algeria that Antoine starts understanding Tamar's feelings. The last sentences of the film are symbolically as strong as the last images of Antoine and Tamar as Pierre declares: "Indifference is the crime (...) Justice is inside of us, in our vigilance."

This film is entirely structured around the pain and the necessity of remembering the Holocaust. Eichmann's trial is presented less as an efficient way to punish the murderer—because he could not care less—than as a necessary step in honoring the memory of the victims by forcing the world to remember their fate. The detailed analysis of Sonia and Pierre's suffering while remembering experiences that cannot be shared leaves, however, a ray of hope as long as the world will remember why it was necessary to create Israel. For this reason, the film ends with images that include a Gentile, the journalist Antoine, as he falls in love with an Israeli on a beach near Tel-Aviv.

Whereas Arthuys' film was set in a very explicit time and place, Marcel Hanoun's *L'Authentique procès de Carl-Emmanuel Jung* (1967) was based on a much more abstract vision of the trial of a Nazi. Hanoun's film narrates the imaginary trial of a Nazi, Dr. Carl-Emmanuel Jung, who was responsible for scientific experiments led in a camp and for the selection of victims for the gas chambers. The whole film is structured around the soundtrack constituted mostly of the testimonies of the survivors describing various tortures and scenes of extermination, some questions from the judge, some of Jung's reactions, some brief interventions of the lawyers and Hanoun's voice-over commenting on the image, introducing the characters or repeating key words. There is almost no direct sound in the film. Most of what is being said is heard through the voice-over of different translators.

In consequence, the image always precedes or follows the soundtrack. Using very strong contrasts, the scenes of the trial are filmed with a totally black background on which characters seem totally isolated, fighting with themselves in order to remember, imagine, understand or judge one man and the atrocities he committed. The soundtrack with the narration and the testimonies of the survivors is constantly superposed with brief sequences showing Jung eating with his family, in his apartment; the journalist in a café or in his hotel room; and most of all, with enigmatic images of a young bride rearranging her veil in front of a mirror.

Hanoun purposefully deleted any anecdote from his film that would have allowed the audience to relate the trial to a specific event. He does not once use the words "Jews" or "Jewish." However, the first witness talks about "the final solution of the foreign problem." The chronology of the imaginary events depicted clearly situate the crime during World War II. Each crime is described with a minute and horrifying realism. Marcel Hanoun, as the journalist, explains later that Jung prevented his daughter from marrying a "foreigner." The eighth witness alludes to the "definitive solution" and the "special treatment" of the victims. Finally, two testimonies describe very precisely the death of the victims in the gas chambers.

As a result, Jung is seen as both a Nazi criminal and as any criminal guilty of crimes against humanity in any period of history. Because of the extreme fragmentation of the image series, the spectators are forced to build their own interpretation of the film and as they do so they realize that their various reconstitutions reveal different personal interpretations. In this respect, Hanoun succeeded in creating, with the spectator, a work of synthesis as if "one was being watched by the film" while becoming conscious of his or her own vision of reality.

Hanoun's work is often and rightfully characterized as that of a poet. However, his dealing with the Holocaust in poetic, general and abstract terms raises various key questions. This is the case, for example, with the most famous sequence of the film that puts in parallel images of the beautiful naked body of a women lying down, slowly scrutinized by the camera and a minute oral description of corpses piled up in a gas chambers.

First, one of the judges asks a witness to describe the gas chambers. Then the witness starts with the words: "In the administrative language of the camp it was called... the special treatment." The testimony is then interrupted by the long sequence slowly showing the beautiful naked body moving on a white indefinite background. At the same time the spectator hears extracts of Gluck's opera *Orpheus and Eurydice*. It is only in the middle of that sequence that Hanoun's voice is heard saying: "I think about you... It could have been possible that you suffer this death..." According to the soundtrack, the body of this woman belongs to the lover of the journalist who could also be Jung's daughter who never got married. The soundtrack makes it clear that the director/journalist is trying to relate to the testimony by imagining the body of the women he loves as the body of a victim. As he admits that this is totally impossible, the image goes back to a shot of the witness and the appalling oral description.

This sequence is disturbing because it puts in parallel sensual images of a beautiful body with the most atrocious oral description. In doing so, Hanoun's sequence juxtaposes a sensation of visual pleasure with the most terrifying words. As is often the case in this film, the emergence of an unexpected image is explained only much later, thus providing the spectator at first with a violent feeling of discomfort and uneasiness. In the case of this sequence, the sudden appearance of a beautiful body creates the impression that Hanoun imagines that such an image is comparable to what took place in the gas chambers. However, the sensuality of the images is in direct juxtaposition with the unimaginable violence alluded to in the sound sequence.

At this point Hanoun takes an enormous risk by trying to turn the evocation of the exterminations into a work of art. Many spectators can be led to believe that Hanoun is thus representing what cannot be or should never be represented. The extreme fragmentation of the film makes it even more hazardous. This parallel between the most extreme horror and beauty can be totally and rightfully seen as unacceptable and offensive to many spectators. However, the sentences added by Hanoun in the middle of this sequence make it much more understandable if one accepts replacing these images in the film as a whole.

Hanoun's comments in the middle of the sequence are exactly the following:

> I am thinking about you... It could have been possible that you'd suffer this death, that you'd be undressed, that you'd breathe death... I can imagine you naked in a gas chamber... I cannot stand this... How could it be possible? Was it possible? Is it possible? Will it still be possible? It was the total destruction of love... To destroy love.

From this the spectator understands that these images do not represent a scene in the gas chambers but the efforts of Hanoun, as the journalist, as he is trying to imagine the extreme horror of what happened. He does so from what he knows, from his own reality, putting together images of the body of the woman he loves in parallel with the words uttered by the witnesses. In the middle he admits that putting the two together is impossible and even intolerable. This attempt allows the audience to begin to understand the terror felt by the victims: "it was the total destruction of love." However, many will judge Hanoun's attempt itself intolerable and disrespectful.

The strengths and the beauty of Hanoun's film lie in the fact that the director uses the specificity of his medium to transmit the confrontation of a criminal with the reality of the horrors he committed. Faced with the evocation of what cannot be represented, he often chose to create violent contrasts in order to force the audience to try to imagine what cannot be put in words nor in images—dark backgrounds; blinding white images; Jung described as a remorseless murderer and shown with his family or holding his head in his hands; descriptions of tortures; images of a young bride, etc. In many respects, Hanoun's work is a technical tour de force.

Shown in 1966, Claude Berri's *Le Vieil homme et l'enfant* (*The Two of Us*) is a traditional film in its form but, because of the themes it deals with, it can be considered as a precursor of the seventies. By telling the story of a Jewish boy in hiding in the house of a conservative old couple in the country, the film clearly describes the reasons for the popular support Pétain's government enjoyed during the Occupation as well as the power of Vichy's anti-Semitic propaganda. Confronted with the daily escalation of the anti-Semitic measures and the inability of their son to fully understand the threat put upon them, Claude's parents decide to hide him in the country with the elderly parents of a friend. At that point however, Claude understands that he must always keep his Jewish identity secret as he has just been beaten up by his schoolmates, one of whom called him a "dirty Jew."

The old man (Michel Simon) is a veteran of World War I who always admired Marshal Pétain as the Hero of Verdun. He is also nourished by radio propaganda against the British and the Jews. It soon becomes obvious that the old man, "Gramps," and his wife love Claude as the grandson they never had. Gramps is presented both as a sweet, loving old man who loves his dog, enjoys kidding around and playing tricks, and as a bigot who knows how to identify or "smell" a Jew. At that point Claude starts crying because he says he might be a Jew. After Gramps proves him the contrary, Claude points out that Gramps himself looks like a Jew. The sequence ends with Gramps bewildered, examining his own face in the mirror.

One sunday afternoon, Gramps and his son Victor make Claude buy and write a postcard to a young girl from school. The two men are drunk and they tell Claude to sign the card with a cherry instead of his name. The girl's father brings the card to

school and asks that the sender be punished. After being
identified by the schoolteacher, Claude has his head shaved in
front of all his schoolmates. In the following sequence, Claude
runs back home crying. Gramps is mortified for being the cause
of the child's suffering and spends the following days trying to
console Claude and make him laugh again. In the end, Gramps'
world falls apart as his dog dies, the Allies invade France and
Claude must return to his family.

In one of the final shots Claude sees the village population
parading a woman whose head had been shaved because she had
a German lover. After this parallel between Claude and the
woman's humiliation, the film seems to condemn political fanaticism of all origins. Gramps is a bigot terrified at the idea that his
world was disappearing but the constant changing of the world
does not bring better values either. (Twenty-four years later, this
same violent condemnation of vengeance and of the self-
proclaimed "heroes" of the Liberation will be at the heart of
Berri's film *Uranus* [1990], adapted from a short story by Marcel
Aymé.) Finally, *Le Vieil homme et l'enfant* condemns any
ideological discourse propagating intolerance and hatred and, by
contrast, it praises one's ability to relate directly to individuals
while rejecting any mythology classifying people, races or
nationalities. This is something Gramps himself has not been able
to achieve although his active love has shown Claude how to
evaluate history and judge people.

Berri's film is a very moving one as its long sequences
allow the director to develop the personality of the characters and
to concentrate on the growing friendship between Claude and
Gramps seen from the child's eyes. It gives a subtle description
of many anti-Semitic attitudes while demonstrating how "good
people" can eventually be brought to support politics of hatred
that are directly at the opposite of their actual lifestyle and
values. It is largely based on Claude Berri's own experience as
the child's real name, Claude Langmann, is also the director's
real name. This aspect allows Berri to portray Claude's feelings
in a particularly strong manner.

Le Vieil homme et l'enfant announces many films of the seventies because it is based on the personal memories of a child and tells the story of a Jewish boy who had to hide his identity and separate from his parents to survive. It is also one of the first films that clearly analyzes Pétain's wide popularity and the psyche of part of the French population at that time. However, because it never mentions the Résistance and because it develops according to a psychological analysis based on a linear chronology, Berri's film seems to be somewhat exceptional within the new French cinema of the sixties. In its form it is more characteristic of the realism of the late fifties—it is clear that Berri admires the theoretical work of André Bazin—while the treatment of its subject announces clearly the seventies.

In 1963, Alain Resnais' masterpiece, *Muriel* (1963), had depicted the effects of the Algerian war on French society and individual memory, in parallel with recollections of the Second World War.[22] While many films of the early sixties depicted the effects of the war in Algeria on the French collective psyche, the most important pictures dealing with World War II continued reinforcing the Gaullist myth of a whole nation united against the invader. During these same years, Gérard Oury's *La Grande vadrouille* (1966)[23] gathered the two most famous French comedians of the time, Bourvil and Louis de Funès, in a farce that is still today one of the biggest commercial successes of French cinema. René Clément in *Paris brûle-t-il?* (1969) glorified in a somewhat ludicrous manner the heros of the underground while Jean-Pierre Melville, with *L'Armée des ombres* (1969), created a much deeper and more moving tribute to the Résistance.

Occasionally, one film will incorporate a Jewish member of the Résistance. This will be much more common in the mid-seventies with, for example, Costa-Gavras' *Section Spéciale* (*Special Section*, 1975), and Frank Cassenti's *L'Affiche rouge* (1976). In 1970, Georges Dumoulin's *Nous n'irons plus aux bois* shows a group of Communist Résistants, including one Jew, hiding and fighting in a forest of the Meuse region capturing by chance a small group of German deserters. These young and romantic fighters dream about the proletarian revolution that should follow the Liberation while debating in the characteristic Leninist jargon of the late sixties. Their immediate goal is to free one hundred Russian prisoners from a nearby camp. They do not know what to do with their German captives and they are constantly afraid of being betrayed.

In the middle of the film, one of the main characters tells a friend that he could not go through a police control and fool a perspicacious gendarme because he has Jewish origins. The doctor and Lise (Marie-France Pisier) tell him that, on the contrary, they would have never guessed and that, according to the doctor's own words: "There is nothing to confess." In the following scene, the same man, Lucien, accompanied by Lise, rides his bicycle past a German convoy. A German officer stops him to inspect the stolen camouflage he carries on his fender. Lucien is executed on the spot while Lise sneaks away. Although the preceding scene suggests that Lucien was stopped because he might have looked Jewish to the Nazi officer, the incident itself indicates that he was stopped because he was carrying the camouflage on the fender of his bicycle.

The film makes it clear that Lucien is executed as a Résistant. His allusion to the fact that he "has Jewish origins" is never developed or even mentioned to explain, for example, his personal commitment to the Résistance or what happened to his family. The whole film is organized around the idea that this small group of Marxist Résistants lives a fragile and temporary egalitarian life, some sort of Commune in the woods, in which there is no class struggle. In the end, the Résistants are attacked by the Germans. The German deserters are sent on their own to an almost certain death while Lise escapes with the leaders who know the region perfectly well.

Lise, the main character and the only woman in the film, is married to an absent leader of the local Résistance. After learning that Lucien was secretly in love with her, she has a passionate love relationship with one of the German deserters. Although the group's political ideals serve as a catalyst for its unity, she clearly represents the real but unconscious power that keeps this little clique together beyond any political, sociological, religious or national barrier. She is brave, sensual and keeps away from any ideological debate. She wants to love people for what they are and refuses to classify them as Résistants, Jews or Germans. Indeed the most negative characters of the film are not German soldiers but a middle-aged French couple hiding behind its windows and refusing to open its door to Lise while the Germans are looking for her. This representation of the Communist Résistance recalls directly the solidarity of the leftist students during the riots of May 1968. Moreover, some key intellectual leaders to these riots were also Marxist Jews.[24] Indeed, at the same time Dumoulin's film was shown, French society was going through drastic changes that were directly linked to a reevaluation of its past.

4.   The Struggle for Accuracy, *1971-1985*

The student riots and the general strike of May 1968 paralyzed France for several weeks. If no one was willing or ready to seize power at that time, a perhaps much deeper revolution was taking place as traditional definitions of hierarchy and authority were broken down in the moral, social and political arenas. These changes called for an immediate reconsideration of the interpretation of the war years and the myth of "Resistancialism" as it had been progressively put in place by De Gaulle and many of the parents of the 1968 insurgents.

For this very reason, and in contrast to *Night and Fog*, *The Sorrow and the Pity* (1971) is not articulated around the necessity to remember the Holocaust itself but it develops a minute analysis of various distortions of reality through memory. In continuation of the last question asked by Resnais and Cayrol's film: "Who is on the lookout (...) to warn us of the coming of new executioners?", its purpose is also to remind its audience of the various attitudes that made the Holocaust possible. It does so through showing the terror, the passivity, the resignation, the complicity or the hatred reigning among large parts of French society mostly during the first two and a half years of the Nazi Occupation.

As Stanley Hoffmann[25] noted, the first half of *The Sorrow and the Pity* can be considered as partly based on Ophüls personal experience of war time in France as a teenager. At the same time, it is important to notice that Ophüls declared on many occasions that, in agreement with his wife's wishes, the films he would really love to make are musicals and comedies. His biography enables us to indicate exactly how he was brought to making documentaries and how they progressively made him famous.

Born in a Jewish family in 1927 in Frankfurt, under the name of Marcel Oppenheimer, Ophüls spent the first years of his life in Berlin. His parents (Max Ophüls and Hilde Wall) fled from Nazi Germany in 1933, the day after the Reichstag fire. Since 1928 his father, Max Ophüls, had become an extremely active and well known stage director. He had made his first film, the "comedy featurette" *Dann schon lieber lebertan* in 1930 (Willemen, 4). By the beginning of 1940, Max Ophüls had already directed or co-directed sixteen films and staged numerous plays in Germany, France, Austria, Holland and Italy. He was, however, not to produce his most famous works, *La Ronde*, *Le Plaisir*, *Madame de...* and *Lola Montès*, until his return to France in the fifties.[26]

Marcel was a young boy of thirteen when he and his parents escaped the invasion of France by the Nazis through Spain and Portugal after living briefly in Switzerland in order to arrive finally in California in 1941. In Los Angeles, he attended Hollywood High, where he might have been a classmate of Marilyn Monroe. It is there that he met his parents' friend Bertolt Brecht and his father's best friend, German actor Fritz Kortner whose wife he interviewed in *The Memory of Justice* (1976). One of his favorite movies of the time was Marcel Pagnol's *The Baker's Wife* (1938). It is also at that time that he played the role of a Hitler youth in *Prelude to War*, a propaganda film directed by Franz Capra who is also one of Ophüls' favorite directors.

From 1942 to 1945, Marcel Ophüls was part of an entertainment unit of the American Army in Japan. In 1947, he attended Occidental College in Los Angeles where he wrote a paper against the notion of collective guilt. With the fight against moral relativism, this was later to become a theme common to his most famous documentaries. Shortly after, he became a philosophy major at the University of California at Berkeley.

Back in France, at the age of twenty-five, Marcel Ophüls dropped his classes at the Sorbonne and became an assistant to famous directors such as Julien Duvivier, John Huston and Anatole Litvak. In 1955 he assisted his father in the making of his last and most famous film *Lola Montès*. Then he made a film on Henri Matisse for a TV station in Baden-Baden and was noticed and hired by François Truffaut for the making of *L'Amour à vingt ans.*

After these difficult debuts, Marcel Ophüls finally made his first feature film in 1963 (*Peau de bananes—Banana Peel*). It was a comedy with Jean-Paul Belmondo and Jeanne Moreau, the two most famous young actors of the New Wave Cinema. Unfortunately, this film was more successful with its audiences than it was with the critics. According to Ophüls himself this was in great part due to the fact that his film was not following the rules of the then very fashionable "New Wave" cinema. Two years later, his second film, *Feu à volonté* (*Fire at Will*, in collaboration with Jacques Robert), also called *Faites vos jeux Mesdames*, was a total failure. It definitely closed Ophüls' experiments in the making of entertainment films as the *Cahiers du cinéma* ridiculed it.

Ophüls then started working for French national TV, the ORTF, making reports for the magazine "Zoom!". With the help of Sédouy and Harris he made *Munich* in 1967, the first documentary of a three-part series about the Second World War and France under the Occupation. As the May '68 student riots broke out in Paris and throughout France, Ophüls made a documentary of the events, took a stand for the students and was fired from the National T.V. network.

In continuation of *Munich*, Ophüls made *The Sorrow and the Pity* in 1969, not for the ORTF but for German and Swiss TV. While *The Sorrow and the Pity* is mainly associated with the name of Marcel Ophüls, it is to be remembered that what remains today as Ophüls' best work was also made with the talented and active collaboration of Sédouy and Harris who were later to make their own documentary on the same period of French history (*Français si vous saviez*, 1973).

Filmed in five weeks and assembled in five months, *The Sorrow and the Pity* was a success both in Germany and in Switzerland but it was first censured in France. Finally shown in a small Left Bank theater in Paris, it immediately became a big success among young audiences and was first shown for a month in three of Paris' major theatres and then, in 1971, all over France and in the United States. Thus, in just a few months, Ophüls had become a world famous documentary director whose name and most famous work in post-Gaullist France was attached to violent controversy.

Fifteen years after *Night and Fog*, *The Sorrow and the Pity* brought back repressed memories of the war in a very different manner. It was immediately recognized worldwide as a very controversial masterpiece that was bringing a new light to the study of an infernal spiral of international events, local politics and individual choices that had led to the systematic exter-mination of six million Jews. However, for different reasons the film was violently criticized by both the Right and by the Left, including the *Cahiers du cinéma*. I will study these criticisms in my detailed analysis of the film. The general public, for different reasons, also found the film extremely controversial.

Whereas spectators would leave the viewing of *Night and Fog* like a nightmare, deeply moved and plunged in deep thought, watching *The Sorrow and the Pity* more generally leaves the audience shocked, angry, unconvinced, revolted or doubtful either with respect to the situation depicted in the film or regarding the film itself and its purpose. In fact this film directly reaches the heart of the controversy that was deleted from *Night and Fog* through the censoring of the image of the gendarme watching the camp in Pithiviers. This time, as noted by Stanley Hoffmann, the film could not avoid working as "a mirror presented by the authors to the audiences."[27] Therefore, independent from the film's relationship with historical truth that I will examine later, it is very important to understand how French audiences first reacted and often still react to this documentary.

The Sorrow and the Pity must be seen both as a film about everyday life in a town in Nazi-Occupied France—the town of Clermont-Ferrand—and as a post-May '68 work. The latter helps us understand in part the gaps and weaknesses in the accomplishment of the former. Even if de Gaulle resigned after the referendum of April 27, 1969, in 1971 he was still generally seen as the man who had given hope to France throughout the Occupation, as the President who made his country a modern world power, as the leader who saved France on many occasions from the Communist threat, and from possible total chaos in 1958 and again in May '68. Even if De Gaulle was no longer alive in 1971, the values of Gaullism were still predominant at that time in the French population as well as the vision of a French past these values had put forward. However, all these values were at the same time strongly challenged by a widely shared need to redefine French society after the tumultuous events of the late sixties. In such a context, *The Sorrow and the Pity* appeared to be extremely controversial for many different reasons.

First of all, this film was destroying the Gaullist myth of a French population united and resistant to the invader. De Gaulle's idea of French grandeur was also largely based on France's heritage and the key role it often played both in European and world history. It was to be understood that France had been a great nation in the past because its people had been able to give themselves great leaders. Obviously, the image of France shown in *The Sorrow and the Pity* was a contradiction to such a representation, showing a nation totally knocked out by the defeat and led by Marshal Pétain. Pétain was accepted by the population precisely because he was a war hero, like de Gaulle himself after World War II, and also because, according to the testimony of the Communist Jacques Duclos, many thought that Pétain could not "hurt anyone, that old man, he can only serve the cause of France. At his age, what can he hope for beyond that?" At the time of the shooting of the film, Duclos was also a candidate in the presidential elections to replace General de Gaulle who himself had become a national myth. Such a parallel between Pétain and de Gaulle is emphasized again when, talking about Pétain, Louis Grave declares that any eighty-year-old leader should be "thrown to the pigs."

Moreover, the film also portrayed former German soldiers who had not changed their ideas since the war at a time when a strong and close alliance with Germany played a major role in de

Gaulle's vision of the European Community. It also showed young German soldiers and their admiration for their elders who had fought in World War II. On the contrary, for de Gaulle's politics, it was essential to show that Germany had completely changed and was now an ally of the French economy.

The Sorrow and the Pity insists also on the fundamental role played by the British as the last defenders of a free and democratic Europe for which so many French were said to be unwilling to fight. However, a few years before the showing of Ophüls' work, in 1963, de Gaulle had prevented the integration of England in the Common Market. In many ways, *The Sorrow and the Pity* was directly threatening a certain vision of the present and the past that de Gaulle needed in order to have the French electorate accept his European politics—a vision that was to be continued by his two successors, Georges Pompidou and Valéry Giscard d'Estaing.

In more direct ways, the film offered much open criticism of de Gaulle's role as a leader of the Résistance and a head of state. Pierre Mendès-France, founder in 1960 of the Socialist Unified Party (PSU), insists that de Gaulle played a major role not because of his inner qualities but because he "had no other way. There was no other conceivable possibility than for him to be absolutely inflexible in defending those rights of which he was caretaker." He immediately adds: "Of course, his pride, his harshness, and his often intractable nature did not make things easier. I think that politically speaking, he was right." Sir Edward Spears, the wartime liaison between Churchill and de Gaulle, also comments in a very general manner: "The French strongly believe in the military, and in the end they always turn to the military [...] They have a taste for rank in France." A little further, after mentioning refugees in England in 1940 and their reluctance to fight, Spears insists on the French "blind stubbornness to get out at all costs."

Georges Bidault, de Gaulle's opponent and former successor of Jean Moulin as head of the Résistance, is heard saying about the French: "But at any rate they feel a certain need for protection. They are, in truth, paternalistic." Because of the general formulation of this remark, it could be both interpreted in 1971 as a criticism of the French people in 1940, in 1958 or 1968, at times when the French population chose order at all cost and turned to a military figure to save their nation. D'Astier de la Vigerie declares also about de Gaulle: "He was *already*, plainly and simply the king of France" (my emphasis).

For audiences of the early seventies, such declarations were extremely controversial as they could all bear at least two meanings: one that would directly apply to the period of the Occupation, and one for the France of the early seventies. Such declarations, which tended to generalize about France, de Gaulle or the French people, were formulated by individuals to whom the French could easily relate or by politicians who were still very influential in 1971. For these reasons, such declarations raised key questions at a time when French society was once again trying to redefine itself after a violent political crisis.

The Sorrow and the Pity also reveals the faults of political choices based on fright, and the desire for order above all. It shows a society profoundly divided by the growing influences of socialism and communism. It underlines the passivity and sometimes the cowardice of large sections of the bourgeoisie protecting their assets at all costs, the responsibility of the military in the defeat, and the hatred and anti-Semitism in the conservative parties. It puts in direct opposition to this the heroism of a Jew and socialist leader (Pierre Mendès-France) or the common sense of a heroic peasant (Louis Graves). It questions the glory of officers and war heros who became heads of state. All these themes could easily be transposed and related by the French audience of the seventies to its own reality.

Regarding the anti-Semitism of the bourgeoisie, May 1969 was also the time of the affair of the "white slave trade in Orléans" in which a rumor spread about Jewish shop owners of downtown Orléans kidnapping and drugging women in their fitting rooms to send them abroad for prostitution (Edgard Morin, *La Rumeur d'Orléans*). Since the late fifties, such rumors were not uncommon in towns such as Paris, Toulouse, Tours, Limoges, Douai, Amiens, Rouen, Le Mans, Lille, Valenciennes or Poitiers.

A few years earlier, in a press conference of November 28, 1967, after the Six Day War, De Gaulle had criticized the Israelis as "a dominating people sure of itself." Raymond Aron responded that de Gaulle had just then "opened a new period of Jewish history and maybe of anti-Semitism" (Bourdrel, 541-542). The debates around the representation of the Jews in the French collective psyche, their assimilation in French society and the role of Israel in the world played an important role in the French politics in the early seventies. And so it is also in this context that *The Sorrow and the Pity* was being shown with its denunciation of Vichy France's anti-Semitism and its attacks on Gaullism.

Moreover, besides its rampant violent criticism of Gaullism, the film also shows de Gaulle's rival Georges Bidault, Jean Moulin's successor at the head of the Résistance, recently returned from exile. Bidault is also the former founder of the ultra conservative *Rassemblement pour l'Algérie Française* (Union for a French Algeria). The documentary insists as well on the positive roles played by leftist political leader, Duclos and Mendès-France, still very influential in the France of the early seventies. In many occurrences, Mendès-France can even be considered as the main positive hero of Ophüls' story. It is indeed his interviews, better than Ophüls' extremely rare direct interventions, that situate other segments within the general progression and unity of the film.

For these reasons, *The Sorrow and the Pity* was to be an extremely controversial work in the France of the early seventies. It could be seen, according to Ophüls' wishes, as a study of present distortions of truth in memory and a violent criticism of the general attitude of the French people during the Occupation but also as a leftist criticism of the foundations of conservative French ideology in the late sixties and early seventies. *The Sorrow and the Pity* is therefore to be seen as a work at the border between political-fiction and politically committed cinema (Martin, 86). It directly involves the imagination and the political choices of its director, the witnesses and the audiences in a reconstruction of the past through an active and ironic judgement of the present.

If Ophüls' film cannot be seen as an exception in French cinema, chronologically it can be considered as the first major work of a series of films criticizing a traditional and mostly Gaullist image of French grandeur. It was to be followed, in 1973, by André Harris' and Alain de Sédouy's *Français si vous saviez* about the legitimacy of power in France, Louis Malle's *Lacombe Lucien* about a collaborator who could have also been a Résistant and Jérôme Kanapa's *La République est morte à Dien-Bien-Phu* about the French War in Indochina. The profound intellectual, sociological, spiritual and moral crises that followed May '68 revealed a deep need to reconsider the values and the vision of the past on which the French people had founded a large part of its identity, since 1945. *The Sorrow and the Pity* also became a first step in cinema toward the open criticism of a central and omnipotent state led by a very powerful president and against the archaism of the dominating patriarchal structures and moral values in French society.

However, in order to reach its goals, the relationship of the documentary with reality and historical truth is essential. It is also the main aspect used by Ophüls' detractors to condemn his work and deny its historical value. For this very reason, it is extremely important to consider that in filming *The Sorrow and the Pity*, Ophüls was not dealing only with facts but with emotions, passions, guilt, justifications and many other degrees of distortion of reality. His main technique to restore truth was then to distort the distortions of the witnesses through the art of cinema, mainly using different degrees of a subtle irony that undermines the entire film. As irony can generally be defined as a figure of speech through which a sentence means the opposite of what it says, the film, in the way it was made and edited often gives a different meaning to a literal reading of the isolated images out of which it is made.

The film then involves different levels of signification and it requires a very active and committed reading from its audience. This is certainly another reason why it remains somewhat controversial today. However, the analysis of distortions by the director is still a matter of interpretation and in some cases whether Ophüls really reached a truth remains questionable. The only way to decide on such matters is to closely analyze the film itself and the mechanisms it uses to convey precise emotions or ideas. Therefore, the study of the film's treatment of irony, uncertain testimonies and historical truth will be at the heart of my detailed analysis of this documentary.

Most critics agree that with the first showings of *The Sorrow and the Pity*, 1971 represents a major turning point in the representation of the Occupation in French cinema. Shortly after the riots of May, 68, the fall and the death of Charles de Gaulle, and with an expanding economy, French society needed and demanded radical changes. This generalized push towards political, social and moral reforms was to be accompanied by major reinterpretations of the past combined with a cozy and nostalgic fashion for memories.

In his well documented essay *Le Syndrome de Vichy*, Henri Rousso characterizes this period from 1971 to 1978 with the success of a "retro" fashion and, in cinema, with a diversification of points of view on the Occupation, making this period of French history a "familiar object" and an "usual reference." As opposed to the sixties during which the theme of the Résistance dominated the screen, in the seventies, following the pioneer work of Ophüls, and Paxton's book *Vichy France*, the Collaboration became a favorite topic of French cinema.

Rousso differentiates between four different points of view on the Occupation at that time: the prosecutors who violently denounced and condemned the ideology of Vichy France and the attitude of the French population at that time; the chroniclers who "try to recreate the atmosphere of the Occupation" from the telling of precise historical events; the aesthetes analyzing "the destructuration the Occupation provoked in the bodies and in the minds"; and the opportunists profiting from a fashionable subject with comedies and very mediocre films (Rousso, 266-269). For each group Rousso mentions the following films:

The Prosecutors:

- *Français si vous saviez* (Harris and Sédouy, 1973; documentary)
- *Les Chinois à Paris* (Jean Yanne, 1973)
- *La République est morte à Dien Bien Phu* (Jérôme Kanapa, 1974; documentary)
- *Section Spéciale* (Costa-Gavras, 1975)
- *Au nom de la race* (Marc Hillel, 1975; documentary)
- *Chantons sous l'Occupation* (André Halimi, 1976; documentary)
- *L'Affiche rouge* (Frank Cassenti, 1976)

The Chroniclers:

- *Le Train* (Pierre Granier-Defferre, 1973)
- *L'Ironie du sort* (Edouard Molinaro, 1974)
- *Les Violons du bal* (Michel Drach, 1974)
- *Les Guichets du Louvre* (Michel Mitrani, 1974)
- *Souvenir d'en France* (André Téchiné, 1975)
- *Un Sac de billes* (Jacques Doillon, 1975)
- *La Communion solennelle* (René Féret, 1977)

The Aesthetes:

- *Lacombe Lucien* (Louis Malle, 1974)
- *Portier de nuit* (Lilianna Cavanni, 1974)
- *Monsieur Klein* (Joseph Losey, 1976)
- *Les Bons et les méchants* (Claude Lelouch, 1978)
- *One Two Two* (Christian Gion, 1978)

The Opportunists:

- *Mais où est donc passé la 7e compagnie?* (Robert Lamoureux, 1973)
- *Opération Lady Marlène* (R. Lamoureux, 1975)
- *On a retrouvé la 7e compagnie* (R. Lamoureux, 1975)
- *Le Jour de gloire* (Jacques Bernard, 1976)
- *La 7e compagnie au clair de lune* (P. Clair, 1977)
  (...plus some of the pornographic films from the years 1975-1978)

To this list I will add six films not mentioned by Rousso that directly deal however with the Holocaust: *Une Larme dans l'océan* (Henri Glaeser, 1971), *Pourquoi Israël?* (Claude Lanzmann, 1973; documentary), *Toute une vie* (Claude Lelouch, 1974), *La France et les Français sous l'Occupation* (Daniel Lander, 1974; documentary), *1942* (Simone Boruchowicz, 1975), *The Memory of Justice* (Marcel Ophüls, 1976; documentary). This list could also include two Belgian films and one Swiss film I will not have the space to analyze here: *Rue haute* (André Ernotte, 1976; on this film see Annette Insdorf 34-38), *Au Nom du Führer* (Lydia Chagoll, 1977) and *Konfrontation* (Rolf Lyssy, 1975).

Except for the "opportunists" whose humor is based on the cliches of the easy going and nonchalant nature of the French and their *joie de vivre*, most of these films confront the Holocaust directly or mention the responsibility of Vichy France in its perpetration. While it is easy to see why their necessary and preposterous distortions of war-time history do not allow comedies to even allude to the Holocaust, it is more difficult to understand why films belonging to other categories listed above could still after 1971 give an account of this period of French history without even mentioning the persecution of the Jews in France.

Français si vous saviez (1973) is a documentary in three parts made by André Harris and Alain de Sédouy. Both men had worked very closely with Marcel Ophüls during the making of *The Sorrow and the Pity*; Harris on the script and the interviews, Sédouy as a producer. Consequently, *Français si vous saviez* often uses similar techniques as *The Sorrow and the Pity*. Like Ophüls' documentary, the 1973 film is made out of interviews of both unknown and famous witnesses filmed in their natural settings and they are constantly put in relationship with newsreel and historical footage. In this film Pierre Mendès-France appears less often but he still plays a key role as a central interpreter of the events depicted. This documentary also begins with describing life in a French town—Toulouse instead of Clermont-Ferrand—but this time it starts with the evocation of the liberation and of the local Résistance members being silenced in 1945 and 1946 by De Gaulle's authority and image. The film also develops clearly, almost to an extreme, the parallel made in *The Sorrow and the Pity* between Marshal Pétain and General De Gaulle. Referring to the famous anthem all French pupils had to learn in the glory of Pétain and that started with the phrase: "Maréchal nous voilà!" the second part of Harris and Sédouy's film is entitled: "Général nous voilà!" Moreover, the poster of the film shows the French people building the image of General de Gaulle with bricks taken from the image of Marshal Pétain.

However, *Français si vous saviez* never analyzes anti-Semitism nor the persecution of the Jews during the Occupation. In its global political and anti-Gaullist perspective it "forgets" to consider the constant harassment of the 350,000 Jews living in France and the 75,000 Jews arrested and deported "to the East" as if their fate was irrelevant to the film as a general essay on French contemporary politics and the legitimacy of power. In contrast with *The Sorrow and the Pity* which was also a "Chronicle of a French Town Under the Occupation," Harris and Sédouy's documentary is mainly dedicated to the analysis of political conflicts and various struggles for power. In consequence, it remains a very good documentary and historical analysis but it allows a safe distanciation of the audience with testimonies that appear to be more factual and less personal than they are in Ophüls' film.

Even if its editing gives it a certain irony that recalls Ophüls' work, *Français si vous saviez* loses the main qualities of *The Sorrow and the Pity*. It loses the subtle, ironic and very powerful evocation of individual feelings and choices under the Occupation, including feelings about the persecution of the Jews. For these reasons and in spite of its provocative title, *Français si vous saviez* could not induce the same interest nor provoke the same scandal Ophüls' film did three years earlier.

In a similar manner, the films Rousso calls "the prosecutors" only allude to the persecution of the Jews within a more general denunciation of Nazi atrocities, the Vichy regime and its popularity. *Au Nom de la race* (*Of Pure Blood*, 1975), is a one hour twenty minute inquiry about the "Lebensborn" program secretly instituted by Himmler and the SS in order to create a new Aryan race. As its subtitle indicates, this documentary, filmed by Marc Hillel and Clarissa Henry, is "an investigation into the creation of a super race." Like Ophüls' films, *Au Nom de la race* combines historical footage with recent interviews. It also uses many segments of Leni Riefensthal's *The Triumph of the Will*. This documentary analyzes how the Nazis' racial theories developed in parallel with a secret program intended to select Aryan mothers and SS fathers, fight abortion, and create a pure race of masters that would dominate Nazi Europe. The vast majority of the witnesses interviewed are Germans: an SS doctor, three nurses, administrators who worked for the Lebensborn program, or bystanders who witnessed how the program was run.

This secret program for the creation of a new race is presented as the heart of Hitler's one thousand year Reich. It is described as being separate from the Holocaust, as "the most secret, the most mysterious and most disputed of all Nazi organizations." According to the film, the Holocaust was to make room for the new race. It was a first step towards the one thousand year reign of the super race. Consequently, the film dedicates only a few minutes to the extermination of the Jews in order to indicate that the staff working for Lebensborn were never to mention the Holocaust, and to recall that Jewish mothers were not accepted in Himmler's nurseries because, as a nurse put it: "there were almost no Jews in Germany during the Third Reich."

Such a preposterous precision seems necessary as just before that a Catholic nun and the wife of the SS doctor Ebner were shown saying that Lebensborn was, literally, "a source of life" (*Lebensborn* in German) helping "all the mothers in need," promoting mothering and fighting abortion. Many sequences of that sort indicate that Hillel and Henry have been strongly influenced by Ophüls' irony both in their interviewing techniques and in the editing of their work. The end of the documentary investigates what happened to some of the babies selected or kidnapped within the Lebensborn. In doing so, it demonstrates some of the repercussions of this program in the present. *Au nom de la race* is an excellent film that investigates a subject that is very seldom analyzed in cinema even though it represents an essential chapter for the study of Nazi racial theories.

Along with Dumoulin's *Nous n'irons plus au bois* (1970) and Cassenti's *L'Affiche rouge* (1976), Costa-Gavras' *Special Section* (1975) is one of three films that clearly mentions Jewish participation in the French Résistance. *Special Section* begins in Vichy, in August 1941. During the first sequence, taking place at the opera, a recorded speech of Pétain announces to the foreign diplomatic representations that the Marshal has suspended the activities of all political parties and created a Counsel on Political Justice to protect order in France. Then, *Section Spéciale* tells the story of a group of Communist and Jewish Résistants trying to assassinate German soldiers in retaliation for the execution of a Polish Jew and a Communist, both arrested for demonstrating against the invader and the government. Anarchists, Jews and Communists are also presented as the preferred victims for random executions in retaliation for the Résistants' actions.

Costa-Gavras' film constitutes a fierce denunciation of Vichy's sense of justice and order by showing how various government officials often acted ahead of any German demand for retaliation to protect their own political ambitions or fulfill their own instinct of revenge. The film clearly shows the various justifications one uses to justify a murder such as Pétain's will to sacrifice a human life in order to protect others, the professionalism of many officials that are "just following orders" or the justification of a murder for political purposes. One of the Communist Résistance leaders is shown explaining how, according to the Marxist ideology, the imperialistic war of 1939 became a war of the people against the fascists after the German invasion of the Soviet Union. This reasoning justifies killing German soldiers at random that might be "good guys" or even "anti-fascists." According to Annette Insdorf: "The target of Costa-Gavras is not merely within the French nation (in the upper echelons of power) but within the individual who allows politics to overcome conscience (...) The film's narrative structure is one of accumulation, as each individual repeats the same suspension of conscience until the inhuman political machine has no impediments" (Insdorf, 243).

Frank Cassenti's *L'Affiche rouge* (1976) also deals with the Jewish Résistance, Vichy's justice and the assassination of German soldiers. Cassenti worked with Costa-Gavras, as an assistant director, on *L'Aveu* (1970). In its form, however, his work is extremely different from Costa-Gavras' even if it often approaches comparable themes such as violent criticism of the parody of justice in a totalitarian state. Cassenti's film is based on the real story of the arrest, trial and execution of the members of the *group Manouchian*, a group of Résistants composed of Communist immigrants, many of whom were Jewish.

Made in a Brechtian perspective, *L'Affiche rouge* is also a film on "the problems of cinematographic representation" (Christian Vaugeois, 5). The film is based on a constant parallel between the trial of February, 1944 and its representation on a theater stage in 1976. It also constantly opposes a Nazi theatrical representation of History (Goebbels in the film), to its own. In the middle of the film, Goebbels (Alain Salomon) is heard saying about the trial: "Ah! What a great time for show-business (...) it will be a French-German co-production."[28] The characters in the movie are seen in three different image series which are intertwined throughout the film: as characters in a play, wearing commedia dell'arte masks; as members of the Résistance in 1944; and as the actors discussing the very play they are rehearsing.

This constant weaving of history, a play and a simultaneous reflection on their conditions of representation creates a distancing between the story and the audience that clearly recalls Brecht's theater. Because it breaks away from any nostalgic representation of the past through personal memory and the comfort of a sentimental identification with the main characters, *L'Affiche rouge* is at the opposite of the so-called "rétro fashion" of the early seventies. In this film, as Christian Vaugeois put it: "rudimentary psychology and sentimentalism are replaced with facts, analysis, and a show as they create the structuring on which the relationship with the audience in based" (Vaugeois, 5). The film takes its title (*L'Affiche rouge, The Red Poster*) from a red poster printed by Vichy officials to track down this group of Foreign Résistants it called "The Army of Crime." Showing the pictures and the names of only ten members of the Manouchian group (23 total members, 22 men and one woman), the poster read "Liberation by the Army of Crime!" Unlike the vast majority of films made about the Résistance, *L'Affiche rouge* strongly insists on the fact that these men were foreigners, Jews, or Communists, and that they were hunted down by French members of the Gestapo. All these characters also have a revolutionary past and future in Spain, Hungary, Armenia, Russia, China or Chile. Their commitment to the Résistance is clearly a part of a much larger and unending fight against fascism. The film itself constitutes a significant chapter in the controversial problem of the representation of the Résistance, and particularly that of the Jewish Résistance in France, since the early seventies. In this respect, the so-called "Manouchian Affair" will be at the heart of many heated debates up until 1985 when a TV documentary—Mosco's *Des Terroristes à la retraite*— accused the Communist party of having dedicated its Foreign and Jewish Résistance members to very high risk operations in order to protect its native French fighters (see Henry Rousso, 167, 252, 340; Judith Friedlander, 28-29).

In 1987 Frank Cassenti will make *Le Testament d'un poète juif assassiné* based on Elie Wiesel's famous novel *The Testament*.[29] This film alludes very briefly to the Holocaust. It is structured around the continuity of the persecution of the Jews in Eastern Europe and the Soviet Union before and after World War II. Like Elie Wiesel's book, Cassenti's work is based on a paradox. It presents the silence of a father and his son as a form of resistance to the executioner's perverted logic at the same time that it underlines the necessity to testify and to speak up in order to save the memory of a whole people. However, when the executioner's purpose is to exterminate a people and its memory, to write or to talk about one's memory is to condemn oneself to death while trying to survive. Years apart from each other, the poet Paltiel Kossover and Grisha Kossover face the same dilemma as a father trying to save the memory of his people for his son and a son trying to save the memory of his father for his mother and his own family.

Among the categories Henry Rousso called "the chroniclers" and "the aesthetes," many films directly consider the persecution of the Jews. They also all involve a rather precise representation of the individual responsibilities of the average French citizen. The first films to be considered under this aspect are Michel Drach's *Les Violons du bal* (1973) and Michel Mitrani's *Les Guichets du Louvre* (1974).

The fact that Drach's film represented France at the 1974 Cannes Festival is indicative of the changing mentalities in France since the scandal of *The Sorrow and the Pity* only three years earlier. It indicates the general need and will of France at that time to reinterpret its past as well as the fact that the Occupation was quickly becoming a rather fashionable subject one could deal with using all the new tricks of contemporary cinema—a broken chronology, the intertwining of fiction with reality, narration and comment, using different actors to play the same character, showing the technique and even the equipment employed etc.

Drach's film is at the same time a moving, and technically intricate recollection of a very personal past. Pauline Kael found it sometimes irritating as its use of Rouch's *cinéma vérité* for contemporary sequences is mixed with a certain *qualité française* of cinema and "the height of refugee chic," (Kael, 1976: 421. Quoted by Insdorf, 120) mainly in its use of color images dealing with the past. It seems however that such a critic misses two central points in the film.

First, the contemporary sequences erupting in black and white within the main narration in color destroy in a very efficient way the comfortable critical drowsiness that threatens the spectators as they are watching a story told in the past with few major events, well organized settings, warm and reassuring pastel colors and a clear ideological cut between good and evil.

Such sequences in black and white force the spectators to look for a link between the film and their own present.

Second, such an ideal representation of the past, with pastel colors, shows clearly that the story is not told by a child but by an adult (Michel Drach himself) as he remembers a chapter of his past through the memories of his childhood. For example, on one occasion, Michel Drach, as the director, indicates that in the film the young boy (Drach's own son) wears a sailor's suit he probably never wore himself when he was this age. Therefore Drach admits that these recollections are partly idealized. This explains and justifies what Pauline Kael called "the refugee chic" as it can be considered a technique consciously used by the director to indicate that this story is told through his personal memories. Neither the "refugee chic" nor the contemporary sequences should be considered as mistakes but as elements inherent and necessary to the functioning of the film.

This film suffers however from a few ideological approximations characteristic of the sixties when it offers various parallels between the student revolt of May '68 against De Gaulle's authority and Michel's brother's revolt against Nazism. As the Parisian students of the late sixties were shouting to the French riot police: "CRS....SS" (CRS: *Compagnie Républicaine de Sécurité*), the film suffers from the militant confusion of that time between Fascism, Gaullism and Nazism. In the film, for example, Michel as an adult (played by Jean-Louis Trintignant) helps a student escaping from the police after a riot in May of 1968. In the car he reflects on these events and concludes: "It still exists!" assuming a supposedly obvious parallel between his hiding as a Jew and the student's flight. The repression of the student riots in 1968 was violent and often vicious but nothing allows one to compare it to the persecution of the Jews during the Occupation. Nevertheless, Drach's film constitutes an extremely important episode in the cinematographic representation of the persecution of the Jews in Occupied France.

Les Violons du bal presents us with an autobiographical story told in a very subjective manner. Contrary to the technique used in *Night and Fog*, Drach chose to use black and white footage for the present and color images for the past. As Annette Insdorf noted, this suggests also that the director's memories "are more vibrantly compelling than his contemporary existence" (40). By using black and white images for the present, Drach also insists on the fact that in dealing with the abruptness of contemporary events we are often unable to see how they situate themselves in our personal psyche. In consequence, the present and the riots of May '68 are presented in black and white, as in a newsreel dealing with facts, with history yet to be interpreted.

In contrast, it is the past and the memories, in color, that are presented as an idealized but very present reality allowing the audience to understand better the objectives of the director in 1973. This obsessive aspect of the past within the present justifies the constant jumpcut parallels between the difficulties of making the film (in the present and in black and white), and the vivid memories of the director (in color). This violent resurgence of past events through the encounters of comparable situations evokes an influence of Marcel Proust's work. Indeed, many thoughts that were popular during the sixties could be used to read this complex film. These would include Freud's and Reich's theories of repressed events, Nietzsche's and Spinoza's representations of active and passive forces or Henri Bergson's conception of memory with its analysis of the contraction of the totality of the past in the present (the Bergsonian cone).

One of the great qualities of this film is that it presents us with personal memories of the attempt of a Jewish family to flee France during the Occupation. If this work is structured around the obsessive reminiscence of this past, it is also punctuated with the evocation of both material and personal difficulties encountered by the director to make his film. On the "material" or commercial side, a producer is shown explaining that unless a film includes sex, a dead body, dead Jews or a star in the leading role, it is of no interest to him. The same man adds "I am the one who got Mussolini started!" Only the last of these requirements is fulfilled by the film as the roles of Drach's wife and Michel's mother are played by Marie-José Nat (Drach's own wife).

On the more personal side Drach felt the urgency of representing this key episode of his own past without making it just another event in French history, a story of the past that happened to other people. For this reason, the film ends as it started with a clear reminder that this is indeed an auto-biographical film. The film opens showing the director working on the production of his film and it ends with an image showing a clapboard clacking in front of Trintignant's face (Trintignant playing the role of Drach as adult). Still within the personal aspects of the film, the leading roles were given to Drach's own wife and son (the actress Marie-José Nat and David Drach).

As a chronicle of life in France under the Occupation, *Les Violons du bal* introduces various types of French anti-Semites. As in many other films of this period dealing with the persecution of the Jews in France, Drach's film shows almost no German characters (as in *Le Vieil homme et l'enfant, Lacombe Lucien* and *Les Guichets du Louvre*). Jews are indeed being persecuted by French citizens. Aristocrats are shown ignoring the roundups and socializing with the Germans. The bourgeoisie rejects the idea of a marriage with an "Israelite" (the mother of Michel's sister's fiance) and farmers take advantage of the fleeing Jews in order to steal their money (Monsieur Robert). In this situation, Michel's family barely makes it to Switzerland in a suspenseful but somewhat conventional escape sequence that can be justified by the idealization of a child's memory.

On the other hand, the film also offers a diversified portrait of a non-religious French Jewish family under the Occupation. Michel's family is being persecuted for being Jewish but Michel himself does not understand was a Jew is. With a smile, his mother acknowledges that they are Jewish but both she and the grandmother refuse to provide the young boy with any explanation. When Michel goes back to school and proudly declares that yes, he is a Jew, his classmates insult him and one of them punches him in the face. In this film, being a Jew is first associated with being the victim of hatred and persecutions (cf. *La Cage de verre, Un Sac de billes, Le Vieil homme et l'enfant*).

As he was first targeted by the police, Michel's father is absent in the film, already in hiding abroad. On the opposite side of his mother's and grandmother's low key existence waiting for a means to escape is Michel's brother, Jean who revolts, tries to help a Jewish refugee and then joins the Résistance in Spain. His sister becomes a fashion model and socializes with Germans in Paris while waiting for an opportunity to escape. She is also the one that warns the family that a roundup is being prepared and that they should leave Paris as soon as possible. Finally, his grandmother is shown worshipping in a church and when Michel, because he is Jewish, wants to refuse a Catholic medal a little girl gives him, the little girl replies: "So what, my father's a Communist." In this context the only consciousness Michel has of what it means to be a Jew consists mainly in the progressive discovery of anti-Semitism and in realizing that he and his family are being persecuted and have to flee.

All the members of this family are portrayed as trying their own ways to escape from their executioners. As many Jews in hiding thought that it would probably be safer to split families so everyone would not be arrested at the same time, the father, the brother, the sister, and the little group formed by the mother, the grandmother and Michel all follow their own paths of survival and escape. In the end, this pays off but nothing assures them that the family will ever be reunited and the film gives no detail about the destiny of each person, avoiding a purely conventional "happy ending." When Michel and his mother finally cross the Swiss border, they are faced with a Swiss soldier and a very uncertain future. Nothing is said either about the grandmother that had to cross the border hidden in a coffin because she was no longer able to walk. This explains in part why the last image shows a clap identifying the take directly in front of Trintignant's face (in black and white). In this manner the film ends both as a personal memory (Drach telling his story) and as a representative fiction to be extended to similar events lived by thousands of other Jewish families (Trintignant playing Michel Drach's role).

Finally, Drach's work introduces or utilizes many themes that were developed in fiction films on the same period throughout the seventies and the eighties. The most important are:

- The denunciation of the myth of a population unified against the invader (borrowed from Ophüls' *The Sorrow and the Pity*).
- The urgency to tell what happened to the Jews and to denounce anti-Semitism.
- The endless material difficulties encountered in making a film on the persecution of the Jews (Ophüls' *Hotel Terminus* and Claude Lanzmann's *Shoah*).
- The personal and obsessive character of the memories of that time for a child or a teenager (Doillon's *Un sac de billes*, Malle's *Lacombe Lucien* and *Goodbye Children*).
- Both the personal and historical value of memories of that time.
- Children and teenagers who do not understand what a Jew or a Freemason are (Doillon's *Un Sac de billes*, Malle's films).
- The attempt of some Jews to survive through hiding their identity or fraternizing with Collaborators or German officers (*Lacombe Lucien*).
- The situation of Jews trying to escape from occupied France and find refuge in the country (Doillon's *Un Sac de billes*, Malle's films, Pierre Sauvage's *Weapons of the Spirit*)

Many of these themes reappear as soon as 1974, in Michel Mitrani's famous work *Les Guichets du Louvre*.

Based on the novel *Les Guichets du Louvre* by Roger Boussinot, this film is also known as a very accurate rendition of the massive roundup of July 16-17, 1942. It was shown for the first time on French TV in 1979, late at night, and again for the anniversary of the roundup, in 1992, during prime time. The character of Paul is indeed grounded on Boussinot's own experience. The story line of *Les Guichets du Louvre* is provided by the

unsuccessful efforts of an isolated French university student
"simply" trying "to save a fellow or two" during a systematic
roundup of Jews in Paris (the roundup of the Velodrome
d'Hiver). As his best friend refuses to be "on the side of the
prey," Paul decides to help the Jews because they are "people,
not better or worse than others, that are caught in a trap." Near
the end of the film, Paul asks the Jewish girl he is trying to save
(Jeanne) what Jews are. Jeanne answers: "That's us... me. I
mean... I never knew what Jews were and I live very well like
that... We are a people" ("On est un peuple"). To this, Paul adds
that bankers and those who are on the side of Laval and Pétain
are not part of the people. Then Jeanne concludes: "We are a
group of people" ("Nous, on est des gens").

As in most French films of that time, the main characters of
Les Guichets du Louvre have no precise idea of what it means to
be a Jew except that every Jew is victim of persecution. This
constant fear and distrust of unknown Gentiles is the central
feeling at the heart of the behavior of all the Jews in Mitrani's
film. Before meeting Jeanne, Paul tries to help an old man whose
family has just been arrested, a man feigning blindness trying to
escape, a young woman in a bakery and two children playing in
the street. They all refuse his help because they distrust him or
because they think they have nothing to fear. Many of them
indeed try to convince themselves that they have nothing to be
afraid of because they have a husband who is a French prisoner
of war (the woman in the bakery), because the French police
would never do anything bad to them (a bystander in the street)
or because they are veterans of the first world war (an old man
in the street).

From the very first images of the film there is a strong
contrast between the systematic, cold blooded, flawless trap that
is being set by the French police and the totally terrified and
disorganized Jewish community that never realizes what exactly
is going on. On one occasion, when the runaways find some of
Jeanne's relatives hiding in their apartment, the film mentions a
leaflet from an underground Jewish organization calling for
resistance. To this, Jeanne's relatives reply "One does not resist

against the whole of Europe." The same people refuse to remove their yellow star imposed by Pétain's ruling because they do not want to look as if they were ashamed of being Jewish. Later, when Jeanne wants to find refuge at the UGIF (the "Union Genérale des Israelites de France"), Paul warns her that: "It's to lure you. It's a sinister trap." Throughout the film the vast majority of the Jews climb calmly into the police trucks or buses while one is heard complaining: "*Oh les gaz encore!*" "Oh, the fumes again!"

At the beginning of the film, Paul does not want to save "a Jew" but "a fellow" ("un type"). Beyond the fact that this statement indicates that Jews should have been helped on the basis of universal humanitarian principles and values, it also shows that Paul is not aware of what the systematic persecution of the Jews that lasted for years really means. Paul never realized that since the rise of Nazism most Jews felt totally abandoned by the rest of the world and sometimes by God himself. In consequence, all of his efforts fail either because the victims do not realize exactly what is happening, because they are afraid of falling into another trap, or because they have learned that they can really trust only their own people.

In the end, after multiple obstacles, Jeanne will trust Paul and follow him to the safer Right Bank of the Seine. However, in the middle of the bridge crossing the river, she stops and returns to the people she belongs with while a German soldier takes a picture of the separation. In this final sequence, in contrast with the beginning of the film, Jeanne realizes what it means for her to be a Jew and to belong to the Jewish community. Her first reason for going back is probably to join her parents and family as she understands that if she crosses this bridge she might lose every chance to see them again. At the same time she reveals her identity for the first time: "My name is Jeanne. I assure you, it's true!" In doing so, she "acquires an identity only by becoming a victim" (Judith Doneson, quoted by Annette Insdorf, 86), but mostly, she is proud to tell Paul that her typical French name could easily allow her to start a new and safe life. In spite of this she wants to return to her family and to her community as a Jew, as a French Jew. By giving only her first name and walking back in search of her family, she insists on the fact that she could have but never did renounce her Jewish identity. In this time of persecution she cannot imagine her life without it even if that means she will die in the hands of the Nazis, as her last image will disappear, anonymously, in the hands of a German soldier.

While putting on center stage the isolated efforts of a student trying to save Jews, the film also clearly shows the French police arresting the Jews, a French militia man and former classmate of Paul supervising the roundup, a member of the secret police, some French people looting Jewish apartments during the roundup itself, a poltroon Catholic priest refusing to protect a Jewish woman begging for protection and a bystander agreeing with satisfaction, "That will teach them!"

But Mitrani's film also shows the bystanders growing reaction of disgust and revolt when they were occasionally faced with the reality of the persecution of Jewish families. This increasingly active but very limited empathy for the victims of the mass round ups has been acknowledged by several historians and survivors. Michael Marrus describes it as a temporary but real threat to popular support of the politics of Collaboration. Once, a French woman witnessing the arrest of Jeanne's co-workers exclaims: "Those poor girls!" In another sequence, some people insult the French police as they are arresting a woman. On three occasions, some French people are shown trying somewhat to help the Jews: a woman, a friend of Jeanne's family, hides the runaways in her boutique and convinces Jeanne to remove her yellow star. Another woman promises to take care of a baby whose family has just been arrested and, in a bar, a group of pimps prevents a militia man from arresting Paul and Jeanne. The realism of such scenes is verified by the fact that among the bystanders who had seen the massive roundup of the summer of 1942, many showed their disgust and their anger up to the point that the administration feared a possible massive show of support for the Jews. Many gentiles were arrested but such anger never led to any massive protest.

One of the best aspects of this film is the fact that it rejects all of the fake and easy heroic-melodramatic tricks of the commercial films made about the Résistance and of the archetypal Hollywood rescue films. Paul is presented as a sincere, well intentioned but very naive Catholic boy eager to do a good deed. Jeanne also reproaches him with not really caring about saving her, with just wanting "to feel proud during his vacation time." However, he is risking his life and Jeanne is facing death. In such a situation, and in the film itself, such a criticism seems rather puerile whereas it would be totally justified in other circumstances. One can consider that with this phrase Jeanne does not directly criticize Paul and what he is trying to do but criticizes a naive Catholic boy trying to feel good about himself. Such a remark becomes of greater importance as it insists on the fact that Jeanne is progressively becoming aware of what differentiates herself from the non-Jews, their good intentions and their powerless values.

After the denunciation of the rampant anti-Semitism in the French population presented in Ophüls', Drach's and Mitrani's works, Louis Malle's film directly put in question the ideological motivation of the "official" Résistance itself. *Lacombe Lucien* (1974) is Louis Malle's indirect first step towards the representation of a very personal memory of the Occupation that the director eventually represented in 1987 with *Goodbye Children*. *Lacombe Lucien* can be read as part of the direct heritage of *The Sorrow and the Pity* with its analysis of the Collaboration and the attitude of the French during the Occupation. Considered in this aspect, the film belongs to what many critics, including the *Cahiers du cinéma*, sarcastically called the "mode rétro."

As Malle noted on many occasions, he first wanted to make a film about the Mexican Halcones. Then, as he did not feel ready yet to base his film directly on his personal memories of war time, as he does in *Goodbye Children*, he developed *Lacombe Lucien* around only one of the people of his past (Joseph in *Goodbye Children* "becoming" Lacombe Lucien) and mixed that story with real events that took place in the southeast of France in 1944.

The film can also be read as a mixture of documentary and fiction. On the documentary side, the film is played by non-professional actors playing characters of a social status similar to their own (the young farmer Pierre Blaise playing the role of another young farmer, Lacombe Lucien). Like a documentary, this work was also filmed in a natural setting. Finally its editing plays a crucial role in selecting and organizing the moments in which the non-professional actors would reach an exceptional realism. On the fictitious side, the scenario and the dialogues of the film were written by a professional writer, Patrick Modiano, and Louis Malle while the staging and the acting were directly indicated to the actors by the director. This mixture of history, realism, fiction, and memories with Louis Malle's personal style as a film director immediately provoked in France a scandal that contributed to the success of the film as it was being attacked at the same time by the left and the right of the French political spectrum.

The most controversial or "scandalous" points of the film are the following: First, Lacombe becomes a Collaborator by chance, because he was rejected by the Résistance. Without any ideological or personal commitment, it is the same for him to resist or to collaborate. Second, a young Jewish woman falls in love with him at the same time he persecutes her and her father. Finally, the two Jewish characters of the film, Horn and his daughter, are presented as assimilated Jews occasionally rejecting their Jewish identity. As Annette Insdorf put it: "*Lacombe Lucien*'s references to Judaism contain no positive resonance" (Insdorf, 123). I will discuss all these points in my detailed study of this film.

It is to be noticed that the first point caused the most scandal as it was directly attacking not only the myth of a France united in its resistance to the invader but also the personal motivations of the resistance fighters themselves. As he did in all his other films, Malle tried not to impose a judgement on his main character. He wanted to "show" rather than "demonstrate." In consequence he chose to represent this period of history through an unknown episode of the Occupation featuring no important historical figure and a main character with no ideological commitment. Lacombe Lucien acts instinctively without any elaborated reflection. For this reason, because Lacombe never really makes any choice, one feels all through the film that he became a Collaborator mainly because of circumstances in a chaotic period of history. Such an instinctive relativism was of course totally unacceptable for most of those who had themselves been in the Résistance.

In consequence of his refusal to judge his main character, Malle was once again accused of sympathizing with his main character and with the extreme right. He had already been the target of such accusations when he made *Un Ascenseur pour l'échafaud* with the collaboration of Roger Nimier in 1957, *Feu Follet* based on the novel of the Collaborator Drieu la Rochelle and *Le Voleur* based on the novel of the extreme right French writer Georges Darien. Although he rejects accusations of sympathy for the political ideas of former Collaborators, Malle recognizes that Lucien Rebatet and Pierre Cousteau (Jacques Cousteau's brother), two famous French Collaborators released from jail in the fifties, were interested in his work after *Un Ascenseur pour l'échafaud* (Prédal, 1989: 111).

Each of these films clearly contains a violent criticism of the bourgeoisie that is also a common point among leftist and extreme right writers and aesthetes. In each case, the cinematographic quality of the image, the social criticism and the psychological evolution of the main characters dominate any political analysis. These are also the points Malle uses to defend *Lacombe Lucien* from any accusation of sympathy for the extreme right. According to Malle, *Lacombe Lucien* is to be seen as a psychological analysis, more than an historical representation of the Collaboration.

Nevertheless, this film is based on events that really took place in a very definite period of French history. They were filmed in the very same part of France where they happened in 1944. Considering this, it is hard to believe that the spectator should not pay too much attention to the extreme historic realism of the film because after all it is mostly a psychological analysis. Such inconsistencies between the proclaimed purpose of the film and its making are the cause of many dangerous ambiguities I will analyze in further detail in the chapter dedicated to the close analysis of this film. Ultimately, as Lacombe's actions appear to be motivated only by his instinctive reactions to local events and with no conscious choosing, his most significant deeds happen, as in Malle's other films, like unavoidable accidents, like the incest scene in *Murmur of the Heart*.

Whereas *Lacombe Lucien* and *Goodbye Children* denounce rather specifically the crimes of the Collaboration and the Vichy government, in their details they create many ambiguities that are rather obvious in the former film and better hidden in the latter. Pushed to its limits, one can wonder if this means that for Malle the persecution and the systematic extermination of the Jews happened like in *Lacombe Lucien* mostly "by chance," as the result of certain "circumstances," with no specific reason or no ideological choices. *Goodbye Children* will eliminate some of these ambiguities by showing some very precise anti-Semitic characters including, for example, the scene with the French Militia men in the restaurant or the presence of Nazis. Only a detailed analysis of both films can provide us with precise answers to these questions.

Two years later, Doillon's *Un Sac de billes* presented a rather different point of view on the persecution of the Jews. Jacques Doillon's film *Un Sac de billes* (1975), is based on Joseph Joffo's autobiographical best seller published under the same title in 1973. Like *Le Vieil homme et l'enfant* and *Les Violons du bal*, it tells the story of a Jewish child hiding and running away during the Occupation. Unlike Drach's film however (*Les Violons du bal*), *Un Sac de billes* avoids any overstylization or systematic distanciation from the story which is not presented as part of some idealized memories of childhood. Jacques Doillon uses here direct sound, sometimes difficult to understand, and his children are presented in an extremely realistic manner with their very own language, fears and ways of coping with a most threatening situation.

At the beginning of the film, Joseph and his brother are standing in front of the door of their father's salon in Paris on purpose, so that they are hiding the sign *"Entreprise juive"* "Jewish business," put on its window. As they are playing this game, a German soldier enters the salon to get a hair cut. The children then run away, another soldier sees the sign, warns his colleague who leaves the store in a fury while the father apologizes and looks for his sons to reprimand them. In the following sequences a foreign Jew is shown being arrested and the family is given yellow stars to wear.

A French child is shown reading a book about the Gaulois (Aryan) hero, Vercingétorix, as he asserts "There are still some good Frenchmen remaining in France!" At that point, Joseph's father asks all his family to wear the star proudly and to take a walk together through the neighborhood so that every one will know exactly what is happening to the Jews and that they are not ashamed of being Jewish. However, when he gets to school wearing his star, Joseph is welcomed by a "Here come the Yids!" and a fight breaks out. The Jewish children are punished for starting it.

As it becomes clear that the persecution against the Jews increases in a systematic way, the parents become more desperate. Out of despair and revolt Joseph's father declares: "I am sick of being a Jew." Then Joseph exchanges his yellow star for a bag of marbles (*un sac de billes*) knowing what the star stands for and that not wearing it is illegal and violently punished by the French administration. In the following sequence, the father asks Joseph if he is a Jew and slaps him on the cheeks every time he answers "Yes," until he finally answers "No."

At this point it is clear that the parents are preparing their children to face anti-Semites by themselves. As Michel Drach's and many other Jewish families understood very early, they would have a better chance of surviving by splitting up. The two boys, Joseph under the protection of his older brother, are then sent South on their own in order to cross the Line of

Demarcation and find refuge in Nice where they have family and where the Italians are much less zealous than the French in their persecution of the Jews.

The following sequences of the film show the adventures of the two children helping each other, crossing the Line of Demarcation and helping other Jews to do so against the greedy professional "passeurs." When they arrive in Menton, Maurice, the older brother, works in a bakery and Joseph tries to work for a farmer picking up potatoes and milking cows. When he quits, the peasant refuses to pay what he owes him. Finally, the parents and the rest of the family join them and everybody moves to Nice. In Nice, things are relatively safe until the Germans invade the town and the whole south of France. Then the family has to conceal itself again and the children are hiding "in the mouth of the wolf," in a youth camp called "New Harvest" (*Moisson Nouvelle*). At this camp the two brothers have to play skits in support of the Nationalistic and xenophobic propaganda of Vichy's National Revolution.

Finally, the children are arrested while looking for their leader who is flirting with a Jewish girl. They are identified as Jews by the Nazis but they claim they are not Jewish. While Joseph is held hostage, interrogated and tortured, his brother finds a Catholic priest to assert that they were born in Algiers and that they are Catholics. After their liberation, the two brothers are surrounded with anti-Semitic Frenchmen, Joseph falls in love for the first time and when he learns that the librarian he has been working for had turned the priest in to the Vichy police, he looks at him in the eyes and defiantly proclaims: "I am a Yid!" After the Liberation, Joseph sees the librarian being executed by the Résistance. The remaining family members get together for a picture in front of their new salon. A voice-over explains that the father died in the "showers" at Auschwitz and the last image shows an old picture of Joseph Joffo's father.

Jacques Doillon's film is largely structured around two main themes: the persecution of the Jews throughout occupied France and the many different ways a child learns to resist, survive and fight the brutality and the ruthlessness of the anti-Semites and the adult world. In this respect, this work has many similarities with Lasse Hälstrom's film of the eighties, *My Life as a Dog*. Reinforcing this idea, Doillon added two scenes that were not in Joffo's book and he mentions these additions on the very first image of his film. While the two brothers are running away trying to find refuge in the south of France, they steal a chicken in a farm in order to eat it. A little further, in a brothel in Nice, the older brother asks and obtains permission from a prostitute to caress her breast while his little brother is watching.

On the one hand, these two additional scenes describe the situation of these children having to survive on their own, living in an abnormal situation that puts them in contact with worlds they would otherwise not know so closely. On the other hand, it is clear that Doillon added them because they also reveal how, in most of the worse situations, children often find a way to survive tragedy by continuing to act like children and transgressing the rules of the adult world, i.e. in finding excitement in the stealing and cooking of the chicken and in exploring their own sexual desires. Therefore, the most terrifying scenes in the film will take place near the end, when the Nazis act as if the Jewish children were adult terrorists, when they use Joseph as a slave in their kitchen and then torture him, denying the two brothers any status as children and therefore any possibility of escape, even in imagination.

Another original aspect of this film is the important role played by the father that is missing in other films involving Jewish and even non-Jewish children or teenagers (*Le Vieil homme et l'enfant*, *Les Violons du bal*, *Lacombe Lucien*, *Au revoir les enfants*). In Doillon's film, the father teaches his children to be proud to be Jewish but he also forces them to confront reality, to toughen themselves by learning when it is necessary to hide their identity, to support each other in order to survive. He forces Joseph to grow up as fast as possible so he will not be too vulnerable.

When the family reunites at last, in Menton, Joseph prepares lemonade to celebrate the arrival of his parents. His mother drinks it and thanks her son but, at first, the father does not pay attention to the lemonade and seems to ignore that Joseph is feeling sad and rejected. After some long seconds, the father finally takes the drink and hugs his son. This scene signifies clearly to Joseph that life is not yet back to normal and that it is too early to really celebrate and go back to being a child in a regular family. Joseph has to understand that they have only overcome their first series of serious threats.

It is the father who suspects that their French landlords in Nice are making up the frequent alerts to take advantage of them. The father is also shown in a moment of weakness and despair when he says "I am fed up with being a Jew!" and when he wants to leave the family's hiding place in Nice. Finally the whole film concludes with the family's tribute to the courage, endurance and the memory of the father who died in Auschwitz.

Un Sac de billes is a moving, accurate and very complete film that includes a realistic representation of France under the Occupation, of French anti-Semitism, of a Jewish family trying to survive and a precise description of the psychology of a Jewish child living in France during the war. In the end, like in *Les Guichets du Louvre*, the main hero of the film proudly embraces his identity as a Jew. However, he does it in a defiant manner, as a sign of denunciation and revolt against the anti-Semites ("I am a Yid!"). At the beginning, like in all the comparable films, this child does not know what it means to be a Jew except that it implies being hated and persecuted for no reason by the whole world. In the end, Joseph understands proudly that he is Jewish but, with the memory of what happened to his father, he is very much aware that, even in France where his family decided to stay, some will continue to call him "a Yid."

Like *Un Sac de billes* and many films of the mid-seventies, Simone Boruchowicz's *1942* (1976) is directly based on the memories of the director as a Jewish child living in France at the beginning of the war. This black and white short tells how a Polish Jewish family was caught up by the war and anti-Semitism in Paris itself, how both the director's mother and father where arrested and deported by French and German police officers. The documentary starts with old photographs of Jews standing behind tombstones and personal pictures of the director's family superimposed with a long travelling through the XIth *arrondissement* graveyard in Paris. On one occasion the travelling stops for a few seconds on a monument to the dead victims of Ravensbruck camp.

The story is told from the point of view of the little girl as she sees her parents and her life change every day as death comes closer to them. She tells how, in 1938, she heard her father talk about the persecution of the Jews in eastern Europe while her mother was asking him not to talk about this in front of their daughter, how they were dumbstruck by the beginning of the war, terrified by the air attacks, the sirens and the sight of the first German soldiers in France. Suddenly, on August 20, 1941, her father was arrested by French and German officers. He was deported to the camps of Drancy and Compiègne. Almost exactly a year later her mother was arrested and imprisoned at the local police station. She would write to them later from the camp at Drancy: "Go on vacation my children... be careful!"

Simone Boruchowicz's film is an extremely moving evocation of the sudden disappearance of the director's own parents. Two very short sentences describe how she felt after the arrest of each one of her parents: "Hope remained the strongest," "everything was over except hope." In spite of that desperate hope, none of her parents returned from the camps. The film starts and ends with images of death. All the pictures we see represent dead people. All the streets of Paris we are shown are either empty or crossed by a distant and unidentifiable woman. They all represent places where the director and her family once lived. In the last sequence the director explains that the only graveyard she has for her parents is the City Hall of Paris' XIth *arrondissement* where their death has been registered. After a long travelling through the City Hall corridors, the last image shows a handwritten sign on an office window. The sign reads "*Décès*," "Decease."

This film describes in a very powerful manner how a child saw her whole world being progressively destroyed by an unstoppable and increasingly close death threat. The film offers no explanation to events that were absolutely overwhelming and totally incomprehensible to a child. In its own way, as a fiction film, Joseph Losey's *Monsieur Klein* will offer during the same year a representation of the persecution of the Jews that no logic can explain. This film will also focus not only on a personal experience, but also on the atrocity and total absurdity of the Holocaust.

With *Monsieur Klein* (1976) the American born director Joseph Losey realized what he himself called his most beautiful cinema experience.[30] This film is with no doubt among the most important masterpieces about the progressive disappearance of the Jews and the criminal indifference of the bystanders. It seems however that critics have often neglected at least one important point in their analysis of this film. Pauline Kael, for example, has written a very negative review of this film she calls "a classic example of weighty emptiness" (Kael, 1980: 396). A victim himself of political persecution in the United States in the early fifties, Losey had been blacklisted and had to move to England. Like the Jewish actors and directors in Occupied France, Losey's name in America was replaced by a pseudonym so his first two films could be shown. He had to wait for five years until his name could appear again on the credits of his own works.

In consequence, in making *Monsieur Klein* Losey was using both historical material and his personal experience as a victim of a much more recent institutionalized persecution. The first images of *Monsieur Klein* show the terror and the humiliation of a naked woman being examined by a doctor specialized in racial identification. From the very beginning the film puts in parallel the two main aspects of the persecution of the Jews: a professional, cold, efficient and totally delirious state-organized racism with on the other hand, the complicity in the indifference of thousands who did not want to see what was going on, hoping that they could still go on with their lives almost as if nothing had happened.

Of course, the general evolution of the identity search of M. Klein is central to the film. Most of the power of the film lies in the fact that M. Klein (Alain Delon) is not an open anti-Semite. It is precisely his indifference and his will to continue "business as usual" that make him an active accomplice of the persecution of the Jews. In choosing this theme, Losey puts in question the attitude of the vast majority of the French population during the Occupation that would not have agreed with the extermination of the Jews but refused to see what was happening or did nothing to prevent it from happening.

The first words M. Klein pronounces in the film are uttered when he answers the question "Monsieur Klein?" with "Yes, that's me..." The rest of the film will consist of the presentation of many different possible answers to the question first asked by an anonymous Jew: "Who is M. Klein?" From a complete denial and a total rejection of his possible Jewish origins, the hero of the film will be brought to understand exactly what is happening to the Jews. He will progressively feel sympathy for his anonymous double and the friends who are protecting him. In the end he will silently revolt against the arbitrary nature and the abjection of the state organized persecution through accepting a total transfer of identity that will ultimately lead him to sharing the fate of the six million Jews.

The beauty of the image and the magnificent acting of Alain Delon as M. Klein add to the power of this film as a very realistic nightmare. This film is not however a perfect historical reconstitution of a specific chapter of the Occupation. The massive arrest of Jews parked in a stadium near Paris leads us to believe that the story takes place during the roundup of the Velodrome d'Hiver. But this roundup took place in the summer of 1942 and all of the film takes place in the winter. It would also be very hard to justify historically the fact that M. Klein could travel so easily back and forth from Paris to Strasbourg.

This voluntary slight distance taken from historical realism gives the film a more general purpose and links its action to a more symbolic reading that makes this work what Jacques Siclier called "a metaphysical fable." Constantly searching for his double who he first rejects and then identifies with, M. Klein discovers the meaning of the tapestry he refused to buy at the beginning of the film. This tapestry represented remorse through the picture of a vulture wounded by an arrow. The same remorse will in the end force M. Klein to identify with his Jewish double and to share his destiny as total indifference is no longer possible for him.

As I will demonstrate in the detailed analysis of this film, a constant ambiguity serves the purpose of Losey's work perfectly. Because the spectator will never know exactly who the other M. Klein is and who exactly framed the hero of the film, the persecution of the Jews remains totally absurd. It is given not even a grotesque explanation. Jews have to hide, abandon everything, disappear, reject their identity or they will be arrested, deported and murdered. This is exactly what should have provoked the general outrage of the French population, what M. Klein refused to see for so long. No other "explanation" needs to be given.

In many ways, *Monsieur Klein* appears to be the master work of this early seventies cycle of fiction films evaluating the various degrees of collaboration with the Nazis. As the basic facts of the historical, political and psychological backgrounds of the Occupation become more present in the minds of French audiences, films can concentrate on other and often more intimate aspects of this period.

François Truffaut's *Le Dernier métro* (1980) takes place in the very enclosed space of the Théâtre Montmartre. Even the streets of Paris shown in the opening sequence are made to look like a theater set. Such an organization reminds us of Roland Barthes characterization of the space in Racine's tragedies as an enclosed one. For the characters caught in such a representation, living on the Parisian stage or in the theater itself announces a certain death.

For all the actors working in the Théâtre Montmartre, there is no question of leaving Paris. They all have many different reasons to keep the theater open: to keep the only job they have and ever have known, for the sake of their art's survival, to show the population that not everything has died with the defeat of 1940, to win some key contacts in the Paris of the Collaboration, to get a cover for underground activities or to be able to hide and feed a loved one. As the outside world is entirely controlled by the Nazis and the Vichy government, the theater appears as a fragile safe haven in which each character tries to survive the war in his or her own way.

After evoking the period of the Occupation through the use of black and white newsreel, the film switches to showing a street of Paris at night, with a low angle, as if it were seen from a sewer plaque or from a basement window. Such an angle announces the point of view of the central character of the film, Lucas Steiner, a Jewish Theater director in hiding, literally "underground." The camera follows men's and women's legs and then rises to show Bernard (Gérard Depardieu) as he is trying to pick up a woman in the streets of Paris. Later, Bernard is shown applying for and obtaining a role that Marion (Lucas' wife) has just refused to a Jewish actor. On that occasion, Bernard reveals that he wants in no way to take the place of a Jew, indicating that he is violently repelled by the politics of Collaboration.

At that point, the main focus of the film switches to Marion (Catherine Deneuve), a very competent, reflective and apparently sensitive woman, while the audience is led to wonder about her motivations to refuse a job to a Jew, even under a false name, and to keep on running her theater in Occupied Paris. It soon becomes clear that Marion's main motivation is her love for her husband and for theater itself. Then the film finally switches to the central character of the film, Lucas Steiner, and to the intricate relationship between Lucas, Bernard and Marion within the very limited spaces of the theater and Occupied Paris.

Lucas Steiner, the theater's former director, and a Jew, lives in hiding in the basement of the building itself. His wife told the authorities that he left for South America as she took charge of the theater presenting a play entitled *La Disparue*, *The Woman Who Disappeared*. Lucas continues directing the play by providing his indications, through his wife, to the new director, his old friend Jean-Loup (Jean Poiret).

While it becomes psychologically more and more difficult for Lucas to remain a prisoner in his hiding place and for Marion to keep the unity of the troupe while facing the pro-Nazi critic Daxiat (Jean-Louis Richard), Bernard joins the underground and sets a bomb somewhere in Paris. After Daxiat tore down a play presented by Marion in one of his articles, Bernard wants to break his neck and force him to apologize. At that point, it becomes rather clear that Bernard and Marion both despise the Nazis and the Pro-Nazis and that they have two different but somehow complementary ways to react. Bernard, as a sensitive and revolted man, responds to any humiliation in a sincere, impulsive but extremely violent and hazardous manner. On the other hand, Marion remains always self-controlled and firm, organizing all of her actions to insure the success of her most important goals: the survival of the theater guaranteeing the survival of her husband.

It is therefore Lucas' partly hidden but central role that brings and keeps Marion and Bernard together as the main theme of the film becomes the relationship of these three characters within a theatrical representation of reality and under the constant threat of intolerance represented by the pro-Nazi critic Daxiat. This violent criticism of intolerance is reinforced throughout the film by the showing of the constant condemnation and persecution threatening homosexuals like the new director Jean-Loup and the lesbian designer (Andréa Ferréol).[31] Whereas French anti-Semitism plays a key role, it is not the central theme of the film. Lucas Steiner, as a Jew, is presented as a victim of intolerance and hatred but his Jewish identity is not developed nor analyzed in the film.

What matters most to him are his theater, his art and his love for his wife and he refuses to let the war destroy all three. It is finally these fundamental senses of survival and/or *résistance* through acting and directing that keeps the troupe together. In this respect, this film can also be read as a defense of the continuity of a certain kind of theater and cinema during the war that did not promote any sort of official propaganda and remained necessary to survive and resist during the war.

The real meaning and function of the play presented on stage, on a literally "superficial" or "horizontal" surface, endures thanks to the survival, in the depths of the "underground" of the theater, of a hidden love. The communication between these two levels is insured by the periodic disappearance of a woman (the main character of the play "The Woman Who Disappeared") and by the voices of the actors Lucas can hear from the basement through a heating duct.

Consequently, this representation of a fundamental fight against intolerance during the Occupation is largely based on three major factors: the evolution of the relationship between the main characters, the necessary communication between two very enclosed spaces confronted with the outside world and the (non-) distinction between fiction and reality.

In the last scene of the film, after the narrator announces, "Our story awaits its epilogue," Marion is shown visiting Bernard in a hospital in 1944. As she walks toward him and declares: "He's dead now," the spectator is led to believe that Lucas is dead. However, this scene is revealed to be part of a play as the camera backs up progressively and shows the actors on stage. Then Lucas joins Marion and Bernard to salute the audience. At that point, the last sequence recalls the first filmed in the streets of Paris and the whole film becomes a play about the survival of a play with its troupe. As a very enclosed place itself, its ends as it started with a black and white newsreel.

Edgardo Cozarinsky's *La Guerre d'un seul homme* (*One Man's War* 1982) is a *film de montage* based on a constant parallel between Ernst Jünger's diary and historical footage of the Occupation. While Jünger's text describes the impression of a German soldier in Paris during the war, the footage shows the evolution of everyday life in Paris during the war. The most exceptional aspect of the film is its description of the Occupation from the point of view of a German officer. The film insists on the efforts of the population of Paris to return to "normal" life after the defeat: French lovers in the streets, the town's "friendship" for the German soldiers ("*l'amitié de la ville*"), the new fashions adapted to the war, the reopening of the stock exchange and the cabarets, the German soldiers, etc.

Progressively however, Jünger realizes that this is not only an opportunity that is offered to him to "settle" in Paris. He is ordered to organize the execution of a German soldier. He discovers anti-Semitism in France, the round-ups of the Jews and the French politics of Collaboration. When he sees for the first time someone wearing the star of David he feels uncomfortable wearing a German uniform. He sees hatred in the eyes of a girl looking at him. Then however, the footage insists only on French anti-Semites and their anti-Semitic campaigns, on their assimilation of the Jews with the Communists by French propaganda. It is only in the end of the film that Jünger is told about the extermination of the Lodz Ghetto, the revolt of the Warsaw Ghetto, the gas vans and the Holocaust taking place in central Europe. The film ends with the evocation of French fashion at the end of the war, French propaganda against the Résistance, the last days of French Militia men, Stupnagel's suicide attempt and the final uprising of the Résistance in Paris just before its liberation.

Cozarinsky's film is interesting but it is also disturbing and very ambiguous. It is interesting because it presents the point of view of a German soldier, as an individual, on the Occupation. It also offers a vivid and legitimate representation of the French government's propaganda, and of the life of the upper classes in Paris during the war. However, *La Guerre d'un seul homme* describes the persecution of the Jews in France as if nothing had preceded it. The German army, like Jünger himself, is presented as a group of innocent individuals who were totally unaware of the violence and the wave of anti-Semitism that had spread throughout Germany since the early thirties. One can wonder why Jünger needed to wait until 1941 while living in France to start feeling badly about wearing the uniform of an army lead by Adolf Hitler. Because Cozarinsky's film never raises such questions, because it never questions Jünger's point of view as that of an officer of the Wermacht, it is, in the end, a very ambiguous film.

Shown at the same time as *La Guerre d'un seul homme*, Jacques Rouffio's *La Passante du Sans souci* (1982) offers a totally opposite representation of the Germans' collective responsibility in the persecution of the Jews. Rouffio's film is an adaptation of a novel by celebrated writer Joseph Kessel written in 1937. Rouffio's film transposes the novel both in the present of its making and during the war thus insisting on the permanency of fascism and anti-Semitism and on the necessity to keep fighting them. This constant intricacy of past and present is one of the main characteristics of this film as, for different but comparable purposes, was the case with *Night and Fog*, *La Cage de verre*, *Le Coup de grâce* and *Les Violons du bal*.

At the beginning of the film, Max Baumstein (Michel Piccoli) is a Swiss millionaire at the head of Solidarité Internationale whose name recalls clearly the real Amnesty International. He is presented as a dedicated but overworked middle-aged man constantly attacked by the sarcasm of the press because of his personal wealth and of his simultaneous fight against both leftist and rightist dictatorships. The opening scenes set a clear political background that will prevail throughout the film.

While investigating the disappearance of political activists, Michel meets the ambassador of Uruguay in Paris. He identifies the ambassador as Ruppert Von Leggaert, the murderer of his own guardians during the war and Michel kills him. The rest of the film is a flashback telling of Max's life as a young Jewish boy protected during the war by a German couple. It is told by Max to his wife Lena (Romy Schneider) and then during his trial for the murder of Von Leggaert.

The first scene of the long flashback shows how Max and his father were caught by surprise in the streets of a German town by a group of Nazis. In a very powerful sequence, Max reveals how his father was beaten to death, how his bones were broken by the Nazis and how Elsa, a young German woman (also played by Romy Schneider), came to his rescue and saved his life. In the following scenes, anti-Semitism remains constantly in the background while the main considerations of the film depict Elsa and Max trying to survive in Paris as Elsa tries to find a way to free her husband, Michel Wiener, arrested in Germany by the Nazis for his political commitment as a leftist publisher. In order to survive, Elsa finds a job as a singer in a cabaret in which the main act is led by a nationalistic, anti-Semitic French comedian (Jacques Martin) mocking both Hitler and Mussolini but also attacking the Jews for being the cause of the war and for profiting from the Occupation. Collaborators, French businessmen, Nazis, their wives and girlfriends as well as prostitutes are the customary audience.

Earlier in the film, Elsa had a visit from a French businessman, Maurice Bouillard, who had seen her husband in a train just before his arrest by the Gestapo. He brought her money from Michel. As Maurice sells champagne in Germany, Elsa realizes that he could help her in finding information about her husband. Whereas Maurice seems to feel genuinely compassionate for Elsa and Michel, his will to continue business as usual prohibits him from realizing the extent of the persecution of the Jews and the real character of the people he deals with. At Elsa's request, he accepts going to Berlin to try to find out what happened to Michel.

It is on this occasion that he meets a German Jewish woman, Mrs. Helwig, whose husband has just been assassinated, and Maurice realizes the extent of the persecution of the Jews. This encounter however does not change his life nor does it interfere at all with his dedication to his business. Later on, after Elsa slept with Ruppert Von Leggeart, a Nazi from the German Embassy in Paris in order to free Michel, Maurice becomes mad at her for preferring a German to himself. After that sequence, Michel is liberated, he arrives in Paris and then he is shot by Von Leggeart while he tries to tell the underground what exactly is going on in the concentration camps. The final scenes show the end of Max's trial, the testimonies of Maurice and Charlotte Maupas, a former prostitute and friend of Elsa.

With this conclusion in the present also showing two young fascists spitting in Lena's face because "her Jew" has been acquitted, the film insists once again on the indifference and the apathy of a large part of the French population towards the disappearance of the Jews during the Occupation. The film also clearly involves the present in its criticism. Besides showing two young fascists, it makes clear that many dictatorships in the world protect and employ former Nazis. It also criticizes the French for having a very limited and simplistic view of the German political scene. In her final testimony, Charlotte tells about "the Vichy people" who put the corpses of Elsa and Michel Wiener in a mass grave. In memory of her friends, Charlotte had raised some money to put a plaque with their names at the café of the "Sans souci." She immediately adds that this tribute was not appreciated because many in the local population could not accept the idea of German members of the underground. The title of the film itself constitutes a criticism of French apathy as Maurice Bouillard just wished to live a life "sans souci," "without worry."

While *La Passante du Sans souci* presents anti-Semitism as the most abject part of the general persecutions organized by the Nazi state, it never describes the deportations or the Shoah as such. In the France of the seventies, this film was also to be read as a general pamphlet against state organized repression, against the permanency and the recurrence of racism and intolerance in the whole world and first of all in South America where, with the help of the American secret services, several well-known Nazis were able to provide various governments with their sordid expertise. Without explicitly describing the specificity of the Shoah, it suggests however that the survivors of the Holocaust and the memory of the victims of the Nazis in general must play a central role in future fights against fanaticism and bigotry.

One year after Rouffio's film, Robert Enrico's *Au Nom de tous les miens* (1983) presented his Franco-Hollywoodian version of Martin Gray's life. This film is an adaptation of Martin Gray's best selling autobiography (published in 1971).

Enrico took full advantage of Gray's amazing life but, technically, his film as such offers no surprises. The *Cahiers du cinéma* wrote about the film:

> One feels, in fact, that Enrico is nothing but an entrepreneur (*un forain*) that *utilizes* History without being really concerned by Treblinka or the Warsaw Ghetto—in spite of some strong scenes for which he

knows all the tricks that easily impress the audience. He clearly tries to create his historical epic, his own *Doctor Zhivago*, around an heroic character enduring any difficulty and interpreted, in part, by the young and promising Jacques Penot—a Jew, a Pole, a concentration camp prisoner, an officer in the Red Army, an American... [32]

Its clean cut and conventionally edited images with beautiful actors make his work a very good commercial picture that never takes any chances to try to go beyond the limitations of a book adaptation. In one episode after the other the film follows closely the script without using the specificity of the cinematographic medium to give its characters a life of their own.

Unlike Gray's book, written with the assistance of French journalist and novelist Max Gallo, the film starts with the accidental death of the author's wife, Dina, and their four children in a forest fire in the South of France during the autumn of 1970 (the last chapter of the book). This inversion allows the film to explain in a very dramatic way why, after more than thirty-five years, Gray felt compelled to write the story of his life and also to insist on the impression that this life corresponds to a "destiny" (the last section of the book is entitled "*Le destin*"), as if the author was to be the last Jew remaining with the task to speak "in the name of all of his people." Such a mainstay in the book and in the film makes of Gray himself one of the "Last of the Just" André Schwartz-Bart had told about in his most acclaimed 1959 novel *Le Dernier des Justes* (1959 Goncourt Literary Prize, the French equivalent of the Pulitzer Prize). The recurrence of the same myth will also play an important role in Claude Lanzmann's *Shoah*.

In the film as in the book, the telling of Gray's life provides the opportunity to vividly depict Polish anti-Semitism, the persecution of the Jews in Poland, the Warsaw ghetto, the deportations and uprising, the author's escape from Treblinka, his role as a new officer in the Red Army, his return to normal life in the United States, his discovery of happiness with his family in France until the final tragedy of Wednesday October 3, 1970 that saw the death of his wife and four children.

Unlike Enrico's film, Diane Kurys' *Coup de foudre* (*Entre Nous*, 1983) keeps history at the root but also in the background of her narration of the evolution of two women's friendship from 1942 to the mid-fifties. At the beginning, one of the women, Lena (Isabelle Huppert) is interned in the French camp of Rivesaltes because she is Jewish. She can escape only because she agrees to marry the French cook of the camp (Guy Marchand). Shortly after, she is infuriated when she realizes that her husband has a Jewish name. No other allusion to her Jewish identity or to the persecution of the Jews will be made as the film concentrates on the relationship of two women, Lena and Madeleine (Miou-Miou), with their husbands and with each other. Madeleine's lover was an art teacher (Robin Renucci) killed by the Germans.

The whole film is organized around a close analysis of the failures of their marriages (with Guy Marchand and Jean-Pierre Bacri) and on the progressive discovery that their feminine friendship provides them with a mysterious, irreplaceable and extremely powerful bond. However, as Annette Insdorf noted:

> Lena and Madeleine are the children of this war which has wounded them, stolen their youth and left them fearful and ready to grab the first comfort offered (...) Since the film is based on the experience of Kury's own mother, *Entre Nous* can also be seen as an exploration of the legacy of occupied France—by one of the war's 'grandchildren' (Insdorf, 87).

In 1987 Claude Chabrol's *Une Affaire de femmes* will briefly mention another friendship between a Jewish woman and a woman later condemned to death and executed by Vichy for performing abortions. The plot is based on a real story and on a novel by Francis Szpiner. At the beginning of the film the two women are very close friends and Rachel is the only person Marie (Isabelle Huppert) really enjoys seeing. Rachel suddenly disappears and, later in the film, Marie learns that her friend has been arrested because she is Jewish. Stunned by the announcement, Marie says, unconvinced, "Rachel is not Jewish... she would have told me so." In this context, Rachel's deportation underlines the discreet but unescapable criminal justice of Vichy. It is a sign announcing the upcoming arrest and execution of Marie.

The early eighties were partly characterized in France by a rebirth of anti-Zionism and anti-Semitism. Many terrorist and anti-Semitic actions took place in Paris, the most famous being the bomb that exploded on Copernic Street on October 3, 1980, killing four and wounding twenty-one. At the same time, the Catholic *intégristes* of Mgr. Lefèbvre and the extreme right National Front of Le Pen dramatically increased their popular support that is still very strong today. If this dangerous rise of intolerance, lies and racism seems to have had no direct expression in cinema, it certainly played a role in the extremely strong impact some films had in the mid and late eighties.

5. Facing the Future; Fighting Oblivion, *1985-Present*

Two key events of the eighties had a strong influence on the representation of the Holocaust in French cinema. In chronological order, the first one is Claude Lanzmann's film *Shoah*, in 1985, and the second is the trial of Klaus Barbie, the "Butcher of Lyon," in 1987. In reaction to the seventies, Claude Lanzmann's film is based on a passionate will to fight a new threat to the memory of the Holocaust. As a very large number of spectators and people in general had by then heard about the Holocaust, many felt that they already knew enough about it and that therefore there was no need to continue studying it. *Shoah* was made primarily as an outcry against the real danger of rendering the Holocaust a trite historical fact among others, soon to be forgotten.

Shoah is the result of eleven years of work. This nine and a half hour film was made out of three hundred and fifty hours of film stock. Lanzmann was asked to make *Shoah* by personal friends after he made *Pourquoi Israel?*. He spent the first year reading books about the Holocaust and almost learning by heart Raul Hilberg's *The Destruction of the European Jews*. Then he had to locate the survivors he wanted to interview. He also had to select the interviews he could use in his film according to its focus and to the objectives of its director. As the detailed analysis of this film will show, many witnesses and parts of testimonies were not included in *Shoah* mostly because Lanzmann's goal was "to transmit" the absolute horror of the extermination process of six million Jews who died abandoned by the rest of the world. *Shoah* is not a historical documentary on the Holocaust. Its aim is to be a work of art made by a man trying to make an audience realize the uniqueness of an unspeakable event.

At the heart of *Shoah* there is the death of the "other," of six million Jews. Witnesses are never heard explaining their own

97

lives or destinies unless they are directly related to the extermination process. The whole film is structured like a spider web with Polish villages and Jewish ghettos in its periphery and the extermination camps at its center. In between, the deportation trains never stop running. Consequently, the main quality of this film is that it confronts us in the present with the specificity of the systematic extermination of the European Jews that took place in Poland.

It is perhaps an incomplete and passionate work but no film and no single book can describe by itself the extermination of six million people. Each book and particularly each film must focus on specific aspects of the Holocaust if it does not want to become an accumulation of incomprehensible remarks and data. Moreover the memory of the Holocaust must be saved and transmitted by men and women, with their passions and personal convictions, because it must never be reduced to a chronology of events and a list of statistics. No one was able to make such a fundamental and much needed cinematographic work until Lanzmann, as an individual, started filming the testimonies of the men who had seen the exterminations with their own eyes. *Shoah* is a great film because it was made by a totally committed individual and because it focuses on the most essential aspect of the Holocaust. Consequently, this film is also a great work precisely because it is knowingly and voluntarily an "incomplete" and "passionate" film that focuses on what is essential to the evocation of its subject.

Claude Lanzmann took some great personal risks in order to film some Nazis who had taken part in the exterminations. He mailed two hundred letters pretending that his name was "Doctor Sorel" from the fake "Center for the Research and Study of Contemporary History" located in Paris. He also offered the Nazis three thousand Deutsch marks for each interview. Ten Nazis agreed to be interviewed but the director also tried to talk to those who did not agree to meet with him. On one occasion at least, his hidden camera and microphone were discovered. Lanzmann and his translator were beaten up and they barely escaped from an infuriated group of neighbors protecting the former head of a Nazi extermination commando.[33] Lanzmann's film displays in an extremely powerful manner the core of facts, images and questions our memory of the Holocaust must save for future generations. The impact of *Shoah* in the France of the late eighties was increased by Klaus Barbie's arrest and trial, the various anti-Semitic terrorist actions of the late seventies and early eighties (rue de Médicis, 1979; rue Copernic, 1980; and at Jo Goldenberg's restaurant, 1982)[34], the various scandals surrounding the "theses" of the *révisionnistes* (Faurisson's trial, 1983) as well as the announcement of the trial of various French Collaborators (Leguay, Touvier, Papon; 1979, 1981, 1983). It is a very powerful and original masterpiece that must be studied in parallel with other films of that period and in particular with Ophüls' continuing work.

Ophüls' most recent film, *Hotel Terminus*, was made in 1987. However, before that date, he was to film two other documentaries that also prelude and indicate in part the strengths and weaknesses of his documentary on Barbie's life. *A Sense of Loss*, made in 1972, dealt with the war in Northern Ireland. Unlike *The Sorrow and the Pity*, it was made for movie theaters and not for TV screens. This time however, Ophüls was not dealing with a country he had close, personal ties to nor with past events. His new documentary was about history in the making, made without the historical distanciation from which *The Sorrow and the Pity* had benefitted. In consequence, *A Sense of Loss* was probably best characterized by Vincent Canby as "a beautifully photographed and edited record of incomprehensible events" (Canby, 43).

Nonetheless, this documentary already reveals some characteristics of his next film, *The Memory of Justice* (1976) as well as *Hotel Terminus*. Like the latter film, *A Sense of Loss* has in its center the murder of children: an infant and a schoolgirl as compared to the murder of the forty-one children of Izieu in *Hotel Terminus*. It is a story told in memory and defense of the victims, against state organized violence, repression and killings. Like *The Memory of Justice*, it is a violent criticism of the

inability of justice to deal with the killing of children or civilians;
more precisely, with crimes against humanity. However, like
some confusing segments of *Hotel Terminus*, *A Sense of Loss*
does not present clearly the historical and political issues at stake
because, as Canby wrote: "Ophüls' documentary style, which
allows the subjects to speak for themselves (...) simply is not
adequate for the job of explaining the issues." In all his
documentaries, as in *The Sorrow and the Pity*, Ophüls is at his
very best when underscoring individual responsibility through his
ironical studies of individual choices, personal lies and distortions
that cripple our sense of justice.

Marcel Ophüls started working on *The Memory of Justice*
(1976) in 1973, right after the release of *A Sense of Loss* (1972).
Like *The Sorrow and the Pity*, and maybe more so, the making
of the final version of *The Memory of Justice* was very turbulent
arduous and romanesque. The project was first financed by one
German and two British companies: the BBC and VPS (Visual
Programme Systems Ltd.) from London and Polytel International
based in Hamburg. The producers soon became dissatisfied with
Ophüls' work, particularly David Puttnam, as the director did not
or could not include interviews of some key contemporary
American officials in his film. As in *Hotel Terminus* a few years
later, he tried but failed to interview McCloy, the former High
Commissioner for Germany. Ophüls refused also to present any
simplistic parallel or analogy between Nazi and American war
crimes, the SS and the Marines. His final version of the film
insists indeed on the specificity of the extermination of the Jews
while at the same time strongly condemning other war crimes.

In consequence the producers gave the material of the film
to a German director "who hacked it into a truncated, routine
documentary that was released in Germany" (Moritz, 331-335).
Finally, in March 1975, an Irish friend of Ophüls "recuperated"
the reels from the offices of VPS and brought them to the United
States where the director was able to make his version of his own
film, thanks to the support of Hamilton Fish, Max Palevski and
the Paramount.

The Memory of Justice is a four and a half hour documentary divided in two equal parts: "Nuremberg and the Germans," "Nuremberg and other places." The most controversial aspect of the film is indeed its few comparisons between Nazi and American, French or Russian war crimes. However, if the different attitudes that led to the construction of the extermination camps can be found in various degrees in different places of the world, Ophüls' film makes it clear that the extermination of the Jews constitutes a unique event in the history of humanity and that "to compare is not to equate" (Des Pres, 1977: 88).

The title of the film is based on Plato's belief that after having drunk in the river of forgetting in order to become human, our souls can only have a vague or very imperfect memory of the ideal of Justice. This title emphasizes one of the main ideas of the film which suggests that although the Nuremberg trial was necessary it was indeed inadequate in really punishing war criminals and totally inefficient in assuring that war crimes would not take place again. At the same time, Ophüls' work is also a film about individual lack of "memory of injustice" as it clearly documents the absolute guilt-free conscience of the Nazis, of their economic partners and of the population who supported them.

Astonishingly, while six million Jews were exterminated by the Nazi "order" and millions of Germans supported the Nazi regime, a few years later it appeared that no one saw or knew anything and most of all no one seemed to be responsible for these crimes, not even the highest ranking Nazis who pleaded "not guilty" at their trials. In consequence, Ophüls' detailed analysis of denial, hypocritical innocence and "controlled stupidity" (Daniel Ellsberg) based on interviews of Nazis, former Nazi supporters and their children after the war can also be expanded to similar attitudes towards war crimes in the United States and in France.

In many respects, this documentary fights hypocrisy, chauvinism, nationalistic propaganda and good conscience in Germany and in the United States just as *The Sorrow and the Pity* did in France five years earlier. It is however regrettable that these two former countries have been unable to give *The Memory of Justice* the same consideration and public recognition *The Sorrow and the Pity* was given not only in France but worldwide. As opposed to what has been happening in France since the early seventies, it seems that the problem of war crimes committed by nationals suffers greatly from a convenient "lack of interest" both in the United Sates and in Germany. A detailed analysis of *The Memory of Justice* should then enable us to show how Ophüls reveals the mechanisms that constitute our very partial and selective memory of injustices.

   Ophüls started working on *Hotel Terminus* at the time of Barbie's arrest and expulsion from Bolivia for financial fraud (January 25-February 5, 1983). The sequences were filmed in the following order: Peru, Bolivia, the United States, Germany and finally Lyon. The almost totally reversed order in which these sequences appear in the film is enough to stress one more time the importance of Ophüls's montage. Indeed, the structure of the final version of this documentary evolved throughout Barbie's trial that took place in Lyon from Monday May 11 to July 4, 1987. As Ophüls explained to Francine Du Plessix-Gray during the trial itself: "As each new witness appears, a new theme arises that can affect the whole emphasis and structure of the work; I may be revising my structure daily until the very week I finish the rough cut. This project is a nightmare, an absolute nightmare" (Du Plessix-Gray, 46).

   Such a statement reveals some very important points about Ophüls' work. It indicates first that the trial played a central role in the final organization of the film. Whereas the documentary is also entitled "The Times and Trial of Klaus Barbie," it appears that it is not essentially a biography of a Nazi. Just as *The Memory of Justice* did in 1976, *Hotel Terminus* analyzes the ability or the lack of ability of our judicial systems to face and punish war crimes. Through the constant opposition of the horror of Barbie's crimes with the various protections he enjoyed throughout his life, *Hotel Terminus* is also entirely organized around the testimonies of Barbie's victims and, ultimately, around the memory of the deportation and murder of the forty-four children of Izieu. Like the *Sorrow and the Pity*, this film is not a didactic study and its weaknesses are often to be found in its poor explanation of the exact historical situation and the role played by some of its witnesses.

Like all the other documentaries made by Ophüls, *Hotel Terminus* is primarily an analysis and a revelation of many different characters. It is a film which speaks out against moral relativism, against the moral weakness leading to total amnesia according to which we should not judge others. Faced with crimes like the Holocaust, such attitudes lead to relativism, forgetting and eventually turning the most horrible crimes into trite facts. Besides the horrifying loss of remembrance of the millions of victims it implies, making murder look banal also becomes an indication that anyone who would plan to repeat such crimes in the future would indeed have very few chances to be punished for them.

"After all, aren't we all human beings with the same weaknesses and strengths? Who can pretend he is better and judge the others?" Confronted with Barbie's crimes, such questions are not only absurd but highly immoral and politically extremely dangerous. *Hotel Terminus* also speaks out against the attitudes towards justice these questions represent. It was started at a time when many were not sure Barbie's trial would really take place because of the consequences it might have on the French population and on internal politics. There were fears of what Barbie could say about French Collaborators, the betrayal of Résistance leader Jean Moulin or about the Résistance itself. Some thought that Barbie would die in jail before he could be judged. Indeed, none of this happened.

The trial remained Klaus Barbie's all along and none of the attempts of his lawyer, maître Vergès, to transform it into the trial of Vichy France or of French war crimes in Algeria worked. Special issues of France's leading magazines such as *Le Nouvel Observateur* and *L'Express* had announced the "trial of the Résistance." However, as in *Hotel Terminus*, the trial was clearly freed of any historical confusion or moral relativism that corresponded to the main lines of Barbie's defense. It stuck to

and completely fulfilled its purpose. Other trials and other
documentaries will be necessary to examine other crimes.
Of course, it is no accident that this film was made between
1983 and 1987. François Mitterrand was first elected President on
May 10, 1981. His very first official action as President was to
visit the grave of Jean Moulin, the former head of the Résistance,
betrayed and then tortured to death by the Nazis. After the 1981
elections, Mitterrand also officially honored Pierre Mendès-
France, founder of the United Socialist Party and the "hero" of
The Sorrow and the Pity. This official honor was repeated by the
French President at the time of Mendès-France's death in 1982.
It is also at that time that Régis Debray was named President's
advisor, twenty-two years after his release from a Bolivian jail
and ten years after his failed attempt working from Salvador
Allende's Chile to kidnap Barbie in Bolivia. These attitudes,
events and the election of President Hernan Siles Zuazo in
Bolivia on October 10, 1980 led to Barbie's arrest and
deportation.

It is also to be remembered that Ophüls never considered
himself as a specialist of the Holocaust or even of France under
the Occupation. As he declared to Joan Juliet Burk: "I have never
considered myself passionate, obsessed, expert, or a specialist on
the Holocaust, Nazi terror, torture, and the criminal activities of
Klaus Barbie. When I am not making these films, I do not keep
up with these subjects" (Burk, 455). Indeed, Ophüls started
making his film on the invitation of Hamilton Fish III and Victor
Navasky, the former publisher and editor of *The Nation*. Thus the
need to make *Hotel Terminus* was dictated according to the
importance of current events.

However, like all of Ophüls' productions, *Hotel Terminus* is
a very personal film, anti-didactic, non-commercial in its
techniques and non-"objective." Its long segments on the
complicity of the American Counter Intelligence Corps (CIC) in
Barbie's escape from justice play a central role in the originality
of the film and it should have insured it better attention from
American audiences. Unfortunately, in the United States of the
eighties, as Oliver North became for many a National hero

simply because he is an anti-Communist and in spite of his lies to the American Congress. Ophüls' criticism of the CIC hiring Nazis to fight Communism had no influence. For similar reasons, *Hotel Terminus* can also be read as an indirect criticism of American pragmatism and of its lack of a developed sense of global historical responsibility in the eighties.

Regarding the same point, one could enlarge the meaning of Ophüls' declaration about the relationship between the agent Kolb and Barbie: "There were probably affinities at work and common prejudices" (Burk, 456). In such a context, it is however very reassuring that Ophüls' film was financed with a one million dollar budget and distributed by Americans, completed and shown in America in 1987. The evolution of its success in the United States could then be compared to the controversy surrounding *The Sorrow and the Pity* in France since 1969. Unfortunately, as a consequence of its very limited distribution, *Hotel Terminus* has yet to be seen by millions of Americans.

As for *The Sorrow and the Pity*, Ophüls followed his basic working rules. He started by shooting interviews and not writing a script. All the discoveries took place during the shooting. After that, in order to familiarize himself with the text of his film, he had a team recopy the texts of the interviews before starting the final montage giving the film all its strengths but also revealing its weaknesses. I will analyze them in the chapter dedicated to the detailed analysis of this film. Following his father's advice, "waste, waste, waste," he filmed one hundred hours of stock film in order to reach his final four and a half hours of documentary. As always, Ophüls needed to film hours of any given testimony in order to catch the "nuances and ironic disjunctions" (Du Plessix-Gray, 38) that reveal a character. The film has an apparent linear and chronological structure that soon reveals its much deeper and more important spiral analysis of characters. Moreover, *Hotel Terminus* also has many involuntary characteristics of Ophüls' production.

The limited budget and current events forced the director to make his documentary with different camera crews. He was also continuously confronted with unending practical obstacles that made the film almost impossible to finish. Such obstacles include: financial limitations, witnesses refusing to talk in front of the camera, witnesses refusing to participate in a film because of the presence other participants (like Vergès), general controlled amnesia or support for former Nazis or Collaborators and last but not least, the general indifference as Ophüls ironically repeats that, after all, these questions do not matter much, "more than forty years after the events took place."

Such constant limitations and frustrations also create in the film, starting with Ophüls himself, some kind of sarcastic humor and irony that are also present in *The Sorrow and the Pity* but often much more developed in *Hotel Terminus*. Indeed, Ophüls recognized that the making of this film was "by far my most difficult and least good-natured movie" (Du Plessix-Gray, 46). Another reason for such a feeling is also the extreme contrast specific to this film between Barbie's cruelty and his victims' courage, moral strength or plain innocence, between the anger one experiences at witnessing Barbie's impunity and the deep sorrow felt at hearing about his crimes and witnessing the suffering of his victims in the eighties.

Contrary to what the Revisionists or even, for opposite reasons, Claude Lanzmann proclaimed, Barbie's trial was anything but useless. *Hotel Terminus* offers in its four and a half hours of cinema many reasons why indeed it was necessary to judge Barbie. The first one is to have justice done at last, to remember and honor the memory of the children of Izieu and through them all the victims of the Holocaust. It is, through the trial of the murderer of forty-one Jewish children, to recognize once and for all the specificity of the extermination of the Jews. The trial, and beyond it *Hotel Terminus*, must also constantly remind all the generations to come what anti-Semitism and racism lead to. This is more than ever of utmost importance since the recent increase of anti-Semitism in Europe and all over the world.

Therefore, as Marek Halter put it, the trial has its place in a very old tradition "that does not so much judge the criminal by desire of vengeance but rather in order to try to understand the crime, and that does not seek to correct the accused, but all mankind through him" (in B.-H. Lévy, 1986: 45). The trial also reminds us that the Holocaust was directly made possible and carried out by specific individuals who are accountable for their behavior. As Eric Ghebali put it, the trial had to take place "so that never again in debates or conferences we would hear pseudo-humanists say: 'Can we really condemn them? Do we know what we would have done in their place?' It must be clear to everyone that this (the deportation of the children of Izieu), we would never have done" (in B.-H. Lévy, 1986: 24).

Finally, as Elie Wiesel put it during his deposition, the trial must prevent the amnesiacs and the falsifiers from killing the dead again because "if they were to succeed, it would not be their mistake anymore but our own." Through and much beyond its cinematographic importance, *Hotel Terminus* serves all of these fundamental purposes of the trial. The film also allows key issues to remain very well-defined and vivid in both places and times that are not or will not be aware of the actuality of Barbie's trial.

It is however this very same reason that not only clearly shows the importance of Ophüls' work but also the key role played by *Shoah* in this fundamental and continuous struggle against oblivion. Claude Lanzmann himself pushed this argument so far as to question the relevance of the trial in favor of the key role played not only by cinema in general but by his own film *Shoah*:

> I will tell you right away why I am certainly partial in this matter: precisely because I have made *Shoah*. And it is a matter of transmitting, in the sense of transmitting what really happened, making *Shoah* was a lot more worth it than having a trial forty years later. A trial that does not reveal anything we did not already know, for which there is nothing at stake, without talking about this confusion between the specificity of the destruction of the Jews with all the stories about the Résistance. I know that the trial has been justified in the name of its pedagogic virtues. I do not believe in

them and we will realize that in times to come. All of
this will be forgotten while *Shoah* will not be forgotten
(in B.-H. Lévy, 1986: 51).

Shown two years after *Hotel Terminus* and the trial of Klaus
Barbie, Louis Malle's *Goodbye Children* was also centered
around the memory of the persecution of Jewish children in Nazi-
occupied France. As after the first showing of *The Sorrow and
the Pity* in 1971, with *Hotel Terminus* Ophüls seemed to be once
again caught up in the "mode rétro." One more time however, the
differences between Malle's and Ophüls' films clearly show that
they belong to two radically different and often opposed film
genres.

With *Goodbye Children*, Louis Malle finally made the film
he had been thinking about for so many years and that he almost
made in 1974 before he finally decided to film *Lacombe Lucien*.
Contrary to *Lacombe Lucien*, *Goodbye Children* is completely
based on Malle's personal memories in his own world rather than
being based on what Malle and a Parisian writer think about what
young farmers were like in 1944. Here the script was not co-
signed by a professional writer and Malle is totally responsible
for all the scenes of the film.

This very personal involvement of Malle in the script and
his proximity to his main character, Julien, make this film greatly
superior to *Lacombe Lucien*. In contrast to what happens with
Lacombe, Malle makes the psychology of Julien very clear and
explicitly complex. However, throughout the film, the positive
character of Julien and the negative character of Lacombe have
many common points.

On many occasions, the character and psychology of Julien
present us with a bourgeois version of Lacombe. During most of
the film, like Lacombe, Julien does not understand what the war
and the Occupation are all about. Like a child who never saw
himself the destructions of war, he is not scared during the
bombings. Being brought up in the very enclosed world of the
high bourgeoisie of the thirties, like Louis Malle himself, Julien
has had very little contact with the "real" world.

Like Lacombe who was never interested in the political speeches on the radio, Julien has a very vague idea of the political situation of his own country. For all these reasons, he asks his mother: "What is exactly a Jew?" "Aren't we Jewish ourselves?" In that same manner, after denouncing one of the chiefs of the Résistance in his village as "by accident," while being drunk, Lacombe asks other Collaborators: "What is a Freemason?" Both remarks are realistic from the position of two teenagers that have had very little contact with reality and that have only heard about Jews and Freemasons that which anti-Semite, anti-Socialist and racist propaganda have told them mostly since 1936.

Both Lacombe and Julien feel rejected by their mothers while their fathers are missing. Both are fascinated by Jews in hiding as they do not understand what exactly is happening to them. Both commit minor or major crimes as "by accident," without apparently knowing exactly what they are doing. This is how Lacombe becomes a Collaborator and Julien becomes an active part of a small black market network, by chance, almost without knowing it. Moreover, both Lacombe and Julien are fascinated by death. Lacombe enjoys killing a bird with his sling, hunting rabbits, staring at a dead horse or beheading a chicken with a stroke of his hand. Julien is fascinated by a drip of blood running on his hand and admits that he always thinks about death.

However, and this is a major difference, Julien fears death while Lacombe does not. Julien has had no direct experience with death while for Lacombe, on the farm, it is almost a daily experience. Julien is also constantly being told what is just and unfair while Lacombe has no authority to remind him of his responsibilities. Finally, Julien is shown as constantly debating within himself, as having a very active conscience of his own feelings while Lacombe is shown as an individual having almost no feelings or at least refusing to face and analyze them.

Regarding their behavior when they are confronted with Jews in hiding, Julien and Lacombe also have similar feelings but their actions are completely opposite. Both are presented as being jealous or resenting the success of the Jews they meet. Julien is jealous when he sees that Jean plays the piano so well that the piano teacher enjoys his playing. Jean is also presented as extremely gifted in class and in direct competition with Julien. This competition provokes the interest of Julien for Jean. On his side, Lacombe wants to be accepted by Horn and his daughter because they also stand for a social status much higher than his own. He is intrigued by their way of life and wants to become part of it using the power of terror the Collaboration gives him. Both Julien and Lacombe are also intrigued by and attracted to Jews that are of their own age (Julien and Jean; Lucien and France) and that will ultimately make them realize what is really happening in their own worlds.

All these elements show clearly that *Lacombe Lucien* and *Goodbye Children* are much more similar than it seems at first sight. Indeed, all the common points between the characters of Julien/Lucien (Julien is almost an anagram for Lucien) characterize Louis Malle's vision of a teenager living in an intermediary world between childhood and adulthood (They can also all be found in the character of Laurent in Malle's *Murmur of the Heart*). However, both are led in opposite directions toward opposite actions. Lucien collaborates and persecutes Jews as well as members of the Résistance while Julien helps Jean and feels a strong friendship and a certain solidarity with him through fear.

Unlike what happens in *Lacombe Lucien*, references to Judaism in *Goodbye Children* contain some very positive connotations. Jean stands up for his best friend "Négus" against all the other students and Julien himself. He prays at night and never rejects his Jewish identity. Confronted with Jean, Julien is extremely intrigued and a little jealous but he feels very close to him because they share unconsciously some of their most important feelings: they both miss their mother and their parents in general, they are both terrified and trying to hide their real feelings. Lucien, on the other hand, can do none of this with anybody, except maybe a little bit at the very end of the film while he is running away with France and her grand-mother.

The large international success of *Goodbye Children* as opposed to the more limited success due to scandal of *Lacombe Lucien* can be explained in great part by the great compassion the film shows for the character of Jean Bonnet, a very tight and precise narration, the progression of suspense and by the minute analysis of teenage psychology the film is based on. All of these elements are combined within Malle's "classical style." They make the film easily accessible to a large audience through what appears to be a certain revival of the French "cinema of quality." My detailed analysis of this film will, therefore, be based on a reevaluation of Malle's often noted "classicism" and how it influences a particular representation of the Holocaust.

Since *Goodbye Children*, several French films have depicted the persecution of Jewish children as well as the efforts of a few Gentiles who tried to rescue some of them. More recently, Pierre Sauvage's superb documentary *Weapons of the Spirit* (1988), Véra Belmont's *Milena* (1991) and Andrzej Wajda's *Korczak* (1991), have been entirely dedicated to the representation of individuals or communities, Gentiles or Jews, trying to save some Jews or openly taking their defense. By contrast, Christian de Chalonge's *Docteur Petiot* (1990) is based on the story of a doctor who pretends to help runaways and Jews in order to assassinate them and steal their belongings.

Pierre Sauvage's *Weapons of the Spirit* is an inspiring tribute to the five thousand villagers of Le Chambon-sur-Lignon who rescued five thousand Jews, mostly children, in Occupied France. The director himself was born in Le Chambon in 1944. His documentary is based on the story of his own return to Le Chambon, on his discovery of the villagers' sturdy, life-saving values and on Pierre Sauvage's continued quest for understanding why it was so "natural" to the people of Le Chambon to save Jews at a time when the world seemed to have turned its back on them.

The greatest achievement of Sauvage's documentary, as a cinematographic work, is the perfect adequacy of its form with the "spirit" of the villagers. Like the people of Le Chambon, *Weapons of the Spirit* is simple only in appearance. It is a story with no hero, no traitor, no liberator, no ideology to justify. It is a profound description and analysis of the complex "simplicity" of a "conspiracy of goodness" that saved thousands of lives. Sauvage clearly presents the story of Le Chambon as an extraordinary one. He always reminds the audience that the Shoah was to exterminate every European Jew, including the elderly and the children. For this reason, Sauvage's work never creates hope from the Shoah but from a few very ordinary people who always opposed bigotry and intolerance without fail and without agonizing about their decisions. Because of the memory this film saves, because of the importance of the questions it raises for our future and the exceptional skills of its director in rendering faithfully the heart of his subject, *Weapons of the Spirit* is a modest but irreplaceable "little brother" of *Shoah*. These points will be analyzed and demonstrated in the detailed study of this film.

In violent contrast with Sauvage's documentary, Christian de Chalonge's feature film *Docteur Petiot* is the meticulous portrait of a monstrous murderer who assassinates Jews and runaways. Based on a real story and the famous trial of Doctor Petiot, the film presents the murderer as a vampire who tricks his victims by offering to help them. Two Jewish men are among his prey. The first one is a married man trying to go to Argentina, the second has been released from the camp of Compiègne by the Gestapo on the condition that he spy on Petiot. He is assassinated by the doctor after telling him why he was released.

Docteur Petiot offers the sharp and frightening description of a criminal who took advantage of the Occupation to commit atrocities that, otherwise, he could not have accomplished with the same facility. The image constantly recalls fantastic cinema, German expressionism and particularly Murnau's *Nosferatu*. Petiot lives at night, underground, in the enclosed spaces of his office and the private mansion where he commits his crimes. His costume and his make-up accentuate his fantastic vampire appearance. During the day, the Doctor takes care of a little girl and her poor family. He also gives free consultations and free drugs to his poorest patients. During the night, he brings victims to the French and German Gestapo or, he himself burns the corpses of his own "clients." In the third part of the film, after the Liberation, Petiot changes his identity and becomes a hero of the Résistance until he is accidentally identified. The persecution of the Jews plays an important role in de Chalonge's film. However, the director's main focus is the fantastic portrait of "a monster" who is praised during the day for the good he does around him while, at night, he is a cold blooded murderer. The last part of the film offers also a fierce criticism of the so-called "Résistants of the last hour" that was developed at the same time and to a much larger extent in Claude Berri's *Uranus* (1990). As two archetypes of Doctor Petiot's many blind victims, the two male Jews are presented as desperately confident (because Petiot represents their last resort), in a constant panic, and terrified. They do not realize what is happening to them until a few seconds before they die.

More recently, Véra Belmont's *Milena* (1991) told the story of Franz Kafka's confidant and translator who loses her life in the concentration camps for refusing to take off the star of David Kafka gave her. Through telling Milena Jarenska's life, Belmont creates a vast and powerful evocation of the richness of intellectual life in Prague and Vienna in the thirties. From a myth of world literature, Milena (Valérie Kaprisky) becomes a "real" and passionate woman caught up in the midst of the rise of European fascism and intolerance. As a medical student, a reporter, a politically committed artist, the lover of a Jewish art critic and an admirer of Kafka, she is very much aware of the intensification of the persecution of the Jews. However, she never thinks about them as being Jewish as only the anti-Semites of the film characterize the Jews as such. She dies because she refuses to repudiate her love not only for Kafka but also for her former lover. She refuses to adjust to the criminal absurdity of her executioners even if it is a matter of saving her own life.

Andrzej Wajda's *Korczak* was shown for the first time on Parisian screen on exactly the same day *Milena* was. Long before its official release, this film created a scandal after Claude Lanzmann and various French critics accused its director of betraying the memory of the victims. The film relates the last days of the famous Jewish and Polish writer, doctor and educator Janusz Korczak who died in the gas chamber, in Treblinka, with the two hundred Jewish orphans he was taking care of. *Korczak* was very well received in England, Sweden, Germany and also Israël. In Paris, however, it was the source of a violent controversy. The polemic started after the very first showing of the film at the May 1991 Cannes Festival. It was revived by the end of 1991 even after a private showing for the Parisian intelligentsia at the end of which Claude Lanzmann left the room declaring to the producer of the film and Mrs. Rocard, the French Prime Minister's wife and organizer of the showing: "You produced this. I do not congratulate you. (...) Madame, you have no idea how bad this is."[35] On the other hand, the philosopher Alain Finkielkraut, the historian André Burguière and many other critics stood up for the film. All the major French distributors, except UGC, refused to finance the film. The public release of *Korczak* was delayed one week after a series of financial difficulties obtaining government funds for its distribution and several rumors about its possible censoring (Bouzet, 41-42).

The film was first criticized because of its two final scenes showing the deportation of the children. The orphans are shown walking together in the street, carrying a flag with a star of David and singing while we do not hear their voices but the loud beat of a drum. Korczak leads the group. In the very last scene, the wagon in which the children are being deported to Treblinka miraculously gets detached from the rest of the train. Its doors open, Korczak and the children jump from the wagon (in slow motion), carrying their flag, and they disappear in a field covered with midst. A final image recalls that they all died in the gas chambers.

Finally, the film was also criticized by Lanzmann for telling the life of "the Poles' good Jew," of a "Polonized Jew," for showing Jewish black marketeers, wealthy Jews, the Jewish police, and Jewish thieves while showing very few Polish anti-Semites or even German soldiers (Lanzmann, 1991: 96-97).

Lanzmann did not say that what is shown in the film did not exist in the Warsaw Ghetto but for him: "it has no importance whatsoever, this exists in every society and it happened there less than in other places. The truth, the only thing that matters, is to represent the tragedy in its immensity, in its purity" (Lanzmann, 96). Lanzmann then goes on explaining why he succeeded with *Shoah* while Wajda failed with *Korczak*. Consequently, Wajda's *Korczak*, like his preceding film *La Terre de la grande promesse*, would become known as the work of an anti-Semite.

After seeing this film, these reproaches seem either largely exaggerated or unjustified. The film mentions Polish anti-Semitism on several occasions, especially at the beginning of the film, before the deportation of the children to the Ghetto. I will give only three examples. First, some of his older students criticize Korczak for not preparing them to face the outside world's virulent anti-Semitism. Also women doing the children's laundry refuse "to wash the shit of the Jews." And finally, a young girl is told by her boss to stop seeing a boy because he is Jewish. The rest of the film takes place inside the Ghetto itself. Therefore it could not show many Poles nor many Germans. As the historian André Burguière put it: "What average anti-Semite Pole would go inside the Ghetto? Is it a reason to accuse Wajda with leading us to believe that all the Poles behaved like Korczak?" (Burguière, 1991: 96).

As for the two final scenes, the film, the soundtrack, the slow motion, the flag, the mist and the violent black and white contrast in those scenes make it clear that they are symbolic. Jerusalem's audiences interpreted them as symbolizing the birth of Israel, an interpretation that is reinforced by the central role played by the flag with the star of David. All these elements make it obvious that the final scenes are not an historical "reproduction" of what happened but a symbolic representation of the deportation and of the survival of Israel in spite of the Holocaust. We are to be reminded however that, in Rossif's film *Le Temps du Ghetto* (1961), a survivor and eyewitness to the deportation of Korcak's children says that "the children were singing" on their way to the deportation train. According to the same witness, Korczak had told the children that they were leaving for "a country where there is no suffering." The final image clearly recalls what really happened to these children. Moreover, as André Burguière recalled, the final sequence is "a mere transposition of the last scene of a play by the Indian poet Tagore (1913 Nobel prize of Literature), "The Messenger," that Korczak had the children play—as we see in the film—only a few days before their deportation" (Burguière, 96). Other spectators reproached Wajda for including in his black and white film some of the footage shot by the Nazis in the Ghetto. The degree of success or failure of Wajda's cinematographic choices in reaching its goal can be debated but they offer no ground for accusing the director of anti-Semitism.

Regarding the representation of the class divisions and the rivalries existing inside the Ghetto, Lanzmann recognizes that they existed as they exist everywhere else. In France, without creating any controversy, Frédéric Rossif described the same divisions in his 1961 *film de montage Le Temps du Ghetto* which received worldwide appraise. They are used in *Korczak* to characterize its main character because the very subject of this film is Korczak himself, whose real name was Josef Goldszmit (played by Wojtek Pszoniak). Korczak was very proud of being Polish but the film makes it clear that he died because he was Jewish and because he refused to abandon his two hundred Jewish children. Consequently, Wajda's *Korczak* remains a unique and striking tribute to the memory of an exceptional man who remained faithful to the children he loved until the very end.

According to Henry Rousso, the eighties correspond to a "banalisation" of the Holocaust, after the scandals of the early seventies followed by a few charges or trials (Darquier, Leguay, Touvier, Bousquet, Papon and Barbie). For Rousso, this "banalisation" has mainly negative but also a few positive aspects (183-184). On the one hand, among often shown images of more recent atrocities, there is the risk that the Holocaust will always be seen as one genocide among others. Rousso indicates also that because everyone and anyone talks about the Holocaust, "sometimes too much, and often in poor manner," it has become a popular subject whose recurrence might exasperate many. Finally, being necessarily dealt with in a "scientific" way by historians, "the Final Solution looses its status as a unique and, to say the word, sacred experience." On the other hand, Rousso believes that if one insists too much on the specificity of the Holocaust, it become impossible to refer to Nazi anti-Semitism "in denouncing new forms of racism" (184).

Indeed, an important part of the new anti-Semitism of the late eighties and early nineties is based on a "banalisation" of the Holocaust. Through comparing and equating other genocides to the Shoah, anti-Semites were able first to make relative the extermination of the Jews as one, "minor," historical event among others. The next step was to make Israel responsible for "similar" war crimes against Palestinians taking as points of reference the massacres of Sabra and Shatila or other more recent killings of Palestinians.

Alain Finkielkraut and Claude Lanzmann have regularly and violently denounced this new anti-Semitism hidden behind an apparently "good-willed" anti-Zionism. This threat was taken very seriously as not only the extreme right but also many Marxist intellectuals confused anti-Imperialism, anti-Zionism, anti-Racism and anti-Semitism.[36]

While the Palestinian cause gained more and more international support in the seventies and eighties, mostly in 1989 through the Intifada, the memory of the Arab terrorism of the seventies and the open threats of Irak on Israel in 1990 reminded the world that an important part of the Arab world demands not only a territory for the Palestinians but also the total obliteration of the state of Israel altogether.

In this context, the support of Jean-Marie Le Pen, the French leader of the National Front, for Saddam Hussein's invasion of Kuwait in the summer of 1990, is consistent with the traditional anti-Semitism/anti-Zionism of the extreme right in spite of its also traditional racism against the Arabs living in France. In consequence, 1990 was marked by a slow but important step back in the frighteningly wide popular support the National Front Party enjoyed during the late eighties.

In this respect, both nationally and internationally, 1989 served as a warning signaling for the resurgence of a worldwide rebirth of a violent anti-Semitism. The Carmelites in Auschwitz, new pogroms in Russia, the new persecutions of the Jews in Eastern Europe, the migration of thousands of Jews out of the Soviet Union and Ethiopia, the desecration of the oldest French Jewish graveyard in Carpentras, France, the fall of the Berlin Wall combined with the German reunification obscuring the memory of the Crystal Night and the Holocaust as well as the vitality of bigotry and anti-Semitic actions in the United States constituted many signs of various importance proving that the "old beast" is still very much alive. If, when and how French cinema will deal with these events remains to be seen.

PART II

CINEMATOGRAPHIC STUDIES

6. Alain Resnais' *Night and Fog*

Night and Fog starts with images of a banal European landscape and then deals with the most dreadful event of recent human history. Following the movement of its first images, Resnais' whole documentary can be considered and analyzed as an archeological study exploring various layers of our recent past. Throughout the movie, the spectator is asked to consider different regions of our very selective collective memory. Alternating between landscapes and ground level shots, the present and traces of the past, the first and last images of *Night and Fog* clearly justify such a leading strand that takes us back and forth through time in search of a few remaining traces of the Holocaust in the strictly delimited space of a concentration camp.

In 1955, Resnais was already famous for his studies on time and memory. However, as Marcel Oms recently noted: "Memory is also a dimension of the imaginary, even if it is turned towards the past. To remember is to make an effort to reconstruct in imagination what has already been lived. To forget is also not wanting to remember or relive" (Oms, 53-54). Resnais also stressed this fusion of memory and imagination when he declared, "I've always refused the word 'memory' *a propos* my work. I would use the word 'imagination'" (Yakir, quoted by Monaco, 11). Finally, John Ward noted, "Resnais never tires of affirming [that] memory does more than preserve; it also creates" (Ward, 14). The complexity of the consequences of such a remark will be analyzed throughout this study, linking in an essential manner memory, imagination and creation.

Resnais' archeological study of collective memory in *Night and Fog* is also inseparable from the mid-fifties definition of what the work of a "committed artist" should be. As Henri Laborit explains in Resnais' film *Mon oncle d'Amérique* (1980):

> We are only the others. When we die, it is the others who are going to die, the ones that we have interiorized

121

in our nervous systems, that have built us, that have built our brains, and filled them.

Such a point of view must be debated as it also plays an important role in the various effects *Night and Fog* produces on its audiences. Even if Resnais has refused to characterize his work as that of a committed artist,[37] he has never denied that tight relationship linking the arts, politics and collective history. Laborit's remark adds a new perspective on our need to talk about the Holocaust, about the massacre of millions of "others." It will lead us to confronting *Night and Fog* and Resnais' cinematographic art in general with the mid-fifties definition of a committed artist.

The archeological structure of this documentary leads us progressively to the discovery of traces of the Holocaust, putting them together to offer a general overview of the questions they raise in the present. Such a movement suggests possible interpretations to be considered by the spectator. In this progressive search, the different means of cinema are being simultaneously used as tools with their own specific powers in order to give a precise, global, powerful and current view of the Holocaust. Nonetheless, the feeling of uneasiness that dominates the film is not only due to the horrifying images it shows. It is also due in great part to the complex time lags and intertwinings of the documentary's main signifying series.

There are two obvious series in *Night and Fog* —one of images and one of sound. They illustrate each other, precede one another or diverge completely. In Resnais' later works they will become more and more independent. The image series splits into two dimensions: color images, belonging to our present, and black and white historical footage. The two elements which make up the series of sounds are the commentary as it is read by an anonymous voice-over and the music composed by Hans Eisler.

The black and white images are taken from three different sources: Leni Riefenstahl's *The Triumph of the Will*, historical footage, or old photographs. The text splits into two series: an historical series which either follows the chronology of historical events or describes everyday attempts to survive; and a poetic series evoking not only what an individual human being feels in such a universe but also the evaluation by all humanity, starting with the audience, of the consequences of this dreadful chapter in our history. This poetic series opens and closes the film. Its basic function is to allow us to penetrate the past and to preserve the memory of the Holocaust in order to prevent its reoccurrence in the present of our own lives. The different elements constituting the film can be summarized as follows:

- from Leni Riefenstahl's *The Triumph of the Will*
-» **black and white**
- historical footage selected by Resnais
- photographs filmed by Resnais

Image Series

-» **color**
- present; all filmed from the inside of Auschwitz
- historical
- general chronology
- everyday survival

- -

-» **Cayrol's text**
- poetic
- individual feelings
- universal consequence

Sound-track

-» **music**
- a link between the image and the text
- replacing words impossible to find

The purpose of this analysis will first be to characterize Resnais' search and the powerful evocation it creates through its complex use of these parallel series. Such an analysis should enable us to study Resnais' documentary as a totality in constant metamorphosis using all the specific devices cinema offers to create a work of art that directly addresses both the spectator's intellect and imagination in both the present and the future of the viewing.

a. Images to Be Seen

The first shot of *Night and Fog* indicates clearly that underneath the apparent normality and tranquility of a contemporary landscape lies traces of the atrocities of the Holocaust. Between the background of the first image representing a ploughed field and the images of Auschwitz which follow lines of furrows dividing the screen in countless parallel lines that meet in the lower right-hand corner of the frame and cross the first image diagonally. As the camera pans vertically to ground level, the line of the horizon and the lines of the furrows give place, in the foreground, to the barbed wire and the posts of a concentration camp as if, by going under the surface of this peaceful landscape, the movement of the camera would reach another layer of European history in the heart of the present.

In the second shot, the movement of the eye is no longer vertical. The camera retreats, panning slowly to the right. This time both the furrows and the horizon (now in the middle of the screen) are parallel, like the wires discovered in the first shot. Retreating, like a frightened spectator discovering an unexpected world, the camera reveals again, in the foreground, the barbed wire that soon crosses the whole screen. Moving slowly from the upper left to the lower right corner of the screen, this shot combines both the directions indicated in the first shot by the furrows and, in the second shot, the direction indicated by the barbed wire just revealed. From shot to shot, an irresistible movement is developing. This movement is basic to the film itself as it evokes a major chapter of history from the few traces remaining, in spite of all the efforts made to erase them. Such a movement will be used frequently during the film as it goes from one detail to a much bigger picture, from one trace to the general scenery; following the railroad track to the entrance of Auschwitz and connecting further the same image with a rising tracking shot of the latrines; going from a close up of a few hairs to the filming of a huge pile of women's hair, etc. The documentary never allows the audience to forget that the Holocaust concerned the extermination of millions of individuals. Accompanying such images, the text insists:

> Today, on the same track there is sun light. We run through it slowly. In search of what? Of traces of corpses that collapsed as soon as the doors were open, or in search of the first unloaded passengers pushed to the entrance of the camp among the barking of the dogs, the lighting of the projectors. In the distance, the flames of the crematorium.

Concluding a tracking shot of the cubicles where the prisoners slept (moving forward and, again, from the left to right) we hear: "Of these dormitories made of bricks, of the sleep threatened, we can only show you the bark, the color." From the position of the camera's eye, we know that the heart of this European landscape is inside the camp. It is also in the heart of our recent history whether we want to see it or not. For Cayrol, the author of the film's text, it is at the foundation of the post-war literature. Every line of the documentary converges at the camp. Even following a flight of crows, the eye ends up inside the camp.

In these opening sequences, the images seem to illustrate ideas expressed by the text, ideas that led to the making of the film. Very soon, this relationship will be balanced, the text and the montage completing and inverting the intended effect of the images of Leni Riefenstahl's *The Power of the Will*. At times it will be inverted, the text explaining what we see—like the hierarchy in the camps—or completely broken, the text not being able to find words to describe what is shown: "These images are taken a few minutes before an extermination... But we can no longer say anything... When the Allies open the doors...." The film works here as a totality. None of the series constituting it will absolutely dominate (images in color/images in black and white/text/music). They intertwine and exchange their powers in order to give a total image of reality reaching both the intellect and the imagination.

In the third shot starting from the landscape, the horizon is in the upper third of the screen. The camera follows a country road panning again from left to right. As it goes toward the horizon, this road could indicate a possible escape. However, in the very same movement, the camera discovers first a watchtower and then two rows of barbed wire. We are again, once and for all, trapped inside the camp, whatever line of this landscape the eye chooses to follow.

The fourth introductory sequence is shot completely in the camp itself, in its labyrinth of barbed wire. The search in a labyrinth is a constant in Resnais' as well as Alain Robbe-Grillet's works. It can be a representation of memory but it stands first of all for the necessary search and confrontation with death, with the Minotaur, the monster hiding in the labyrinth's heart. Even if, on the surface, life seems to have resumed its normal course, the ghost buildings of Auschwitz remain in spite of the efforts of the Nazis to hide and destroy all signs of the genocide. We have no choice but to face what happened and more importantly, we must try to understand how it could have happened. *Night and Fog* then really insists for the first time in French cinema on the necessity of facing the most important repressed event of our collective unconscious.

In this same fourth shot, whether we follow the slow, continuous movement of the camera from left to right or whether we follow the perspective of the shot, we see only ruins, empty buildings, and barbed wire. The eye of the spectator is now searching for traces that would facilitate an understanding of what had happened here and why "even a quiet landscape... even a prairie with flights of crows, harvests and grass fires... even a road where cars pass by, farmers, couples... even a vacation village with a fair and a church can simply lead us to a concentration camp" (my translation).

The equality in length, tone, and speed of the first five introductory shots in dull colors creates the atmosphere of a necessary but anguished search, indicating already the fear of what we might find and the uncertainty of our ability to face it. The intriguing melody and the monotonous voice reading the poetic and enigmatic text add considerably to this strong feeling. These techniques combine to thrust the audience into the heart of our collective memory and imagination.

In this introduction to the documentary, the line of the horizon has been successively placed at the lower, the middle and top third of the screen to disappear finally in the perspective of rows of barbed wire crossing the depth of the screen. Such lines form a recurring image in the documentary, seen in the rows of barbed wire, railroad tracks, latrines, trucks of prisoners going to work, etc. The historical footage can only begin when the line of the horizon has completely disappeared. This progressive disappearance of the horizon, the subsequent domination of the lines of a concentration camp and the frightening marching of military boots plunges the spectator suddenly into the history of Nazi Germany starting in 1933. A little further, it will thrust the spectator onto "another planet."

In the first dive into the past, the last color image of successive rows of barbed wire running from the left angle of the foreground to the center of the background has been suddenly replaced by innumerable rows of soldiers parading at exactly the same angle. From a low angle black and white shot, the screen is covered by the boots and the uniforms of parading soldiers, almost as if they were stepping on the camera itself.

In these first images, as often happens in Resnais' work, the unexpected, the unusual, emerges suddenly to form a very balanced image. In a more general context, Resnais himself declared: "I have a certain taste for mixing sugar and salt, for little unusual encounters."[38] René Prédal noticed that "this search for sometimes explosive oppositions brings Resnais and Cayrol to destroy the tragic and lyrical image of the death camps" (Prédal, 1968: 12). Such "explosive oppositions" are of course very frequent in *Night and Fog*. The most famous might be the documentary's presentations inside a camp of a symphonic orchestra, a zoo, green houses, Goethe's oak, an orphanage, a hospital for invalids, etc. Such sequences are immediately followed by the incredibly violent punishments, humiliations and executions of the prisoners.

In the inverted world of the camp, the simulacra of an ordinary life exhibited by the Nazis become monstrosities, signs of a terrifying irony, of constant psychological torture, instead of signs suggesting a temporary relief. Indeed in *Night and Fog*, as Ilan Avisar noted:

> There are those within that infernal reality who conduct a quite ordinary life. The kapo's room is spacious and neatly organized, containing a comfortable bed, desk, chairs, and night lamp. The Commandant lives in a villa, relaxing at home with his wife and dog. They entertain guests, who chat, drink, and laugh while another couple plays chess (Avisar, 9).

Such an irony was introduced at the very beginning of the film with the presentation of the different styles used in the construction of watchtowers. The effects of this particular sequence are particularly subtle as the contrasts of the film very often push the spectators to snicker as they know that these constructions played a key role in the organization and the perpetration of the Holocaust.

Thus the documentary creates a supplementary uneasiness as well as an automatic and necessary distancing between what the spectators see and how they will react to it. The juxtaposition of the sordid aspect of many images and the irony of the comments reveal that this film will be as much about what happened as it will be about how we react individually to its complex reality and its consequences. This very same kind of study and reaction will be developed in Resnais' feature films, most particularly in *Hiroshima mon amour*, about which James Monaco wrote: "Your reaction is the subject of the film, and its objective. Some of us see nothing in *Hiroshima*. Nothing. Others see *everything*. *Everything*. That is the point" (Monaco, 37). This also explains in great part the importance of the subtle irony throughout Resnais' work as a process based on the divergence and inversion of the relationship between three main series: the series of what is being said or shown, what it usually signifies and what it really means in the actual sequence.[39]

These encounters, as well as the ruptures of style, are a very efficient way to avoid the trap of the completely out of place melodramatic and nationalistic tone of Hollywood-type productions. In *Night and Fog*, ruptures and encounters insist on the perversity of the Nazi order but they also directly oppose the traditionally comfortable, irritating and misleading dichotomy Hollywood productions make between the mad, dirty and sweaty-looking "bad guys" and the good, pitiful, sometimes dirty but always clean-looking "good guys." Hollywood productions always reinforce these aspects with a purely illustrative, extremely melodramatic and redundant music. On the contrary, Resnais' aesthetic of ruptures and subtle transitions warns us about the apparent normality of our lives as well as the Manichean and dangerous ideology of the tall, good, handsome, sensitive but in the end always self-controlled and very nationalistic hero.

Thanks to such techniques Resnais insists on the responsibilities of the Nazis but also avoids simplistic Manicheism that would make us believe that normality and abnormality, humanity and monstrosity are neatly separated and easily differentiated in history as well as in each nation or individual. Even if the universe the Nazis created is presented in the documentary as "another planet," it is clear that the executioners themselves did not come from another world and their story could be repeated today. As the film proclaims in the end, "Who among us watches in this strange observatory to warn us of the coming of new executioners? Are their faces really different from ours?" The combination of such statements with the utterly disturbing images that accompany them do not help sell a film for prime time TV in Europe or the United States.

Thus we note four of the main rupture lines of *Night and Fog*: the emergence of horror in the heart of banality; the reverse emergence of frightening banality in the heart of horror; the ambivalent reactions of the spectator, both intellectual and sensitive; and the insistence that the horror is still present among us today (distancing and identification at the same time). However, the same oppositions are crucial parts of the profound moving unity of the film. They create metamorphoses and inversions of the same reality. The first necessary task for both the filmmaker and the spectator who wish to comprehend what happened is to interpret traces and signs in their metamorphoses.

The first such complex metamorphosis and inversion of this kind that we see in the image series of this documentary concerns extracts of Leni Riefenstahl's *Triumph of the Will* as they are used by Resnais. While using this propaganda film or more trustworthy historical footage and photographs, Resnais could not direct the making of the image. He was free however to select the segments that were interesting to him and to insert them in his film in a way that would best serve his purpose. I already mentioned how the first brutal switch from color to black and white is legitimized by the metamorphosis of the rows of barbed wires into rows of parading soldiers and how the angles and the movements of the camera are similar in both cases. In so doing, Resnais has turned Riefenstahl's images, filmed by order of Hitler to symbolize the growing power of the Nazi party, into symbols of the crush of Europe by Nazi troops and the beginning of the Holocaust.

In fact, if we remember that the Nuremberg Rally was staged and organized to best serve the making of Riefenstahl's film, *Night and Fog* then appears as the perfect opposite of a propaganda film as the camera becomes modest in front of the reality instead of forcing reality into its ideology.[40] Because the Nazis inverted reality and the meaning of images and words, Resnais must in turn invert their effects. After bringing back to memory what the Nazis wanted to hide and make disappear—i.e. the site of the camps—this inversion is the second most important task of *Night and Fog*.

Another echo between the first series of shots in color and then in black and white can be seen in the similarity of the almost right angle, formed in the very first shot by the L-shaped post holding the barbed wire and, in the footage, the very similar shape of the Nazi salute made by Hitler standing in his car as the army parades in front of him in Nuremberg. The repetition of such a shape evokes clearly the structure of a gallows.

In the first historical images borrowed from Leni Riefenstahl the camera does not move, filming either with a low angle as if it were crushed, or from a high angle to give a better impression of a huge, anonymous, enlisted crowd. The same angles will be used constantly to show the horror and the extent of the Holocaust: filming the picture of a pile of women's hair; a color panning shot of Auschwitz filmed from a watchtower; footage filmed from an airplane flying over a camp, etc. This use of Leni Riefenstahl's *The Triumph of the Will* has the opposite effect from that intended when this documentary was ordered by Hitler. The low angle shots were of course made to indicate the strength of the army and the power of the Nazi leaders and the high angle shots to insist on the extent of this power on the German people as well as to express their support to the Nazi regime. Resnais, by his selection and his montage technique, thereby reverses or destroys the original function of the German propaganda film.

The feeling of oppression increases as the rows of soldiers cross the screen first from right to left then from left to right and finally come from the background toward the camera filming in a low angle to turn skimming past it, just before the parading swastikas cover the whole screen. It is at that point that the camera pans to the right, in the street of Nuremberg, following another parade, and discovers Himmler and Hitler dominating the entire scene with a Nazi salute. As in the desperate frenzy of a nightmare, the camera runs through the streets of Nuremberg, seeing one smiling individual after another repeat the Nazi salute. Here, in the black and white footage as much as in the first colored shots, there is no escape possible. The space is closed, the individual crushed, and the horizon has disappeared.

Inversions, encounters, distancing, constant interpretation and ruptures of signifying series are also different ways to avoid overstylization. Such techniques, to use an expression of Elie Faure, make of cinema, and particularly of Resnais' cinema, an "architecture in movement."[41] Stylization therefore represents at the same time a chance to reach the imagination and to evoke the reality of a human experience. However, as Ilan Avisar noted, it "might affect the perception of historical truth and distort the authentic nature of the concentration camps" (Avisar, 16).

Resnais' close collaboration with Jean Cayrol helped him to protect his film from distortion. As he declared to Annette Insdorf:

To make a film about the concentration camps, it seemed to me that you had to have been an inmate, or deported for political reasons [. . .] I accepted only on the condition that the commentary would be written by Jean Cayrol because he was himself a survivor. I agreed to make the film with Cayrol as the guarantee of the montage and the images" (quoted by Insdorf, 213; see also Avisar, 6).

This fear of distortion through excessive lyricism and over-stylization also explains in part the abrupt rupture in style produced by the sudden merging of historical footage taken from *The Triumph of the Will*, with very short and fast successive shots in black and white accompanied by a purely historical documentary read with a louder and faster voice.

The use of the "real" historical footage in *Night and Fog* serves in part the same purpose, as "Resnais' film usually relies on the arresting power of its documentary photos without any additional stylization which might only cheapen or trivialize the authentic enormity" (Avisar, 17). However the "arresting power" of the historical footage is also considerably increased and modified by Resnais' montage constantly intertwining the past and the present in search of an interpretation that directly concerns our future. Such plays of differences and repetitions indicate a very complex functioning that directly involves Resnais' conceptions of time and memory as they appear in *Night and Fog*.

The image series in *Night and Fog* were the creation of only one person, the director Alain Resnais. From the very beginning they split into two other dimensions: color images, belonging to our present, and the historical footage, in black and white. At the beginning of the movie the ruptures between these two series are extremely brutal and obvious. They are always reinforced by parallel ruptures in the soundtrack. However, through different metamorphoses of shapes, lines and structures, the film keeps its unity and its strength without disseminating the reactions it creates in an overcast of a purely impressionistic horror. This constant coming and going between both the present and the past, the necessity to understand and the necessity to imagine what happened through the constant metamorphoses of shapes, ideas and feelings, plays a key role in the perfection of Resnais' art in *Night and Fog*.

When the film first switches from color to black and white, the description of a landscape and the evocation of a site are being replaced by the telling of a long and real nightmare. As if by lightning, four series have been brutally ruptured, two in the images and two in the soundtrack, color; camp in a countryside; harmonious melody; poetic text are replaced by black and white; historical footage; machine-like music; historical commentary. The contrast in the image appears first through the acceleration of rhythm in the switch from color to black and white. The slow meditation of the present is then replaced by the frenetic rhythm of the Nazi machine.

With the same kind of extremely powerful montage, Resnais follows the start of what the movie calls the "Nazi machine." With sustained and uncontrollable rapid rhythm opposed to the slow meditation of the color images, we see successively: the leaders, drums and the bringing to heel of the all German nation. We see militarized children, disciplined factories, thousands of militarized workers. We see the assembling of the first camps conceived as major projects attempting different architectural styles for constructions that no one had built before. We finally see the end of the arrangements preceding the first deportations.

Then, with the same anguishing and unstoppable rhythm, comes the roundup of the deportees from all over Europe, crossing the screen in every direction and waiting for departure. We see images of deportees boarding a train, officials verifying papers, children and the disabled embarking, masters delivering directives, alarmed and terrified faces, wagons crowded with people, doors closed by Jews, employees and Jewish deportees. The train departs, first from the left to the right then from the right to the left of the screen, towards an horizon completely covered by the train itself. At the night time arrival of the train, from the upper right to the lower left corner of the screen, the documentary gives us the code word for this entire operation as the convoy arrives: "... in the night and fog."

In spite of all its ruptures, the film maintains a strong unity. Beside some of the major structural lines of the images already mentioned, the movements of the camera are consistent from the first color shots into this first selection of historical footage giving a definite unity to the documentary accompanying the brutal flashback: 1 - fixed camera with vertical movement, 2 - a panning from the left to the right, 3 - a tracking shot moving again from the left to the right. This can be interpreted as the setting in motion of the memory search and of the consciousness of the spectator.

Following the thrust in time I see as an archeological study of collective memory, the recurring movements of the camera from left to right can also be interpreted on a more symbolic level. Indeed, in the ancient divinatory science of the oracles, a flight of birds, especially of crows, coming from the left and moving to the right was a sign of catastrophe, an omen of disaster coming from the "sinister" side of the sky (in Latin, *siniestra*, left, became in English, sinister). The most recurrent movement of the camera exploring the camp throughout the documentary also goes from the left to the right. To pursue further this analysis of movement within the relation between black and white and color images in *Night and Fog*, we also have to consider, following the progression of the movie itself, the next switch, this time from black and white to color.

After showing the arrival of a "special train," "in the night and fog," using historical footage, the film switches abruptly to color images, in the present. The text underlines the rupture by starting with the word "Aujourd'hui..." ("Today..."). However, even if this rupture comes unexpectedly, the transition in the images themselves is again insured by a similar structure used both in black and white and color images. The last black and white image shows a train arriving in a camp station, from the center background to the lower front left corner of the screen. This movement is amplified by a parallel line of Nazis waiting for the train to stop in order to unload the wagons. The horizon is drowned in the fog and the smoke (this will happen again with the images of trucks taking prisoners to work). In the following color images the camera follows the railroad track leading to Auschwitz today with the two parallel lines of the track replacing the train and the soldiers shown in the previous image. Inverting completely the backward lowering movement of the camera in the very first shot of the documentary, the camera now moves from the layer of the past to ground level and rises up moving forward, from the left to the right, to reach the horizon (similar to the movement chosen to film Hitler at the beginning of the documentary).

As in an inescapable nightmare, going from the present to the past or from the past to the present, the place the camera discovers is the same. The horizon lost in the fog in the footage now shows for the first time in the film the arrival at Auschwitz with the now famous building surrounding the main gate appearing like a monstrous mouth.

In a similar image, two lines in perspective leading to the horizon end up in a closed space toward which the movements of the whole universe seem to converge irremediably, inside Auschwitz. This first image of the Auschwitz platform clearly marks the end of this section of the documentary. The next image, in black and white, moving from building to building, will start the description of what Elie Wiesel called "the Night," and of the organization of the everyday struggle for survival inside the camp. This closing of space and the horizon by a massive building crossing the background of the screen will be used again by Resnais in *Last Year in Marienbad*, in 1961, to characterize the imprisonment of the three main characters of the movie, the impossibility of escape from the territory of the castle, the necessity to face their memories and their metamorphosis in time and space.

In addition to the introduction and the conclusion of the documentary both filmed in color with a commentary in the present, *Night and Fog* is regularly punctuated by sequences in color. Here is the general organization of the documentary as I characterize it:

Introduction:
> (in color and in the present tense)
>> The slow descent into memory and imagination from the exploring of the present enclosed space of a camp.

First part: "The machine gets under way."
> a — (in black and white and in present tense)
>> "1933—the machine gets under way."
>> The construction of the first camps
>> The first deportations
> (color//present tense)
>> Today, the same track, in search of traces of the corpses.
> b — (black and white//imperfect and present tense)
>> The discovery of "another planet"
>> Organization and hierarchy
> (color//present and imperfect)
>> Impossible to ignore the camp, or to talk about it.

Second part: A finite universe of suffering
> a — (black and white//present)
>> Working, suffering, dying
>> The first worry: to eat
> (color//imperfect)
>> The latrines, a center of nocturnal encounters
> b — (black and white//present)
>> The orders and the words of the SS
>> Simulacrums of normal life imposed by the SS
> (color//imperfect)
>> A finite universe seen from the watch tower

Third part: Life for death
> a — (black and white//present)
>> Punishments, humiliations, executions
>> Individual resistance through craft work
>> Taking care of the others
> b — (color//imperfect)
>> The hospital: a false relief
> c — (black and white//present)
>> Amputations and medical experiments

Systematic dehumanization
The life of the masters
d — (color//imperfect)
The brothel and the prison
Fourth part: The final acceleration
a — (black and white//present)
1942 Systematization and acceleration of the extermination
Amplification of the techniques
b — (color/b.w./c./b.w./c.//imperfect and present)
The gas chambers
c — (black and white//present)
What to do with thousands of corpses?
d — (black and white//present)
1945 camps become gigantic
Towards a permanent economy based on the extermination
Fifth part: The revelation of the extent of the horror
b — (black and white//present)
The defeat
The amplitude of the massacre
c — Who is responsible?
Conclusion:
a — (color//present)
What does this mean for us today?

As it appears in this brief summary, images in color first evoke the impossibility today to describe what it was like to be in a concentration camp. Color images allow us to imagine what the footage cannot show. The first three "chapters" end with color images of the search today for what remains of these events. As they flit from past to present and back, the images suggest how we must remember the events.

Here again, the film works as a totality in which none of its series dominates absolutely. As the latrines, the brothel or the prison appear on the screen, the text describes what no image can show. The filming of the bodies and the mass graves combines with the music to show what no words can describe. The segments dedicated to the hospital and the surgical block maintain a more even balance among the four series.

At the same time, the abrupt shifts between present and past progressively become smoother in order to present a pure past that is very active in the present. Finally, a shot of the crematories, in color, will include black and white images of the ceiling and the walls of a gas chamber. The picture of a black corner makes a smooth transition in the continuous movement of the camera from the left to the right. The images of the ceiling and the walls of a gas chamber are in color and in black and white at the same time, recent and part of the historical footage.

This gas chamber shot is the center and culminating point of the movie, where the two main series of images join the series of the soundtrack. This is a shot whose function is to bring the audience into a collective recollection of a past which is in danger of being forgotten or replaced by the audience's own present. Here, with more intensity than anywhere else in this documentary, the spectators have to imagine and interpret what they see and hear.

The gas chamber images take the whole movie, along with its audience, into a "pure past,"[42] a "memory of the world,"[43] where the monstrous Nazi machine and the agonizing of ten million people, including six millions Jews, become much closer to us. This constant intertwining of the past with the present is made more apparent since the historical footage is accompanied by a text in the historical present tense while the images of the present, in color, are accompanied with comments first in the present, when it seems extremely difficult to talk about this past, and then in the imperfect. After the first direct opposition of two presents, the past becomes a new present and the present tells us about the past. The film ends in the present with questions concerning our future.

The last historical images of *Night and Fog* thus have an extreme power over our imaginations as we have just encountered this collective memory. The film can then end with the threat of a horror that is still upon us, in the same present with which the film started. This time however the film is oriented towards the future.

After presenting the ovens, color is not used until the conclusion of the documentary. Nothing in the present can really make us share, not even in our imagination, the inhumanity of the last year of the camps. No color images mark the fourth chapter. However, they are testimonies of what had once been a very real present for millions of people. Nothing can be compared or related now to the horror evoked in the last minutes of a documentary which ends with a question still looking for an answer in our present: "Who is responsible?" The present of our collective memory then becomes the foundation for understanding the limited present of our daily lives.

b. Words to Be Heard

The spoken text of this documentary was written by Jean Cayrol, a poet and a Catholic who survived the Holocaust.[44] His *Poems of the Night and Fog* were published in 1945. Thus, the subject of the documentary directly concerns both his life and his work. In modern French literature, Cayrol is known as the theoretician of the *romanesque lazaréen*, the Lazarean novel, mainly because of his article "Pour un romanesque lazaréen"[45] first published in 1950, five years before the making of *Night and Fog*. For Jean Cayrol, the experience of the camps profoundly changed his personal life, his theory and his literary work. According to Cayrol, every writer publishing after World War II, whether a prisoner of the Nazis or not, was thus affected.

The universes created in novels published in the fifties are often similar to the world of the concentration camps in which the characters are prisoners of a given space, looking for an ever absent meaning to their experience as well as for a sign of hope. Therefore, the text of *Night and Fog* starts with a now well known feeling about the difficulties of working on the Holocaust; that is to say, it is impossible to really tell what happened in the camps and yet it is necessary to bear witness and analyze what the Holocaust means to us.

The Lazarean heroes are also caught between the impossibility and the necessity of communicating with the rest of humanity. They are isolated and vulnerable but this solitude itself becomes their passion and strength: "One must not make himself vulnerable, that is the main point."[46] However, at the same time the Lazarean heroes "cannot do without love, whatever name is given to it: attachment to a political party, abandonment to a religious faith, approach of a feminine love. This uprooted man, a prey to the untiring indigence haunting the world, can live only through others" (Prédal, 1968: 107).

Of course in *Night and Fog* there are no characters, no heroes. The dehumanization of the extermination process and the incommunicable suffering isolated the victims and made them anonymous. In that sense, they all became Lazarean heroes for the very short time separating their "dehumanization" and their death. In part, due to this singularity and anonymity, all of us can identify with each victim of the Holocaust; we discover a brotherhood of fear and suffering that allows us to start to understand what they lived. A few years later, in *Last Year in Marienbad*, Resnais and Robbe-Grillet's characters as well as their viewers were anonymous prisoners in another labyrinth, trying to remember and understand what happened, what had happened to them before they became prisoners of the castle, as well as how those events directly concern their present.

In Cayrol's texts as in Resnais' images, the extraordinary is conjured up in banality. As Roland Barthes wrote about Cayrol's characters: "In a unique movement, beings are, in his texts, mediocre and unusual, natural and incomprehensible."[47] Cayrol, like Resnais, avoids any kind of sentimentalism to create characters with an "affective silence" which could be "a sign of modesty or a sign of insensibility" (Barthes, 246).[48]

These central themes are key to the collaboration of Resnais and Cayrol on *Night and Fog* as well as to their very personal friendship. The influence of Cayrol's theory on Resnais' work is constant. It has been carefully studied and summarized in the essay of René Prédal, et al.: a world similar to life in the concentration camps; characters that are prisoners, solitary, anonymous, traumatized, unstable, worn out, mediocre and strange, never in the right place; the central experience of death, suffering and fear; the need to love and to communicate in spite of everything; a distrust of any kind of sentimentalism (Prédal, 1968: 103-120).

The text of *Night and Fog* uses the same processes analyzed earlier in the series of the image and which will be seen later in the series of music. In the same way the first images all lead inside the camp, all the ruptured sentences of the introduction end with the same words: "a concentration camp." Ruptured lines are equally underlined: "No footstep is heard but our own."—switch from color to black and white—"1933, the machine gets under way." Smooth transitions, comparisons and balanced parallels are also used to try to bring to present comprehension what happened in the past: "A second sorting is made on arrival in the night and fog." —switch from black and white to color—"Today, along the same tracks, it is daylight and the sun shines"; and further: "Here is everything left to us to imagine this night. . ."—switch from black and white to color—". . . interrupted with calls, lice controls. A night of chattering teeth."

The key to the film is the denunciation and the inversion, in the text, of the inversion of reality imposed by Nazi power. The names of villages secretly turned into names of camps become, with this documentary, camp names every spectator must know if other villages hope to avoid becoming synonymous with "death camps" and have a chance to remain "ordinary" villages.

The text also quotes precise names of deportees and cities from all over Europe to insist that the anonymous corpses seen later in unmarked mass graves were once the bodies of individuals, just like us, from our towns, exterminated in a banal countryside. From the beginning of the film, the dehumanization process of the Nazis fails because the film creates links between the victims and the viewers. By inverting the propaganda, the dehumanization, and the enforced anonymity of the victims, Resnais reverses the process of the Nazis' Final Solution.

A complex distancing/identification technique characterizes the documentary as each spectator feels very close to the victims while aware of the impossibility of ever completely understanding their experiences. A few years later, *Hiroshima mon amour* will present a situation that is also personal and historical, exploring the love between two characters as they attempt to survive Hiroshima and criminal hatred.

The necessary distancing justifies in part the literary tone of the text. As Resnais wrote:

> I yearn for a cinema in which the text would play the role of true music. I dream of a great film in which we would hear a language that would be like Shakespeare's or Giraudoux's. I do not see why we should not have the right to hear a text with true literary value, simply because we are sitting in a dark room (Resnais, 1966: 25).

Indeed, the darkness of the movie theater lends itself very well to the subject of the literary text being listened to. At the same time a complex network of ruptures and inversions remind the spectators that they must constantly interpret what they see and hear. It is also important to note that all the victims of the Holocaust went through their own distancing-identification process as they discovered in their own hearts reactions of basic survival—reactions at the same time cruel, selfish and heroic, of a being they had until then never known.

Through its denunciation of the perversity of the Nazi order, Cayrol's text insists on the violent opposition of the horrible euphemisms or lies of Nazi phrases written above the porches at Auschwitz with the reality that lay therein. Regarding this precise point, Ilan Avisar noted:

> Unlike the deceptive straightforward Nazi slogans—'Cleanliness Is Health,' 'To Each His Due'—the narrator's tone is cryptic, questioning, almost distrusting the power of words to describe or explain. The Nazis used words to distort reality, to inflame their masses, and to rain death and destruction (Avisar, 14).

The most striking example of this active denunciation and inversion of Nazi propaganda is the title of the documentary itself. The movie inverts completely the intent of the Germans' use of visual signs and words. The words "night and fog" were used by Hitler and the Nazis as a military code name to indicate their will to hide and make disappear any possible trace of the Holocaust. Resnais and Cayrol use it to express the anguish of the deportees upon their arrival and the horror of their extermination. As already mentioned, Cayrol chose these words as the title for a collection of poems.

Thus, these words are turned from a coded military sentence into a symbolic formula expressing the despair, the coldness and the horror that reigned over the camps. But the use of this phrase by the Nazis already corresponded to a perverse use of a traditional German phrase. Avisar explains that

> the choice of the film's title reflects the distortion of word meanings in Nazi slogans. The Nazis adapted the common German phrase 'bei Nacht und Nebel dahon gehen,' meaning to get away or to escape under cover of darkness or night, to designate one of their rules of terror, the 'Night and Fog Decree' (Avisar, 14).[49]

A few years later, the phrase "Night and Fog"—in French "Nuit et Brouillard"—became the title of a very famous French song written and sung by the *engagé* French singer and poet, Jean Ferrat, to remember the atrocities of the Holocaust. This double inversion is yet another example of this process of distancing, denunciation and inversion of the Nazis' own perversion of reality.

The tone of the voice reading Cayrol's text reinforces all these aspects. It is a voice-over, read by a professional actor, Michel Bouquet, not by Jean Cayrol. The voice is never identified as belonging to someone in particular. It never says "I." Such an avoidance of the first person prevents sentimentalism as it creates a necessary distancing between the spectator, the author of the text, and the images. A similar technique was used by Resnais, in 1966, in *La Guerre est finie*

(Prédal, 1968: 45). The voice could be that of any survivor, being at the same time precise, collective and anonymous.

The deeply human, not indifferent but monotone sound of this voice, chosen precisely for those qualities, creates in and of itself an atmosphere of threatening fate. The voice never tries to imitate or recreate what might have been said in the camps. It never pretends to be the voice of any one prisoner as the footage is always commented upon in the present tense. Neither is it the voice of God passing judgement on history. If, because of this monotone, there is no strong and overwhelming melodic value in this voice, the voice does have many variations in the length of its discourse and in its intensity. The voice supports the text and insists on its meanings but creates no melody, leaving that to the musical series itself.

Three main levels of intensity are used in the narrating voice. The first is quiet, slow and "affectively silent," intoning long sentences, asking the spectator to imagine what happened in the now mute camp. This voice is used for imagining, for evoking what cannot be shown but only suggested, like the extreme horror and suffering experienced by the millions of victims and the degradation of their bodies. The same slow tone is also used for the final meditation and interpretation in the present of the consequences of the Holocaust.

Accompanying the narration of events or the sequences describing the hierarchy of work according to the Nazi order, the rhythm is faster, the sentences shorter, the voice a little louder, often with *pizzicati* or *staccati* in the background. The voice narrates the deportations with short or broken sentences to accompany the rapid succession of different sequences or photographs. Starting with "Nineteen thirty-three—the machine gets under way," the voice continues with sentences such as: "Factories have women's names," "The SS watches," etc. In 1950, Resnais used similar techniques in *Guernica*.[50]

When the voice imitates the reading of orders or slogans by the Nazis, it becomes both louder and faster, accompanied by louder music: "We must have a nation in tune, without any quarrel," "A louse means death, and an SS, my boy!" "A bed not well made: twenty club strokes," etc. However, as the low angle shots of *Triumph of the Will* used by Resnais reversed their intended effect, this voice always remains the voice of an anonymous witness evoking the sound of the Nazi orders. In contrast with what happens in Claude Lanzmann's *Shoah*, the narrator never transmits the characteristic feeling of pleasure or self-contentedness felt in the voices of old Nazis reading the same phrases.

Such changes in rhythm as earlier noted in the image series serve to insist on the opposition between the urgent pace set by the Nazis to complete the Final Solution before the war's end and the slow pace of life for the prisoners who hoped to survive long enough to be alive when liberation would come. This slowness most often turned a long suffering into an isolated and anonymous death.

On two occasions the film uses complete silence to underscore the fear the prisoners felt. After the musical phrase of the opening credits, *Night and Fog* employs silence to instill immediately a strong feeling of strangeness and fearful waiting, a feeling increased by a very distant rolling of drums. After this there is only one very brief complete silence in the movie. At the beginning of the fourth part of the film, total silence precedes Himmler's directives to accelerate the extermination process. Other than these two passages introducing descents into hell, there is no complete silence in the documentary nor any release of tension. The tension just switches from one series to another, alternatively imposed by the images, the black and white footage (like the piles of personal belongings), the music or the text.

Pauses in the text are first created by suspended sentences that allow the spectator to imagine the words impossible to find that would describe each scene. Such ruptures in the text allow the music to accompany the image with variations on a given theme (for example, the different musical variations accompanying different images of mass deportations). Sometimes, the text gives way to images and scenes that words cannot describe. For example, the film shows what is being done with human bodies: "But nothing can be said anymore..." or shows the mass graves discovered by the Allies: "When the Allies open the doors...." Finally, mostly in the second half of the documentary, pauses are used to give spectators time to draw their own conclusions.

Similar techniques are used in the music of *Night and Fog*. Here again, in Resnais' movie, there are two types of music. The first is melodic and harmonic, often involving two parallel motives and always creating a feeling of fear and of strange languidness. The second kind is characterized by its loud, almost machine-like rhythm and sound. If it is true that music directly addresses the imagination and sensitivity through vibrations of the body, we can understand the variations, the ruptures and the intertwinings of these very different kinds of music in this powerful, poetic evocation of the Holocaust.

The music itself varies from the long, quiet, sorrow-laden violin strokes of the credits and conclusion to the rolls of drums and the nervous *pizzicato* or the very detached notes of a trumpet. During the introduction, the parallel dissonant melodies played by a flute and a clarinet accompany the first confrontation of two incompatible presents, the images of Auschwitz today and the effort to remember what happened there. The melody of a flute, a clarinet or a trumpet, is always sustained in the background by the incessant repetition of a motif, a chord, a single note, a *pizzicato* or a *staccato* played by a trumpet or a piano. Sustained, piercing bow strokes that sound like a musical saw often accompany the evocation of suffering.

Although the music often suggests an interpretation or counterbalances the violence of the image, it can also be purely descriptive. Drums imitate the sound of the first departing trains. They also accompany images showing soldiers, Nazi youth or Nazi officers. However, the dissonance and isolation of one solo instrument avoid any sentimental effect. In more conventional sequences, the image series dominates, reinforced by the music.

Violent ruptures in the image or in the text are always accompanied by an equivalent rupture in the music: a drum roll, the loud resounding of a trumpet, two loud notes from the tympani, a chord violently struck on the piano, each succeeding a quiet melody played by violins, a flute or a clarinet. However, when images in color succeed images in black and white on the same theme, the continuity of the music assures the sweet transition between past and present. The rupture is violent between two opposing themes: for example during the switch from the sequence showing prisoners eating their soup in order to survive and the following tracking shot of the latrines, in color, turning this will to survive into a new threat of death: "But the soup was diuretic."

While smooth transitions reinforce the efforts of remembering, ruptures indicate clearly the separation between different layers of the past and opposed but simultaneous aspects of the same reality. They jolt a spectator's sensitivity. Ruptures awaken the critical sense of the viewers, forcing them to consider different aspects without letting them be hypnotized by an overwhelming feeling of terror.

However, this coincidence of structures between the sound and the image series mainly concerns passages introducing new sections of the film. These processes of illustration and reinforcement never last too long. As the power of the image increases, the music always becomes more discreet. When the doors of the first trains are closed, the imitating sound of the drum disappears. When the mass graves are shown, the text disappears and the music does not produce the expected feeling of extreme violence or aggression. Slow, low, respectful and peaceful, the music gives background support to the necessary interpretation and fights any overwhelming feeling of horror that would prevent the viewers from thinking about what they see. Resnais himself points out that

> In *Night and Fog* the more violent the image the lighter the music. Eisler (the composer who wrote the film's music) wanted to show that man's optimism and hope always exist in the background (quoted by Oms, 68).

Such an opposition prevents melodramatic representations and keeps the critical senses of the spectator alert. It protects against the domination of one style as well as against the domination of a purely impressionistic reaction on the part of the spectator. It also indicates the profound unity of the different series and thus of the film itself. Throughout the documentary, the illustration, reinforcement and domination of the four main series weave together in different patterns (color; black and white//text; music), without any overall domination of one element.

Finally, the technique of double inversion found in the text and in the images has its equivalent in the musical series. A very discreet adaptation of the "Deutschland über alles," Haydn's 1797 string quartet and Germany's national anthem, is arranged in the style of the music of the film (very detached, spasmodic notes with a threatening bass drone in the background). The anthem accompanies scenes of the loading of the first trains bound for the camps.

Once again, the Nazis' misuse of Haydn's beautiful piece as the symbol of the Nazis' domination of Germany, is in turn reversed in *Night and Fog*. Eisler's orchestration maintains the general atmosphere of uneasiness and fear musically sustained throughout the documentary. However, as always in Resnais' films, a note of hope survives in the background with the memory of the original work of Haydn. In spite of its Nazi use, "Deutschland über alles" remains first of all Haydn's 1797 string quartet, the promise of a beautiful piece surviving the present distortion by the Nazis, surviving the horror and suffering.

With all these ruptures and fragmentations of the text, the film becomes a totality in which images, commentary, music and voice are subtly woven to provoke simultaneously the intellect and the imagination of the spectator. The commentary is always modest and conscious of its own limits. The simplicity and precision of the text will be a common mark of Resnais' later works and of his collaboration with different writers.

The use of ruptures in the reading allows Resnais to insist on an increasingly tighter intertwining of the different series that compose the documentary (images, music, text, black and white, color, past, present, future). The film is a totality in which no element dominates absolutely even if some of them play extremely important roles. René Prédal notes that with

Resnais insisting on making of all his movies a total
show addressing all the senses, music in itself holds a
key role as a cohesive element between the images
(Prédal, 1968: 34).

The constant presence of music throughout the film, imposing
itself, accompanying the images, independent, divergent or barely
distinct, underscores its key role in uniting this masterpiece.

c. The Art of Alain Resnais

We have thus far characterized Resnais' aesthetic as one of
violent ruptures, subtle transitions, inversions, sudden encounters,
and distancing allowing the imagination to bring traces of the
past to the present through an intricate weaving of different series
of signs. These techniques are some of the main trademarks both
of *Night and Fog* and of Resnais' work in general.[51] Because he
was not writing criticism for the *Cahiers du cinéma* or any other
review, because "his training was practical rather than
theoretical" (Monaco, 9) and because he always gave the
responsibility of writing the script and the music of his film to
well-known writers and musicians, Resnais is often considered as
a "pure" man of cinema. What does this characterization mean
for the author of *Night and Fog*?

According to Christian Metz, the essence of cinema is to be
found in the re-production of movement in the image.[52] As this
re-creation must have a beginning and an end—at least the
beginning and the end of the projection itself—a film can also be
characterized as the metamorphosis of a delimited temporal
sequence based on the difference between the real time of the
event narrated and the time of the narration itself. Continuing his
general analysis of cinematographic narration, the three stages
Metz defines apply surprisingly well to the first images of *Night
and Fog* and reinforce the notion of Resnais as a "pure" man of
cinema. Metz wrote:

The example of the cinematographic narration easily
illustrates these three possibilities: the isolated and

immobile shot of a desert stretch is an image (space
signified -> space signifier); many partial and
successive shots of this desert stretch constitute a
description (space-signified -> time-signifier); many
successive shots of a caravan travelling through this
desert stretch form a narration (signified-time ->
signifier time) (Metz, 27).

This general and simplified example illustrates very well the
movement of the beginning of *Night and Fog*. Each sequence
starts with a different static shot of the same landscape,
continuing with the juxtaposition of extremely different
successive and partial images of the same landscape (inside the
camp), creating the movement which begins the narration through
the montage and movements of the camera itself. These three
elements are woven through constant variations (for example, the
filming of photographs).

At the time he made *Night and Fog*, Alain Resnais was
already famous for his artistic shorts dealing with painting,
history, genocides and memory through the use of both color and
black and white techniques. He was first influenced by the
techniques of Robert Hessens and by the Belgian school of Paul
Haersens. This interest in cinema as an art brought him directly
to the analysis of one's consciousness of reality, representation
and interpretation of the surrounding world. As a consequence,
Resnais quickly became known as a committed filmmaker.

In Resnais' cinematographic career, *Night and Fog* is the
second of a series of three major films about memory and the
annihilation of civilizations before and during World War II. The
two others are *Guernica* (1950) and *Hiroshima mon amour*
(1959). For the French public, these three works gave Resnais a
very strong reputation as a committed director. Between the first
film of this series, based on Picasso's famous painting, and the
third, which already belongs to the cinema of the *nouvelle vague*
developed in parallel with the movement of the New Novel,
Night and Fog, as a work of art, belongs to a precise research in
aesthetics which renewed a very important part of both French
cinema and French literature in the late fifties and early sixties.

As it was for Sartre and the collaborators of the *Les Temps Modernes*, Resnais' commitment is fundamentally both political and artistic. His commitment appears as much in the political ideas his works express as it does in the techniques he employs. Therefore, the study of form and meaning in his films cannot be separated. *Night and Fog* can be studied in relation to two other themes: Resnais' studies of memory/imagination and of worlds similar to the universe of concentration camps. The first series includes *Les Statues meurent aussi*, *Toute la mémoire du monde*, *Hiroshima mon amour* and *L'Année dernière à Marienbad*; the second series is more precisely limited to the second and the last films of this list. All deal with death; indeed Marcel Oms notes that "death is at the heart of Alain Resnais' cinematographic work" (Oms, 23). Gaston Bounoure put *Night and Fog* together with *Hiroshima mon amour* because they both deal with the Second World War. For each classification, this documentary gives prime examples of the key themes of Resnais' work.

With *Guernica* Resnais' commitment became even more obvious. As Oms recently noted, this film is not "about this painting but rather about the place of the aesthetic of this painting in the evolution of the painter and in his consciousness of the century" (Oms, 12). For Prédal, *Guernica* is first of all a "violent indictment of war":

> Conceived as a scream of horror, this work wants to strike out at the spectators, to shake them out of their blissful torpor, to touch them straight in the heart without even passing through their logical minds (Prédal, 1968: 24).

These characterizations are apt for many shots of *Night and Fog* considered both as works of art and as the representation of a silent scream of horror (for example, with shots of dead bodies or shots of the mass graves). Besides the problem of movement already mentioned, a comparison with Munch's famous painting *The Scream* raises the problems of the functions of memory and imagination and the use of color or black and white in Resnais' work.

It has been often noted that *Night and Fog* overwhelms the spectator with some sort of terrifying spell. Even if, as Annette Insdorf wrote, "this movie addresses intelligence" (Insdorf, 42), it is certain that after seeing *Night and Fog*, to quote François Truffaut, "we leave the place 'devastated,' muddled and not very proud of ourselves" (Quoted by Insdorf, 43). Jacques Doniol-Valcroze's 1956 article on *Night and Fog* makes the same point (Doniol-Valcroze, 37-38).

This documentary evokes a concentration camp universe for the audience not only with historical footage, but also with the commentator's descriptions of a typical day. The general descriptions and the poetic style combine to mesmerize the spectators while the various ruptures in style force them to remain critical and analyze the film. At the same time the film ends with an invitation to ponder the actual meaning of what has just been shown.

Throughout this documentary we notice a definite will to compose a work of art, a sort of cinematic poem[53] based on a very precise formal structure and an "ineluctable progression" (Valcroze, 37) whose purpose is to capture and preserve the memory of what happened in the pure past of a collective memory. It is important, therefore, to recall that in the years following *Night and Fog*, Resnais was to become famous both for his studies on time and memory and for his joint work with avant-garde French writers such as Marguerite Duras and Alain Robbe-Grillet. In Resnais' career, this documentary was preceded and followed not only by two major works that characterized their author as committed, but also by two shorts studying the importance of memory and popular art for a community, and the distinction between a living and a dying memory through books that are still read or completely forgotten. I am referring here to the two films entitled *Les Statues meurent aussi* (1953) and *Toute la mémoire du monde* (1956).

The deepest link between these two shorts and *Night and Fog* is forged in this sentence of *Statues also die*: "An object is dead when the living eyes that came to rest on it have disappeared" (quoted by Oms, 60). This defines the ultimate

function and power of Resnais' cinema as the movement of the
camera becomes the movement of the eye and of the consciousness of the spectator that brings to life the memories of beings,
communities and cultures that have been exterminated. However,
in order to reach its goal, to become "real" and "lively," the
image cannot address only our intellect. It must at the same time
put in motion our own memory, our sensitivity and our imagination in order to understand and to start sharing experiences lived
by fellow human beings. Remembering becomes interpreting and
imagining as we start understanding. For this reason, *Night and
Fog* could not be a mere documentary. As James Monaco noted:
"Resnais thinks of himself as incapable of a straightforward
documentary realism" (Monaco, 4). *Night and Fog*'s ultimate
goal had to be to become a committed work of art.

Commissioned by the review *Présence Africaine*, *Les Statues
meurent aussi* was first conceived as a documentary about "l'Art
Nègre." However, as Resnais himself noted: "At first it was not
our idea to make a film against colonialism. But we have
naturally been led to ask certain questions that provoked the ban
of the film."[54] For both Resnais and Chris Marker, the study of
African Negro Art was inseparable from the denunciation of
colonialism and of the destruction of African cultures by western
civilization.

In the French context of the fifties, the notion of a
"committed artist" refers directly to the work of Jean-Paul Sartre
and, more precisely, to Sartre's essays such as his book *What is
Literature* and his article "Intentionality: A Certain Idea of
Husserl's Phenomenology" published in 1948 and 1947 respectively. Its first meaning is that the work of the artist is a direct
product of the "situation" of a free consciousness in the world, of
a "consciousness of something" of a "being-in-the-world" to use
Husserlian and Heideggerian concepts popularized by Sartre in
the late forties and the early fifties:

> Being, says Heidegger, is being-in-the-world. Under-
> stand this "being-in" in the sense of movement. To be
> is to burst into the world; it is to start from a
> nothingness of world and of consciousness to burst

suddenly as a consciousness-in-the-world [...] This
necessity for consciousness to exist as consciousness of
something other than itself, is what Husserl names
"intentionality" (Sartre, 1947: 30-31).
John Ward noticed about *Muriel*, another Cayrol-Resnais film,
that

Cayrol's script, in common with the work of Robbe-
Grillet, owes its technique to Husserl's phenomenology
and, in particular, to the theory of intentionality. The
physical detail of appearance reveals character far more
than dialogue (Ward, 65).

In that sense, Resnais' film *Van Gogh* (1948) and his
Gauguin (1950) are both committed as they study according to
Resnais' own words, the "Van Gogh myth" (quoted by Oms, 12)
and the quest of the painter for an absolute. Both works are
studies of the "consciousness of something" and of the "being-in-
the-world" of two artists. This more philosophical definition of
the "committed" artist is inseparable from its polemical and
political version that has been much more publicized. It has,
however, the advantage of showing how Resnais' characterization
as a "pure man of cinema" is also inseparable from his work as
a politically committed filmmaker.

At the same time, Sartre's review *Les Temps Modernes*
never separated the work of the artist from his political
commitment:

I recall indeed that in committed literature, the
commitment must on no occasion make us forget
literature and that our preoccupation must be to serve
literature instilling new life into it, to serve the
collectivity by trying to produce the literature that suits
it. (Sartre, 1948: 30).

Such a declaration definitely puts aside any kind of propaganda
art such as that of the Nazi or the Stalin regimes. The continued
influence of Sartre's thought on Resnais' work is also confirmed
by different uses of Sartrian texts for the making of feature films
such as *La Guerre est finie* (1966) or *Stavisky* (1974).[55] At the
same time, Resnais remains primarily a man of cinema.

From the beginning of *Night and Fog*, we know that the camera's search for traces of life will almost completely fail. From the very first images of the film the spectator enters into the heart of the monstrosity of the Holocaust where the necessary movement of life and reality must directly confront the heavy and static emptiness of the death camps as the danger of forgetting is symbolized by the grey, cold, empty and silent buildings remaining at Auschwitz.

There are no characters in *Night and Fog*. The people, the victims seen in the historical footage, were given no choice but to remain anonymous and silent. All their movements, filmed in the past and reproduced here, led them to the camps and to the gas chamber. At the same time, the montage and the movement of Resnais' camera aim to reveal who these people were, where they were from and what exactly happened to them. They insist that all this was/is real and directly concerns our "being-in-the-world." The film tries to destroy the effect of the documentaries made by the Nazis and goes much further than the documentaries filmed by the Allies when they freed the camps. Resnais creates a sense of reality that directly captivates the audience.

Once the audience realizes that the banality of the landscape is deceptive, the movement of the camera simultaneously discloses illusions and searches for truth and being through the encounters of various leads of reality. As Christian Metz noted in his seminal work *Essai sur la signification au cinéma*: "it is movement that gives a strong impression of reality" (Metz, 1968: 16). Metz also points out that "the spectator is 'disconnected' from the real world; but he still has to get involved in something else, he has to accomplish a 'transfer' of reality[56] that implies a complete affective activity [underlined by Metz], perceptive and intellectual, that itself can only be started by a spectacle that only remotely resembles those of the real world" (Metz, 1968: 21).

It is precisely the movement of the camera that effectuates this "transfer of reality" because the film is not merely a reproduction, that is, the static reproduction of material objects appearing in the image. It is more precisely a "re-production" of movement in the actual present of the film, because movement is already essentially visual (Metz, 1968: 19). For this very reason, even if the film deals with elements of the past, its major indication of reality, its editing, its movement, situates it automatically in the present of the viewing. Therefore "the cinema spectator does not look for a has-been-there[57] but for a living being-here" (Metz, 1968: 16).

In *Night and Fog*, we experience from the very beginning an acute feeling of uneasiness precisely because there is no "living being-there" to discover. The fundamental movement of the film is an indispensable search for what we already know is essentially missing. However, in spite of this monstrous absurdity, there is still life—grass growing in Auschwitz itself—and Resnais' film helps us to understand this paradox. The movement of the camera is in itself a search for life, even if little hope remains. This movement is similar to the search for survivors of the Warsaw ghetto at the end of *Shoah*. All that remains is the searching movement of this one last survivor, eyes running through the ruins. The last survivor is impelled to remember and to testify so that history will not repeat itself.

This subtle but fundamental optimism led Resnais to make his films. In Hiroshima also: "As early as the second day, precise animal species have re-emerged from the depths of the earth and from the ashes" (quoted by Oms, 25). Oms remarks that "even after the horror of the concentration camp, the will to survive wins" (Oms, 25). Even after the hatred of Nevers and total destruction of Hiroshima, there is always a fundamental need for "crazed love" for the characters of *Hiroshima mon amour*.

This optimism is part of the originality of Resnais' art at a time when, during the Cold War, the Korean war and the beginning of the War of Independence in Algeria, the literature and the theater of the absurd prevailed through the works of Vitrac, Ghelderode (both rediscovered in the fifties and the early sixties), Ionesco, Beckett, Sartre and Camus. These last two writers were fighting each other to redefine the precise role of the intellectual and of the individual confronted with an unavoidable political choice. Following a violent debate around the publication of Camus' essay *L'homme révolté* (1951), Resnais' commitment consisted in directly orienting his research towards working with a team (musicians, writers, technicians) and exploring the functions of memory and imagination in the present.

Optimism through an extraordinary encounter of the unusual in a banal or gloomy situation (for example the grass growing in the camp site in Auschwitz) also links Cayrol and Resnais' work to the surrealistic notion of the *hasard objectif*, the objective chance, developed in André Breton's works such as the second *Manifesto of surrealism* or *Nadja*. Based on Freud's study of the surfacing of the inhibited in the ruptures and abnormalities of everyday life or speech, Breton believed that through wandering at random, with no defined purpose, we open ourselves to the apparently gratuitous encounter of objects, words, situations or beings that reveal in us unconscious drives or hidden truths that otherwise we would have never discovered. In this manner, we can learn much more through "losing our time" than we do trying to assimilate sophisticated theories. Such a point of view was already very important in Proust's work, which the young Alain Resnais admired very much (cf. Oms, 11; Prédal, 4; Monaco). This same belief drove the surrealists to their experiments with automatic writing.

In *Night and Fog*, when the camera wanders in the existing streets of Auschwitz, the audience experiences a very similar feeling. The viewers do not exactly know what the camera is looking for but wait for an encounter to happen without knowing exactly what it will be. Like Resnais and Cayrol, the audience is looking for possible traces, signs that would give any information about the millions of people who have been exterminated in this place. However, as the extermination process, its hiding, and the destruction of all its traces were systematically organized by the Nazis, the signs that would tell us what really happened can emerge only by chance, thanks to a completely unexpected but necessary and violently desired encounter. As Simon Wiesenthal has often noted, it was a similar illogical chance that allowed very few people to survive the Holocaust, few corpses to escape total destruction in the ovens, few buildings to remain in order to testify to the most frightening reality of the extermination of at least ten million people.

Resnais' optimism also links him to the surrealists, as he explains,

> I am for *l'amour fou* (crazed love), in spite of the myth and mystification it includes. And I consider André Breton one of the great poets of *l'amour fou.*[58]

Resnais' art constantly wonders how this *amour fou* is still possible after the Spanish Civil War, Guernica, Auschwitz, the hatred of Nevers, the atomic bomb and the Algerian War for Independence.

At this stage of the archeological study of memory, in the second sequence of the film, the camera moves horizontally in order to explore a particular level of our memory, one of the actual few remaining traces in our present of the Holocaust. The colors of the first landscape become greyer and darker in an intermediate polychromy tending to the black and white. After a brutal rupture introducing the next sequence, the spectator is directly plunged into a deeper layer of our collective memory, in a past represented in black and white.

This search then becomes very similar to the process of psychoanalysis. Resnais himself noted that one of his major films, *Last Year in Marienbad* could be of strong interest to a psychoanalyst:

> I do not know what a psychoanalytic study of *Marienbad* could find because there are too many themes voluntarily employed, but what would be interesting for a psychoanalyst, would be to find out what a spectator feels when confronted with the dream that is *Marienbad.*[59]

Indeed, with its haunting atmosphere, its implacable progression and its anguishing logic, *Night and Fog* often resembles a dream, or more exactly, a nightmare. The resurgences in the present provoked by the film itself allow us to compare it, like *Marienbad*, to a psychoanalytical session.[60]

The documentary is a search for what the audiences of the late fifties first did not want to see or hear about their recent history as well as a search for what later audiences might have forgotten of a past which shames them because so little was done to prevent its reoccurrence in other parts of the world. Certainly at that time in France, it was much easier to talk about the heroism of the Résistance fighters than it was to mention the roundup of the Vélodrome d'Hiver or French camps like Drancy and Pithiviers. Although *Night and Fog* did not go that far it was nonetheless censured for showing, in a five second shot, a French gendarme in uniform watching over the Pithiviers camp.

However, in 1955-56, at a time when for many intellectuals and politicians of both the right and the left of the French political spectrum the only hope of building a peaceful world started with the building of a unified Europe, it was a major task to face once and for all the Holocaust as the most important repressed reality of recent European history. With the Holocaust present in every memory, it was clearly impossible to dream of a better Europe without first facing what had made possible history's most horrifying genocide in the so-called "civilized" world. In this sense, applying the study of the psychoanalyst Léon Grinberg on *Hiroshima mon amour*[61] shows that *Night and Fog* accomplishes for its French and European public a necessary grieving process, finally recognizing the impossibility to forget what happened and the impossibility for the survivors to live without ever "going back." It is precisely in recognizing the indelible image of the Holocaust on the European collective memory and imagination that the documentary does not allow anyone to forget while, at the same time, it makes hope possible again.

By force of circumstances, in a world where "ethnocide" and genocide destroy direct human testimony, certain objects become "more eloquent than beings."[62] In *Night and Fog*, this point of view led to the strong shots of enormous piles of victims' belongings classified and organized in gigantic depots. The filming of these sequences can also be linked to Resnais' other short filmed in 1956.

In *Toute la mémoire du monde*, the camera runs through the labyrinth of the French National Library much as it runs through the streets of Auschwitz. Here, books as objects enveloping the memories of dead beings and of forgotten ideas are classified, numbered by a gigantic enterprise in what Oms called "the prison universe of catalogues and shelves, cells and bars where works are piled that can only live again by the eye of the reader" (Oms, 63).

Resnais' well-known early passion for Proust's *A la recherche du temps perdu* led to the filming of an unfinished and lost adaptation of Proust's text in *Le sommeil d'Albertine* (also called *Les yeux d'Albertine*), in 1945. The obvious similarities between these two works, famous for their studies of time and memory, can be analyzed through two aspects that link Resnais' work, particularly *Night and Fog*, to Proust. These, to my knowledge, previously unstudied aspects are: the spider web structure and the function of the objects.

On the one hand, as we saw in the first pages of this study, all the spacial and temporal lines of Resnais' documentary converge irremediably towards Auschwitz. A little later, all the descriptions of the camp converge towards the filming of the gas chamber and of the crematory revealing the monstrous heart of the extermination process, the first center of the spider web, with history, the Nazi trains, and time playing the role of the spider who takes the prisoners to their death. In the same movement, the remembrance and the study of this past with death in its center must metamorphose itself into a lesson that will teach us how to find hope again and continue life without forgetting. It is precisely because we will not forget the history of the extermination camps that we will have a chance to live. It is by using this optimistic interpretation as a new center that the centripetal movement of the web is inverted by a centrifugal interpretation that directly concerns our future. A similar structure has also been used by Resnais' placing the castle of Nymphenburg[63] in the center of *Last Year in Marienbad* (see Prédal, 1968: 33, 56, 71, 79, 101). Moreover, as Prédal wrote: "All of Resnais' movies have a concentric structure" (101).

On the other hand, in Proust's work, the past first appears as a destructive power, the first center of the spider web of the work. The convergence of all the books of *Remembrance of Things Past* towards the last volume, *Le Temps retrouvé*, reveals also how, through a study of memory in a work of art, the past and the future intertwine in the present and, to use Rimbaud's famous phrase, are able to "reinvent life."[64]

In such a representation of time and memory, objects become traces, vivid images of events or lives that have disappeared. Their appearance may suddenly bring into the present bits and pieces of instants we thought had disappeared for ever. In *Les Jeunes filles en fleur*, Proust writes:

> Each hour of our lives, as soon as it dies, incarnates itself and hides in some material object . . . . We can very well never encounter the object—or the sensation—in which that hour hides.[65]

We already saw that in *Toute la mémoire du monde* the books of a library can live again only through the eye of the reader. The same could be said about the function of the eye of the viewer of *Les statues meurent aussi* as well as in *Night and Fog*.

In its third part, Resnais' documentary isolates and insists particularly on four different kinds of objects separated into two even more interwoven series. These are the objects made or brought by the prisoners and the objects made or used by the Nazis. Each object is an anonymous trace of a life or a testimony of daily horror and unimaginable suffering in the camps. In the first series, the making of objects describes a process that, through work and imagination, enables the prisoners to resist, to survive. They make spoons to eat the always-insufficient soup, puppets and monsters to create imaginary worlds, empty boxes to concentrate on precision skills, recipes for impossible feasts and prayer books.

All these objects allow the imagination to make believe that there might still be life outside the world of the concentration camps. They are weapons against total despair, the only escape of which the prisoners can dream. Filming these objects is followed by a succession of static images indicating the persistence of a care for oneself in each prisoner. This is directly followed by the evocation of the care for the other, of the mutual aid between prisoners. However, this caring leads to the surgical block and a more atrocious death. For the next series of objects seen is comprised of surgical and "medical" tools used by Nazi doctors or the kapos to practice their experiments on the prisoners. The viewers automatically remember the extermination process and the vicious circle is once again closed.

The following succession of images shows objects brought by the prisoners or made from their bodies. The lives of the victims are cut into pieces, classified, and recycled by and in the Nazi war machine. The metamorphosis of the imagination and creation is destroyed to be replaced by the metamorphosis of horror and death. Objects and body parts become products. Bodies become anonymous corpses. Viewers learn of the perverted order of the inverted "life" invented by the Nazis, with cloth made with material made out of women's hair, food grown on fields fertilized by human bones, good hygiene maintained with soap made out of human bodies. The series closes with Nazi artists drawing and painting on human skin to create works that serve to reaffirm the incredible but very real horror of the Holocaust and the sadism and perversity of the executioners.

Objects in Alain Resnais' art function in a similar way in the work of Alain Robbe-Grillet. Of course, for chronological reasons and because Resnais had read none of Robbe-Grillet's novels before first meeting him to make *Last year in Marienbad*, we can only talk about very strong similarities or affinities that developed more and more in Resnais' later works with Alain Robbe-Grillet or Marguerite Duras.

Even if, in 1955, Resnais is still creating a style that will soon culminate in *Hiroshima mon amour* and *Last Year in Marienbad*, the treatment of the objects in *Night and Fog* already reveals many important connections. Like the writers of the New Novel, Resnais refuses to impose upon his spectator any sentimental or lyrical attitude traditionally conveyed by the easy use of affective adjectives, pathetic music, a linear chronology or the domination of only one significant series. All the aspects of the film may vary their relations, intertwine their effects and be reorganized by the audience.

Unlike what happens in commercial drama, the author must not become an omnipotent god ordering the world in order to produce one single and precisely desired effect on the reader or spectator. The film itself must acquire its own power and address freely both the imagination and the intellect of each reader/spectator. The dominant message of the film is that the audience must think about what the Holocaust means for us today. On the contrary it is precisely through the rupture of a fake "natural" continuity, of the omnipotent role of the author and through such precise descriptions that a new image of reality can emerge leaving the readers/spectators free to compose their own interpretations.

In 1954, just before the filming of *Night and Fog*, Robbe-Grillet was writing one of his most significant pieces, "Le Mannequin,"[66] published in 1962 in the collection entitled *Instantanés, Snapshots*. From the very beginning, the links between photography, cinema and literature were extremely strong both for Resnais and the New Novel. The succession of static images just analyzed in *Night and Fog* already isolate objects, piles of the same objects put in relation with other objects in the same enclosed space, to evoke precisely the reality it describes, rejecting any sentimental dramatization by the author. In some cases, as in the filming of a pile of women's hair, the camera moves slowly backwards to film a picture and then slowly rises, moving forward, to give a striking view of the totality of the victims' hair stocked in this place. Such a movement allows us to feel the reality of the non-representable number of victims massacred in the camps. It allows us to imagine the reality of a horror the intellect is too often unable to represent without falling into the traps of sentimentalism.

This film, as a poem, is structured on many different heterogeneous series whose many ruptures, alternations, intertwinings and superpositions force the imagination of the audience to make successive jumps in order finally to elaborate the present unity of the evocation. Resnais' film works as a complex totality in constant movement and metamorphosis because it is essentially an open work made out of disparate

series. This will become more and more obvious as Resnais'
work develops. As James Monaco underlined:

> Conversations with Resnais are liberally punctuated
> with the word 'process.' It is a hallmark for him, and
> it is clear that he considers his movies to be products
> of that process rather than willed art objects. Often, it
> seems, he is almost a bystander as the film grows by
> itself, according to its own rules of process (Monaco,
> 30).

While being a general evocation of a recent historical event,
Night and Fog is constantly refrained from overdeveloping purely
stylistic problems. In this sense, *Night and Fog* is more
traditional in appearance than most of Resnais' works. It remains
extremely different in its form and its effects from documentaries
made mainly of personal testimonies. This explains in part the
very controversial absence in *Night and Fog* of a clear presentation of the central role played by the extermination of the Jews
in the Holocaust.

The overall general tone of the documentary addresses each
member of the audience as a human being and concludes with
the importance of fighting, in the future, any genocide victim-
izing any definite group. Obviously, this is done at the expense
of the central fact of the Final Solution, that is to say the
systematic extermination of the Jews. Ilan Avisar points out that

> Resnais and Cayrol, it should be noted, never mention
> Germans or Germany either. Still, in my opinion, the
> distortion is minimal, nor is there any vicious attempt
> to falsify history. It is not true that 'the script never
> mentions the Jews-not once.' Referring to the potential
> victims who live in blissful ignorance during the rise of
> Nazism in the thirties, the narrator talks about a "Stern,
> a Jewish student from Amsterdam," although the
> English subtitles somehow fail to give the full identity
> of Stern. Moments later, when we see those 'rounded
> up in Warsaw, deported from Lodz, from Prague,
> Brussels, Athens, from Zagreb, Odessa, or Rome' it is
> clear from the pictures and the Jewish stars on their

clothing that these victims are Jews. In particular, the first image in this sequence, the frightened Jewish child raising his hands before a German trooper during the liquidation of the Warsaw ghetto, is one of the most well-known photographs of the Holocaust. Also, when the hierarchy inside the camp is discussed, the viewer understands that those wearing the Jewish star are at its bottom and are the most miserable victims. The flaw of *Night and Fog* is not one of distortion or even of totally ignoring the Jewish suffering, but rather a failure to present the assault against the Jews as an essential pillar of the Nazi phenomenon (Avisar, 15-16).

However, such a "failure" has certainly played a significant part in the success of the movie in post-war France. Its main effect on the audiences of the fifties and sixties was to assimilate the victims of the Holocaust to all victims of the Germans in general. Showing French gendarmes watching over the camps or mentioning the Jews as the principal victims of the Nazis would inevitably have led a French audience to analyze anti-Semitism in France as it would have put together the film's allusion to the people "interned at Pithiviers," "arrested at the Vel-d'Hiv," with the persecution of the Jews in France. Instead, the film's reference to the French internment camps ends with the evocation of the "members of the Résistance herded at Compiègne." For this reason, the above mentioned censure of a shot showing a French gendarme was to erase any direct mentioning of French responsibilities in the persecution of the Jews and that of the Résistance members.

When this movie came out, France was certainly not yet ready for such self-criticism. Ophüls' *The Sorrow and the Pity* was to be made only fifteen years later. Therefore, Jean Cayrol's text remains one of a survivor but had to be written about anonymous victims of the Nazis, read by an anonymous voice and addressed to the whole of humanity. This distancing probably made testifying possible for Cayrol, as well as facilitating the poetic style of the film.

Indeed, the process of testifying for a survivor, an executioner or a bystander is extremely complex and involves very specific skills from the filmmaker in order to catch the significant phrase, tone of voice, sight or attitude that will either bring back to memory or betray a piece of the truth. It is this very different kind of work that will be at the heart of the power of Marcel Ophüls' and Claude Lanzmann's documentaries.

7. Marcel Ophüls

a. *The Sorrow and The Pity*

In his excellent introduction to the script of *The Sorrow and the Pity*, Stanley Hoffmann insists that Ophüls made his film in order to show "the discrepancy between present testimonies and past reality, the distortions of memory and the soothing role of oblivion for many souls who need to find peace" (XVI). In fact, as Hoffmann wrote: "There are no lies here." There are no lies but there are distortions. It would therefore be a mistake to read *The Sorrow and the Pity* in a purely literal manner. Because we are dealing here with cinema, the different ways testimonies are expressed and presented is as meaningful as the verbal testimonies themselves. It is the reason why a detailed consideration of the way this film was made is extremely important. Ophüls' skills in interviewing witnesses from all sides and in editing the documents he gathered play a fundamental role in his discovery of truth. However, they also create different traps not always avoided by Ophüls' critics.

In a long review of books about France during the Occupation, John Sweets briefly analyzed Ophüls' film and wrote:

> [...] my detailed research on Clermont-Ferrand and the Auvergne during the war years has demonstrated that this 'documentary' film was highly distorted. Contrast, for example, the comments of the Wermacht officer interviewed in *The Sorrow and the Pity*—'People in Clermont liked us very much: our relations were good, and as far as they were concerned, there was no distinction between Frenchmen and Germans'—to the reports written at the time by German officers and French police who note month after month the consistently hostile attitude of the overwhelming majority of

Clermontois toward the Germans and toward the idea
of collaboration (Sweets, 747).
After giving another similar example, Sweets concludes that:
It is a simple matter for a historian to find flaws in the
version of life in occupied France presented by the
Ophüls film, but through skillful interviewing techniques the cinematographers dramatically and effec-
tively left on the mind of *an average viewer* the image
of a France in which the mean and petty clearly out-
weighed the heroic and noble (748. The emphasis is
mine).
However, the declaration of the German soldier Sweets
refers to is not to be read as a direct expression of the truth but
as the statement of a former occupation army soldier who needs
to live in peace with his past as he is testifying for a film that he
knows will be seen by thousands in the future including his
friends and relatives. This is not to say that this man is consciously lying but that his memory has selected, saved and
magnified only some very specific aspects of that time for some
very personal reasons. Among others, the following sequences of
the film about German soldiers being attacked and killed in the
streets of Clermont are enough to tell the audience that one must
look beyond the surface of this man's remarks to understand
what he is saying.
Next, Sweets rejects as inaccurate Verdier's (the pharmacist)
testimony in which he explains that he over-fed his son because
of his fear of lack of food. I will analyze this point a little
further. It is also to be noted here, however, that the expression
of this fear is important to the film as it explains incoherencies
in some testimonies as well as many reactions of the population
at that time. The subject of the film at this point is less the real
lack of food than the various fears that pushed the population
toward accepting the armistice. Ophüls presents the importance
of such a reading of distortions in the very beginning of his
documentary.
Besides its lack of trust in the intelligence of the "average
viewer," I would then reproach Sweets' reading for its literal

approach that reads a film as if it were an isolated document or historical footage made by a reporter. Indeed, from the very first images and throughout the film itself, what we see or hear in *The Sorrow and the Pity* cannot be separately considered as the plain truth because the strength of the film is precisely based on its treatments of a variety of distortions of the truth through the creation of various and complex relationships between its image and its soundtrack. This is a trap John Sweets could not avoid because of his literal and purely verbal reading of the two examples he quotes, as if he were quoting from a book.

And yet, the short sequence preceding the opening credits of this documentary gives the audience the necessary clues to read the film. We first see a wedding procession in Germany, 1969. On this is superimposed some popular German tune played with a ridiculous-sounding Hawaiian guitar that has nothing to do with the solemnity of the ceremony being shown. Already a clear disjunction is indicated in the film between what is being shown and what we hear. The image and the soundtrack do not coincide well and in some cases not at all. The Hawaiian guitar also gives a certain sarcastic humor to the film that the image does not have in itself. This humor will often turn into irony as it reverses the effect or the meaning we would experience by only watching the image or only listening to the soundtrack.

This opening sequence shows a wedding—that is to say, an institutionalized ceremony through which a bourgeois society reproduces its nucleus and insures a permanency to its values and way of life. Ophüls' film develops this point of view in the wedding sequence by showing the three pillars of bourgeois society—religion, family and the army. Such an opening recalls distantly the themes of Marshal Pétain's National Revolution: "Family, Work, Homeland" (*Famille, Travail, Patrie*). At this point the spectator knows that this film will probably also be an examination and a critique of traditional social life and social institutions, of values that may not have changed that much in twenty-five years.

As the image continues, the parents lead the young couple to the altar watched by young soldiers and the music continues its comic irony. We then see, in the same church, a monument to soldiers that fell in World War I. The irony becomes more bitter, the film more serious, the music intriguing rather than funny. Then, at the wedding reception, the father, Helmut Tausend, tells the newlyweds that he hopes they will never have to experience the hardship he and his wife had to go through shortly after they were married, thirty years earlier. Using a dissolve, this sequence is paralleled with the next one introducing the city of Clermont-Ferrand. Until now, the image (the wedding) was self-explanatory and the soundtrack (the music and the speeches) added some precision or various ironic nuances to what was being shown. In this second sequence this relationship between the image and the soundtrack is inverted. The soundtrack (the text of a tour guide) becomes predominant as it could be read without any image at all. What we see in this segment (views of Clermont-Ferrand) illustrates the text of the tour guide we hear. This passage constitutes a rather comic parody of a traditional documentary on a provincial town.

However the images indicate clearly that this is much more than a tourist documentary about the town of Clermont-Ferrand as the soundtrack ironically wants us to believe. There is first a clear parallel with the preceding sequence indicated through the showing of a church also with resounding bells (as bells ring in France for the beginning or the ending of a war), and the image of a French monument to soldiers fallen in World War I. The film will also be about two societies that share similar values and a common history even if, or precisely because, they have been old enemies. It will present two sides of the same story, interpretations from the German and the French, the victors and the vanquished.

The last sequence of the introduction shows a French bourgeois family filmed in its living room in Clermont. The family is sitting in a half-circle with the camera in its center, facing the father who is the witness being interviewed. It is important to notice here that the witnesses are talking to Ophüls and Harris, that they agreed to be filmed and that they are aware that everything they say will be shown to a large audience. The camera and the director/interviewer represent privileged spectators to whom the testimonies are addressed. Therefore, each testimony must also be considered in relation to the specific position of the camera and to the audience the witnesses address.

For the second time in this opening sequence, the film deals with a bourgeois family and bourgeois values but this time the wife is missing. In the German wedding she was silent, prudent but admiring of the role played by the head of the family. Her husband is responsible for saying the important words both at the wedding and for the film. Mrs. Tausend will say very few words; Mrs. Verdier is totally absent visually and orally and there will be very few women testifying in the documentary, all of them holding a rather negative role. We will have to consider the function and the effects of the discreet and often minor role that they play or were given in this work.

Finally, in the French bourgeois family, like in the German family, we see the audience, the faces of the people listening and watching the father as the main speaker. Admiring and amused, sitting "naturally" at the right of his father, the son listens carefully as the daughter pretends not to be interested, as if she had already heard those old stories a hundred times.

In these shots, like in the movie theaters of the seventies, the audience is mainly composed of young people who want to hear something else besides the official Gaullist version of history taught in French high schools. As Stanley Hoffmann noted in 1972:

> It is no surprise if the audience in the movie houses where *The Sorrow and the Pity* is shown are largely composed of young men and women, who have found in this film a way of learning without indoctrination. (XIII)

With the focus of the camera on the listeners within the film itself, it becomes clear that this "documentary" is also about its audience, about the way listeners and spectators will react to what will be said and the way they will show sympathy or contempt for certain witnesses. The film is also very much about the feelings and the ideas it will make the audience discover within itself.

Then Marcel Verdier, the father of the French family answers a question asked by his own daughter:

> *Daughter*:   In the Résistance Movement, was there anything else besides courage?
>
> *Marcel Verdier*:   Well, there certainly was that. But personally what I felt most often in those years was a sense of sorrow and pity.

At that point we understand that this film is not going to be another feature about the bravery of the Résistance. Its heart will be the study of individual passions and choices ("personally") of persons living through an ordeal ("what I felt most often") rather than deliberate political choice. It will be a study of feelings or of their lack, both towards oneself and towards others ("a sense of sorrow and pity").

Then, very abruptly, with its loud music, comes a jovial and paradoxical song of Maurice Chevalier with the title of the film and the opening credits. The success of Chevalier's song and some of its verses indicate clearly the general attitude and feelings of the people the film is going to analyze first:

> Yet they all march in step
> And they are all terrific Frenchmen [...]
> And they all agree on wanting just one thing:
> To be left alone, once and for all.

During the opening credits, the sound track is completely opposed to the literal meaning of the image. Maurice Chevalier laughs, dances and sings a funny song for soldiers as we see on the screen, in bold characters, the words "THE SORROW AND THE PITY."

The film is not saying that the French were having fun during the Occupation. It is not saying either that the French were always living in sorrow and pity. The reality and the meaning of the film are much more complex than this and everything the film will show us will be put in context by contradictory signs. Contrary to what John Sweets assumes, the spectator does not need to be a professional historian to really understand the film. Apparently, it might even help if he or she is not as he or she might more easily avoid the traps of a too literal reading. First of all, the audience must remember Ophüls' warnings and clues given in this very important introduction to the film. This film is about people, their selective memory, their feelings, their choices and their subjective reasons to remember their actions. It is not merely about easily identifiable and classifiable facts.

As the complete title of the film indicates, it is also a "chronicle of a French city under the German occupation" with two parts: "The Collapse" and "The Choice." As the triple meaning of the French word *chronique* suggests: this film will follow a chronological order; it will be dedicated to a very specific subject; and finally, it will gather some extremely varied points of view about an often scandalous subject. It will be a chronicle about local history, rumors and passions. After this sort of "viewers guide" at the beginning of the documentary, this complex chronicle can really begin according to the chronology of events.

- A Chronicle

If the spectator can hope to find any truth at all in the feelings and passions presented in this film, it will be through the interpretation of a large variety of disjunctions, paradoxes or contrasts that will produce a new meaning, often different from the literal meaning of what is being said or shown. For this reason, the word irony can be used as a key word for the reading of this chronicle, the developing of its techniques and their implications. However, before analyzing Ophüls' different kinds of disjunctions, it must be made clear that they concern only the main subject of the film, i.e. the study of passions and individual choices. Ophüls indicates clearly that there is a solid and irrefutable background to this project: historical events themselves that no one can question.

As a chronicle, the film follows a chronological order as the backbone of this "story/history" (*histoire* in French) of Clermont-

Ferrand. Newsreels are often used here to remind us of the historical context in which the witnesses had to make choices. Events happened in a certain order and were presented by the authorities in a certain way that is capital to the evolution of the mentalities of that time. In this sense, Ophüls is the complete opposite of a "Revisionist" historian, in the meaning of this word since 1978 (denying the existence of historical facts—cf. introduction), even if his work leads to the "revision" of an official interpretation of the Gaullist myth of a united and resisting France (corresponding here to the literal American definition of a Revisionist).

According to this preoccupation, the film will also use segments that are non-contradictory, redundant or that develop an idea, mainly at the beginning and at the very end of the documentary. In such situations dealing with basic historical events, images reinforce what has been said, the soundtrack develops what has been shown, images develop previously shown images, more comments repeat what has just been said. The music or the silences reinforce the triumph of the conqueror and the despair of the vanquished.

For example, after hearing about the rose bushes planted on the Maginot Line or the invasion of France, the audience will see a newsreel about the same rose bushes or about the invasion of France. After seeing images of the German victories we see the contemptuous face of Helmuth Tausend smoking his cigar in 1969. After seeing images of the *débâcle* we hear Pierre Mendès-France talk about the *débâcle*. When we hear about the hatred and the "purges" of 1944-1945, we see images of hate and of the purges, etc. These are the facts and the general feelings we as an audience, and Ophüls as a director, are dealing with. They are not so much a matter of doubt or irony but rather the justifications and attitudes various individuals will use to face or fight these facts.

In a similar manner, Ophüls does not let his interviewees tamper with facts and statistics. However, he obviously lets them sincerely omit or modify part of the truth as if it were the best they could do considering their character and their experiences.

What interests Ophüls the most are individual and local reactions to key events that explain how the politics of Collaboration could enjoy great popularity for a few years.

In consequence, this chronicle is constituted of two main chronological series that will constantly intertwine in the film: the series of events of national and international importance and the series of individual and local reactions to those events. For the logic of the film itself, the second becomes progressively more and more important as the documentary evolves from the historical chronicle to a more scandalous chronicle: the chronological study of public attitudes or opinions that go against general beliefs or values. Thanks to this alternating movement, the heart of the film will be progressively uncovered with its very specific subject: the analysis of irony and distortion of truth that led many French people to directly and indirectly support politics of hatred and the extermination of the European Jews.

In the beginning of the first part of the film, three witnesses explain why they have good reasons to remember the Occupation. We first hear statements by Louis Grave, who remembers because he was betrayed and deported to Buchenwald. Then, Pierre Mendès-France remembers the prejudice, the hatred fed by propaganda, and Emile Coulaudon recalls the shame and the degradation he felt living in his defeated and occupied country. The film does not start with a direct narration of events but explains why and how individuals remember them.

The chronology of events followed in the documentary is constantly accompanied by examples of its official interpretation presented to the public by the authorities and by explanations of the individuals' dominant feelings of the time. This progression can be summarized with three columns. As it would take too much space to analyze in detail the totality of the film in this essay, I will only give three examples. The first example will aim at explaining the foundations of the film. The following examples will deal specifically with the representation of the persecution of the Jews in this documentary.

Following the warnings of the introduction and the reasons why three individuals remember the war period, the film can start its chronological study

1 - *Facts and Main Events Being Dealt With*
    2 - *Propaganda; Official Interpretation (newsreels, press)*
     3 - *Individual Feelings*

1 - Preparation/lack of preparation of the French army for the war

    3 - In 1939-40: *Lack of motivation* of French soldiers to fight an enemy they did not know (L. Grave)

2 - Patience, courage, vigilance resolution, confidence of the French soldiers ready to fight and win the war (French Newsreel: FN)

    3 - *Boredom* of the soldiers, sympathy of "well-intentioned circles" planting flowers on the Maginot line *Desire of the population to forget* the possibility of a war, to hide the front with rose-bushes (Mendès-France)

2 - The population supports the morale of the army with Rose-bushes put on the Maginot Line (FN)

1 - The sudden attack by the German army, the fast defeat

2 - Germany attacks a decadent nation; a German tank destroys a giant French distillery (German Newsreel: GN)

    3 - *Contentment* of the German soldiers, *desire to return* to their families: everything worked as planned (Tausend)

2 - German images of the invasion

3 - *Satisfaction* of Tausend remembering while smoking his cigar (in 1969)

2 - German images of the invasion with the voice of L. Grave

3 - *Total disorientation* of the ill-equipped French soldiers lost without organization of the army (L. and A. Grave)

3 - *Surprise of the German soldiers* that are winning so easily: Hitler was right, the French are decadent (Gal. Warlimont)

1 - The "débâcle," panic and massacre of refugees

2 - An extremely easy invasion compared to 1914. France is "a cultural shame for the white race" (shots of African soldiers dancing among French prisoners). They declared war, they must pay. They are the barbarians, not us (GN).

3 - *Satisfaction, amusement and slight embarrassment* of Mrs. Tausend in 1969 (facial expressions)

2 - "The Jewish warmongers and Parisian plutocrats" flee the advance of the German army. The French suffer because of them while "the German peoples are spared all this misery" thanks to the Führer (GN).

3 - *Terror among the refugees* (Mendès-France)

3 - "We saw destroyed villages... It was rather a shaking sight" (Tausend)

2 - German images of destroyed and abandoned vehicles on the roads with the voice of Tausend

3 - *Appeasement*—Some civilians realized that the Germans were not the "wicked enemy" and that "we meant no harm" (Tausend)

1 - Total disorientation of the French army and admiration of some French military for German discipline and organization

2 - Images of French officers getting acquainted with German officers, with the voice of Mendès-France.

3 - Some French military would rather be led by Hitler than by the socialist Blum—*exploitation of hatred for the Socialists and the Communists* (Mendès-France)

2 - Images of the German army in Paris (GN)
We must not accept the defeat (Laval's article; with comments by Ophüls on Laval's desire to prepare France for surrender and a new order)

1 - The French government moves to Bordeaux; opposition Reynaud-Pétain; last contacts with the British

2 - The government retreats to Bordeaux but does not surrender (photograph with Ophüls' voice)

3 - *Hope* that Pétain would take over (Ophüls' commentary) *Admiration and trust* for the "hero of Verdun"

3 - Gravity of a choice between plain surrender and collaboration. Pétain is ready to collaborate. Feeling of a final separation (Anthony Eden)

3 - *Hatred, cynicism and disagreement* in Bordeaux between the different leaders
Desire to put the responsibility of the defeat on the Popular Front and socialist politicians (Mendès-France)

1 - Pétain becomes head of the new government

2 - Photo of Pétain and Reynaud (with an explanation by Ophüls)

2 - Triumph of Adolf Hitler SS Division entering Vichy (GN)

3 - *Disorientation and humiliation* of the French population that discovers its territory is being occupied (Verdier)

2 - Images of the German army invading France with the voice of Verdier

1 - The German army occupies all of France (directly introduced by Ophüls' commentary)

2 - The French do not want to fight any longer. Large regiments hand over their arms (GN) with the voice of Tounze

3 - "I did not understand anything" (Tounze)

3 - "There must be someone who can stop this massacre" (Verdier)

1 - An armistice will be signed

2 - The French population listens to Pétain: The enemy was "superior in number and in arms"; "I (Pétain) make to France the gift of my person, to mitigate her misfortune"; "We must stop fighting" (FN)
Distress of the vanquished (FN)
Joy of the German victors (GN)

3 - *Joy of German civilians* (Mrs. Tausend)

3 - *Humiliation of the defeat*, "I do not like to lose right away" (Verdier)

[...]

The first effect produced by the structure of this brief chronicle of the defeat is to show the contradictions between the propaganda of the newsreel, facts and the reality of human experiences. While they describe the same events, the first testimonies destroy systematically the planned effect of the official news. In its first sequences, Ophüls' documentary often works as an anti-newsreel or at least as an anti-propaganda film.

The first major event in the documentary (i.e. the sudden German attack) is represented by a brutal switch from a French to a German newsreel followed by Tausend's commentary. From now on, it is the official German interpretation of reality, through the German and soon the Vichy propaganda, that will dominate the news and say what the populations at war should think. The first part of the film is based on this constant confrontation between the frenetic movements of history, its official interpretation and its acceptance or rejection by various individuals. As the chronology of events is extremely important but already well-known, what interests Ophüls the most is the evolution of the feelings of individuals as he often asks them how they felt during such a time. Consequently, the chronicle of the defeat reveals a most important chronicle of emotions that will ultimately explain the wide popular support Pétain's government enjoyed (emotions underlined in my summary of the first sequence).

At the end of this segment two newsreels are put next to each other again as they introduce a new official representation of reality with a surrendering France and a victorious German army. On the French side, testimonies of the late sixties confirm the prostration and the total disorientation of the French population we see in the film. However, Verdier's remark putting in parallel losing the war and a game already indicates that the defeat did not mean the accepting of total submission to the occupying army. Already, Verdier's remark indicates a deep desire for, somehow, getting revenge. This does not fit completely with the total submission asked for by Pétain in the newsreel. If despair could be used by the National Revolution, it is still different from the implementation and total support of pure politics of Collaboration. As a consequence of the prostration following the defeat, Verdier's passivity is, however, undeniably one of the foundations allowing the development of Collaboration politics. On the other hand, for the German side of the film, there seems to be no rupture between the official propaganda shown in the German newsreel and the actual feelings of each German individual. Even the German testimonies of 1969 either reinforce or complete the official German accounts of the 1940 newsreel.

After the German newsreel explains that the German army was freeing France of Jews and plutocrats, Tausend explains that the French quickly understood that the Germans meant no harm. Tausend still sounds convinced that he was sent to France to free it from the Jews and the plutocrats. He also wants to ignore the fact that the German army was the cause of the destruction that "shook" him as he can not possibly see himself as a member of "the wicked enemy" the French were talking about. Moreover, the pride and the satisfaction on his face or on his wife's face regularly punctuate the film. Tausend is still convinced in 1969 that the war started merely because France and England declared it to Germany as he is still convinced, in 1969, that the Alsace-Lorraine *is* German. General Warlimont will also testify that the events proved that Hitler was right about the decadence of France. What matters here is that the propaganda coincides totally with individuals' feelings. Moreover, all these feelings were experienced and filmed thirty years after the events.

Consequently, the fact that each witness testified in 1969 and 1970 must be underlined. In most cases, the feelings they mention are still very much alive at the time of their testimonies. Ophüls' montage insists on this point, for example, as it inserts images of a smiling Mr. or Mrs. Tausend between the German newsreel showing the German victory. If the events mentioned took place in the past, the feelings and the emotions are still very much present. This is also a major reason why this film was very controversial after 1971 at a time when the Franco-German Collaboration was the key-stone of Pompidou and Valéry Giscard d'Etaing's European politics. We will also notice a very similar effect in Claude Lanzmann's *Shoah*.

Regarding the French side of this segment, individual feelings do not completely overlap the official propaganda shown in the newsreels. The official interpretation of the events changes from the confidence of the victors before the war to the acceptance of the surrendered. Individual feelings evolve from a lack of conviction to fight, to varying degrees of resignation, to moral defeat, through terror of death and a violent will to survive at any price. The immediate popularity of Pétain's government is therefore largely attributed by the film to Pétain and Laval's ability to use the ethics of survival on a population terrorized by sudden defeat and very recent memories of World War I. Vichy's political tricks first manipulated passions and instincts. They consisted of using this enormous prostration following the defeat to feed hatred through anti-Parliamentarianism, anti-Communism, anti-Socialism, anti-Semitism and Anglophobia in order to free the army of the responsibility for the defeat and to start its National Revolution.

The next step for the new government was then to find scapegoats responsible for the defeat, to purge the country of its internal enemies, mainly Communists, Socialists and Jews, to consolidate the unification of the people in support of the National Revolution. It is however this step that showed the population's limited support for the new regime. In this sense, the two sequences Ophüls dedicates to the persecution of the Jews are central to the film and they reveal both the extent and the limits of the popular support given to Pétain and Laval, as they directly address the problem of the French responsibilities and participation in the carrying out of the Holocaust.

There are two sequences dedicated to the persecution of the Jews, one in each half of the documentary. The first and largest segment starts with a newsreel. It is made out of two sequences, one dedicated to the progressive revival of anti-Semitism, the other to the role of cinema within such politics. The first sequence starts right after a report on "painted legs" (look alike panty-hose). It is presented in the same newsreel as just another way the National Revolution will make the best out of the worst situation towards the reconstruction of the national economy. At this point it is very clear that the National Revolution can be a success only thanks to the politics of Collaboration:

1 - *Main Theme*
    2 - *Newsreel, official interpretation*
      3 - *Predominant feeling, individual interpretation*

1 - (The politics of Collaboration)

    2 - France is the spearhead of the new European order thanks to the politics of Collaboration (FN—Chateaubriant)

      3 - *Hatred* easy to revive—Such propaganda based on *Anglophobia and anti-Semitism* worked. Such impulses were only momentarily dim in the French population (Mendès-France).

1 - (The French anti-Semitic tradition revived by Vichy)

    2 - Official celebration of the memory of E. Drumont. Images and success of the exhibit "The Jew and France" (FN)

      3 - *Surprise and wondering* in front of the disappearance of Jewish friends—"I started asking myself questions..." (Tounze)

1 - (Daily persecution of the Jews)

      3 - *Passivity or indifference* of the witnesses—"Always the same—no one said a word" (M. Dionnet)

2 - Photographs of the publication of anti-Jewish laws in the press (FN)

3 - *Cowardice or selfishness* of some—"Well, because it seemed I was thought to be Jewish, and they were arresting Jews, you see. So I said: This is not fair. I cannot call myself a Jew if I am a Catholic" (Klein).

3 - *Concern and justifications* of others—"I had two student helpers working in my pharmacy who were considered evil-minded because they were Jewish [...] No one would have anything to do with these two children, they had been banished ..." (Verdier).

Here once again, the documentary moves progressively from historical reminders to the analysis of individual attitudes. This movement characterizes in part the evolution of the film from its first toward its second chapter, from the history of "The Collapse" to the analysis of "The Choice." In the sequence just reviewed, the newsreel progressively gives way to testimonies as the audience feels it is reaching the heart of the film through the analysis of opposite individual reactions to propaganda. The documentary becomes a study of a variety of individual attitudes that made possible the complicity of France in the extermination of the European Jews.

The opening newsreel of this sequence was made to appeal strongly to the defender of a certain French tradition representing France as the "spearhead" of ancient European values. The speaker, Alphonse de Chateaubriant, was the director of the collaborationist newspaper *La Gerbe*. He was to be condemned to death, in his absence, in the Fall of 1945. It is made clear in the newsreel that his speech was attended by an audience of three thousand.

The comments by Mendès-France that follow are presented as results of a historian's own research. Unlike Chateaubriant the fanatic, Mendès-France is filmed in an empty room, as an isolated and wise man. This reveals once more a very particular role

Night and Fog (Nuit et brouillard 1955) Museum of Modern Art/Film Stills Archive

The Two of Us (Le Vieil homme et l'enfant 1967) Museum of Modern Art/Film Stills Archive

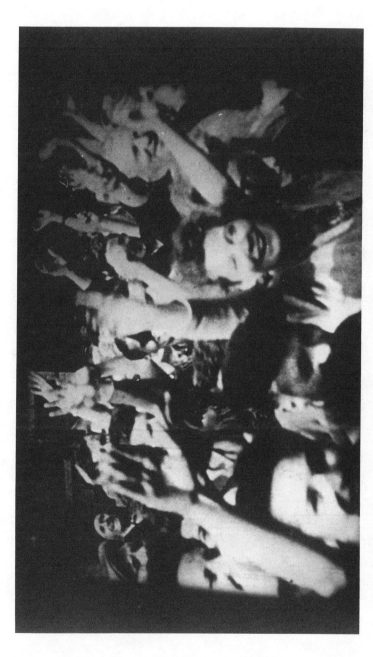

The Sorrow and the Pity (Le Chagrin et la Pitié 1971) Museum of Modern Art/Film Stills Archive

Lacombe Lucien (1973) Museum of Modern Art/Film Stills Archive

Black Thursday (Les Guichets du Louvre 1974) Museum of Modern Art/Film Stills Archive

La Passante (*La Passante du Sans-souci* 1982) Museum of Modern Art/Film Stills Archive

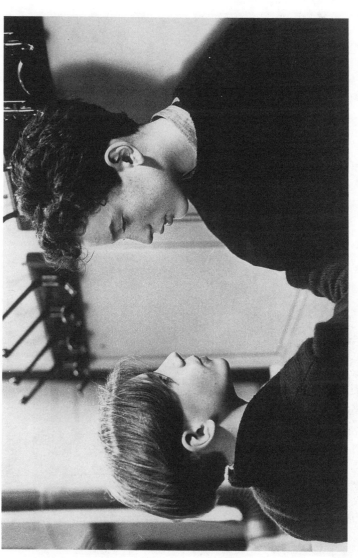

Goodbye Children (Au revoir les enfants 1987) Museum of Modern Art/Film Stills Archive

Weapons of the Spirit (Les Armes de l'Esprit 1988) Courtesy "Friends of Le Chambon"

played by Mendès-France in the film. Most testimonies in the
film have to be compared to others that contradict them or that
do not coincide completely with them. This is not true for
Mendès-France. His commentaries are of two different types.
Either they express a personal experience that nothing will further
contradict in the film, or they become the basic commentary that
makes us understand the succession of events mentioned and its
meaning.

When filming Mendès-France or his lawyer, Ophüls avoids
breaking the continuity of the sequence by using different points
of view of the camera. In doing so he facilitates the identification
of the spectator with these two witnesses. They appear to be dis-
passionate, self-controlled and thoughtful, filmed by a fireplace
in a country house or at work, behind a desk. Earlier in the film,
when Mendès-France is deeply moved while describing the
extreme hardship that his wife and Madeleine Zay went through
during their husbands' trials, the camera remains very respectful
of Mendès-France's deep emotion and does not try an extreme
close-up. It stands still and waits for the testimony to go on.

As we will see further, the same treatment was not used for
other witnesses as close-ups at particularly moving moments will
be used to try to point at a hidden truth. According to Ophüls'
treatment of the interview, Mendès-France appears as a sincere
man directly telling the truth. This remark does not aim at putting
in question Mendès-France's sincerity. However it seems
important to indicate how Ophüls' film reinforces the audience's
point of view toward a witness, independent of the testimony
itself. The camera and the montage do not play tricks on Mendès-
France's testimonies like they will do with others.

Many books and TV documentaries of the seventies in
France attest to Mendès-France's general image as a passionate,
sincere, intelligent and honest politician. This was also confirmed
by the tribute French politicians in general paid to his memory at
his death in 1982, at the beginning of the presidency of François
Mitterand. Ophüls' film conveys the same image of Mendès-
France as on many occasions the politician becomes a double of
the director, ordering the facts and the possible interpretations. As

Ophüls rarely intervenes to justify the continuity of the film and never to explain directly the feelings of the time, Mendès-France is the one that tells the spectator how things really were at that time. He presents a general overview with a credibility that Ophüls' montage gives to no other witness except the farmer, Louis Grave. When other witnesses present a similar, very general interpretation of their time, their words remain as parts of one testimony put in balance with others. Mendès-France's words provide the audience with a general interpretation that the film will illustrate.

Mendès-France's long political experience and perspicacity give him all the credentials to play such a role. However, this role was given to him by Ophüls' montage and it indicates clearly Ophüls' political point of view in the film. Ophüls does not believe in the existence of a so called "objective" representation. It is clear that in making this film he has chosen a side from which to tell the story. It is precisely because this choice is made clear to the audience that *The Sorrow and the Pity* keeps and gains great historical value.

Ophüls' sympathy goes to Léon Blum, to Pierre Mendès-France, to Louis Grave and his brother, to the socialists, to the persecuted Jews, against Pétain, against Laval, against de Gaulle, etc. The director is never trying to hide it. This honesty leaves all critical freedom to the audience who can always interpret the testimonies *and* the way they are being presented by Ophüls from his honest but subjective point of view. With such a topic, claiming to have attained pure objectivity would only reveal the naive technique or even the incompetence of a director presenting the audience with an artificially unified truth.

This sequence does not only indicate that the Vichy government actively participated in the persecution of the Jews on its very own convictions. It also shows that such politics could not have been carried out without the fear, the passivity, the indifference, the cowardice or the direct complicity of thousands of individuals. This point is clear despite the fact that no explicit anti-Semitic idea is presented in the interviews themselves. The conclusion of the film is that the propagandists and the anti-

Semites were able to carry out their persecutions thanks to the passivity and the apoliticalism of the masses supporting actively or passively Pétain's ruling. Such conclusions drawn directly from this sequence make the film seem aggressive toward any French person who lived during the Occupation.

The montage of the film itself also creates several dialogues and contrasts between witnesses that never met in reality. When Tounze expresses his worry for his Jewish friend that had disappeared, he is looking to the right side of the frame, talking to someone outside the scope of the camera. In the next image two teachers, Dionnet and his colleague, are filmed looking to the left side of the frame, as if they were directly conversing with Tounze. This way, their passivity and lack of commitment toward the persecuted Jews is put in contrast with the evidence of the persecution and the awareness the population had of it.

From the confrontation of various testimonies, the interview moves to the observation of one's desire to forget or ignore the persecution of the Jews because of fear of reprisal, anti-Semitism or mere indifference. The interview of Dionnet and his colleague that started with profiles ends with a front view of a confused face. The next sequence starts with a similar medium shot insisting on the uncomfortable posture of M. Klein, a shop keeper, and the expression of embarrassment on his face as he justifies the fact that, during the war, he had put an add in a local newspaper, *Le Moniteur*, to say that he was not Jewish. Here, like in the interviews of de Jonchay, de Chambrun or Mme. Solange, as opposed to the interview of Mendès-France, extreme close-ups are not used in moments of reflection but instead to underline a lie, fanaticism, passions, embarrassment or confusion.

Such close-ups are enough to tell the audience that the witness is hiding something, that he or she cannot say what is most important. Indeed, the expressions that accompany such close-ups do not deny the cameraman's intuition. One could argue however that all the politicians filmed have already had great experience with being filmed for TV purposes as opposed to the other witnesses. Therefore, the interpretation of the embarrassment shown by many witnesses that have never been filmed before must also be considered, in contrast with their previous experience or non-experience dealing with the media. It is most certainly much easier for the politicians being interviewed to feel comfortable in front of a camera than it is for other witnesses and Ophüls' montage does not mention this difference. Even a very positive witness like Louis Grave once looks directly at the camera with a silence asking the cameraman if he is done with his work, if he has caught what he wanted.

Such a montage also poses the question of Ophüls' subjectivity as it uses a grotesque witness to depict ideas he disagrees with and as it decides to ignore completely the Stalinist orientations of the French Communist party until the late sixties and the dangerous judgement mistakes French Communists made in seeing the Stalinist army as an army of Liberation, being completely blind to the massacres it committed and to Russian anti-Semitism. The distrust of Communist Résistance throughout Europe could have been introduced with another witness and in a very different manner recalling also, for example, the Katin massacre or the extermination of the Warsaw Ghetto the Russian army did nothing to prevent.

The second sequence of this segment is dedicated to the study of a theme that directly concerns Ophüls' and his father's works. It analyzes the function of anti-Semitic propaganda within cinema. It is organized as follows:

1 - *Main Theme*
  2 - *Newsreel, official interpretation*
    3 - *Predominant feeling, individual interpretation*

1 - (Persecution of the Jews in the cinema industry)

  2 - Jews like Bernard Nathan have "cost the economy almost 700 million francs" (FN)

1 - (Popularity of cinema during the Occupation)

3 - A place to hide from persecutors and a clear testimony of the disappearance of the Jews—"Their names were now erased from the credit titles" (Mendès-France).

1 - (French cinema as an anti-Semitic industry)

2 - Eviction and public humiliation of the Jews. The trial of Bernard Nathan (FN).

3 - Excitement for ordinary cinema and insertion of propaganda films (P. le Calvez)

3 - German propaganda films presented as French and dubbed by French actors (Mendès-France).

2 - *The Jew Süss* presented as a historical feature

1 - (Reaction of the audiences)

3 - General disgust and rejection of propaganda films (Mendès-France)

2 - Long final segment of *The Jew Süss* dubbed in French—"May our descendants remember it forever. By respecting this decree they will be spared much suffering and much misfortune, and they shall preserve the purity of their blood from the blemishes of this accursed race."

3 - Eighty percent of the audience went to see those films without knowing what they were. Other German films had a lot of French actors in them—"La Continentale was a company which made French films. Tino Rossi and all those people used to work for La Continentale" (P. le Calvez).

2 - Famous French actors leaving for Germany, invited by the President of the German Cinema Corporation (FN).

2 - Heydrich's visit to Paris, meeting with Bousquet, Hiller, Darquier de Pellepoix and de Brinon, the General Commissioner for Jewish Affairs (FN)

This segment has particular value in the film for two specific reasons: first, the director deals directly with the history of cinema; second, as Stanley Hoffman noted, Ophüls, whose father was a Jewish director who had to flee from France with his family in 1941, deals here with the cinema of "those who stayed." This segment is also particularly powerful as it allows a deeper identification of the audience with the people of the time.

Like the spectators watching films during the Occupation, the contemporary spectators of Ophüls' film have to interpret the newsreels and the footage being shown while they also have to interpret *The Sorrow and the Pity*. The spectator must be aware of the reactions of the audiences of the forties to films of that period as well as his or her own reactions to Ophüls' film. This necessary double distancing allows us to analyze the film's key influences on its audiences.

In the first two newsreels of this sequence, the camera is presented as a powerful tool of propaganda and of persecution of the Jews as it supports the anti-Semitic campaign of the government and humiliates Bernard Nathan shown during his own trial. Ophüls then rightfully insists on the exclusion of the Jews from the cinematographic profession and on their persecution by the official French media. Regarding this point, Robin Buss's position is extremely dangerous when the author of *The French Through Their Films* writes that the collapse of Pathé-Nathan was due to "a notorious fraud which ended in Bernard Nathan's imprisonment" (Buss, 18). Indeed, Buss never mentions the violent anti-Semitic campaign that surrounded Nathan's trial. In omitting such a major point, Buss's comments become very ambiguous.

The first newsreel insists also on the economic justifications of the persecution of the Jews and the tricks first used by the authorities to disguise its racist policy. This segment is about cinema because it is about new politics regulating what had to be seen as "real." After this general introduction, Ophüls' film allows a direct and strong identification of the audience with Mendès-France, a victim of Vichy's anti-Semitism.

Mendès-France describes his experience hiding in the dark, among a cinema audience, in order to become anonymous and to protect himself from his persecutors. The audience watching *The Sorrow and the Pity* finds itself in a similar situation when an anti-Semitic newsreel is shown right after Mendès-France's intervention. Moreover, after Mendès-France mentions that Jewish names were erased from credit titles, Ophüls adds "Don't I know it!" Ophüls' intervention recalls his father's and his own experience of the Occupation. A triple identification Ophüls/Mendès-France/spectator is thus put in place: first, Ophüls' own experience and his father's are indirectly recalled by the disappearance of Jewish names in film credits; second, the disappearance of Jewish names is put in parallel with the hiding of Mendès-France in the movie theaters; third, the anonymity of the spectators in the dark theaters, watching Mendès-France testifying in Ophüls' film, recalls the disappearance of the Jews from public life as it is being described. In this complex movement, cinema is characterized as a source of persecution, as a source of protection and as a possible waking of consciousness.

Immediately after this, the newsreel showing the trial of Bernard Nathan provokes disgust and rejection. From the previous images, the spectator strongly identifies with Nathan as he is trying to escape from the sight of the authorities' camera. Here, the camera represents the perception of the authorities persecuting this man. Such an identification was wanted by the authorities ordering the filming of the trial. They also wanted German propaganda films presented as French and, if at all possible, made with French actors.

Thus, *technically*, the audience is forced to identify momentarily with the executioners because it is through the eye of their camera that it sees Nathan. At the same time, this forced identification provokes a much more powerful counter-identification with the victim and creates in the spectator a violent rejection of the propaganda film as such. This rejection of pure propaganda, in the forties and in the seventies, is precisely the theme of the following segments. The next film segments of the time show the credits and the end of *The Jew Süss*, the final achievement of this sort of cinema. Mendès-France's and le Calvez's testimonies are superimposed to insist on the general disgust of French audiences for pure propaganda films.

However, the two sequences of the newsreel that conclude this segment create a direct and extreme parallel between the collaboration of famous French actors with the German cinema industry and the visit in Paris of the SS leader, Heydrich. After what has just been shown, French cinema is fundamentally accused, beyond and often against the population's desire, of collaborating closely with a foreign order and a government that gave itself the task of exterminating the European Jews. According to the newsreel: Albert Préjean, Danielle Darrieux, Suzy Delair, Junie Astor and Viviane Romance left for Germany while, in the next sequence, General Heydrich was coming to Paris. These two sequences are clearly put in parallel by the montage of the newsreel. However, the parallel was meant to illustrate the collaboration between France and Germany while, in Ophüls' montage, it directly illustrates the extent of anti-Semitism and Franco-German propaganda in French cinema.

Such a parallel to conclude a sequence is rare in *The Sorrow and the Pity*. It implies an extremely judgmental point of view from Ophüls directly linked to his own experience of the time. The lack of counterpart implicitly suggests that the cinema of the Occupation was fundamentally a cinema of Collaboration whose heart was anti-Semitic. Like Vichy's politics, French cinema also went further in its participation in the persecution of the Jews than the defeat and the Occupation could have explained. Such a point of view can be sustained but, regarding cinema, it remains highly controversial and in any case rather schematic. It also introduces a problem Stanley Hoffmann summarized this way:

> The first half of the movie—'The Collapse'—is almost
> unassailable: Marcel Ophüls was there, lived through
> this, and gives us the best account since the first half
> hour of René Clément's *Forbidden Games* [...] But
> Marcel Ophüls was not there later on: hence the
> weakness of the second half, 'The Choice.'[67]

In this segment, the testimonies of witnesses who "were
there" are enclosed within Ophüls' very suggestive newsreel
montage and its abrupt conclusion. Indeed, Pierre le Calvez
indicates that most of the cinema of that time was not for propaganda and that people were in fact disgusted by propaganda
and films like *The Jew Süss*. However, because no segments of
the majority of other French films made at that time are
presented, the central idea here is that cinema was a key tool of
the anti-Semitic propaganda and that the audience was often
tricked by it because of its passivity, its need for entertainment,
and its oblivion to reality.

Ophüls does not examine at all the complexity of the production of that time and of its messages. He does not mention
either the work of the Comité de Libération du cinéma or the
situation of Jewish producers and directors living in Nice at that
time. Only two options are represented here: the cinema of
propaganda and the implicit story of Ophüls' family who left
France in 1941.

The only positive aspect of cinema mentioned here is,
paradoxically, that it provided persecuted individuals like
Mendès-France with a good hiding place. Regarding the industry
of cinema, this segment leaves the audience with the wrong
impression that all of those who stayed in France and did not join
the official and active Résistance were indeed collaborators. Such
an extreme point of view ignores totally the situation of Jewish
members of the profession in hiding in Nice and the production
of important films made during the war such as *La Symphonie
fantastique* by Christian Jaque (1941), *Le Corbeau* by Clouzot
(1943), *Les Visiteurs du soir* or *Les Enfants du paradis* by Carné
and Prévert (1943 and 1944. On these points, cf. the first chapter
of this study).

This problem takes us directly to the analysis of Ophüls'
technique in presenting "The Choice," as it concerns more
directly individual representations of reality and a time during
which Ophüls and his family were no longer in France. More and
more, the historic chronicle will give way to a more detailed
analysis of passions, to a more private chronicle.

- Disjunctions, Distortions and Irony

It is to be noticed that the title Ophüls chose for the first
part of his film—"The Collapse"—suggests that the French
population was first completely crushed by the defeat and more
or less taken advantage of by official propaganda. The title of the
second part indicates, however, that after the invasion of the free
zone, there was no doubt possible about the goals of Collaboration politics. Each individual then became directly responsible for
his/her own choices. However, Ophüls' title insists on the fact
that, for him at least, there were not "choices" but only one
choice to make between resisting and collaborating: "*The
Choice*." However, many witnesses rejected and still reject such
a clear cut interpretation and Ophüls' technique does not always
respect such points of view as the ironical structure of his film
often opposes extreme and contradictory statements according to
a binary or "black and white" logic leaving almost no room for
what Primo Lévi has called the "grey zone."
    Consequently, there are two major kinds of ironical
situations, or complete reversals of meaning, depicted in this
documentary. The first kind of irony is produced by history and
the succession of events themselves. In this case, further events
completely reverse the meaning of prior occurrences, symbols or
places. Facts themselves invert their own symbolism or meaning
in history. This is not even a matter of evaluating, denying or
making up facts or statistics to serve a certain ideological
purpose. However, Ophüls plays a progressively more important
role emphasizing this irony. The second kind of irony, central to
the film, is produced by the confrontation of testimonies with

facts, behaviors or with other testimonies. Both ironies are underlined, organized and commented on in many different ways by Ophüls' explanations and montage.

Regarding the first kind of irony, Ophüls insists that the Germans wanted a reversal of the Versailles Treaty and the defeat of 1918. The Nazi *mise-en-scène* of the signing of the Armistice in Rethondes, for example, reverses the memory of the German defeat of 1918 by having the Armistice of 1940 signed in the same place, in the same wagon. The symbol of French victory becomes the symbol of its defeat, the symbol of German defeat becomes the symbol of its victory. In a similar manner, Pétain, the war hero of 1914-1918, will soon become the traitor of 1945. De Gaulle, the traitor of 1940 will become the hero of 1944, etc. In this segment there is no further comment added by Ophüls or his montage to the newsreel. The footage is self-explanatory. Rethondes reverses its original symbolism through the Nazi staging of the signing of the Armistice.

However, Ophüls' intervention underlining historical irony quickly becomes more and more apparent. Ophüls' very first direct and obvious ironic statement comes a little before this newsreel, to insist on the opportunism of some political leaders and their quick switch of politics with the evolution of the events. After a German newsreel shows the German army parading down the Champs Elysées, Ophüls shows a page of Clermont's newspaper *Le Moniteur* with an article calling for the French citizens to resist. After that, we see, also in the same newspaper, a drawing for migraine medicine depicting a man holding his forehead. Accompanying these images with an amused tone of voice is the following commentary:

> The local paper of Clermont, *Le Moniteur*, calls upon its readers to keep up the fighting, to struggle valiantly, to hold on, to stay free. Who is the owner of this antidefeatist newspaper? [We see a drawing of a man holding his head in an advertisement for aspirin.] Pierre Laval, Auvergne politician, who at the same time is preparing France's surrender in Bordeaux.

The insertion of the drawing is typical of Ophüls' irony. It is used to denounce the total inversion of values, meaning and truth so well organized by the Nazis and their collaborators. At this point the spectator cannot help sniggering and feels a sort of complicity with Ophüls while being reminded one more time that everything he/she will see or hear regarding choices and commitments will have to be interpreted. Once again, these contradictions and inversions of meanings and values are historical facts. They do not depend on what we might think of those events. However we are still free as an audience to reverse in our turn the meaning and the values of such inversions and criticize the way Ophüls presents them.

Until now, we have dealt mostly with historical aspects that carefully lead us to the heart of the film. For Ophüls, and for most of us, there are historical facts and statistics that cannot be contested. The director never lets his interviewees tamper willingly with these. The best example of this is provided in the interview of the Comte René de Chambrun, Pierre Laval's memory rehabilitator.

When de Chambrun tries to misinterpret statistics of Jewish and Résistants survivors of the extermination camps, Ophüls interrupts him immediately. This film cannot become a stage for de Chambrun's propaganda and distortions of history. This is the only time Ophüls interrupts one of his interviewees to directly restore the truth:

> *De Chambrun*: In all countries occupied by Germany, except for France, the number of Jews arrested and deported—the number of Jews who never came back—is terrifying. In 1946 only 5.8 percent had survived. But if you take the statistics for French Jews alone, a statistic which no one disputes, it shows that only 5 percent *did not* come back. In the army for instance...
>
> *Ophüls*: I'm sorry to interrupt. I'm quite familiar with that statistic, and it refers only to those French Jews who had not lost their citizenship. It so happens that, of those Jews without citizenship—that is, foreign Jews,

or Jews whose citizenship had been stripped away by the Vichy government—that indeed only five percent came back: in effect, the same percentage as in other countries.

Immediately following this testimony, Claude Lévy reminds the spectator that the Vichy government was not aiming to protect the Jews, as de Chambrun wants us to believe, but, on the contrary the "French racial criteria were even more demanding than the German racial criteria." The example of the deportation of the four thousand children from the roundup of the Vélodrome d'Hiver is the most well known example of Vichy and particularly of Laval's very zealous and innovative role in the Holocaust. Ophüls makes clear that historical events and the reality of the extermination of the Jews are not matters for personal interpretations and cannot be tampered with.

The second major kind of irony found in *The Sorrow and the Pity* deals with the central interest of the film. Indeed, this films brings to light many different varieties of opportunism, propaganda, inversions of meanings, contradictory attitudes or lies. Such a process progressively introduces the heart of Ophüls' work: the study of the ideas, the feelings, the passions, the cascades of choices that explain and lead to those facts, those lies, those crimes or those acts of heroism. Dealing with such material, Ophüls lets us make up our own minds, emphasizing the disjunctions between what is being said or shown and what it might mean.

Within this type of "ironical study," I was able to distinguish nine different kinds of disjunctions in the testimonies that have been selected and underlined by Ophüls' montage. Ophüls signals each one of them with a different technique. In each case, it is up to the audience to decide who is closer to the truth or what is the predominant feeling that determined the consequent action or attitude. Such a situation often makes one uncomfortable as it reinforces the polemic surrounding this film. In most cases, it forces the audience to reveal its sympathy, its understanding or antipathy for a certain witness, for or against Ophüls' intertwining techniques.

Such a mechanism is completely opposed to what happens in Hollywood-type films in which the sympathetic and the odious characters are always clearly defined by the director acting as an "objective" storyteller. With *The Sorrow and the Pity*, it is up to the audience to make, in its turn, its own choices, precisely because we are made aware of Ophüls' point of view on the question. This can be explained with a few examples of these nine types of disjunction.

1) *Inconsistencies and self-contradictions*:

A first type of irony can be found within the testimonies themselves; many of them carry contradictory statements that, however, could all be correct simultaneously. It is the case, for example, when after a long speech explaining that the main pre-occupation of people at that time was food, M. Verdier tells that "for fear of giving too little" to his new born son, they fed him too much and he became "a sort of giant" (29). It is very possible that M. Verdier exaggerates this story and it does not fit with the research of historians of Clermont like John Sweets. However, being a pharmacist, M. Verdier had to be in touch with a very large number of people in Clermont and it was probably much easier for him to find some way to get extra food for his family. But this does not really matter for the film. What does matter is the insistence of the testimony on the survival instincts of a population, on the very individualistic worry for one and for one's family. For M. Verdier, the main event of 1942 is not the invasion of the unoccupied zone nor the intensification of the arrests and deportations of the Jews but—the re-opening of the hunting season. It meant obviously more food for those who had a gun.

This scene also reveals ethics of survival and the lack of concern for what happens to anybody beyond the individual's or the family's borders. This is made clear by the disjunction between two statements within one testimony: "We were lacking of any kind of food" and "My son ate so much that he became a giant." A simultaneous and more optimistic interpretation would emphasize the sacrifices families made for the survival of the youngest. Such a reading would however be inconsistent with the general tone of the film. Variations on the same kind of irony in a witness' statements can be found throughout the film. It is the case again when M. Verdier declares that he does not like to lose so quickly while he explains later that he never fought or wanted to fight. Here, the idea of the passivity of the majority of the French population is given through many disjunctions between judgement, feelings and actions.

2) *The slip of the tongue*:

A second type of irony is uncovered through the means of unconscious mistakes or various slips of the tongue. It happens, for example, when M. Leiris talks about his commitment as a *Résistant*:

> *M. Leiris*: The Legion of Veterans of the First World War. Every Sunday they went, *except me—I was the only one that never set foot there.* They went to raise the colors in the marketplace over there, every Sunday morning, *with the sickle and the hammer, the sickle and.. not the sickle, the sword. The francisque, the sword... no, that's not it.* And they were all given a beret. A beret! Of course, *I myself never ever set foot there, not on your life. When I saw all that, I understood right away what it was all about* (24. The emphasis is mine).

More than what M. Leiris says about such meetings, what matters here is the way he tells the story. A confusion between the Legion of Veterans of First World War and the Communists is ironical not only because it confuses ultra-nationalist and internationalist groups that could not stand each other, but because while M. Leiris wants to say that he never hesitated to join the Résistance to fight Collaborators, his overinsistence and his slip of the tongue lead us to think that an important motivation of his political choice was and maybe still is oriented against Communism. His worry was also to fight "the sickle and the hammer" and probably the strong influence of the Communists in the Résistance. This becomes even more ironical when we remember that one of the main slogans of Nazi and

Vichy propaganda was calling for the unification of the people to fight international Communism. At this point, Leiris' loud insistence denying his support to Pétain becomes very confusing. Leiris ends up being trapped by his own words. The final confusion is the opposite of the clarity intended by this witness. Once again, the true meaning of the film rises in the heart of such tensions, discordances and inversions.

3) *Irony between what is being said and facial expressions*:

A third kind of irony is encountered when the Royalist Résistant Colonel R. du Jonchay explains how he was such a good patriot when he provoked Mendès-France in a restaurant in Rabat because he was held responsible for the defeat. At the same time, the contempt shown on his face and his falsely relaxed attitude reveal the hatred, the anti-Semitism and the typical anti-Parliamentarianism of many conservative military personnel of that time. Thanks to a close-up and his montage, Ophüls insists here on the disjunction between what a witness says and what his facial expressions reveal.

Throughout the film, there will be many examples of such revelations by Ophüls' montage or techniques. Another example is provided in the interview of de Chambrun ending with a close-up that insists on de Chambrun's uncomfortable feeling with the camera. This close-up gives a strong idea of de Chambrun's deep embarrassment in facing an audience with his quite personal and unsustainable explanation of Laval's innocence. A similar use of the close-up can be noticed during and in the end of Klein's interview.

4) *Irony between what is being said and body language*:

The fourth kind of irony generally works in conjunction with the preceding one. It is based on the interviewees' general position or movements of the body as they reveal a faked easiness and a real discomfort. This is obvious for example in the way M. Klein stands uncomfortably leaning against shelves in his store, faking a very relaxed attitude. It is noticeable also in the way du Jonchay stiffly sits on a chair in Vichy's park. The most famous example however is provided by Madame Solange, accused of having collaborated with the Germans, as the nervousness of her hands reveal that there is probably much more to her story than what she says. However, in this case, as Hoffmann noted, we will never now what really happened.

Hand movements are very important for Ophüls. The camera very often insists on them with a close-up. Mendès-France's and Henri Rochat's hand movements are didactic and they punctuate the clarity of their explanations. In contrast, De Chambrun's hands seem to mimic this clarity with similar movements but their ostentation and exaggeration as well as the count's desperate attempt to sound convincing indicate that he is overdoing it and that he is trying not to convince but to impose fake evidence on his audience. On the contrary, the very repetitive, nervous movements and embarrassment of Mme. Solange's hands indicate the recollection of painful memories, real embarrassment and real suffering that did not disappear with the ending of the war.

5) *Irony in Ophüls' montage*:

Ophüls' fifth kind of irony occurs thanks to the montage, in the succession of divergent statements by different people. There are at least two examples of this, one in the beginning, one at the end of the second part of the film. First, after hearing the bicycle champion, Geminiani, declare: "In fact there were not too many Germans in Clermont, because after all it was the unoccupied zone" and then "Well, we saw them... (after 1942). No, we only saw them when the Maquis came. But after all, we were not occupied." Right after this, Marcel Verdier is heard saying: "I saw too many of them. I used to see them everywhere. I saw them by day, and when I was sleeping I saw them in my dreams [...] All I saw was helmets, all I saw was Germans."

What makes such a scene important is less the truth about the actual number of Germans in Clermont after 1942 than the variations in perception of reality according to different personalities. For Geminiani, 1940 was a dark year not so much because of the defeat but because at that time no bicycle race was possible. On the contrary, 1943 was much better and it gave him the opportunity to start his cycling career. On the one hand, Geminiani adapted quite well to the Occupation while M. Verdier did not at all. The confusion of Geminiani about what really happened in 1942 and after is necessary because it allows him to live at ease with the good memories he has of this time when he started racing.

Another example of successive contradictory testimonies is given after Emmanuel d'Astier de la Vigerie describes his years with the Résistance: "I'll say it again and again— that is the only period in my life when I lived in a truly classless society." Marcel Fouche-Degliame further adds: "The problems of everyday life no longer existed; we were very free...." After, this comes Jacques Duclos talking about the role of precursor played by the Communists in the Résistance. Then Colonel R. du Jonchay admits his inability to unify the Résistance as he declares: "I did it very poorly. As regional leader for Limoges, I never once contacted the Communists. Not once."

This disjunction indicates the fundamental fragmentation of the Résistance, the idealism of some and the strategies of others, both already preparing for the after-war period. In this particular case, the side taken by Ophüls is obvious as it directly opposes very positive statements by the Communist leader Jacques Duclos and the distrust of the already very negative figure of du Jonchay. What appears here is the survival of an instinctive anti-Communism within the Résistance that recalls the traditional and instinctive anti-Communist feeling of the Conservatives either supporting or fighting the Vichy government. The parallel is continued as the next images show posters of Vichy accusing the Résistance of being a bunch of gangsters and murderers. It appears that, in spite of being a Résistant obeying de Gaulle's order to "stand by and wait," du Jonchay had the same ideas about the Communist Résistance as about Vichy propaganda.

6) *Irony between the testimonies and newsreel of the war:*
A sixth kind of irony is used to oppose the testimonies to the newsreel and to different kinds of propaganda of the war time. It is, for example, the opposition between the German

newsreel depicting the escape of the plutocrats and of the Jews during the invasion of France. Right after this, Mendès-France's testimony insists on the massacres, the misery and extreme confusion of the vast majority of the population fleeing the advance of the German army. This makes very clear that thousands of people were far from welcoming the invader as the force that would "free them from the Plutocrats and the Jews."

7) *Irony between the newsreel and the audience's historical knowledge*:

The seventh type of irony opposes the newsreel to what the vast majority of the audience already knows. It is used when we see hundreds of Waffen SS soldiers laughing and enjoying the show of a German comedian. As these men are shown by the newsreel as a nice bunch of young men, the audience knows that they are the main group within the German army responsible for carrying out the extermination of six million Jews and for the most horrifying massacres perpetrated throughout Europe. No comment and no montage effect is necessary here to underline the irony of this sequence and its consequences in our evaluation of our own present.

8) *Irony in Ophüls' questioning and staging of the interviews*:

The eighth form of irony deal directly with certain questions Ophüls asks his witnesses. The irony is created when Ophüls asks a question pretending he does not know its answer, just to force a witness to reveal who he or she really is. The best example is provided when Ophüls asks colonel du Jonchay if he is a Republican:

> *Ophüls*: Are you a Republican?
> *du Jonchay*: Not very much.
> *Ophüls*: Not very much?
> *du Jonchay*: No.
> *Ophüls*: More of a Monarchist?
> *du Jonchay*: Yes, more of a Monarchist.

Du Jonchay's terseness reveals clearly his embarrassment and the fact that he knows Ophüls is trying to analyze the value of his judgement in relation with his political commitments. The testimony abruptly ends here and these last words put a new light on everything du Jonchay just said. Ophüls' ironic question, asked in the Socratic sense of pretending not to know the answer, obliged the witness to reveal exactly who is speaking.

9) *Irony in the staging of an interview*:
    The ninth and last kind of irony also deals directly with Ophüls' interviewing techniques. It is revealed when the director obviously creates special staging which works as a direct comment on what a witness says. The clearest example is given when Ophüls and André Harris interview Georges Lamirand, the former Minister of Youth of Vichy. The interview is conducted in the meeting hall of La Bourboule's city hall, the town in which Lamirand was mayor. Lamirand is sitting in his very official and dominating mayoral chair; Ophüls and Harris are then shown sitting around the meeting table like two good bourgeois counselors of the mayor, candidly listening to his justifications. This staging first insists on the popularity and the continuity of the political career of some high ranking officials of the Vichy government. It also automatically distances the audience from the witness as Ophüls, and Harris' location in the room clearly indicates that what is being seen and said have to be interpreted because we know that the interviewers are playing a very active and parodic role in the interview itself.
    All these different kinds of irony used or underlined by Ophüls' work—and especially the last two—indicate clearly that this film is much more than a mere documentary. Moreover, Ophüls himself often said that he could not stand documentary as a genre. This "documentary" is really a film, with its fiction and its reality effects. Therefore, its study must be concluded with a general study of Ophüls' precise role as a non-objective and very skilled director.

- The Art of Marcel Ophüls

Irony is a key concept in the functioning of *The Sorrow and the Pity*. It is also an indispensable tool to read the film properly and make clear the point of view of the director. It is clearly the case, for example, when Ophüls builds up a parallel between Pétain and de Gaulle and ends both parts of his film with a picture of these military men shaking hands with a crowd, accompanied by a nonchalant song of Maurice Chevalier. Somehow, according to Ophüls' ironical montage, the more things change, the more they look the same as history seems always capable of repeating itself. With such warnings, the audience can more easily understand Ophüls' large variety of ironies used to deal with witnesses and their testimonies.

Moreover, as many critics noted, as soon as someone grasps a camera, selects a shot and starts filming, there is already a manipulation of reality. Ophüls is very much aware of this phenomenon. For him, moreover reality is infinite but film is not. Making a film involves constant decision making before, during and after the filming itself. Those decisions involve both artistic and budgetary questions that strongly condition the film as a final product. In this respect, the reality shown in a film is always based on a precise point of view that determines its evolution. This is not to say that the reality seen on the screen is only a matter of opinion and that therefore we can dismiss it as personal and partial. On the contrary, for the human eye, there are only points of view, constant interpretations and diagonals that cross those points of view and interpretations to give us a general perspective on reality. What is seen is always real. The best films could therefore be defined as the ones that trace the best diagonals whatever the unavoidable and necessary personal point of view of the director. Pretending to the pure objectivity of a film dealing with various interpretations of reality or to reach a pure objective truth in this matter constitutes the only but very destructive lie. It is precisely because *The Sorrow and the Pity* forces us to create our own interpretations that it makes us accountable for our own reactions to the facts being presented.

The audience can never find refuge behind a "neutral" scientific point of view that would observe a purely objective truth. The facts of the war and of the Holocaust are undeniable, "objective" and real. The interpretations, the attitudes and the choices surrounding them were a matter of collective and subjective human perceptions. They must be seen and analyzed as such while they totally engage the individuals who study them and are also responsible for their own interpretations.

As we saw throughout the preceding pages, Ophüls' film is structured on connecting ideas, emotions and a precise chronology. Even the determination of a chronology can be seen as subjective as it demands a pre-selection of significant events that will follow each other as a chain of causes and effects to illustrate a certain interpretation of history. Each ideology selects in history its chronology and interpretations of significant events that serves best its interpretation of reality. Such a selection is unavoidable and it does not necessarily constitute a lie. However it must reveal itself as an interpretation more valuable than many other interpretations, or else it directly threatens to reduce reality to the single point of view of its ideology. Therefore, the first quality of Ophüls' montage can be found in its presentation of different interpretations of the same events which its witnesses selected as extremely significant. Such a process does not imply that all interpretations are equally valuable. On the contrary, this process allows one to illustrate why false truths and lies constitute dangerous idols while still demanding that each interpretation be constantly evaluated in relation to its coherence when confronted with detailed observations.

Again, regarding the ethics of action and commitment, it is then extremely important to add immediately that all these points of view and interpretations are not equivalent. Some led individuals to join the Résistance while others led many towards the perpetration of the most horrible crimes. As *The Sorrow and the Pity* shows, there is a certain emotional logic in all points of view but this does not mean that the gravity of what happened is a matter of opinion. Therefore, the film concentrates on the study of the evolution of different individuals as their individual freedom, always active in the ability to make choices, was constantly challenged by the succession of historical events and their official interpretations according to different ideologies. The first quality of Ophüls' film is therefore to stick to a very personal study of the evolution of various individuals' psyche throughout the war.

This very personal study of ideas and emotions is never based on a preplanned structure. It directly follows the intuition of the director, shot after shot, according to the inner development of the interview or of the events being narrated. As Francine Du Plessix-Gray noted writing about *Hôtel Terminus* and Ophüls himself:

> (For) those aspects of Ophüls' personality that have made him notoriously difficult to work with have less to do with his character than with a special philosophy of film. It is based on a mystique of spontaneity and prodigality that Ophüls credits in part to his father, Max Ophüls, whose advice he often quotes: 'never mind the quality of ideas in your films, it's the quantity that matters. You must splurge generously with your medium, you must waste, waste, waste.' (Du Plessix-Gray, 48)

There are two points in Du Plessix-Gray's paragraph I will analyze separately.

The very personal "mystique of spontaneity" of Ophüls' work derives directly from his distrust of any "objective" technique. Ophüls' documentaries are not based on notes nor on a script. Each question he asks is based on previous answers. This is also why witnesses in *The Sorrow and the Pity* so often seem to be in dialogue although they never met during the filming. The film develops its own logic from its own material. It creates and follows its own rules according to what the witnesses say or do not want to say, and according to the questions they raise.

However, such a progression requires at least two basic rules. First, Ophüls is always, at least "technically," very respectful of others' own rules. Very often, he goes along developing one's point of view to see where it leads without trying to tell the witness that his or her logic is extremely personal. But even in those situations, Ophüls always follows his own pattern of thoughts while respecting others'.

This takes us to a second rule according to which the director must never let his film be controlled by the point of view of one of his witnesses. He must continue to switch points of view according to the questions raised and not to stay with one single interpretation expressed by a witness. The best example of Ophüls' constant vigilance is given when the director corrects de Chambrun's wrong statistics about the Holocaust in *The Sorrow and the Pity*. These two rules of the director always work in parallel: respect others' points of view and always follow your own pattern of thought.

The respect of such a pattern requires a continuous vigilance on the part of the director. According to the first rule, the commentary can only be used for secondary purposes and not for structure. It cannot be presented as the voice of a universal and ubiquitous commentator. According to the second rule, the interviewer must present himself or herself as a real person dealing with real people and not as a purely objective and neutral recorder of a collective memory. In consequence, when conducting interviews, Ophüls always gets away from abstractions. He asks very personal questions that directly involve personal choices and experiences. It is also a very important part of the strength of *The Sorrow and the Pity* as the film is not presenting its audience with abstract and general interpretations but rather with a succession of very concrete and personal choices.

However, this spontaneity is not easy to obtain, from the director, from the witnesses or the audiences. According to Francine Du Plessix-Gray, it also requires a characteristic prodigality—that is precisely the second characteristic of Ophüls' technique. This prodigality is due in great part to the ability, the patience, the time and the enormous quantity of work it requires to obtain a genuine and spontaneous testimony from a witness. It might take a very long time before the interviewer can obtain only a few minutes or even a few seconds of real trust, confidence or a mere release of vigilance from a witness, particularly if this witness feels very uncomfortable about his or her past.

Following his father's advice, Marcel Ophüls does always "waste, waste and waste" film stock. As Du Plessix-Gray recalled, he needed an average of forty hours of film stock for one hour of film to be included in *The Sorrow and the Pity*. For *Hôtel Terminus*, the ratio was fifteen for one. Such a method has deep implications; the film becomes the final product as the result of hours of manipulations and required montage that reorganize, underline or change completely the effect intended by a witness during his or her testimony.

As the filming itself was very spontaneous and invented progressively its own rules rather than following a pre-written script, one could argue that Ophüls' real work with the script exists mainly during the montage, only after the filming. According to Du Plessix-Gray, Ophüls requires an extremely close and almost sensual contact with the script (Du Plessix-Gray, 48). Thanks to this deep familiarity *with the text* of the testimonies, the director can then organize his film following its own logic, that is to say according to the various echoes and contradictions he finds in primary film documents.

It becomes much easier then to understand precisely how and why irony plays such a key role in Ophüls' films. First of all, Ophüls deals here with a past repressed by most of the witnesses he interrogates. What interests him is the parts of this past that have been repressed. Therefore, the kind of truths Ophüls is interested in seldom appear from one single testimony. It is most often to be found through various slips of the tongue, many juxtapositions, parallels, echoes or contradictions. In this context, the first literal meaning of a testimony is never sufficient to explain and understand the extreme complexity of the reality it describes. It must always be confronted with what contradicts it in order to evaluate its validity as a statement that describes what really happened.

For this reason, even though the basic structure of the film is text oriented around the text of the testimonies, the dynamism of the film is definitely to be found in its montage and in the parallels Ophüls built between what is being said and what is being seen. For this reason, Ophüls' questions often take the witnesses by surprise. This is the case when M. Klein is being reminded that, during the war, he had put an add in the *Moniteur* in order to deny that he was a Jew. At this moment, as Ophüls himself indicated: "An ironic disjunction begins to reveal character" (quoted by Du Plessix-Gray, 48).

In this sequence, Klein is taken on a footing he did not expect. He becomes embarrassed, clumsy and does not control his reactions as much as he would like in order to provide the most positive image of himself possible. At this point, the camera offers a close up of Klein, then films his nervous hands, goes back to another close up, and then retreats to a medium shot showing the generally fake ease of Klein's posture leaning against the shelves of his store as if he were having a very casual discussion with Ophüls. In this occurrence, it did not take long at all to reveal the truth about M. Klein's embarrassment dealing with his past. In many other situations, Ophüls, and Harris' strategies are different, less direct, less provocative, more patient or more subtle depending on the aptitude of the witnesses to give a personal answer or to reject an embarrassing question. It is obvious for example that de la Mazière or de Chambrun have much more experience and more powerful skills than M. Klein in getting rid of personal guilt and feelings of uneasiness. Ophüls knows that very well and always adapts his strategies according to the personality of the interviewee.

In conclusion, and as opposed to Macbean and Ilan Avisar's opinions, *The Sorrow and the Pity* is neither "a politically vacuous"[68] film nor a work without "any compelling artistic vision" (Avisar, 19). It is a chronological, personal and ironic study of individual emotions, choices and justifications. It is a chronicle of the individual confusion, fright, blindness, passivity, complicity or direct commitment that made possible the perpetration of the Holocaust. On a third level, it is a chronicle that analyzes the evolution of the psyche of a local population caught between direct collaboration or confrontation with the Nazi order.

For this reason, this complete documentary develops in a continuous come and go between different pairs of notions.

First, the title of the film presents it as a study of the different degrees of sorrow and pity of individuals for themselves and for others. At the beginning, two worlds confront each other through the interviews of two German and French heads of family in a German and a French town. The film develops also in two parts: "The Collapse" and "The Choice." In the first part, witnesses explain their attitudes for or against the government of Pétain and Laval. In the second part, the choice is between opposing or working directly with the occupying armies. Finally, we saw that Du Plessix-Gray characterizes Ophüls' techniques with the two notions of prodigality and spontaneity.

At the heart of the binary confrontations presented by Ophüls' film and techniques we find the problem of the representation of what made the Holocaust possible. As of now, almost half a century after the end of the war, the so called "choice" seems obvious and easy to make. It is extremely important to understand however what made it so difficult for millions of people at the time of the war. Such an analysis is important as it reminds us that no matter how good our intentions, reasons or self-confidence, our most personal decisions and backgrounds can lead us to a chain reaction of choices or passive behaviors in support of politics we might refuse to endorse consciously. This film also appears as a condemnation of reactive political choices based on fright, survival instincts and emotional disarray. The great irony of the final images of the film putting de Gaulle in parallel with Pétain is to remind the audience that we can in no way disregard the problems of that time because they were developed in another time or in another country.

b. *The Memory of Justice*

Ophüls was already working on his next documentary when *The Sorrow and the Pity* was being shown in France. He was gathering information and interviews on the civil war in Northern Ireland for *A Sense of Loss* (1972). This time he was dealing with actuality and interviews made more or less at the same time the events talked about were taking place. Consequently, this film could well be Ophüls' most "subjective" work as in order to edit his film and select relevant passages he had to organize his own reading of history with almost no distance in time.

The interviews in *A Sense of Loss* allude twice to the Holocaust in a very explicit manner. The first time is when a political analyst compares the propaganda of the Protestant agitators against the Catholics to the Anti-Semitic propaganda of the Nazis. The second time is when a young boy draws a war picture with a Nazi flag. When Ophüls asks him why he drew this flag the boy answers that it is because the British army is acting towards the Catholics the same way the Nazis were acting towards the Jews.

Each of these segments is reinforced with images showing either a Protestant agitator making a frantic speech clearly recalling the Nazi leaders' speeches in Nuremberg, or with images showing British soldiers. More implicitly, the black and white clandestine pictures of the detention camps for I.R.A. activists recall also the few black and white pictures remaining to testify to the systematic extermination of the Jews. There is no irony at all in the treatment of these comparisons which clearly indicates Ophüls' sympathies. On the contrary, his treatment of the interviews of British officers, political agitators or British occupation "collaborators" are often dealt with in an ironic manner.

One of the recurrent themes in Ophüls' films is the denunciation of hatred propaganda. In *A Sense of Loss* he asks a publisher who printed songs of violent hatred against the Catholics if he thought there was any relation between his publications and the ongoing violence in the streets. Like the

Vichy politicians in *The Sorrow and the Pity* or the Nazis in *The Memory of Justice* (1976), and Admiral Doenitz in particular, this man denies that there is any relationship at all between his propaganda and the civil war taking place. Like most anti-Semites, he denies any relationship between his repeated calls for violence and hatred and the actions they obviously encouraged or led to. Like the Nazis in the opening images of *The Memory of Justice*, this man pleads "not guilty" without any hesitation.

Because it uses the same techniques of other documentaries made by Ophüls but dealing this time with current events, *A Sense of Loss* appears to be somewhat confusing. As usual in Ophüls' films, the audience is faced with a long and interwoven series of individual testimonies. This time however, the film cannot take advantage of a historical background that would be more or less known by every spectator. Moreover, *A Sense of Loss* does not offer any equivalent to the sagacious and unifying role played by Pierre Mendès-France's interviews in *The Sorrow and the Pity*. Consequently, most of the chronology and the basic historical knowledge necessary to interpret testimonies can only be provided by bits and pieces found in the interviews themselves as Ophüls selected them. This is certainly the main reason why some critics consider *A Sense of Loss* a failure because its techniques are not suitable to deal with the complexity of current events.

However this critical problem becomes much less annoying if, based on the example of *The Sorrow and the Pity*, we consider this documentary as a "chronicle of life in Northern Ireland during the early seventies." With such an angle this film becomes a detailed analysis of Irish people's everyday life in the midst of the hatred of a civil war. If Ophüls' political choices are once more very clear, the first images and the conclusion of his film make it also very obvious that he is focusing this time on the victims.

While *The Sorrow and the Pity* insisted clearly on the various degrees of individual responsibility in Vichy and in Occupied France, Ophüls' following films progressively give a much more central role to the victims themselves. This movement starts very clearly with *A Sense of Loss* (1972) to end up with *Hotel Terminus* (1987) that is entirely organized around the memory of the Jewish children of Izieu. In this regard, if Ophüls' documentary does not succeed in explaining the complexity of the war in Northern Ireland, it is nonetheless a very powerful document about the perseverance of hatred and about the almost inexpressible "sense of loss" experienced by the friends and relatives of the victims of this war.

Because of its general project of combining lessons of past events with the analysis of recent comparable situations *The Memory of Justice* (1976) can be technically considered as a mixture of both *The Sorrow and the Pity* and *A Sense of Loss*. After insisting on different kinds of responsibilities in Occupied France and on the continued suffering of the Irish people in Northern Ireland, this long documentary directly questions the ability of modern societies to put an end to war crimes on the basis of a clear definition and application of the ideal of Justice.

The title of this film is ironic in itself as it indicates clearly that, according to Plato's philosophy, modern societies can only have a partial and imperfect conception, a "memory," of what Justice is. In consequence, if the ideal of Justice is at the same time necessary but unattainable, no society can proclaim to be totally or forever free of the threat of injustice. From these premises, Ophüls starts his remarkable documentary analyzing how the vast majority of war criminals see no relationship between their deeds and war crimes, how their sense of Justice becomes so crooked that they can institutionalize murder in the name of the law that was supposed to protect the ideal of Justice itself. This documentary can be considered a long analysis of its own images showing a Nazi at the Nuremberg Trial pleading: "Not guilty." Millions died while at the same time those who ordered these crimes think they can openly plead not guilty; who then is responsible?

Like all of Ophüls' documentaries, this film directly faces the complexity of the questions it examines. The introductory sequence, for example, gathers a variety of contradictory individual reactions about war crimes in general that the documentary will try to untangle. First, a Nazi proclaims he is not guilty. Second, Yehudi Menuhin says that everybody is responsible for what happened. Then, images of civilian victims of the Vietnam War brutally remind us that we are not talking about abstract ideas but that indeed millions were killed by "someone." Then Telford Taylor (the former Chief Prosecutor for the U.S. at the Nuremberg Trials) declares that anybody caught under certain pressure could eventually become a war criminal. After this, a French deserter from the Algerian War of Independence explains how he saw the murder of a little girl being committed "by accident" and how the officer who ordered this execution felt fine about this while the soldier who had executed the order lost his mind.

Finally the introduction concludes with the interview of two young men, an American and a German, who always refused to learn about Nazi concentration camps as if the camps had no relationship or influence on their own world. The next image shows a close up of the fuzzy picture of an anonymous Nazi executioner. Consequently, one of the main purposes of the film will be to try to put a face on this picture. Does this war criminal look like a monster, a pervert, a very committed and ambitious professional, an irresponsible idiot or, most of all, does he really look like anyone of us? The last images of this opening segment show a little girl victim of the Vietnam War and then Mrs. Vaillant-Couturier reminding us of the deportations of the Jews, while we hear Ophüls' own daughter playing an interrupted melody on the piano. A similarly interrupted piano lesson of a little girl will be used by Ophüls in his introduction to *Hotel Terminus* to suggest an appalling death threat upon innocent victims and ultimately, the murder of the children of Izieu by Klaus Barbie.

Throughout *The Memory of Justice*, every time an interview leads us to believe that no one can be pointed at as being responsible for the extermination of the Jews or for the perpetration of specific war crimes, Ophüls' ironic editing immediately presents petrifying images of a mass grave, of some victims, or a newsreel showing Nazis to insist that "someone" however has committed such atrocities and is responsible for them. Like in *the Sorrow and the Pity*, Ophüls' ironical montage in *The Memory of Justice* plays a key role as a very active and subjective criticism of the interviews by the director himself. The montage replaces the direct commentaries or objections Ophüls refuses to make during most of the interviews themselves.

The first part of this film, "Nuremberg and the Germans," is divided into three sections, each of them punctuated by a characteristic line pronounced by a Nazi. At the beginning of the first part an accused at the Nuremberg Trial declares: "I have a clear conscience." This part is dedicated to the analysis of the way various individuals experience the denial of individual responsibility. On one level, Admiral Doenitz denies any responsibility because he "did not know" what was happening to the Jews and because he only saw "one side" of Hitler's personality. At the same time he denies any connection between his violent anti-Semitic speeches and the persecution of the Jews.

On a second level, and in a much more subtle manner, Albert Speer recognizes his deeds but he presents himself as a victim of the times, blinded by ambition and propaganda and "a lack of interest for the subject." Unlike Doenitz, he recognizes that the Nuremberg trial was "necessary" but paradoxically, it is thanks to this trial that Speer can now say that after all he was not that guilty and that he has paid his debt to the world community. In consequence, he should even be accepted now as an objective witness telling what really happened. In the end both Speer and Doenitz see themselves not only as innocent but mostly as victims of their times.

Consequently, victims feel guilty for surviving and executioners present themselves as victims of propaganda. This will become a recurrent idea in Ophüls' documentaries. It is also corroborated by many personal testimonies of survivors in many other contexts. Nazis (like Doenitz) see themselves as victims because they were prosecuted by the justice of the victors and because they were also forced to see unbearable images of the concentration camps while they had "of course" nothing to do with this. Doenitz even explains how he personally saved many Jews by asking for slave laborers from the camps!

Ophüls' montage opposes to this a newsreel showing one of Hitler's most famous speeches of 1939 directly calling for the extermination of the Jews. In the end of this section, every Nazi has a "clear conscience" because they "did not know," because they "did not see." No one wanted to see the camps and the mass graves we are now being shown on the screen. In the present, Ophüls' wife herself declares that the Holocaust is "too much" to face for her children and she wishes her husband would make other, more pleasant, films such as *My Fair Lady*.

We then see a poster of *The Band Wagon*, and we hear the songs "New Sun in the Sky," "That's Entertainment," and "I Guess I'll Have to Change My Plans" all taken from that film. At the same time we see beautiful images of a German landscape. Continuing the same ironic parallel, Ophüls notices that Nazis always lived in these wonderful Hollywood-type landscapes of Germany bathed with sun and white snow. In fact his film is also a search for a certain kind of beautiful and "fair lady." Her name is Frau Oberheuser. She was condemned at the Nuremberg Trials to twenty years in jail for crimes against humanity.

The continuing sequence shows clearly the profound and general indifference of the older German population of 1976 towards the fate of war criminals. These people saw no problem in sharing their everyday lives with mass murderers as after all, according to everybody in the village, they were all victims of a past that had to be forgotten. This segment ends with a long interview of an old farmer praising the good old days of Nazism when there was no crime like in our modern societies. While a young women is telling him not to talk so much, the old man regrets that unfortunately, men like Hitler, Bismarck or Napoleon come around "only once in your life time." The interview ends ironically with pictures of this beautiful landscape and a happy tune with the words: "It happens but once in your life time!"

The second segment of this first part is introduced with the declaration of another Nazi at the Nuremberg trial: "To order and to obey: that's when the conflict started." This section examines closely how Nazi doctors, professionals, and some Germans with their children in the seventies reject any responsibility because they or their parents had no other choice other than to obey orders. Executioners like the Nazi doctor Rose, explain that they were innocent because they could not see the camps themselves and therefore they could not know what their actions led to.

In the same manner, because the majority of the Germans did not see the camps or even did not want to hear about them, their anti-Semitism and their wide support of the Nazi regime had supposedly nothing to do with the extermination of the Jews. Consequently, some of their children conclude that their parents cannot feel guilty for something they did not know about and that they could not prevent anyway. As everybody had to obey, only one person must have been responsible for the murder of six million, the conveniently missing Adolf Hitler.

The most ironic, powerful and well-made sequence of the film is probably the one showing a group of young Germans in a sauna. Only a few minutes after having seen thousands of corpses in the mass graves of the camps and starved dying survivors at their liberation, the audience is confronted with color images of nude, healthy and happy young Germans in a sauna. The contrast is even more violent as the sauna itself clearly recalls a gas chamber.

In this derisive *mise-en-scène*, Ophüls himself is shown as having a lot of fun because (of course!) no one is responsible for the past and none of this has anything to do with the systematic murder of the Jews. In this very ironic scene, the interviewees explain that in a sauna everyone is equal, even the Germans and the Jews like Ophüls (!), the workers and their bosses. Another one feels however the need to add that even with their clothes on, they are equal. The same man explains that anyway the Jews had always been persecuted. He refrains from using the verb "gassed" because twenty percent of people in his business are Jews. In parallel, Telford Taylor explains how in America, 1959, a teleplay on the Nuremberg Trials had to delete any reference to gas because one of its sponsors was the Pacific Gas and Electric Company ("Judgment at Nuremberg," *Playhouse 90*). In the end we see various close ups of healthy bodies in a sauna and three beautiful nude young women playing in a swimming pool like Rubens' three graces just a few minutes after having seen the emaciated body of a dead women thrown into a triangular mass grave. In this very ironic conclusion, it appears that time has passed, "good times" are back and no one really cares about being disturbed by dark memories.

The last section of this first part is dedicated to the rejection of responsibility not only by Germans as individuals but also by the German people as a whole. It is developed around the central declaration of the Nazi doctor Otto Kranzbueler, explaining that he has found a perfect answer to the questions of his children and grandchildren. When asked what his responsibilities were, he replies that considering the common representation of the war time derived from the Nuremberg Trials, it is up to them to decide whether he was "an idiot, a coward or a criminal." He goes on explaining that as they know he is none of these, they understand that he had nothing to do with war crimes nor with the concentration camps. Once again, no one is responsible for the extermination of six million Jews, not even the Nazis as they were all, of course, "intelligent, courageous and very decent people."

Consequently, this section also insists on the ineffectiveness of the Nuremberg trial. It appears that according to Ophüls' montage, this trial could not be effective because it could not ask the right and basic questions on war crime responsibilities as they would have led to admitting that the Americans and the Russians were also guilty of committing other atrocities (i.e. the bombing of Dresden, Hamburg or Nuremberg, and the Katin massacre). This is the main reason why Nuremberg was mostly perceived in Germany as the trial of the vanquished by the victors.

According to M. Kogon, the young Germans "listen but they do not understand" what happened at that time. In contrast, Ophüls shows the exceptional "understanding" of Beate Klarsfeld who totally left her "a-political" mother and other Gentile German family members to dedicate her life to the hunting of the individuals who were indeed directly responsible for the murder of her father in-law and of six million Jews.

This first part of *The Memory of Justice* ends on the evocation of the great confusion of the Nuremberg trials based on the different goals the prosecutors were trying to reach, their different conception of justice and everyday technical problems making the sessions a long, repetitive and laborious process. In the end, and thanks to this growing confusion, very few criminals were punished, often for a very short time. Moreover, everyone agreed on the impossibility of judging a people as a whole. The final images and interviews indicate also that the German people themselves paid dearly and were victims of the Russians', of others' war crimes. This section on "Nuremberg and the Germans" leads to a dead end facing the Berlin wall as a German woman reveals that she was raped by Russian soldiers.

"Nuremberg and other places," the second half of *The Memory of Justice*, can be divided in two sections: the representation of Nazi Germany in the post-war world followed by a comparison with American and French war crimes. This part starts with images of Hamburg totally destroyed by the Allies and with the need of the German population for music or any kind of entertainment to forget their hardship. Through the interview of Mrs. Kortner, an old friend of his parents, Ophüls learns that in Hollywood, his father was one of the very few Jews who were proud of being a German in spite of the Holocaust.

After making distinctions between German artists that were Nazis, active Nazis, anti-Nazis and active anti-Nazis, this long sequence constitutes a tribute to the persistence of some rare artists in exile like Max Ophüls, Gurtz, Kortner, Brecht and others who never forgot the incredible wealth of German culture that preceded the Nazi era. In a similar manner, through various interviews of Yehudi Menuhin as the first world renowned Jewish artist who played in Germany after the war, the film recalls that the complete German culture cannot be ignored and forgotten because of the Nazi era.

Various pieces of the post-war play, *The Devil's General*, oppose clearly the guilty and blind obedience to military authority and military courage to the moral courage that should have led responsible officers to refuse to "execute" inhumane orders. At the same time Frau Lueber in the company of her son explains how her husband was such a good and dedicated Nazi judge and how much the SS loved their wives.

This sequence on Germany ends on various historical reminders of the richness of German-Jewish culture before the war; the assimilation by the Nazis of Jews to decadents and left-wing activists or communists. Other sequences remind us that the Germans had seen what was happening to the Jews before the war, how Goering logically but also "by chance" met Adolf Hitler and how Hitler became so popular because of his speeches against the harshness of the Versailles Treaty. At that point, after a brief reminder of the ineffectiveness of the Nuremberg trial by American students at Princeton University, the film closes its circle on Germany and switches to various comparisons between the Holocaust and other war crimes committed by other nations.

In a gripping parallel, Ophüls interviews alternatively Mrs. Keating who lost her husband in Vietnam and Mr. and Mrs. Ransom who lost their son in the same war. The pride and extreme patriotism of Barbara Keating contrasts with the overwhelming "sense of loss" expressed by Louise and Robert Ransom who find no consolation in the idea that their son died for his country. Their conviction that their son's life was "wasted" by the American government contrasts violently with the opinion of Mrs. Keating who takes so much pride in showing her husband's military decorations which she exhibits in a cabinet. In the end, the loud and happy patriotic music Ophüls puts with images showing the American flag and Mrs. Keating's house turned into a shrine becomes rather ironic compared to the very respectful and silent images that accompany the interview of Mr. and Mrs. Ransom. Once again, it is the soundtrack and the editing that indicate clearly the director's own opinion and subjective irony. It is correct to say, with Annette Insdorf, that these interviews are being "objectively" made as the questions asked by Ophüls allow the interviewees to express themselves completely and freely (Insdorf, 247). However, the filming and the editing of these segments are very personal and not "objective" at all. Once again, Ophüls' own convictions and interpretations are made very obvious both by the editing and by the soundtrack on these interviews.

The rest of the film compares the Nazis' war crimes to others perpetrated by the American, the Soviet or the French armies. Concerning the United States, the film insists on the genocide of the American Indians, the bombing of the civilian populations of Nuremberg, Dresden, Hamburg and also on the My Lai massacre. Each time however, a clear distinction is made to avoid any confusion between the specificity of the systematic extermination of the Jews by the Nazis and other war crimes.

In the following segments, the film develops the idea expressed by the Ransoms according to which influential civilians and officials in the government are also responsible for what happens during a war. The following sequence is then dedicated to the presentation of the totally guilt-free consciences of the industrialists who profited directly from the Nazi era and finished their lives wealthy and influential. In a comparison with the Watergate scandal, Daniel Ellsberg explains that "not to know requires a great deal of effort" for politicians and key officials not to see the direct consequences of their policies. In opposition to this "controlled stupidity" (Ellsberg) Ophüls shows interviews of American and French deserters who fled when they saw what was being asked from them by their direct superiors. In contrast, Mrs. Keating explains that such deserters are responsible for the death of men like her husband.

During the final sequence dedicated to torture and war crimes in Algeria, Edgard Faure explains that fighting to keep colonies, like France did in Algeria, is extremely different from what the Nazis did when they invaded neighboring countries. However, as Anette Insdorf recalls, this statement is preceded by the interview of a French soldier who explained that he deserted because he felt like a Nazi. More importantly, the same segment is followed by a speech of the French prosecutor in Nuremberg recalling that the Nazis wanted to colonize all of central Europe. Therefore, according to Ophüls' montage, like the French in

Algeria, the Nazis were fighting for what they saw as being their colonies.

The Memory of Justice then closes like it opened, with Yehudi Menuhin being interviewed and playing the violin. As this world renown Jewish artist who fled Nazi Germany returns to Berlin, the film ends on a positive note showing musicians of all ethnic and national backgrounds playing again in Germany and returning to the limelight, even if our memory of Justice proved to be inefficient in preventing or even punishing war crimes to the full extent of our principles. With such a sequence, and in agreement with his father's feelings, Marcel Ophüls' film ends with the same pride of being a German in spite of the Nazi era.

c. *Hotel Terminus*

When compared to *The Sorrow and the Pity*, *A Sense of Loss* and *The Memory of Justice*, *Hotel Terminus* often seems to be identical in its techniques but different in its subject and its effects on its audiences. Like the three preceding documentaries, the introduction, the title and the conclusion of *Hotel Terminus* provide major keys to the reading of the film. Like them, it is also divided into two chronological parts—i.e. Barbie's life until and after his escape to South America. As in all of Ophüls' work, irony plays a key role throughout this film and the montage gives real significance to the interviews. Like *The Sorrow and the Pity* and *The Memory of Justice*, *Hotel Terminus* is also articulated around two main themes indicated in its complete title: *Hotel Terminus: The Life and Times of Klaus Barbie*.

Like *The Memory of Justice*, *Hotel Terminus* deals primarily with the inefficiency of justice when faced with war crimes or with crimes against humanity. Like the *Sorrow and the Pity*, it also analyzes distortions of the past and the importance of finding out who needed them and who benefitted from them since the end of World War II. Like *A Sense of Loss*, *Hotel Terminus* ultimately constitutes a tribute to the memory of the children who lost their lives in the Holocaust and to the handful of bystanders who tried to save a few lives or to fight the murderers.

At first sight, *Hotel Terminus* consists of two main themes that intertwine from the beginning to the end of this documentary. These two themes are: the life and times of Klaus Barbie. However, these two topics only provide the audience with a convenient but superficial structure which makes the film easier to follow. Indeed the film does not start nor end as a chronological biography. The first and the last images of *Hotel Terminus* recall the freakish personality of the "Butcher of Lyon" and the atrocity of the crime he was convicted for, fifty-three years after he committed it: the roundup of the forty-one Jewish children of Izieu on April 6, 1944. The telex signed and sent by Barbie on the evening of this "operation" reads as follows:

> The Jewish children's home in Izieu (Ain) was closed down this morning. A total of 41 children aged 3 to 13 were arrested. Additionally, all the Jewish personnel—comprising ten people, including five women—were also arrested. Money or other valuables were not discovered. Transport to Drancy follows 7.4.44. Signed Barbie.[69]

Two of the children arrested were deported to Estonia where they were shot. All the others were deported to Auschwitz where they were gassed. Out of fifty-one, only one survived (Lea Feldbaum).

As in Ophüls' film on Clermont-Ferrand during the Occupation, this documentary unfolds on a first level according to a precise historical chronology, that of Barbie's life. Building up around this chronological backbone, with the movement of a spiral, Ophüls creates a complex depiction of Barbie's times. However, the beginning and the end of *Hotel Terminus* make it very clear that there is more to the film than just the biography of a famous Nazi. The very first sentence of the film, right after the title and the opening credits, is pronounced by a Jew whose family has been exterminated by the Nazis. This man, Raymond Lévy, declares: "Barbie's life in itself is of no interest to me." By using this line as the very first phrase in his film, Ophüls indicates clearly that Barbie's biography provides only a helpful backbone to the film, but that it does not represent the final purpose of the film itself.

Before Raymond Lévy's declaration, the introduction, the credits and the title of the film already gave us important clues to reading the documentary. Once again, the introduction and the conclusion of Ophüls' film give us important keys with which to read this documentary that constantly takes us back to three central locations, the three infernal circles evoked during Barbie's trial with their progressive ascension into horror: the city of Lyon, the Terminus Hotel, and the village of Izieu.

At the very beginning of the introduction to *Hotel Terminus*, the screen remains black and we hear the slow melancholy beginning one of Chopin's famous *études*. This music is interrupted and then starts again. This interruption on a screen remaining black immediately creates a feeling of anxiety as if some sorrowful child's piano lesson had been abruptly interrupted by a terrifying memory, vision or event. Then the music starts again and Klaus Barbie's picture appears on the screen as if this face could somewhat explain the mystery of the previous interruption.

This picture of Barbie shows a joyful man in his late fifties celebrating some happy event. The voice-over of Johannes Schneider, the German cultural attaché in Bolivia, then explains how this man, Klaus Altmann-Barbie, while otherwise very pleasant and cheerful, one day became suddenly crazy in order to defend the honor of Adolf Hitler. Following this, Schneider laughs and the camera offers a close-up of a Christmas decoration—a candle and a Christmas tree—next to the cultural attaché. Then, a German traditional song starts with the opening credits showing the Saint Joseph jail in Lyon with the title of the film: "Hotel Terminus."

With this introduction the audience is provided with key elements to read the following documentary. It tells us that, as with each one of Ophüls' works, the music plays a key role in its relationship to the image and to the subject of the film. This relationship will be a disjunction. However, as opposed to Chopin's melody that opens the film with an anguishing mystery and interruption, the rest of the music will mostly be very happy and ironic. As during the opening credits it will mainly consist of traditional, patriotic or religious German songs sung by the Vienna Boys' Choir. It will soon become synonymous with the totally guilt-free indifference of many towards the extermination of the Jews and the murder of the children of Izieu. After a point, the joy of this traditional song will become unbearable as it accompanies a succession of pictures showing different views of Izieu.

The first image of Barbie insists on the enigma hiding behind this happy face capable of the most inhumane crimes and on the silence of the Nazi about his past at his trial.[70] It insists also on Barbie's extreme talent for hiding who he really was. At the same time, Schneider's first interview introduces the idea confirmed by many of Barbie's victims according to which the "Butcher of Lyon" would first give the appearance of a very well-educated, able and well-mannered man who would then suddenly break into the most vicious, "efficient" and unbound Nazi torturer. It is precisely these qualities that will explain the usefulness of many men of his kind to intelligence and police organizations both in Europe, the USA and in South America. Schneider's interview indicates the film's constant attempts to understand the witnesses' ways of thinking which at some point, for many different reasons, allowed them to become friends and co-workers of Barbie, not knowing or not wanting to know what he had done, or hiring him for what he could still do—i.e., organize and direct a secret police.

Finally, the end of the introduction brings the film back to its real center, the necessary remembrance of Barbie's victims. As Schneider's interview ends on a recurrent close-up of Christmas decorations, it reminds us first of all that the witness is a Catholic. Given Ophüls' constant use of irony throughout the film, his insistence on the celebration of this holiday so important to Catholic children brings to mind, *ad contrario*, the absence of the Jewish children of Izieu and the Jewish holidays they never knew and will never know. Many of the film's interviews were indeed conducted during the Christmas season and the Christmas decorations next to Schneider, the SS Gusman or the former CIC agent, Eugene Kolb, remind us throughout the film of Barbie's unforgettable crimes and the different levels of complicity of the men who agreed to hire him or work with him. Such a "natural setting" for the interviews—as opposed to a setting that would have been staged by Ophüls—reveals an important degree of irony in the film I will study in further detail.

For all the preceding reasons, I propose to represent the progression of the film with the following schema. The film itself develops as a wave centered around the telling of Barbie's life and crimes. Each high and low in this curve correspond to a point where the film offers an analysis of a specific theme brought up by a specific testimony—i.e. the Jean Moulin affair, the mentality of a German village, various complicities, the responsibilities of the CIC etc.:

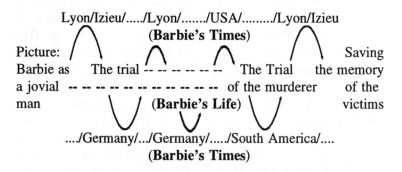

Lyon/Izieu/...../Lyon/......./USA/........./Lyon/Izieu
(Barbie's Times)
Picture: Barbie as a jovial man   The trial   The Trial of the murderer   Saving the memory of the victims   **(Barbie's Life)**
..../Germany/.../Germany/...../South America/....
(Barbie's Times)

Such a schema is only a convenience to start to understand how the film develops.

After the introductory segment, we see images of the Saint Joseph jail in Lyon where Barbie was held just before his trial, we hear a traditional German song, and we can read on the screen the title of the film: "Hotel Terminus." The title of this documentary is in itself very revealing of Ophüls' style. Like "The Sorrow and the Pity," "A Sense of Loss" or "The Memory of Justice," it is made out of two notions between which different degrees of irony progressively infiltrate. Thus, just by briefly analyzing the use of "Hotel Terminus" as the title of this film, one can easily underline key aspects of Ophüls' work.

First, the Terminus Hotel is a hotel that still exists today near the Perrache train station of Lyon. It has only recently changed its name to the Pullman Hotel, possibly in order to avoid bad publicity since Klaus Barbie's arrest and trial. Any irony we might find in its name was not created but strongly underlined by Ophüls. As often happens in Ophüls' work, places or witnesses bring their own meaning to history. The talent of the director very often consists in revealing or underlining it. Irony is in reality itself.

According to Ophüls, as we saw through *The Sorrow and the Pity* and *The Memory of Justice*, the problems developed during the war did not end in 1945 when the French population was already revering another military man, when the American Army and Secret Services were engaging in conflicts in Southeast Asia and judging some Nazi criminals of war while, at the same time, hiring others, like Klaus Barbie, in order to fight Communism. At the same time, the Terminus Hotel remained at the same place with the same name, like an ironic reminder that not everything had changed with the end of the war and that many men like Klaus Barbie still had very promising careers waiting for them. It is a massive, square nineteenth-century stone building with a black slate roof located right next to the Lyon Perrache train station. Like all the other Terminus hotels in France, its original purpose was to provide comfortable lodging for travelers who needed to rest at the end, or terminus, of a long journey. When Barbie was using it as his headquarters, its name became synonymous with terror, torture and death.

The bitter irony of the film's title can be found if we compare the apparent banality of its meaning with the gruesome reality it is hiding. Indeed, thousands of French towns still have a "Hotel Terminus" near their train station. Obviously, in the case of Lyon this apparent banality immediately reveals the real function of the place that became for many years the building from which the so-called "Final Solution," the real "Terminus" of the Nazi politics, was applied to the region of Lyon. With its location near a train station, its use by Barbie and the double meaning of its name, this building in itself is directly related to three major elements of the persecution of the European Jews: the trains; the Gestapo, its collaborators and the torture of their victims; and the deception of the victims about the real meaning of the deportations to the East until the very end.

There is only one reproach I would make towards the very strong symbolic use of the name of this hotel as the title of the film. While some victims of Barbie mention the fact that they were tortured in the hotel itself, many others were in fact tortured in the Montluc Fort or in what is still today the Ecole de Santé Militaire, the Military Medical School, of Lyon. On one occasion, we even see parts of this building and one of its gates while we are led to believe that it is in fact the Terminus Hotel. Such an omission obviously increases the central role played in the film by the Terminus Hotel and helps its general interpretation. It creates however some confusion for the audience that does not know the city of Lyon at all.

Finally, a shot in the opening credits of the Saint Joseph jail where Barbie was held for a short time before his trial reminds us that this film was made and edited before, but mostly during and after the trial. As if he were still in this jail at the beginning of the film, Barbie is awaiting his trial by the audience. Similar to *The Memory of Justice*, the actual trial will be in great part oriented toward the redefinition of a "crime against humanity" and why these processes of redefinition, instruction and trial are so important in the present.

With these implicit indications, the alert spectator can start watching the documentary with its two basic series, the life and times of Klaus Barbie, with the omnipresence of the victims of Izieu in its center. As the second series constantly duplicates and complicates the first one through Ophüls' art, I will start analyzing the more obvious—how Barbie's life is being told—followed by the more complex—the understanding why it took forty-two years to try him and the meaning of this delay for our own world.

- How to Tell the Life of a Nazi

Hotel Terminus is not merely a film on Barbie's life. Many chapters of this life are just alluded to in the film, or completely omitted, like Barbie's persecution of Amsterdam Jews. For these reasons, the way Barbie's life is told in this film is very important for the present analysis. The apparent linear structure of the film is indeed completely centered around the tragedy of Izieu, the importance of remembering the victims of a crime against humanity and, ultimately, the trial. However, the film is also entitled *The Life and Times of Klaus Barbie*. On a basic level, Ophüls' film can also be read as an inquiry into the life of a specific Nazi. This provides the spectators with three different threads—Barbie's life; the trial of the murderer of the Jewish children of Izieu; and a typical Nazi's life—with which they can enter the complexity of the documentary. Such a subtitle also makes a film more marketable and at least more "appealing" to the media and a larger audience often more interested in the life of the torturer than it would be in the fate of the children of Izieu. I would also interpret it, however, as a parodic allusion to the very limited interest of many media for Barbie himself, especially the American media focusing on the most gruesome anecdotes of a Nazi's life and too often situating his times in remote foreign countries, in a convenient past that barely concerns American politics today.[71]

Indeed, Ophüls' film answers many questions a commercial documentary on the life of a Nazi would ask: "Where was he born?" "Who were his parents and their friends?" "Who were his friends?" "What kind of education did he receive?" "What were the values of the society in which he grew up?" "What was he like as a child?" "How and when did he join the Nazi party?" "What were the turning points in his life?" etc. As American audiences are accustomed to through TV shows like the weekly *60 Minutes*, this documentary indeed conducts an investigation answering all these questions and many more such as: "What were Barbie's responsibilities in Lyon?" "Who betrayed Jean Moulin?"[72] "How and why was Barbie hired by the American

Secret Services (CIC)?" "What was he doing in Bolivia and Peru?" etc. However, the documentary itself, as a whole, works in a totally different manner. The length and the unhurried pace of this study, its final editing and the way in which all of these questions are asked and answered make this film very different from conventional documentaries or TV investigations as it carries all the distinctive marks of Ophüls' style. For this reason, I will not tell Barbie's life. This has been done in many articles and books.[73]

As it is much more important for my subject, I will examine the way Ophüls investigated and told the biography of "the Butcher of Lyon."

To start with, Ophüls never appears in person as the master of ceremonies to directly tell the audience what they should pay attention to nor does he pretend to be perfectly objective. The film stands for itself with its specific montage, as Marcel Ophüls' production, not under the cover of the pretended objectivity of a professional reporter. The film reveals characters and various degrees of complicity more than the story already told by the press of the time or by many books. The events and the truths it depicts are real but they are always put in relation with individual choices and responsibilities, not only as the consequences of a mere demonstration of logic, of rational causes and effects.

Indeed the film never lets individuals find shelter for their guilt by justifying their actions with "circumstances." This is mostly prevented by Ophüls' use of irony. The "objective" reasoning of a good-willed and well-trained reporter is not at the basis of the organization of the documentary. Ophüls' film organization is at the same time much more simple, based on the chronology of one's life, and much more complex than that, admitting its personal choices and weaving all the testimonies throughout the film, not only in a linear manner but rather in the form of a spiral thanks to a large network of resonances, contradictions and contrasts. It deals not only with facts but also with their interpretations, their consequences and the passions they developed from or nourished. It requires extremely active audience participation and interpretation beyond the mere factual logic of the events depicted. An excellent example of all this is provided at the beginning of the film itself.

Following the opening credits, *Hotel Terminus* itself starts in a billiard room in Lyon where three old friends are playing while Ophüls is asking them some questions about the possible implications of Barbie's trial. This very casual conversation first contrasts with the gravity of the subject. The setting creates the relaxed atmosphere comparable to the one of a café conversation allowing the three men to reveal various widespread feelings in the local population at the time of the trial. First, the three men playing billiards, bouncing three balls interminably on the same surface, represent the three basic attitudes of the public confronted with Barbie's life as told through his trial: it is useless and too late to judge these old stories (Marcel Cruat); without conviction but by a matter of principle Barbie should be tried merely because nobody should be able to get away with such crimes (Henri Varlot); and finally Barbie's crimes were so atrocious for relatives of his victims that whether or not he should be judged should not even be discussed (Raymond Lévy).

Then, as the film shows images of corridors and stairways inside the Terminus Hotel, we hear, one after the other, the voices of various witnesses assessing Barbie with the following contradictory statements:

- Barbie was really a... a brutal man.
- Very jovial.
- He was a sadist (*C'était un sadique*).
- Someone who was succeeding well and who was without mercy. He was frightening (*Quelqu'un qui réussissait bien et qui était implacable. Il faisait peur*).
- He was sure that he was the greatest intelligence officer.
- I never got the impression that he was really guilty of any atrocities.
- I remember this fellow who was rather calm and who suddenly would start screaming (*Je me souviens de ce type qui était plutôt calme et qui se mettait à hurler d'un seul coup*).

It is only after the introduction, the opening credits, the billiard game and this sequence closing on images of the Lyon Perrache train station that the narration of Barbie's life can start. At this point we do not know who formulated these final judgements on Barbie. We will find out later, throughout the film. This succession of discordant statements repeats the two warnings given at the beginning of *The Sorrow and the Pity*: everything we will hear or see will have to be interpreted and the image and the soundtrack will constantly comment on one another.

Thanks to this sequence, *Hotel Terminus* begins with a brief evocation of the trial in Lyon, the major event that brought Barbie's life into the limelight. The documentary then develops through different chapters corresponding to different phases in Barbie's life:
- his childhood in Udler and his adolescence in Trier
- his Catholic devotion and his beginnings as a devoted SS
- his excellent skills as a leader and as a policeman
- his formation and promotion in Nazi Germany
- his exceptional skills as a torturer in Lyon
- his responsibilities in Jean Moulin's death
- his hiding at the end of the war
- his hiring by the American CIC
-- End of the first part // beginning of the second part --
- the role the CIC and the Vatican played in his escape
- his excellent qualifications for his new "jobs" in Bolivia and Peru
- his relationship with local officials and neo-Nazis
- his identification and his capture
- his life as a good and loving father
- his trial and his conviction for the murder of the Jewish children of Izieu.

The first section, on the Nazi's childhood and high-school years, begins with Ophüls reading Barbie's autobiographical text. In doing so, Ophüls has to say "I" and to pretend he is Barbie himself describing his own life. This odd situation has many possible interpretations. First, Ophüls reads this text in a very casual manner, as if he were reading any biographical note. This insists on a recurrent and ambiguous idea often used to present the torturers as mere victims of their social and political surroundings: Barbie would have been a little German boy like any other, even like Ophüls himself who grew up in Germany at about the same time. It is obvious however—according to the film—that Barbie as a young man became "different" from his classmates very early, with a clear consciousness of being a respected or feared leader, somewhat "superior" to them. Moreover, the fact that Ophüls says "I" for Barbie, as if the two men could be switched, gives a certain ironic twist to this narration as the spectators already know that this film will conclude with the trial of this specific Nazi and that Ophüls' family fled Nazi Germany and Vichy France because of the persecutions of men like Barbie.

At this point, Ophüls' irony suggests that, in spite of all the appearances and the propaganda, Barbie was and is not a man like any one of us who just happens to have a darker chapter in his past. This rejected interpretation will be used throughout the film by the people who worked with Barbie before, during and after the war and who need to feel good about it at the time of the documentary's making. Finally, one can easily feel a feigned casual or innocent tone in Ophüls' voice saying "I" for Barbie. This in itself indicates the irony put in place in telling Barbie's life, especially when contrasted with Ophüls' extremely respectful tone of voice when he interviews Barbie's victims.

Much later in the film, while examining the fate of other Nazis who escaped from Germany after the war, Ophüls will imitate someone else's voice and this time in a much more theatrical, ironic and parodic way. This takes place almost at the end of the first part of *Hotel Terminus* when Ophüls and his assistant act out a telephone call to the wife of a Nazi who was hired by the CIC and had died. In this scene we see Ophüls giving directions and acting as the old German woman as he changes his voice to imitate her. His assistant plays the role of Ophüls trying to get some information. In this parodic reenactment, the SS's wife (played by Ophüls) refuses politely to meet with Ophüls (played by his assistant) because, of course, she does not know anything about her husband's situation after the war and because she has nothing to say about these old stories. As he always does in such a situation, Ophüls ends this useless conversation with an extremely polite and ironic tone of voice, thanking the woman for her time. Once again this strange scene has different functions.

First, it is extremely important to most German interviewees to forget or at least not to talk about this period of their history. This scene indicates clearly the difficulties Ophüls encountered making this film as Nazi criminals, like Barbie during his trial, or anyone who was directly related to them, did not want to testify. Indeed, some of the most frightening moments of *Hotel Terminus* take place in Germany and in Bolivia when we see with what passion Nazi criminals, or their memories, are protected from Ophüls' camera, not by their families but by their neighbors of the eighties.

In a final ironical twist typical of anti-Semitic propaganda, Nazis would have become the pitiful victims of vengeful Jews or of the Israeli Secret Services. At least seven people directly reinforce that interpretation in the film making war criminals helpless victims of mean-spirited Jews: two neighbors protecting the Nazi Barthelmus; an old German man and a gas-station owner accusing Ophüls of making money out of the misery of these now old people; Albert Rosset, a leader of the French National Front in Lyon; a former neighbor of Barbie in Bolivia; Ive Omrcamin, a former American agent; and the French journalist, Albert Brun. Only Ophüls' complex irony can fight such myths or reverse such lies conveying rampant modern anti-Semitism disguised as anti-Zionism that has continued to prosper since 1933.

Finally, the segment of the reenacted phone conversation clearly shows Ophüls' exasperation and his very personal reactions as most people he interviews or tries to interview, except the former victims of Barbie who are still alive, just wish to forget about this subject. This obvious exasperation is new compared to what happens in *The Sorrow and the Pity*. With *Hotel Terminus*, the audience is always very conscious of all the concrete obstacles Ophüls had to overcome in order to make this film. It also discovers on many occasions the varying moods of the director and his continuous uncertainties about the final success of his enterprise. In such conditions it always remained difficult for Ophüls to tell Barbie's life.

On a couple of occasions, however, Ophüls was able to interview some former members of the SS or some former Nazis in spite of the general rule of silence that usually prevents such men to talk about their past with outsiders. Such an exception to this rule is the interview of the Nazi, Gusman, placed by Ophüls in the section dedicated to the hiding and the survival of Barbie in Germany right after the defeat of 1945. Indeed, in contrast with the rest of the film or with the tricked interviews directed by Lanzmann in *Shoah*, Gusman is an SS who agrees to be interviewed, in spite of all the warnings his family and neighbors might have given him not to do so. The extreme serenity Gusman exhibits while talking about his friend Klaus Barbie constitutes a clear defiance as he knows he is proudly talking about his past as an SS to a Jew—Marcel Ophüls—knowing at the same time that nothing can happen to him anymore. Gusman's behavior is indeed characteristic of the attitude of the vast majority of the Nazis faced with their past. As they express no remorse whatsoever for what they did, as they were "just obeying orders" or "fighting a war like any good soldier," Nazis do not regret actions for which they do not want to take personal responsibility. This allows them to carry on with the same discourse they had since 1933 and keep on protecting the memory of Hitler as a great leader fighting a war. This memory, in return, continues protecting them from individual guilt.

Moreover, Gusman's interview quickly becomes very similar to the kind of defiant interviews Barbie was giving the world press before his extradition from Bolivia. At this point, this interview becomes a masterpiece within Ophüls' work as the art of the director/interviewer must by itself restore the truth while an SS is trying to use the film for his own propaganda. I will therefore analyze this confrontation in the following section dedicated to the study of Ophüls' art of irony in this film.

As we have seen since the very beginning of this study, Klaus Barbie's life only provides the documentary with a "story line" for the convenience of its reading. It is not the main subject of the film; the film is not a biography of some evil hero. As M. Varlot stated in one of the first sequences, the life of Klaus Barbie is of "no interest in itself." Then, what is of interest? Why continue telling the story of a Nazi at the risk of turning him into some kind of major historical figure? Answers to these questions can only be found in the way Ophüls tells that story.

Throughout the film, Barbie's life is told through the points of view of three major groups of interviewees: the victims, like M. Varlot, Mme. Lesèvre or Mme. Lagrange, who know Barbie is a criminal; those, like former agent Kolb or journalist Brun, who think that, after all, he could not be that bad as he was a good father, victim of the circumstances of a Jewish conspiracy or because he helped fight Communism; and finally those, like Gusman and de Castro who think he was and still is a great fellow. It is important however to notice that whereas they are all handled with the same extreme attention and seriousness, these points of view do not play equivalent roles in the evolution or the general structure of the film.

In the first part, for example, there are two different kinds of transitions between the different chapters of the film as well as of Klaus Barbie's life: thematic and factual transitions. These transitions are extremely important after the film has insisted on the violent contrast between different blocks of interpretations such as: "Barbie was a vicious criminal" versus "He could not have done such things"; "He took a very personal and active role in the persecution of his victims" versus "Barbie was just a good boy swallowed by the Nazi regime." Transitions will therefore be extremely important in understanding how all these statements can be made by different people about the same man at the same time. As we already noticed in *The Sorrow and the Pity*, in the final montage, an interview always leads directly to the next, the film following the inner logic of what is being said by a witness. However, we have also seen that Ophüls never lets his opponents use his film for their own propaganda purposes. These two rules also apply in *Hotel Terminus* and they are applied to the thematic or ironic transitions.

In the beginning of the narration, with sections about Barbie's youth and his time in Lyon, the transitions between one chapter and the next are always insured by the testimony of a former Résistant or a victim of Barbie. After the film opposed the nice but authoritarian boy and classmate to the young Nazi of twenty-seven in Lyon, Mme. Aubrac mentions how she threatened the Germans with retaliation from the Résistance if her husband was not immediately freed. It is this episode Ophüls uses to switch from Barbie's youth to the organization of the Résistance and to the Jean Moulin Affair.

At the end of the inquiry about who betrayed Jean Moulin, M. Cordier, a former Résistant, recognizes when answering Ophüls' question, that, on the French scene, the Moulin Affair overshadowed all the other war crimes. Then the film switches to the search for other Nazis posted in France during the Occupation. After this, Serge Klarsfeld's linkage of Steingritt with Barthelmus introduces the segment about the search for Barthelmus. At the end of this section however, Nazi Barthelmus' wife tells Ophüls that war crimes were not only committed by Germans but also by French citizens.

It is to be noticed here that Ophüls refuses to use this statement as a direct transition. He first goes to the interview of Mme. Lagrange and it is only when Mme. Lagrange herself mentions that she was tortured by a French man that the film really starts examining French Collaboration. It seems rather clear that Ophüls will not let his opponents tell him how he should organize his film. Even when transitions cannot be insured by testimonies of victims, Ophüls will not let Barbie's sympathizers take over the logic of each chapter's succession in his documentary. This prevents the film from becoming, in spite of itself, a justification of pro-Nazi attitudes. *Hotel Terminus* remains all along a very respectful tribute to the victims of Nazism and to the children of Izieu.

When it is not possible to end a section or to articulate two segments using the testimony of a victim, Ophüls relies on his characteristic sense of irony so that the film will not fall into relativity or worse, into the hands of pro-Collaborationist propaganda. Such a procedure is very common in the sections of the film depicting Barbie's life after 1945. In these images, Ophüls used no testimony of Barbie's victims except one, Mirna Murillo, tortured by Barbie in Bolivia in the early seventies. Like the trial, the documentary also focuses on the killing of the children of Izieu and on other charges of crimes against humanity held against Barbie. It considers only briefly the crimes committed by Barbie in South America. The testimony of Mirna Murillo, as well as the images introducing her interview, insists on the continuity of the Gestapo officer's career and on the utility of his "skills" for other governments. It does not constitute a detailed examination of Barbie's crimes in Bolivia and Peru. All the testimonies about Barbie's life in these countries will constantly be linked to what he did in Lyon and ultimately, in Izieu.

Irony will then be the most frequent thematic transition used in the film. Its function as articulation is clearly introduced at the end of the section dedicated to the Collaboration and the Occupation in Lyon. Concluding her long interview during which she wants to prove that she had nothing against the Jews and nothing to do with Collaborators, Mrs. Hemmerle declares that anyway these stories are too old to be judged and that they do not make any more sense than judging the British now for the execution of Joan of Arc: "They will tell you about Joan of Arc!"

Ending unintentionally her justification with such a ludicrous comparison, Mme. Hemmerle shows her admiration for one of the greatest heros of Vichy's Nationalist and anti-British propaganda. In one sentence, she destroyed all of her preceding efforts. This is the end of the testimony on the Occupation of Lyon. Its use by Ophüls is clearly ironic as the director chose not only to include this apparently stupid remark in his film but also because he uses it to conclude his analysis of Lyon during the Occupation. This is followed by official images, newsreels of the liberation of Lyon, as the film switches from individual and local to national and international history.

From this point on, Ophüls' constantly uses ironic transitions. As was the case in *The Sorrow and the Pity*, Ophüls employs irony and disjunctions not only as transition tools but throughout his documentary. Once again, an important part of Ophüls' art will reside not in the manner in which he stages an interview, tricking his interviewees, but, on the contrary, in filming them in their natural environment, in selecting and editing extremely significant segments of the film stock during which witnesses are completely spontaneous and finally show who they really are. As opposed to Claude Lanzmann's technique in *Shoah*, all of Ophüls' witnesses agreed to be interviewed in front of a camera. This implies that Ophüls had to use great skills as an interviewer and as a film editor in order to prevent his film from being used as a medium for propaganda by the Nazis and the various anti-Semites he interviews. For this reason, as we have seen throughout this study of his various films, Ophüls' great mastery as a film director is essential to the success of his enterprise. There is however one exception to this rule in *Hotel Terminus*, one short part of a sequence during which an interviewee is being filmed without noticing.

One instance in which Ophüls actually tricks one of his interviewees is when he continues filming after the reading of a message from the German Ministry of Justice by Dr. Knittel who thinks that the camera has been turned off. At that moment, Dr. Knittel had just finished presenting the official reasons why Dr. Wolfgang Rabl, the public prosecutor in Munich, had German justice drop Barbie's case on June 22, 1971. Then Ophüls pretended the camera was turned off and asked for more explanations. Dr. Knittell started explaining that Rabl himself "has no comment" to make on this subject. Then he stopped talking immediately when he realized the camera was still filming. In this case, Ophüls' technique becomes similar to Claude Lanzmann's. It is however important to notice that, as opposed to Lanzmann's technique, Ophüls does not use this trick in order to record the testimony of an SS but to show the discrepancy between the "official story" and the truth about various complicities that enabled Barbie to escape from justice.

Once again, the director's purpose here is to show a disjunction, to indicate a lie and the irony of administrative double-talk.

The "official" segment about the reasons why charges against Barbie were dropped by German Justice is presented as a farce. It provides us with one of the most significant examples of Ophüls' irony that will metamorphose the mere narration of Barbie's life into the successive revelation of various well hidden truths and very official lies about the real politics of German, American, French and South American administrations since the end of World War II.

- Irony and the Official Story

Dr. Knittel's reading of why German justice did not prosecute many Nazis is preceded by the interview of a self-satisfied SS, Gusman, comfortably seated in his living room and by images of a street in Germany at the time of Carnival. In this introductory segment, people are shown wearing masks in the streets, hiding their real faces, moving to the rhythm of the happy nationalistic song often used as a theme of the film. After Knittel's *faux pas* and embarrassed reading, the camera shows these masked people again with the same happy tune. This time however, one of the masks represents Stan Laurel as it announces the future job of Barbie for the American Counter Intelligence Corps (CIC). From now on Klaus Barbie's life becomes a farce with its lies, tricks and *pirouettes* that would be quite funny, as the smiles of some American agents want us to believe, if it did not have in its heart the torture and the murder of hundreds of people before, during and after the war. But, of course, nobody really knew who Barbie was and what he had done. Particularly not the European based secret services of the most powerful nation of the war whose agents, according to Kolb and Browning, never read French newspapers.

Such incredible statements bewilder the spectator. Whether it is true or not that these American agents in Europe never read Europe's local national newspapers has only two possible interpretations for the audience of the nineteen-nineties. Either these men knew the French were looking for Barbie and they were just lying to Ophüls to protect their former employer or their own reputation, or they never did know what was in the French press after the war and, in this case, they were incompetent. This interpretation however does not fit very well with the responsibilities they had. In fact, Ophüls' montage suggests only one very coherent interpretation.

In the following statement Eugene Kolb, a retired CIC agent, recognizes that for him, the French Résistance was nothing but a bunch of "Commies." For that reason, Barbie having already worked for the CIC could not be turned over to the French as what he knew could have been used by the French Communists against American interests in the reorganization of Europe. According to Paillole, the former head of the French secret services, and Browning, a former CIC agent, it is true that many French officials did not want Barbie in their hands as the French government already feared revelations about fights within the Résistance and about the betrayal of Jean Moulin.

At this point, it is clear that, as in *The Sorrow and the Pity*, the fight against socialism and communism was at all times one of the main priorities of Nazi collaborators, protectors and employers. It is indeed such a political choice that enables the SS, Gusman, to declare, addressing the audience directly by staring at the camera, that the Western World must be grateful to the SS divisions for protecting it from Communism. Such statements do not diminish in the least the horror of Stalinist crimes but they also recall that one crime can in no instance excuse another. They also recall that for many responsible men and women, anti-Semitism and the Holocaust were past events not important enough to reorganize or to risk a slow down in the war for influence in the newly liberated Europe.

This theme is introduced in the documentary by an official speech of President Truman and idyllic American images of American-Soviet collaboration for the liberation of Europe. Accompanying these images of party and celebration, the charming voice of Fred Astaire sings the happy tune "Teacher teach me something...," recalling the information the US army was getting at the same time from the Nazis in order to fight Soviet influence in the world. The very ironic use of Fred Astaire's song here takes the place of Maurice Chevalier's tunes in *The Sorrow and the Pity* as it symbolizes the opposition between the official propaganda of a government hiding the real political issues.

Obviously, in this long section of the film which ends the first part and starts the second, almost none of the interviewees ever mentions the children of Izieu or the six million Jews murdered by these not so bad anti-Communists. Only Daniel Cohn-Bendit, a German Jew and a well-known Marxist, recalls that in Germany, it is much easier to gather a crowd to fight for six million trees than for six million Jews. In such a context, Ophüls' irony plays a key role in revealing the real issues at stake as well as the character of the individuals he interviews.

As in *The Sorrow and the Pity*, Ophüls uses in this film many different techniques to underline disjunctions and irony in order to reveal progressively bits and pieces of the truth. I will analyze the categories used both in the 1971 film and in *Hotel Terminus* in order to be able to indicate what is new in the irony or the disjunctions in the more recent documentary. Indeed Ophüls again uses here the nine different kinds of irony we noticed in his first major documentary:

1) *Inversion and irony in history itself:*
Perhaps, the more obvious example of this kind of irony is provided by the constant fluctuations of the notions of ally and enemy in *Hotel Terminus*. For the CIC, after 1945, some of the official enemies, the Nazis, became more reliable allies than some official allies, like the French Résistance. Indeed, American agents like Eugene Kolb trusted men like Klaus Barbie much more than they would have trusted even Jean Moulin because of his links to the French Communists. In consequence of such an ironical twist in history, the CIC ended up making some of the same choice as Pétain's government did: against the French

Résistance, against French Communists, preferring to work with Nazis in order to institute a new political order in Europe.

In another ironic twist, in the nineteen-eighties, President Ronald Reagan placed flowers on the graves of SS officers in Bitburg more or less at the same time the American government was officially apologizing to France for having hired Klaus Barbie. Ophüls insists on this paradoxical behavior after Erhard Dabringhaus explains that the excuse was made only because "they feel bad." Dabringhaus was the CIC agent in charge of handling Klaus Barbie and Joseph Merk's network of informants in Augsburg, Germany, in 1948. After this, the film will regularly insist on the discrepancy between official good intentions of American politicians and the actual politics being implemented by various responsible administrators like McCloy, Browning, Kolb and others.

Finally, the irony of recent history shows that 1945 did not end the reign of the Nazis. In many cases it just moved it to other parts of the world. Ophüls' film then insists on the important Nazi network developed throughout South America, on the parallel between book burning against a German bookstore in Bolivia and the *autodafé* of Nuremberg and finally, on the reproduction of neo-Nazi governments in Bolivia and Peru as, even after the arrest of Barbie, one of his former neighbors threatens Ophüls with reporting him and his crew to the police. Also, like M. Klein who denied being Jewish in *The Sorrow and the Pity*, another of Barbie's former neighbors explains that he was worthy of being Barbie's friend because he told him he was not a Jew but a Bolivian. Ironically, history keeps on repeating itself.

2) *Disjunction and irony within one's testimony:*

Like in *The Sorrow and the Pity*, disjunctions and contradictions within a testimony are common here with witnesses that were not victims but friends, collaborators of the Nazis or Nazis themselves. In these cases the primary intentions of a testimony are often completely reversed by a slip of the tongue, by the way a story is being told or by the personal values an interviewee reveals.

The best examples are provided by the testimonies of Hemmerle, Zuckner and Gusman. Hemmerle uses Vichy's propaganda hero Joan of Arc in order to prove she was not a collaborator and quotes *Night and Fog* as a propaganda film. She first states that she was arrested with the torturer Payot, and then that she was then arrested by him. Finally she describes her horror upon seeing the shaved heads of other women accused of collaborating, and thus reveals that she was among them and that, on the contrary, she was not arrested as a member of the Résistance. Zuchner, the policeman in charge of Franco-German relations, explains that he was a Résistant because "by the end" he tried to free some very influential people that could have him released when, in his turn, he was arrested at the Libération.

There is also irony in the testimony of the SS, Gusman, stating that because his dogs loved Barbie, it was obvious they instinctively knew he was a "great guy." Thanks to Ophüls' questioning we also find out that these dogs were German shepherds, probably the kind Gusman and other Nazis trained to attack Jews and other prisoners in concentration camps. The dogs knew indeed right away what kind of man Barbie was.

3) *Disjunction and irony between what is being said and facial expressions of the interviewee:*

Mrs. Hemmerle provides us with the best example of this kind of disjunction. As opposed to the direct eye contact, the sorrow and deep emotion one reads on the faces of Barbie's victims, Mrs. Hemmerle is having a very hard time looking at the interviewer while she prepares her explanations. The frenetic succession of expressions on her face all reveal anger, threat, worry and total panic as she is saying that her soul is very peaceful because she has nothing with which to reproach herself.

Much closer to our own history, a similar reaction can be noticed on the faces of the two representatives of the French National Front (PFN). It is the now famous expression of panic of Jean-Marie Le Pen caught on the French radio Europe 1 declaring that the Holocaust was a minor point in the history of World War II. It is also the same expression of panic we see on

Albert Rosset's face feeling trapped by Ophüls following his own reasoning and asking him if he is saying that the Jews are responsible for the recent anti-Semitic waves. In each case Le Pen's and Rosset's facial expressions participate in and aggravate the self-destruction of their own sophisms.

We must also compare the direct look of Gusman and of former CIC agents like Kolb which reveal a very self-controlled professional trained to look his adversary straight in the eye. Precisely because such a look is clearly intended to make one believe that a man is telling the truth, it provokes a systematic disbelief in the audience as these totally emotionless eyes indirectly insist on untold truths they will always hide. The same looks were used in *The Sorrow and the Pity* by De Chambrun explaining Pierre Laval's alleged good will.

4) *Disjunction and irony between a testimony and the behavior of the interviewee:*

In part for the reasons just mentioned, the professional self-control of many interviewees, this irony and the preceding one are much rarer in *Hotel Terminus* than they were in *The Sorrow and the Pity*. It is found mainly in the testimonies of Nazi collaborators or supporters who do not have strong political training nor any experience with the media. However, *Hotel Terminus* deals much more often with officials or professionals such as politicians, SS or secret agents that are used to structuring their arguments and controlling their expressions in front of a camera or a microphone in a very disciplined manner. Moreover, as the film often recalls, for many of them, Barbie's life and crimes are just another part of World War II history.

According to these witnesses, no one could seriously see in them any relevance to the present. This "old story" interpretation is of course the point of view of Nazis, former Nazi supporters, former collaborators, former American agents having worked with Barbie, recent collaborators of Barbie in South America and of all the politicians trying to revive anti-Semitism and racist politics freeing them of the memory and of the consequences of the Holocaust.

Indeed, *Hotel Terminus* is filled with witnesses that calmly and surely state with straight forward gazes and a very natural tone of voice that Barbie did not need to engage in torture (Kolb), that he was not an anti-Semite (Kolb and De Castro), that he was a great guy (Gusman), that no one should reopen these old wounds, bring to the surface these old stories, etc. Their next argument is usually that Barbie, like any other SS before, during and after the war was also a good fellow, a very skilled professional, a very caring head of family and a loving father. Such statements do not constitute lies or direct distortions. They are made out of more subtle distortions, of a subtle mixture of controlled ignorance and extremely partial vision of reality that enables other men to live with their own past hiding behind the notions of hierarchical irresponsibility, professionalism and a very convenient sense of duty. Therefore, one would in vain look for any sense of remorse or any apology from such witnesses. Faced with such an horrifying recurring "professionalism" and such a decency in horror, Ophüls must insist on other types of irony to restore the truth.

5) *Disjunction and irony in two consecutive testimonies:*
    Often faced with an openly declared lack of responsibility or the astounding casualness of the various people who appreciated Barbie for his infamous "skills," Ophüls often juxtaposes several testimonies to show their incoherencies and underline distortions. It is the structure Ophüls uses most often throughout his film. As we already saw, it is made very clear from the opening of the film juxtaposing divergent statements on Barbie as a man with images of the Hotel Terminus corridors. In particular, Kolb's judgements on Barbie will constantly be opposed to the judgements of Barbie's victims.
    On another level, we hear American agents Browning, Dabbringhaus, Robert Taylor and Kolb, successively declare that Barbie was arrested as a war criminal, that he escaped, that he was target number three of the Operation Selection Board searching for Nazis and then, minutes later, stating that they did not know what Barbie had done in France because they did not

read French newspapers! At the same time of course, the very same men (except Thomas) admit that they "had to" work with Barbie and to protect him because they new enough about France to figure out it was about to fall into the hands of the "Commies" (Kolb again) that had complete control of the Résistance and of the French secret services. Kolb probably did not read this in French newspapers either.

Therefore, according to the logic of CIC men like Kolb, the official enemy, the Nazi, was a natural ally while the official ally, the French, were indeed the real enemy... *quod erat demonstrandum.* At this point of course, it does not matter anymore how the Communist Jean Moulin was killed. The mere fact that Barbie was able to arrest and kill him was good enough to insure the Nazi a position working for this section of the CIC:

> *Taylor*: On March of 1947, Merk gave me a text written by Barbie on René Hardy.
>
> *Kolb*: Barbie said that Hardy had betrayed Moulin. I did not know Moulin had died under torture.

Throughout the film, Ophüls also juxtaposes contradictory testimonies that still constitute unresolved and controversial issues. This is the case of Hardy's trial to which the film offers a clear but still partial answer suggesting for example that many different people had an interest in somehow getting rid of Jean Moulin. This is also the case of the relationship or the non-relationship between Régis Debray's arrest in Bolivia and of its consequences on concurrent events such as the death of Che Guevara after Debray's arrest, just mentioned by Ophüls, or the non-expulsion of Barbie from Bolivia or Peru until 1983.

First the French TV journalist, Ladislas de Hoyos, says that the French secret services knew about Barbie since 1966-67 and then he suggests that Barbie was not expelled from Bolivia in 1970 because at that time French officials wanted to free Debray first and they could not ask for both men at the same time. Right after this, we see Debray declaring that the French secret services identified Barbie only by the end of 1971, a few months after Debray was freed, on December 29, 1970. Alluding to his close ties with the Mitterand government since 1981, Debray adds with a smile that he would have been told later if the French secret services had identified Barbie before December 29, 1970.

This final argument is anything but convincing as absolutely nothing explains why the French or the Bolivian secret services at any time would have provided such information to an ideologist and a former guerrilla member who had left France to join Che Guevara's army. Moreover, to a French audience aware of the constant self-admiring and self-justifying tone of Debray's work, his argument leaves the question wide open. Indeed Debray's interview ends with another self-justification explaining that after all "he" was right all "his" life as "he" went to South America to fight fascism. In contrast, it is noticeable that this aggressive/defensive attitude and such statements are completely foreign to Serge Klarsfeld's interviews. This segment is more revealing of Debray's personality than it is of the events that did or did not take place.

6) *Disjunction and irony between a testimony and the official propaganda:*

This type of irony plays a less important role in *Hotel Terminus* than it did in *The Sorrow and the Pity*. The obvious example, however, is the discrepancy between the American newsreel showing President Truman declaring that Americans will not be making friends with the Germans and all the interviews surrounding it justifying the hiring of Nazis by the Counter Intelligence Corps. It is also the newsreel images of American and Soviet soldiers making friends as the real enemy of the American army is already the Soviet and Communist influence in Europe. It is finally the opposition of a recent newsreel showing Reagan honoring SS graves while the American Government is officially apologizing to France for having hired Barbie. Ophüls uses this kind of opposition mainly with regard to American politics. Apparently he chose not to use similar opposition between the official positions and the real lack of action regarding the Nazi hunt by French officials. Such constant discrepancies on the French side, mainly during Pompidou's and Giscard d'Estaing's presidencies, appear only in the verbal testimonies, but they could have been an easy target for such a kind of irony using newsreels in the montage itself. In this regard, Ophüls' choice is really to insist more on the responsibilities of the American secret services.

7) *Disjunction and irony between a testimony and what the audience knows:*

This type of irony plays a very important role in the film as at the time of its first projections, most audiences already knew quite a lot about the Holocaust, the Collaboration and the Cold War. A large part of *Hotel Terminus* audiences had already seen *Night and Fog*, *The Sorrow and the Pity*, *Shoah* or at least some film, documentary or docu-drama made about the Holocaust. Moreover, most of the spectators of this film do not represent average members of a population but various groups that had voluntarily made very clear political choices. The audience knows if the person who is talking was a convinced Collaborator, a secret service agent, a Résistant, a victim of Barbie, an SS, etc. Therefore Ophüls' interpretation and position are easier to identify in *Hotel Terminus* than they are in *The Sorrow and the Pity*. Mrs. Hemmerle for example is a more easily identifiable convinced Collaborator than Mrs. Solange was in *The Sorrow and the Pity*. Gusman is still and very clearly an SS while the French SS, de la Mazière, was expressing bad feelings about his past. American secret agents like Kolb never apologize for their past work while even the former Minister Lamirand—in *The Sorrow and the Pity*—did not feel too good about it, etc. Probably, as time goes by, it is less and less necessary for these people to fake remorse.

8) *Irony in a comment or in the way a question is asked:*

For many different reasons, this kind of irony is much more common in *Hotel Terminus* than in *The Sorrow and the Pity*. As we already saw, it is the main component of Ophüls' use of German traditional music and songs to comment on his film. It is also present in the interviews themselves. First, as we just saw, Ophüls often deals with former Collaborators or even direct friends of Barbie that do not express the least remorse for what they did and as time goes by, even see the way they acted as more and more natural. Faced with such aplomb, Ophüls is often led to make a direct ironic remark or to ask an ironic question in order to remind the witness and the audience that such behavior was and is not that simple and easy to justify.

When Zuchner, the former collaborator, explains that he is responsible for the release of some very influential Lyonnais from Nazi jails, Ophüls immediately asks him: "I have a feeling that in certain times one is much better off being rich and influential than poor and forgotten!" A little further, when after the reading of a statement by Robert Taylor saying that Barbie is "an honest man both intellectually and personally," Taylor comments: "I wish I could rewrite that." Ophüls immediately adds: "Perhaps especially right now!"

In these two examples as in every situation where this occurs, the interviewee does not react to Ophüls' ironic statement probably for two main reasons. Either they feel trapped, they know Ophüls is right and they cannot defend themselves logically any further (Taylor) or they feel that, Ophüls will never agree with them, that he is on the "other side," but they still want to try to take advantage of his film to justify themselves, expose their ideas, or just make some money out of the publicity they might get from the film (Zuchner, Hemmerle, Gusman, De Castro, Fiebelkorn, etc.)

Finally, Ophüls' ironic remarks often express the director's frustration or well withheld anger in front of the hundreds of obstacles he had to overcome or could not overcome during the making of his film. The clearer example of this occurs when he is trying to interview a former Nazi in the hallway of an apartment building, asking him what trouble a two year old girl could cause the Third Reich. The Nazi closes his door in front of the camera. Ophüls remains standing silent in front of the closed door and then adds "Merry Christmas!" This goes much further as Ophüls is sometimes forced to only show how many interviews were denied to him.

Ophüls' frustration is shown also with other segments that are not part of the film itself but that are included only to reveal the difficulties faced to make it. This is the case, for example, when a former neighbor of Barbie in Bolivia runs after Ophüls' crew in order to prevent them from filming his apartment building. Such an image of unusual violence in a film made out of otherwise quiet interviews, reveals both the support Barbie still enjoys in some circles and the concrete obstacles, besides facing silence, lies and distortions, one has to overcome in order to make a film about a Nazi.

Finally, in some instances, anti-Semitism or distortions are so obvious that Ophüls remains bewildered, speechless or cannot help adding a terse "I see!" This happens in at least three segments, during the interview of Gusman, still very proud of being an SS, with the American agent, Omrcamin, and with the French journalist, Albert Brun, both convinced that Barbie is nothing but the victim of a Jewish conspiracy.

9) *Irony in the staging of an interview:*
There are mainly two kinds of such staging: involuntary or "natural" but particularly convenient and voluntary ones. First, as we saw in the beginning of this analysis, it happens that many interviews were filmed during the Christmas season. Therefore, many witnesses (Johannes Schneider, Robert Taylor, Eugene Kolb and Wolfgang Gusman) are filmed next to a Christmas tree or some Christmas decorations. This is particularly ironic because the center and the unity of the film are represented by the murder of the Jewish children of Izieu. Therefore, without the witnesses noticing, the Christmas decorations constantly recall to the audience the Catholic faith of all of Barbie's friends, the total innocence of all children in general, and by an ironic extension, the absence and the killing of the Jewish children of Izieu. Such an effect cannot be considered as a trick played by Ophüls on his witnesses as they themselves accepted to be filmed in their own houses at Christmas time, with their own decorations. It is however to be noticed that none of the Résistants and none of Barbie's victims are interviewed in similar surroundings. Their

interviews are completely free of this type of irony and possibly contain no irony at all.

Considering staging consciously and voluntarily organized by Ophüls, I could find only one rare example with, in fact, what could be called the only "non-interview" of the film. It is the case of the mocked phone conversation with a former SS and CIC agent's wife in front of the building in Memmingen where former Nazis were hired by the American secret services (Ophüls playing the role of the woman and an assistant playing Ophüls' role). This interview could not be taped. We are not even completely sure it really took place. Then, even if it had taken place, the background does not correspond to the "natural" background for this witness. It is imposed only by the coherence of the film and had the interview really taken place, one can imagine it would have been in totally different surroundings. As such a radically ironic and somewhat surprising scene sticks out from *Hotel Terminus* and is totally absent from *The Sorrow and the Pity*, it leads us directly to the final analysis of the weaknesses, the strength and the originality of this documentary.

In spite of its very powerful interviews and montage, *Hotel Terminus* has not provoked the same enthusiasm from its audience as *The Sorrow and the Pity* or Lanzmann's *Shoah* have. I attribute this to different factors. First of all, the film was shown after Barbie's trial. By the time they saw this documentary, five years after Barbie's arrest, most of the audiences knew about Barbie's life, they knew about his police work in South America and they knew about the Collaboration in France. There are very few segments in the film that could have shocked the audience in the way *The Sorrow and the Pity* did when it came out right after the fall of De Gaulle. Since that time, French audiences became very much aware of the Collaboration. The mention of *Gueule tordue*, a French executioner, and interviews of Hemmerle and Zuchner could be directly interpreted as part of the historical truth, without any controversy.

Moreover, this film insists on the inhumanity of a German officer—Klaus Barbie—helped by some vicious French misfits, and it also gives a large part to the heroism of some members of the Résistance, producing a balance between Collaborators and Résistants that is definitely favorable to the latter. As some critics said of *The Sorrow and the Pity*, one could not reproach *Hotel Terminus* with leading the audience to believe that all the French population collaborated with the Germans. For this reason also, *Hotel Terminus* could not stir a violent controversy or benefit from the success of scandal.

Then, the fact that the film is entirely centered around the murder of the children of Izieu forbids any denial of the reality of the events it depicts. The problem here is not any more to decide how much of the French population really collaborated with the Nazis, supported Pétain, ignored the destiny of the Jews or resisted in some way invasion and occupation. The horrifying heart of *Hotel Terminus*, Izieu, is absolutely no subject for interpretation or ideological debate. This is enough to impose respect and eliminate any kind of subtle arguing about what was the right attitude at that time. The problem here is not any more to find out if there were different possible choices or to evaluate if Pétain's government spared France more atrocities. In front of the murder of forty one or of thousands of children, such questions become systematically absurd and atrocious. This also eliminates much controversy around the film itself.

The most controversial part of the film may have been Ophüls' depiction of the considerable help and protection Barbie enjoyed from the American secret services. Unfortunately, *Hotel Terminus* has still to be shown on American TV. In fact, one can hardly imagine a worse time and place for this movie to come out than during the nineteen-eighties when America made Oliver North a national hero. In such a context, one can doubt that the interviews of Kolb and others saying that Barbie was such a great guy merely because he was a safe anti-Communist would have been very controversial. Moreover, as American audiences watching videotapes or going to movie theaters to see this film are already made up of the minority who is very much aware of the events it depicts in its details and consequences, such a film will not reach a large American audience as long as it will not be distributed in major movie theaters or shown on American TV. It seems, therefore, that as long as TV programmers are more worried about ratings, popularity, the box office record of such a film, and the support of sponsors than they are by the actual quality of what is shown, the public who most needs to see such a documentary will have very little chance to actually see it. It is true, however, that *Hotel Terminus* is not completely exempt from the characteristics of commercial cinema and that it is distributed by some major video-stores in this country. Such characteristics often play against the best qualities of the film itself while they certainly help sell it.

I already mentioned the first example of a commercial element of the film, the subtitle of the film itself: "The Life and Times of Klaus Barbie." Undeniably, such a title sells the documentary as the biography of a Nazi, some sort of a anti-hero in horror and abjection, and a depiction of Nazi regime, all categories that have produced many best sellers and popular films in the past. Fortunately, the documentary is not in itself the biography of a Nazi as it remains all along faithful to its main title and to its tribute to the children of Izieu. The film starts indeed with Raymond Lévy stating: "Barbie's life in itself is of no interest to me."

The second and more important aspect that makes it more similar to a commercial film or documentary is its initial appearance as an investigation. Unlike *The Sorrow and the Pity*, *Hotel Terminus* can be partially watched as an investigation of one man's past. It follows in part a precise chronology that is the biography of its main character. It gathers testimonies to find the truth about one mysterious man. However, it is to be immediately added that the spectator watching this film with such a thread will be very disappointed. *Hotel Terminus* is not a segment of *60 Minutes*. There are indeed entire segments or chapters of Barbie's life that are missing in the film mainly because once again, the goal of the film is not merely to tell the life of Klaus Barbie in itself. Everything written on this particular point in the preceding pages should be enough to prove that.

Therefore, the weakest chapter of the film is probably the part that looks the most like an investigation while the deepest structure of the film goes much further. I am alluding to the interviews of the former CIC agents. This chapter links the first and the second part of the film. It is an extremely difficult section to follow for the audience as no presentation reminds us what were the exact responsibilities of each man involved during and after the war. In order to really understand who is who and who did what, a spectator would have either to watch the film many times or to read the Ryan Report or any good book on the subject. The large majority of the spectators I talked to thought this segment was too long because it was very confusing.

In contrast, such a segment becomes much clearer and much more fascinating as soon as one starts paying attention to the disjunctions between various judgements on Barbie, all the arguments used by the many witnesses to justify their past, to project responsibility on others, to live in peace with their memories or simply to explain that Barbie is a victim of a Jewish conspiracy because he was not such a bad guy after all. It remains, however, that the weakest parts of this film are the few segments where the montage seems to be ruled more by Ophüls' own investigation rather than by his study of the various attitudes that allowed Barbie to continue his "job" on various continents even after Izieu.

There are mostly three reasons for the confusion sometimes created by *Hotel Terminus*. First of all, Ophüls interviews a very large number of witnesses without always recalling who they are, how they came to be close to Klaus Barbie and what their responsibilities were. Second, the telling of Barbie's life and the presentation of his times brings Ophüls to analyzing many much broader subjects such as: the truth about the Jean Moulin affair, the rivalries within the Résistance, the organization and the responsibilities of the CIC, the sympathy governments in Bolivia and Peru for the Nazis, etc. Each time the film dedicates a long segment to one of these themes the spectator loses the relationship between these events, all the points made and their precise relationship with Klaus Barbie's life itself. *Hotel Terminus* cannot provide all the elements to fully analyze such complex issues. In these sequences the film is presenting too much and too little information at the same time.

Finally, *Hotel Terminus* creates some ruptures both in its spatial and chronological continuities that sometimes make the film very confusing. Because of their constant come and go between Barbie's life, his times, and trial, a few segments that are more clearly a study of choices and passions seem misplaced. This is the case with a debate between various Lyonnais and journalists around a table in Lyon, situated close to the end of the second part of the film. Before this we see interviews of Barbie's daughter and daughter-in-law talking about him both during and after images of the trial. According to the predominant chronology, the spectator is led to believe that this segment is about Barbie's trial and the trial of Nazi Germany. However, the discussion of the Lyonnais takes us back to the now abandoned theme of living in Lyon during the Occupation. For this reason, this discussion brutally breaks the chronology.

This segment makes sense in the montage only if one notices Mrs. Crozier's—Barbie's daughter-in-law—last sentence about Barbie being a Nazi: "I had an idea but I did not know. There was a discordance for us." After this, in the segment in Lyon we hear a group of old Lyonnais describing their main worry of the time: eating and also not letting the Germans eat their lobster. The opening ironic theme of the sequence is: "Nazis are also good fathers and they were very bad because they ate our lobster." The common theme of these two segments (Mrs. Crozier and the group of Lyonnais) explain why various people did not realize what atrocities men like Barbie were able to commit. However, Ophüls' rupture of both spatial and chronological continuity in this sequence make it extremely confusing. Then, at the end of this mundane conversation, Ophüls takes advantage of the remarks of a young student on the divisions of the Résistance to assure the transition back to Barbie's trial.

The film goes back to the heart of Barbie's trial: the definition-redefinition of the crime against humanity through the killing of the children of Izieu. This theme provides the perfect ending for the film joining at the same time the main reason why Barbie was arrested at the end of his long life and the real heart of the film: Izieu. *Hotel Terminus* ends as it started, not as Barbie's biography but as a tribute to the memory of the children of Izieu and of the victims of the Nazis. In this respect, its long interview of the rejected witness of the round-up, Julien Favet, plays a critical role.

Julien Favet was a witness of the arrest of the children of Izieu. He was however rejected as a witness in the trial for three major reasons: what he saw happened in forty seconds, it was forty years ago and he later had a lobotomy. In consequence, his testimony could not be considered "realistic" and Barbie's lawyer, Jacques Vergès, ridiculed him.

This rejection represents one of the most important threats to the memory of the Holocaust for three reasons. First, the Nazis knew that because their crimes were so horrible they would be hard to believe and it would be hard even for the survivors to convince others that the Holocaust really took place. Every survivor has many "unrealistic" but horribly true stories to tell. Simon Wiesenthal's biography is filled with such occurrences as, according to the strict organization of the extermination by the Nazis, a Jew could survive only by some extraordinary and unexpected chance. Second, as is often repeated during the film, the Holocaust took place more than forty years ago and this time lapse is used as an argument either to put in question the memory of the witnesses or to diminish the relevance to the present of the crimes committed then. Finally, ever since their return from the camps, the survivors have been looked at by many as people who were unable to give an accurate account of the events precisely because they were a part of it. Others would even sarcastically argue that, if they survived, there must have been "a reason."

This last argument was particularly clear during the debate following the showing of the film about Simon Wiesenthal on French TV in April 1990. In this debate, two survivors, Simone Veil and M. Corrin testified that for at least forty years after the war, they stopped talking about what they had lived through the camps because no one was really paying attention to what they were saying. They were often accused of distorting the truth, of making up stories, of surviving because of some secret and shameful reason. Unfortunately, the Nazis were partly right. It was and still is sometimes extremely difficult for the survivors to be heard and believed, partly for the same reasons Julien Favet's testimony was rejected at Barbie's trial.

As the very last images of the film show, victims like Mme. Lagrange are often still isolated and misunderstood. The neighbor she is talking to remains far away, talking from her third floor window in her apartment in Lyon. She feels no need to come any closer. She feels bad about what happened but it remains a story of the past. This situation is quite ironic as even "more than forty years later" and in spite of all the sorrow expressed, the neighbor feels sorry but remains distant behind her closed door. Then the film finally ends with a tribute to the people who tried to help, as a somewhat desperate call to imitate Mme. Lagrange's other neighbor who opened her door to try at least to save a twelve year old girl. The film is then dedicated to the minority of thousands of French Gentiles who, even hopelessly, tried to help. Such an ending is very similar to the final lesson of *Night and Fog* and very different from the ironic parallel ending of *The Sorrow and the Pity*. The last words of *Hotel Terminus* allude to a group totally absent from the rest of the film but it underlines a slightly more optimistic tone in Ophüls' work as Barbie was finally tried and condemned for his crimes, even if it was "more than forty years" after the war.

8.   Ambiguity and Mastery
in Three Renowned
Fiction Films

a. Louis Malle's *Lacombe Lucien* and *Goodbye Children*

Within Louis Malle's eclectic work, *Lacombe Lucien* and *Goodbye Children* clearly indicate the persistence of very personal and mature themes and techniques. Both films were in Malle's mind for years before he was actually able to make them. Moreover on a very personal level, as we saw in the introduction to this study, *Lacombe Lucien* could also be read as a preparatory work for *Goodbye Children*. As the masterpiece of a director in his full artistic maturity, the latter gathers all the characteristics of Malle's work, including its very controversial ambiguities. However, mainly because of its focusing on the victims rather than on the psychology of the executioners, this film was not surrounded by any of the violent controversy and the scandal accompanying the release of *Lacombe Lucien*. One could argue, nevertheless, that within Malle's work these films are not contradictory at all; they offer two opposite but complementary angles on two similar situations pertaining to the same general interpretation of life in France during the Occupation.

Both films, for example, are very different and yet comparable in their representation of the persecution of the Jews. According to Annette Insdorf:

> *Lacombe Lucien*'s references to Judaism contain no positive resonance. "Monsieur is a rich and stingy Jew" is how the easy-going fascist Jean-Bernard (Stéphane Bouy) introduces Horn to Lucien (while taking money from the tailor). When Lucien asks Horn, "Aren't the Jews the enemies of France?" Horn answers, "No, I am not" (as opposed to *we are* not). His identity is rooted

in having been the best tailor on Paris' chic Avenue
Pierre-Ier-de-Serbie, an assimilated individual of
exquisite taste (...) And the blond, blue-eyed France
[Horn's daughter] cries, "I'm fed up with being a Jew,"
before throwing herself tearfully into Lucien's open
arms (Insdorf 123).

In contrast, in *Goodbye Children*, Jean Bonnet hides but protects
and never denies his Jewish faith and identity. He hides himself
to pray at night. During a game in the courtyard, he openly takes
the defense of his friend "Négus" fighting "Richard Coeur de
Lion." But such differences are not irreconcilable.

If Horn seems to reject partially his Jewish identity—in
Lacombe Lucien—he is still furious when he sees that his
daughter might consider having a love affair with Lacombe.
When he insists that "he" is not an enemy of France, he knows
that the only idea of a Jew Lacombe can have is the one he was
given by anti-Semitic propaganda. He also knows that it is
useless to argue with men like Lacombe. His reply is addressed
to a man who learns only from his own experiences and from
anti-Semitic propaganda. In this context, Horn's reply can
therefore be interpreted as meaning: "I am not an enemy of
France and you know I am a Jew therefore Jews are not enemies
of France and your propaganda is a lie."

As for Horn being characterized as a "rich and stingy Jew,"
this judgment is formulated by a Collaborator and it cannot be
taken as Malle's own representation of this man in his film. Horn
and his daughter are Jewish and they do not try to deny it. They
are assimilated Jews both desperately fighting to escape from
their executioners. If the references to Judaism in this film do not
contain *direct* "positive resonance," Horn and his daughter cannot
either be considered, like Annette Insdorf suggests, as assimilated
Jews rejecting their identity.

Regarding the relationship between Lacombe and France
(Horn's daughter), it can never be characterized as a loving one.
When France declares: "I am fed up with being a Jew!" it is to
be remembered that she is talking to Lacombe in 1944 and not
directly addressing a general audience in 1974. France is fed up
with being "labelled" as a Jew according to the definitions of

Vichy. She is not referring to a general definition of Jewish identity, but fed up with being trapped in that short period of history. The film does not say anything about her personal conception of her Jewish identity. Her relationship with Lacombe can be interpreted as a desperate attempt to escape from history, to save her family and then her grandmother by showing Lacombe that maybe he himself was trapped by propaganda and circumstances.

This brings us indeed to one of the most controversial aspects of both of Malle's films: the feeling that the key actions of his heroes are only the results of circumstances. This poses serious problems when it comes to confronting the actions of the Résistance, victims or bystanders, with actions of Collaborators.

However, Horn and his daughter, like Jean, live in the same constant state of terror knowing that, at any time, French officials or Nazis can come and arrest them. They are all presented as Jews trying in their own desperate way to escape from the same "creatures of amoral impulse" (Insdorf, 123).

In general, the audiences of *Goodbye Children* did not directly perceive this unity of both works because of Malle's fundamental style of not showing the technical artifices he uses and having his entire film evolve around the psychological analysis of one or two characters. Therefore, *Lacombe Lucien* became automatically a "scandalous" film on a French Gestapo agent and *Goodbye Children* a "masterpiece" on two innocent victims of the Nazis. However, in both films, the French boys who became members of the Gestapo (Lucien in *Lacombe Lucien*, and Joseph in *Goodbye Children*) are both presented as being led by a chain of circumstances or accidents to collaborating with the Nazis. They are not presented as being totally responsible for the atrocities they support or commit. According to the narrations of both films, their actions can be explained, understood and may be justified by a chain of "circumstances." The persistence of such an extremely controversial position of the director in both films did not provoke the same reaction from audiences partly because this point was the central focus of *Lacombe Lucien* while in *Goodbye Children* it is only a part of the final episode of the film otherwise centered on the victims and bystanders.

In order to go beyond the very partial analyses contemporary to the release of both works, the analysis and the understanding of both films should not be separated. *Lacombe Lucien* must be read beyond the interpretations and the various scandals of the seventies that followed the release of *The Sorrow and the Pity* and the reinterpretation of the Occupation at that time. *Goodbye Children* must be seen beyond the interpretations of the late eighties, shortly following the release of *Shoah* and the trial of Klaus Barbie, the murderer of the children of Izieu. Within Malle's work, both films constitute a major chapter within the evolution of the representation of the Occupation and the Holocaust in French cinema. In this perspective, the scandal caused by the first work and the almost unanimous praise provoked by the second shed new light on what audiences can or cannot accept in a film dealing with the Holocaust.

These two films reveal very clearly the three main characteristics generally noted by critics in Malle's style: its stylistic "classicism"; the importance it gives to the gaze or psychological analysis of teenagers; and its very personal rhythms and interpretation. The popular success of Malle's films both in France and in the United States leads us to consider how these characteristics apply both to *Lacombe Lucien* and to *Goodbye Children* and how they are also part of the commercial success of films that deal very closely with the representation of the Holocaust.

In his analysis of Louis Malle's complete works, René Prédal noticed that the main traits of classicism "characterize rather well" the films of the French director.[74] The traits he lists are: a great rigor in composition; a search for spontaneity and verisimilitude; a taste for a just measure; subtlety in the moral and psychological analysis; purity and clarity in the style as well as admiration of the ancients (Prédal, 1989: 53). Applied to *Lacombe Lucien* and *Goodbye Children*, these characteristics seem indeed to work very well. However, they also indicate the limitations and the originality of these works.

One of the first or most obvious qualities of *Goodbye Children* noticed by general audiences is that it clearly narrates a story with well-mastered logic of suspense, mystery and positive, negative, partial or total identification to the various characters. As opposed to the films of many French directors of Malle's generation—directors like Resnais or Godard—the traditional laws of narration are here well respected. In both films the story line remains linear and the events presented follow the chronological order of the main action. The psychology of the characters seems to be very coherent even when it appears to surprise us.

Goodbye Children is generally read as a personal telling of the discovery of the persecution of the Jews by an adolescent through the story of a friendship. Some spectators could also see in it the first film about Père Jean (in reality Father Jacques) and the Collège des Carmes, in Avon. It could also be read as a personal testimony on the persecution of the Jews during the Occupation; the brutal discovery of the reality of this period by a teenager and perhaps as a presentation of various personal attitudes and mentalities during that period. All of these aspects however are clearly and totally subsumed under the only story of the film, that of Julien's investigation about Jean Bonnet's real identity.

Julien is present in each and every shot of the film. The audience is told nothing Julien is not. The audience can understand historical or cultural allusions only if it stops identifying completely with Julien in order to refer to what it knows now about this period or the general history of the Holocaust. It is the case for example when, close to the end of the film, Jean Bonnet tells Julien that he did not see his father for almost two years. As we were told earlier in the film that the scene takes place in January 1944, Jean's line becomes an allusion to the large roundups of Jews in the summer of 1942 like the one of the Vélodrome d'Hiver in Paris. Obviously, as Julien was often characterized by his ignorance of what was really happening to the Jews, he cannot understand this allusion.

This is to say that even if it tells different stories at the same time, the functioning of this film is based on the identification of the audience to one character and to the telling of one story. The only times the audience is allowed to differentiate what it knows, feels or sees from Julien's experiences are moments in which a general historical reestablishing sequence is necessary in order to situate the narration within historical truth itself. Thanks to this process the film can never be reduced to what could be seen merely as the telling of the partial or imperfect memories of a child. Indeed, this story is first being told by Louis Malle as an adult remembering his past. At the same time, the audience is never allowed to forget about the main question Julien is asking himself and that is moving the film ahead: Who really is Jean Bonnet and why is he hiding his real identity?

As a classical, rigorous and linear composition hiding the technical devices used behind a linear and well-centered plot, *Goodbye Children* is in great part structured like a seventeenth century French tragedy, the epitome of French classicism in literature. The introductory scenes clearly expose the question and the elements that will be developed slowly throughout the film. In his study, René Prédal found the same progression in all of Malle's fiction films:

> In the beginning many micro-sequences follow each other and either they push forward the action (...), or they introduce the characters (...) After this continuous line, Malle develops large sequences during which the action does not progress anymore, but this does not mean that they are static scenes. The machine is jammed and people stop by the side of the well marked road they were following without thinking. The heart of the film is made out of extremely dense sequences elaborated with a particularly sharp sense of details (...). Then the climax brings the resolution of the crisis, most of the time in a prospective manner (Prédal, 108).

Such a structure is very similar to that of a classical tragedy with its expository scene, its long analysis of characters, the irreversible and progressive tension build up and the sudden and violent resolution of the crisis through death in the end. Two more elements reinforce this structure: the premonitory scene and the omnipresence of death through the films.

In most classical French or Greek tragedies the dream of a character or a prediction announces a threatening, mysterious but unavoidable end. Regarding this point and *Goodbye Children*, Louis Malle recently declared: "I tried to reveal through a series of simple images how, little by little, the film became darker and darker, as when clouds progressively accumulate in the sky" (Decock, 673). In the opening scenes of *Goodbye Children*, the pupils are being read the story of Saint Simon, *Stylite*. The reading starts with the line: "Woe betide him who is laughing now because he will soon be crying." Julien laughs at this prediction like all the other pupils, except Jean Bonnet. Julien gets up and mocks the solitary Saint spending the rest of his life isolated from the world, standing on a top of a column in the middle of the desert. Only in the end of the film will he and the audience understand the meaning of this prediction. In a similar way, when we hear Julien's mother say in the introductory sequence "Goodbye, children" to her sons and, shortly after, Père Jacques say: "Goodnight, children," the audience is lead to believe that the meaning of the title lies in the story of a separation in which a small group of children and Père Jacques will play a key role. These two scenes subtly create a tension and announce the final and tragic "Goodbye, children!" said by Père Jacques when he is arrested at the end of the movie.

Such direct and indirect predictions create in the film itself a subtle feeling for the constant presence of death. Like Laurent at the sanatorium in *Murmur of the Heart* (1971), Julien believes that he is the only one thinking about death in his school: "I am the only one who thinks about death!" (at the beginning of the treasure hunt scene, in *Goodbye Children*). Before that, at the public bath, Julien is shown in a bath tub, thinking of the music teacher he has a crush on. At the same time he feels jealous of Jean who seems to be a gifted pianist. When a young priest asks him to hurry to give his place to someone else, Julien fakes a suicide attempt by pretending he is drowning in order to scare the man waiting for his turn. When he is pulled out of the water, Julien has a hard on. He looks straight in the eyes at the embarrassed priest who asks him to hurry and he adds: "It is not my fault, the soap does not foam!"

This scene condenses in a few minutes a complicated intricacy of sexuality and sensitivity with jealousy, a slight anti-clericalism and death drives. A similar situation is encountered again when the two boys enjoy secretly reading the *Arabian Nights* as these very sensual stories are told by Scheherazade who is trying to escape from death through the telling of imaginary and erotic tales. As many teenagers, Julien enjoys playing with the idea of death until the day he will really and directly be confronted with it through a real loss. Until then it remains a very mysterious and intriguing concept. On this point obviously, Jean Bonnet's attitude is radically different. As he will admit later in the film, Jean is constantly scared. He is never shown "playing" with the idea of death because he already knows too well what it represents. His readings of *The Arabian Nights* make up another desperate attempt to escape from death through imagination while the fascination this text has for Julien is a much more confused one.

For these reasons, I would not say like René Prédal that Jean and Julien become very close because of their common sense of fright. As the film constantly shows, Julien has only an extremely vague feeling of what Jean is going through and there is no way these two boys can experience the same fright. I would rather say that they are both obsessed with death in two opposite ways and that this obsession leads them to a better understanding of each other's feeling. In contrast to Jean, Julien is extremely curious about physical pain (hurting himself with his compass and staring at his running blood) and he acknowledges that he often thinks actively about death. After being scared by a wild boar and Germans in the woods, Julien brags about it with his friends. Jean does not.

On the other hand, the idea of death is one Jean is violently scared of and cannot escape from. Jean is the only student shown praying with fervor. He never talks about death. He says he thinks about it because he is constantly trying to escape from it feeling that somehow, in the end, *"they* will catch him anyway." Jean nevertheless feels that Julien is the only one who can understand the constant terror he lives in because Julien is in his own way scared and mysteriously fascinated by death.

The turning point in their relationship is when the two teenagers experience together the same fear of death. This happens when they are lost in the forest during a treasure hunt. Together, at sun down, they are suddenly faced with a real death threat, a wild black boar ready to charge them. They both hide in the dark and the cold, behind a fallen tree. The boar turns around and runs away. At this point, the friendship between the two boys deepens as they understand better each other's basic fear. However, this understanding remains very intuitive as in the following sequence, when German soldiers find the two children on the road, Jean is the only one who runs away from them as Julien still does not understand exactly what Jean is afraid of.

The first scenes of the film also provide the audience with all the elements that will be combined and the problems that will be developed throughout the narration. Some of the main themes presented during the introductory scene preceding the opening credits are: the absence of the father (in the train station), the physical love of the mother and the revolt against her authority (Julien telling his mother "I hate you" and then hugging her), initiation to adult life by a sibling and friends (the brother smoking on the platform with a friend), separation, isolation and enclosure of children's lives (the departing train, the dead and cold winter landscapes).

After the credits, the first scenes of the film add a few more themes. After this, no new element will be introduced in the narration that will develop irreversibly towards its tragic end. These new elements are presented in the first scenes taking place in the dormitory, at church and in the classroom. These are indeed the three key locations where the education given by the monks will confront the children with three different kinds of discipline: sensual, moral and intellectual. It is within this framework that the children will invent their own lives. In order of appearance the themes are: the Occupation and the black market among children; sexuality (some children hiding a picture of a naked woman); the mysterious arrival of the three children to be hidden; the mystery about Jean Bonnet's real identity; the central role of Père Jacques protecting the children; the importance of reading in the relationship between Julien and Jean; a slight anti-clericalism mixed with a sincere admiration for Père Jacques (a child faints during mass because he had to fast); and Julien's fascination with death (staring at his own blood).

From that point on, all the themes presented will reappear later and intertwine closely in order to build up the tension leading, in the end, to the arrest of the Jewish children and of Père Jacques. Moreover, for the spectator who already has some knowledge of Malle's previous work, some of these scenes suggest some major interpretations that are not otherwise clearly noticeable. It is the case for example when Julien's mother tells her son, in the introductory scene, that she would like to be able to dress as a boy in order to go with him to school. She then adds "it would be our secret." This sentence recalls directly the scene of incest in Malle's *Murmur of the Heart* (*Le Souffle au coeur*, 1971) after which the mother declares to her son "it will be our secret." In this film also the father is constantly absent, the young boy is initiated to sexuality and adulthood by his older brothers and he is constantly required by his mother herself to understand why he has to be separated from her.

After this line, the relationship between Julien and his mother takes on an ambiguous aspect tied to its underlying links of incestuous drives. Such an ambiguous sensuality both needed and rejected is later alluded to through two different scenes when Julien smells his mother's letter and when, after the restaurant scene, he tells Jean that his mother is crazy while it is obvious he suffers a great deal from being separated from her. Other themes just alluded to in *Goodbye Children* gain more importance for an audience familiar with Malle's work. It is the case, for example, with the link between solitary sexual games and reading or the obsession of a central character with death. This last point plays a key role in *My Dinner with André* (1981) which contains a few references to the Holocaust. André also admits that he was "always thinking about death." One of the most important stories he tells concerns his own burying alive, "like in a deathcamp" and his discovery that New York is comparable to a death camp built by the inmates themselves. All of these elements are then unified and wrapped in Malle's characteristic classicism.

The distinctive classicism of Malle's style can then be developed from the central role played in his film by a clear and linear narration, both fictitious and real, articulated around key problems dealing with death, sexuality and morality. All the themes introduced at the very beginning of the film will intertwine according to the narration, from the questions raised at the beginning to their partial answer in the end through the story of the central character, Julien, and of his relationship with Jean. Even the montage of the film will be put at the service of this progression in which the mastery of the director consists in never letting his virtuosity get in the way of the general strength of the film as a psychological analysis with a linear plot.

René Prédal characterized Malle's editing as a "tight cut that leaves generally little room to montage inspirations" (Prédal, 1989: 54). Malle himself acknowledged that:

> Since *Vie privée* and *Feu follet* I absolutely insisted on the audience being able to forget the camera, which supposes the acquisition of a certain mastery in order to obtain a cinematographic style that is so fluid during the shooting and the editing that one would forget the sensation of this recording machine so terribly present in some works (quoted by Prédal, 1989: 60).

This classical idea of hiding the mechanism of a work in order to insist on the *naturel*, the spontaneity, of the action taking place, is also a distinctive mark of Malle's film *My Dinner with André*: "Suzanne Baron and I did an enormous amount of editing so that it (*My Dinner with André*) would look like a spontaneous conversation without feeling the joints" (Prédal, 1989: 61). Such an attachment to a certain tradition of quality and linear transparency in French cinema clearly separates this aspect of Malle's work from the aesthetic of rupture that characterizes in part the French New Wave.

In consequence of this attachment to both the richness and the apparent simplicity of the film, smooth transitions and announcement of upcoming turning points play a key role in the film. On many occasions, a slow panning of the camera to the left or to the right guarantees a very soft transition between two scenes. It is the case, for example, with the scene during which the pupils must go to the shelter during an air bombing. The camera pans slowly to the right from the teacher to Julien and Jean, from the pure narration of an ordinary school day during the Occupation to the analysis of a relationship between two teenagers during the war.

On other occasions, the soundtrack of a shot expands, logically or not, on the following one, providing also a barely noticeable link between two scenes. In some cases, the sound track announces clearly an important upcoming scene. It is the case for example when we hear in the background the violin playing Saint Saëns' theme while the parents are gathering in the courtyard of the school. A few minutes later, the same music comes to the foreground as it is accompanying the projection of Charlie Chaplin's *The Immigrant*. At the same time of course, Malle follows very closely all the basic rules of a realistic filming of narration such as alternating the shots of two conversing characters or following a movement on two consecutive shots through the preservation of the same direction (from the left to the right or the right to the left).

Another aspect of Malle's classicism is his attachment to the text. Like Alain Resnais, Malle is known for working closely with famous writers or for basing many of his fiction films on novels. However, Malle very often worked with writers in order to adapt to the screen a text that had already been published. In contrast, when Resnais worked with famous writers, both the text and the scenario were created at the same time and only for the purpose of making a film. Malle's work is also very different, in this respect, from the New Wave cinema as it remains very faithful to literary works that preceded the making of his films.

This was the case for the making of *Un ascenseur pour l'échafaud* (1957; based on a novel by Noël Calef; dialogues by the novelist Roger Nimier), *Les Amants* (1958; based on the novel *Point de lendemain* by Dominique Vivant-Denon; dialogues by the novelist Louise de Vilmorin), *Zazie dans le métro* (1959; written with the scenarist Paul Rappeneau; based on the famous novel by Raymond Queneau), *Le Feu follet* (1963; based on the novel of Drieu La Rochelle), *Viva Maria* (1965; written with the very successful scenarist Jean-Claude Carrière), *Le voleur* (1967; based on the novel of Georges Darien), *William Wilson* (1967; written with the novelist and scenarist Daniel Boulanger; based on the short story by Edgar Allan Poe). In all of these cases, a text with a strong literary value existed before the film and in some, Malle was helped by famous scenarists and writers.

In the end of this long series, *Murmur of the Heart*, *Lacombe Lucien* and *Goodbye Children* form a somewhat contrasting group. No literary text existed before the scenarios of these films, even if Malle worked closely with the young novelist Patrick Modiano for the script of *Lacombe Lucien*. For all three films, the text was either totally or in great part written by Malle and based on a personal experience and memories. All three are based on the evolution of teenagers isolated in an enclosed world and confronted with the absurdity of the adult world. Finally all three are also characterized by the quality of their writing. *Murmur of the Heart* was nominated in 1972 for the best scenario award in Cannes, *Lacombe Lucien* was written with the Collaboration of an already famous and much appreciated writer and the scenario of *Goodbye Children* was published by a French literary institution, the Editions Gallimard.

Murmur of the Heart and *Goodbye Children* are also filled with direct or more subtle allusions to famous literary texts (allusions to Boris Vian, Proust, *The Story of O*, Dumas, Péguy, *The Arabian Nights*, etc.). Reading, as an isolated, secret and sensual activity, plays a key role for the central characters of both films. In the first film, Laurent masturbates while reading *J'irai cracher sur vos tombes* by Boris Vian. In the latter, Julien and Jean hide at night to read and fall asleep on the most sensual descriptions of *The Arabian Nights*. The case of *Lacombe Lucien* is different as the main character of the film is not educated and never reads a book. Malle himself described both his character and the actor playing his role in a similar manner:

> For me, Lacombe is not unintelligent, but his culture is direct, it comes only from his own experience as a little farmer without any references (...). Pierre Blaise himself, this totally uncultured boy, would become totally fascinating when he would start talking about hunting thrushes, bird migrations and his tricks to hide and take them by surprise (quoted by Prédal, 1989: 112).

It is however in order to write the story of this young man without any literary culture or reference that Malle felt the need to ask for the help of a novelist specialized on the period of the Occupation. According to Malle himself:

> It was a difficult scenario and, without Patrick Modiano, I could not have succeeded. He came with his own world, his instincts of ambiguous situations, a certain perspective on shady zones of the Occupation. With him the characters took shape, and the narration gained a certain thickness and a sinuosity it did not have (Prédal, 1989: 31).

These words make it clear that for Malle, the literary qualities of his scenario and of the text written for a film is directly linked to the realism of the characters, the rigorous structure of a linear narration and the regular progression of suspense. Compared to modern literary movements of the early sixties like the New Novel, all these criteria remain very classical, almost directly opposed to, for example, the cinematographic and literary works of Alain Robbe-Grillet or Marguerite Duras. Still in opposition to these writers who became film makers, Malle seems to be a film director who progressively became a writer, writing films with the rigor of a classical narration, very often looking for the best cinematographic "equivalencies"[75] to a text written by a novelist or later by Malle himself.

Indeed, all of these "literary" qualities and the narration itself serve best another characteristic of classical literature: the rigor of a psychological analysis. To critics that were reproaching him with political ambiguities or historical errors both in *Lacombe Lucien* and in *Goodbye Children*, Malle answered that his films were not meant to be ideological analyses or precise historical reconstitutions of the Occupation but rather very detailed psychological analyses of sometimes illogical characters. However, even seen from such an angle, both films are not exempt of many embarrassing ambiguities.

According to René Prédal's study supported by a long interview with Louis Malle, *Lacombe Lucien* presents us with an "edifying story about love and death" which Malle treats "only at a psychological level, evacuating carefully any theorization" (Prédal, 1989: 112). Within Malle's work, this film tells us once again the story of an isolated character during a few decisive days, living in a well-delimited space, at the limit of two worlds (the Occupation and the Liberation) and of two ages (childhood and adulthood). As he did in his other films, Malle refuses here to impose a moral judgement on his central character. As always, still according to Prédal, he prefers to "show" rather than "demonstrate" (Prédal, 1989: 53).

However, such a remark ignores the fact that any "showing" of a reality through a rigorous and linear narration of the behavior of one individual is forced to present a succession of actions that inevitably produce a succession of events, reactions to these events, chains of causes and effects that constitute in themselves a subjective interpretation and a demonstration. Even if many of these reactions seem "illogical," the order in which the director presents them is never totally free of ideological choices mostly because, as Marcel Ophüls noted: "Life is infinite but film is not."

It is true that Lacombe's enrollment in the Gestapo cannot be explained by ideological reasoning. This however does not free this character from individual responsibility towards crimes he did not directly commit but directly supported by reinforcing the power of the men and women who committed them. For this reason, Lacombe cannot be excused just because, according to Prédal, "he did not commit the irreparable." Indeed it is to be remembered that for many spectators, Lacombe did commit "the irreparable" because it does not require any formal education, ideological conviction or literary culture to realize that the active support of terror and torture constitutes in itself a crime. In consequence I refuse to consider as Prédal does that Malle's character, as opposed to "real" Collaborators, "could maybe benefit from extenuating circumstances" (Prédal, 1989: 121).

This question remains controversial if we consider not only Lacombe as a character but Malle's own interpretation of his film itself. In a conversation with René Prédal, Malle described the days Lacombe spends in the Gestapo as follows:

> It is merely a brief moment in his (Lacombe's) life during which he can enjoy the extreme pleasure of having some money and a gun in order to terrorize the bourgeois of the city. Future does not exist for him; he would not know how to change his mind: this question does not even cross his mind (...). The archaic aspect of Lucien comes truly from the dregs of history and you can find him in every troubled time: the Arabs who helped the parachutists during the Battle of Algiers found themselves, for similar reasons, exactly in the same situation. So, I always thought that the film was almost Marxist in the sense that it shows that the low proletariat traditionally constitutes the troops of fascism. See also the character of the Black man: in this gang of the Gestapo in which Lucien cannot assimilate very well, he is his only friend because both of them are here for the same motives (Prédal, 1989: 118).

According to these statements, Lacombe became a member of the Gestapo only because he is a social misfit who wants to "terrorize the bourgeois" and because he was previously rejected by the Résistance. Such a justification of the character is totally insufficient for many different reasons.

First of all, such an explanation justifies Lacombe's behavior by making the victims partially responsible for the monstrosity of their executioner. According to such a logic, Lucien is a Collaborator because of the Résistance who rejected him and he persecutes the old Jewish man and his daughter as they reject him because of his lack of social status. As Rosset's interview shows in Ophüls' *Hotel Terminus* (Rosset is a member of the Front National), such reasoning leads to the most traditional demonstration used by anti-Semites to explain that the Jews themselves are responsible for anti-Semitism. In a similar way, according to a former German officer in *The Sorrow and the Pity*, the Germans had to use terror against the Résistance in Clermont-Ferrand because the Résistance embodied a bunch of terrorists. These are the dangerous and final consequences of such reasoning, even if Malle would probably never support them.

According to Malle's explanation, Lacombe is a social misfit who enjoys "terrorizing the bourgeois." This last expression put Lucien on the same level as the bourgeois adolescents in *The Murmur of the Heart* or the revolting students of May 1968 in France. Even if it is partly correct, this explanation does not suffice to justify Lacombe's choices. If he is basically anti-bourgeois, Lacombe is a Collaborator who works mainly with the local bourgeoisie and aristocracy. If they despise him, he never revolts against them. He never terrorizes the local bourgeoisie but two Jews from Paris. Moreover, he uses the money and the power he gets from the Gestapo to force this very well-educated man and his daughter to accept him as their possible equal. Indeed, Lacombe never revolts against anything in order to "terrorize the bourgeois." If that was the case he would act very differently and he could easily find ideological justifications for his behavior. On the contrary, Lacombe is only trying to be accepted by the bourgeoisie and suffers violently from being looked down on by the members of the Gestapo and despised by their victim, Albert Horn.

Both Prédal and Malle insist on the fact that Lacombe is not an ideologist. He does what he does by accident, without any conscious choice. According to them, his behavior is just like that of his victims: "Therefore, Lacombe Lucien is not the only one who is acting without any coherent plan and the erring ways of the tailor and his daughter result from the same deliquescence of the time" (Prédal, 1989: 116). Malle adds in complement to this:

> Faithful to the process of my documentaries, I avoided judging Lucien, I preferred to show the character's behavior with all his contradictions and even, in a certain way, I tried to understand him. It was more interesting, more useful than throwing him without appeal to the dregs of History (Prédal, 1989: 117).

Indeed, this process links this film to many others previously made by Malle. The director of *Les Amants*, *Le voleur* and *Murmur of the Heart* refuses to force a judgement on his main characters. He dedicates himself to depict and "show" inter-mediary states or episodes during which the foundations of moral rules are shaken and appear to be often based on social prejudice, not on the respect for life itself. This explains in great part Malle's predilection for subjects staging adolescents as central characters and his interest in the Mexican *Halcones* before he made *Lacombe Lucien* (cf. introduction). In this context, the main characters end up committing, as by accident, what would be seen in other circumstances as a crime. It is "by accident" that Jeanne Tournier falls in love with Bernard and is ready to abandon her children (*Les Amants*). It is also "as an almost unavoidable accident" (Prédal, 1989: 58) that Laurent commits incest with his mother (*Murmur of the Heart*). However, applied to the character of Lacombe Lucien, this poses different problems.

In *Les Amants*, *Le voleur*, *Murmur of the Heart*, adultery, theft and incest happen because of social sclerosis and social injustice acting as elements of repression against desire. All three films develop a bitter and sarcastic critic of the bourgeoisie whose social rules appear as institutionalized stupidity or even as institutionalized crime (*Le Voleur*). In this context, "crimes" of the main characters can no longer be condemned as such. They are the logical consequences of a justified revolt. Lacombe's story tries to present a similar evolution in a context that however does not permit maintaining the same parallel.

As we already saw, if Lacombe is a young man revolting against the bourgeoisie, none of his actions presented in the film correspond to this revolt. Unlike what is shown in the other films, the bourgeoisie depicted through the old Jewish man and his daughter cannot stand for social injustice nor social sclerosis. On the contrary, the dignity of both Jewish characters (Albert and France Horn), their education and their attachment to their social status are the only force they can oppose to protect their deep humanity from the contempt, the insults and the cruelty of their persecutors. Consequently, Lacombe's "revolt" against this type of bourgeoisie can gain no positive aspect at all.

On the other hand, Lacombe's alliance to the local bourgeoisie and aristocracy of the Collaboration clearly make him a strongly negative hero. As Lacombe cannot be presented as a man revolting against the bourgeoisie, Malle and Prédal insist that his revolt is unconscious because the young man is not an ideologist and because he does not have the education to clearly formulate such a revolt. According to Prédal: "*Lacombe Lucien* is more the portrait of an adolescent lost in a society that is falling apart than a film presenting the problem of the Collaboration."

In another interview with Prédal, Malle presented this point of view talking about his past encounter with two famous Collaborators after they were released from jail (Lucien Rebatet and Pierre Cousteau, the brother of Jacques Cousteau):

> After they were released from jail they were very interested in me because I was twenty-one and I represented the generation of the after-war period. For me their intellectual compromise is contrary to Lacombe's and I think that these people must pay for what they did because they committed themselves knowing exactly what was going on whereas Lucien did not have the ideological concept corresponding to what he was doing. Intellectuals on the other hand have

an intellectual responsibility to assume (Prédal, 1989:
111).
The problem with such a point of view is that it tends to make
intellectuals the scapegoats thanks to which, mostly directly after
the war, many actual criminals were able to avoid trial. Like
Lacombe Lucien the unknown and "unaware" Gestapo agent,
many administrators of Vichy were also able to pretend it was
impossible for them to see the real consequences of their
"insignificant" role in the machine of the Collaboration. Many
historical studies have indeed shown clearly that intellectuals like
Brasillach paid greatly for their support of Vichy while hundreds
of administrators and criminals who played a very active role in
the deportation of the Jews were able to avoid justice rather
easily.

This point also raises the problem of historical realism in
Malle's films. According both to Prédal and Malle himself,
Lacombe Lucien is a psychological analysis and not an historical
film on the Collaboration. As Prédal underlines (Prédal, 1989:
111), there is no historical character in Malle's film. It is true that
there are no famous historical characters in the two films
considered, however both stories are based on real events and
their characters on real people (Prédal, 1989: 116). In both films,
as André declares in the end of *My Dinner with André*, reality is
shown as a fiction, as a representation of reality. This is why
fiction can "show" what reality is through destroying various
historical fictions like the myth of a unified French people in the
Résistance, the denial of the responsibilities of Vichy France in
the persecution of the European Jews, and so forth.

Louis Malle's films are both fictitious and real because they
denounce what we commonly call "reality" as a fiction and
because only a certain kind of fiction can reinstate a just representation of reality. For this reason, to keep as close as possible
to the truth, *Lacombe Lucien*, as Annette Insdorf wrote, "feels
like a documentary" (Insdorf, 124). The film was shot on
location, with non-professional actors, a "real" peasant, and based
on a "true" story. The same points could be made about *Goodbye
Children* based on a real story, filmed in a provincial French

school (in Provins not in Avon itself), with non-professional actors.

However, this look alike "documentary" is structured by a very personal process of selection and montage of the shots in order to give the story its linear unity based on Louis Malle's conception of what a good fiction film should look like in order to reveal reality. In consequence, these films are based on the idea that only a very personal and consciously subjective representation can reveal reality itself (as in Marcel Ophüls' work) while Malle keeps on pretending at the same time that it is possible to "show" reality from a totally impartial point of view.

For all these reasons, Malle's attempt to "show without judging" and to "understand" Lacombe's behavior is extremely ambiguous as it always threatens to imply a certain sympathy of the director for the central character of his film. As we have seen in the general introduction, Malle has often been accused of sympathy for the extreme right precisely because of his non-judgmental comprehension. I do not believe such accusations are founded because the general tone of his films dealing with this subject obviously implies a clear condemnation of the crimes committed. It is however a grave mistake to believe that one's themes and techniques can be applied to reveal the truth about an individual's behavior no matter the historical and sociological contexts. Moreover, Malle's criticism of a given social order is always very ambiguous as his "characters in revolt" always reveal a deep desire to protect and be admitted in the society they criticize.

In making commercial films Malle himself, like Laurent in *Murmur of the Heart*, is a son in revolt of the high bourgeoisie who seems very attached to the economics of the society he attacks. Like Laurent and his brother who destroy a copy of a painting by Corot only after making sure they protected the original to put it back in place later, Malle's films often present a violent criticism of the bourgeoisie that remains commercially very successful as it never really threatens the economic status of "the original" bourgeoisie. Like Lacombe with his gun and his money, Malle's films often seem to enjoy "terrorizing the bourgeois."

Consequently, in *Lacombe Lucien* Malle clearly failed to see that he could not treat the "accidental" commitment of an adolescent with the Gestapo in the same way and with the same themes with which he dealt with adolescent sexuality, incest, theft or adultery. For this reason his film remains dangerously incomplete and insufficient to deal with the problems it poses. The same problem remains in *Goodbye Children* with the character of Joseph. However, as Joseph is not the main character of the film, his incomplete portrayal does not pose the same problem and it can be accepted more easily. Here again the behavior of the young Collaborator is not judged but shown, explained and somewhat justified. Joseph is also presented as an uneducated victim of circumstances and also paradoxically as a victim of his future victims. This character suffers from the very same dangerous ambiguities the character of Lacombe Lucien does.

The last aspects of Malle's classicism are his taste for psychological analysis, measure, spontaneous acting, as well as his constant search for a beautiful image, particularly in *Goodbye Children*. It is always possible to identify with Malle's characters up to a certain point. They are all presented as human beings with very realistic behavior. However, they also all reach a certain point at which their unmitigated individuality makes them at the same time stranger and closer to us. It is because like any of us they appear sometimes to act without of any apparent logic that they are revealed not as stereotypes but as unique individuals. It is precisely because we cannot completely understand their actions that they become unique and similar to any spectator.

This explains in part Louis Malle's interest in giving the central roles both in *Lacombe Lucien* and *Goodbye Children* to unprofessional actors. During the making of the latter, Malle just agreed in a general manner with his actors on the scene to be played, the gestures and the dialogue:

> During the filming itself I had to leap at them as I would have done with a documentary. I think that now

> I know well how to do that because I do not put them
> by force in a constraining frame minutely elaborated. I
> try to maintain them in the scenario as much as
> possible but at a certain moment they take control of
> their characters, they give them life and therefore they
> fly off rapidly. One must therefore accept to follow
> them instead of directing them. But this is possible only
> because they have been put in a true state of grace
> representing if you will the absolute spontaneity... the
> spontaneity one gets with professional actors only after
> the seventeenth take! (quoted by Prédal, 1989: 90-91)

Such a technique is directly borrowed from the making of documentaries for which the director must constantly select among
thousands of shots the significant ones he will include in a given
work. It is important however to remember that this "absolute
spontaneity" of the psychology of the teenager is always
captured, selected and organized by an adult, by Louis Malle
himself. The director himself recognized that in *Goodbye
Children*:

> I limited myself to what I think my memories are,
> knowing very well that I reinvented a little bit (...). It
> is more interesting than what really happened. My own
> relationship with Bonnet, in the film, is more complex
> and more interesting than in reality as what we were
> lacking was time (...). I believe that I added all my
> reflection about these events during all these years.[76]

This statement implies that realism in *Goodbye Children* does not
present us directly with the reality of adolescent life but rather
with an adult's reflection on adolescence and the general un-
awareness of the persecution of the Jews during the Occupation.
Unlike Julien Quentin and Louis Malle in 1944, the director and
the spectator of the film know about the Holocaust and the
persecution of the Jews. In consequence they never really see the
film through the eyes of Julien but always through the eyes of
Malle as an adult analyzing this relationship. Moreover, the film
seems to make up for a very personal sense of loss, the loss of
time between Malle and Jean Bonnet who were not given, in

reality, the time to really develop a friendship. This is however a point only Malle himself could analyze in depth.

It remains that with all its "absolute spontaneity" and its classical psychological analysis, the film becomes "more interesting" than reality itself. This confirms one more time that Malle's desire to "show" instead of "demonstrate" corresponds in fact to a very personal kind of demonstration based on his own interpretation and analysis of the confrontation of individual desire and ethics to a repressive bourgeois society with its moral and political oppression.

In the context of this representation, the film keeps a very classical sense of measure. The audience is shown no image of graphic violence or obscenity. As in *The Murmur of the Heart*, such scenes are only alluded to and not directly shown. One can easily imagine that showing and seeing this story directly through the eyes of a teenager would have implied a very different and much more graphic representation of the adolescent's sensuality, physical sensations, psychological pleasures and terrors. On the contrary, the film mentions such episodes from an adult point of view through which extreme and violent sensations or images of adolescence are only alluded to (incestuous tendencies; masturbation; erotic desire and curiosity; extreme cold; enuresis and separation from the mother; terror of death; etc.).

This economy of violent images and emotions serves perfectly well the slow progression of suspense in the film. It reinforces its structure as a classical tragedy concentrating all of its energies toward the final outburst. This general purpose is also very well served by the beauty of the images that serve the unity of the film without letting any misplaced excess disturb the gradual progression of the narration.

Throughout *Goodbye Children* the dominating colors are white, raw umber, ultramarine blue and raw sienna. These cold colors reinforce the location of the story during the extremely cold winters of the Occupation, the isolation of the children and their generalized fright in which this episode takes place. Here again, all the techniques used by Louis Malle and his crew are subsumed to the general progression of suspense and anguish

throughout the film. Louis Malle's works also give great importance to creating an impressionistic or sensual unity for the film
through the use of color to a given work. Writing about Malle's
film on Brigitte Bardot (*Vie privée*), René Prédal recalls:

> As a fundamental element of this approach, the
> sensuality of Henri Decae's image constitutes a
> vibrating tribute to the beauty of B.B. magnified by
> sumptuous colors, a sweet and warm light. Marcel
> Martin talks about an impressionistic palette like
> Renoir's, Monet's and Seurat's (Prédal, 1989: 64).

Moreover, Malle himself often characterized his work as one
of a painter. He declared to the review *Cinéma 62*: "There is, for
the painter and the film director, an identical combat with matter.
I see myself as closer to a painter than to a novelist."[77] It is also
no surprise when comparing his work to that of a writer, he
chooses the classical French tragedians Jean Racine and Pierre
Corneille as the moralist La Bruyère saw them: "Racine portrayed
his heroes the way they are and Corneille the way they should
be." He uses this quote to compare his film on Brigitte Bardot to
Corneille's work. Indeed, as we just saw, Lucien Lacombe and
Julien Quentin are also "portrayed" not "as they are" but as they
"should be" or should have been in order to best serve the impact
Malle wanted his film to have on its audiences.

These words of Malle himself recall the complex relationship we just analyzed within his work between cinema, literature
and painting. The French word used by the director translated
here as "to portray" is indeed "to paint:" "Racine *peint* ses héros
tels qu'ils sont, Corneille tels qu'ils devraient être." Of course,
this use of the verb in literary criticism is rather conventional
within the classical discourse of La Bruyère. Used in its turn by
Louis Malle it becomes the keystone or the final coating of his
own type of classicism tracing a characteristic "classical" triangle
between film, text and image (cinema, literature and painting).
Throughout all these borrowings however, Louis Malle remains
a film director and his work a very personal cinematographic
creation.

I have encountered in both *Lacombe Lucien* and *Goodbye Children* Malle's film characteristics as many of them are analyzed throughout the essay by René Prédal:
- a precise conception of classicism
- the criticism of the bourgeoisie
- the confrontation of adolescents with this absurd world
- the absurdity of prefabricated morals
- the mild anti-clericalism
- the use of anti-heroes placed in intermediary and uncertain worlds
- a conception of realism based on a subtle mixture of fiction and documentary, and on the use of teenagers and unprofessional actors
- the opposition between ideology and psychology
- the opposition between showing and demonstrating
- a great importance given to close-ups
- smooth or imperceptible transitions
- parallel actions converging slowly towards a final explosion
- the development of the plot according to three phases within a short time period (usually one or a few days)
- a very tight construction of the intrigue
- the harmonious and classical beauty of the image as a key element of unity in the film

As two milestones in the evolution of the representation of the Holocaust in French cinema, *Lacombe Lucien* and *Goodbye Children* present us with two fiction films directly influenced by Marcel Ophüls' *The Sorrow and the Pity*. If *Goodbye Children* appears to be a greater work it might be in part because in making this film Malle stuck *subjectively* to the representation of what he knew and felt rather than trying to "show" what he thinks young farmers and Collaborators were like. Creating an historical image of the other requires an ideological representation of history that cannot be rejected even if this film is a partial transposition of personal feelings and memories. In refusing to acknowledge this constraint Malle created a very ambiguous film.

Lacombe Lucien is a complete stranger to Louis Malle or even to Julien. They are two very cultured children of the high bourgeoisie and he is presented as a totally uncultured farmer. With this basis, "showing" what Lacombe did or did not feel required a judgment, an ideological point of view, Malle thought he could do without. In consequence Ophüls' denunciation of any pretention to objectivity in the representation of the Occupation constitutes indirectly the most profound criticism one could make to *Lacombe Lucien*. It is very clear that, as opposed to Louis Malle, Ophüls "shows" reality but he knows that his realism is always the product of a subjective representation and inter-pretation of reality. Instead of trying to ignore this fact, Ophüls works with it and makes it an integral part of his films. In contrast to Malle's position, Ophüls knows that any "showing" or manipulation already constitutes a demonstration.

Goodbye Children is completely centered around the story and the feelings of Julien whose character is directly inspired by Malle's memories of his own youth. In comparison with Julien, all the other characters of this film appear rather schematic and their actions are always shown in relation with the way Julien reacts to them. We know almost nothing about Joseph, the other children in the school, Mr. Moreau or about the other children brought with Jean. We know very little about Père Jean. The case of Jean Bonnet is of course different as the partial and progressive discovery of who he really is constitutes the main thread of the film.

This explains however that in this film, Malle's technique of "showing" rather than "demonstrating" worked better as he knew in this case he could not avoid being subjective. The fact that he carried this subject in himself through his own memories for so many years (cf. introduction) gives a much more realistic approach to his main character, portrayed from Malle's memories as an adult but still from the inside of the character with his fears, his anguishes, his fantasies and his very personal emotions.

b. Joseph Losey's *Mr. Klein*

Joseph Losey's *Mr. Klein* is a powerful and subtly fascinating work that can be considered as the best fiction film made in France about the reprehensible indifference of many bystanders faced with the persecution of the Jews during the Occupation. Robert Klein is not presented as an anti-Semite. However, his everyday behavior plays a very active role in the persecution of the Jews. He has no apparent political commitment. He lives totally ignorant of the turmoil and the atrocities that surround him. He wants to live through the Occupation by continuing business as usual, even taking advantage of any good business opportunity that might be available without embarrassing himself with emotions or altruistic considerations. For this reason, according to Losey's own desires, Robert Klein appears as a callous and stony man from the very beginning of the film.

Robert Klein (Alain Delon) is an art dealer who occasionally enriches himself by taking advantage of the Jews forced to sell the art work they possess in order to survive or to flee. One day, as he is closing such a "deal," he starts receiving the weekly *Information Juive*. He then goes to talk to the paper's publisher, and then to the police, to find out who gave his name for the subscription and, most of all, to explain that he is not Jewish. Throughout the film he desperately tries to convince the French authorities that he is not a Jew while we are constantly shown the French police preparing for a major roundup.

On several occasions, Robert Klein will get very close to discovering who the real Mr. Klein is but he will never succeed. In the meantime he meets many of Mr. Klein's friends and realizes progressively what is happening to the Jews. In the end, without ever understanding what exactly happened, he will be arrested and deported with thousands of other Jews in a scene that is voluntarily an approximate reconstitution of the notorious round up of the Vélodrome d'Hiver.

The first two sequences of *Mr. Klein* put in parallel the two main themes of the historical background of the film: the ferocious and meticulous persecution of the Jews by the French administration during the Occupation and the indifference or even the opportunism of the French population confronted with the crimes being perpetrated in front of their very eyes. The first image of the film shows an expression of terror on the face of a woman being examined by a French doctor in order to determine whether she is a Jew or not. Meanwhile, her husband is going through the same examination in the same building. After this sequence, we hear the first line said by Robert Klein. Being asked if he is "Mr. Klein" by a still anonymous voice, he answers without any hesitation: "Yes, I am Mr. Klein." While he is negotiating to obtain a ridiculously low price for a painting sold by a Jew who needs the money to try to survive with his family, we see Robert Klein's girlfriend in bed, getting up and going to the bathroom to put on some makeup. In order to keep my analysis as clear as possible, I will refer to the main character of the film as "Robert Klein" or "Robert," and to the Robert Klein in hiding as "Mr. Klein."

The parallel between these two opening sequences is ensured by the parallelism of two different themes. First they introduce two different aspects of the terror in which Jews were living while other French citizens were "adapting" to the situation and finding even new occupations and new sources of profit, here as art dealers or racial specialists. Second, these two sequences introduce a clear parallel between two undressed women, one being treated as an animal by the doctor, the other one as a prisoner of Robert Klein's fantasies as he orders her throughout the film to go back to bed or to stay in bed. The violent contrast between a world of terror and a world of pleasure in voluntary blindness is stressed as the medical examination scene started with a close up on the mouth and teeth of a woman treated like a slave while the scene of Robert Klein's lover getting up ends with a close up of her lips while she is putting on makeup. It is clear that these two women live in the same society but in two different worlds, the second woman ignoring the suffering of the first one while profiting from it.

The very thin but constant contact between these two worlds will introduce the major unifying theme of the film: the progressive remorse of Robert Klein and his slow identification with at least one of the victims of the Holocaust. Consequently, Losey's film is filled with recurrent themes and scenes to which Robert Klein will each time react differently. A general interpretation of the film makes it obvious that Robert could not and should not have pretended to ignore the destiny of the other Mr. Klein, the Jew, his double. When he finally realizes that, it is too late for him to change anything in the course of "their lives" and to avoid total annihilation. The price of his total indifference will ultimately lead him to the very same death train that will also take away the Jew he took advantage of at the very beginning of the film.

Such an ending makes Losey's film extremely different from Louis Malle's *Lacombe Lucien* which depicts another indifferent French man during the same period. While the films of both Malle and Losey show men who persecute Jews without any clear ideological commitment (Lacombe works for the Gestapo "by chance" and Robert Klein is never shown as a convinced anti-Semite), one of the great qualities of *Mr. Klein* over *Lacombe Lucien* is that Robert Klein's indifference and total lack of compassion are clearly presented as criminal. Unlike Lacombe, Robert Klein becomes the direct victim of the order of society which his personal way of life supported and from which he even benefitted. On the contrary, Lacombe becomes a victim of some sort of vengeful spirit after the war.

In *Mr. Klein*, Jews are presented as terrified victims hopelessly trying to escape the Kafkaesque machine of persecution of the French administration. There is a clear feeling throughout this work that it is too late to change anything and that a trap is slowly closing itself on the Jews as well as on Robert and Mr. Klein. This feeling is created by the repeated and unannounced portrayals of the French police and French officials getting ready for a major roundup. Without any explanation, we are also shown the central archives of the CGQJ (Commissariat Générale à la Question Juive) where lists of the victims of the up-coming roundup are being made.

At the beginning of the film, right after Robert found the newspaper *Information Juive* on his doormat, the Jew who just sold him a painting at great loss wishes him: "The best of luck *to you*, Mr. Klein." After that, Robert Klein stares for a few seconds at "the other" Mr. Klein, at his reflection in the mirror across the hall. Later, at an art auction a blue and white tapestry representing a vulture hit by an arrow is being sold. It is the same tapestry that was used during the opening credits of the film. As it is being auctioned, Robert explains to a woman: "Something tells me it brings bad luck" and he runs away from it. At the same time, we are being told by the auctioneer that the design of this tapestry represents a symbol for remorse. Right after this, while Robert calls the publisher of *Information Juive* from a cafe, the camera films him from the outside and, as if announcing what will soon happen, his voice is being covered by the sound of passing buses. In the end of the film, the very same buses will take him away to the death trains with thousands of Jews. Finally, when his girlfriend abandons him, Robert Klein realizes that: "Pierre (his lawyer) was right. They are preparing public opinion for something inevitable!"

This constantly growing sense of an inevitable and upcoming catastrophe progressively leads Robert from opportunism and indifference to solidarity and identification with his double, the other Mr. Klein. Whether he rejects it or not, the destiny of Robert Klein is defined from the beginning by the themes of a haunting remorse and identification. The omnipresence of remorse is made clear by the constant reoccurrence throughout the film of the tapestry representing a wounded vulture used during the opening credits. Robert refuses to purchase this tapestry but it definitely represents a sign from which he cannot escape. When he answers an invitation from Florence (Jeanne Moreau), a wealthy Jewish woman living in a castle and probably one of Mr. Klein's lovers, she makes it clear to him that he is a vulture praying on wounded human beings while the other Mr. Klein is a hibernating snake waiting for the end of the war to come out of hiding.

Just before that conversation, we see in the castle a tapestry representing an emblem with a snake. Florence explains that the other Mr. Klein would have compared Robert to an animal because he has a theory which states that, while there is an infinite variety of insect species, there is only one human species. Robert interrupts her with a disinterested "I understand," indicating he might think he belongs to a different species such as a bird of prey, a falcon. However, according to Florence, he belongs in fact to the same species as his victims and the other Mr. Klein. Consequently, the vulture becomes a symbol of the way Robert acts and of his destiny but not of his nature. It is because both men belong to the same "human species" that in the end, albeit through their own opposite ways, they will suffer the same annihilation. According to the theory of the other Mr. Klein, as it is explained by Florence, there ultimately cannot be any winner when death and annihilation are governing a so-called "civilization."

Joseph Losey himself indicated rather clearly what the people living in this castle represent:

> That castle is my family. I wanted that scene—which has been harshly criticized—because it was important to show that there were also Jews who had enough money to simply buy their way out of France without changing their life-style much—and they go to Mexico because of my great love for the country. I made a conscious use of symbols in the scene—which you should pick yourself—which indicate very clearly that it's a Jewish family (Ciment, 353).

This inevitable recurrence of remorse for Robert is represented by the theme of the wounded vulture but also by the omnipresence of the colors of the tapestry throughout the film. The tapestry mainly consists of three cold colors: a light blue, a hazy white and a somber golden yellow (Naples yellow) recalling on various occasions the yellow of the star of David Jews were forced to wear. It is also similar to the color of Robert Klein's coat (dark yellow/light golden brown). These three colors dominate all the images of the film. They are also the colors of both Mr. Klein and Robert Klein's apartments. Moreover, the last

time Robert goes to Mr. Klein's apartment, just before he talks
to "Isabelle" on the phone—she is probably Mr. Klein's
lover—and just before his belongings are seized by the police, he
is shown thinking at the doorstep with a very large portion of a
yellow wall behind him. It is after this last visit that he will
definitely be considered as a Jew and identified by the French
police as such.

In this context, the identification of Robert Klein with Mr.
Klein follows a crooked but irreversible progression. From
violent rejection to obsession, compassion, silent solidarity,
identification and remorse, Robert discovers little by little the
unavoidable character of his common fate with Mr. Klein. In the
France of 1976, when this film came out, Robert Klein's psychological evolution probably parallelled the evolution of the feelings
of a large part of the French population since the war years. No
one could ignore anymore what the "relocation of the Jews" had
really meant. Just as *The Sorrow and the Pity* reminded everyone
in 1971 of the wide popular support the Vichy government had
enjoyed, *Mr. Klein* came exactly at a time when the French were
completely revising their own recent history and acknowledging
their responsibilities in the persecution of the European Jews.
Consequently, *Mr. Klein* could also be read as an allegory of the
evolution of the French psyche in the seventies, regarding their
perception of their responsibilities in the persecution of the Jews.
This is of course not to say that each French person could
identify completely with Robert Klein but that his character
would at least remind many of real people they knew. Many in
the audience could also identify with one of the many stages of
the complex evolution of Robert's feelings towards the hiding
Mr. Klein.

Many critics have insisted on Losey's masterful representation of ambiguities in which clear answers are never given to
the problems developed by his films. In *Mr. Klein*, this complex
ambiguity structures the progression of the film, its suspense and
the interest of the spectator. As the film is completely centered
around the main character which we follow from beginning to
end, we are taken through different possible interpretations
corresponding to the different points of view of Robert Klein on

his own situation. Sometimes, however, the spectator is given more information than the central character. This increases the suspense and the feeling that there will be no escape possible for Robert Klein.

This happens for example in a scene in which, after talking to the police in his own apartment, Robert embraces his girlfriend saying that there is no reason for anyone to put him through so much trouble. While this is going on, the camera offers a close up on the smiling and content face of Robert's former mistress who is standing by the stairs, watching the whole scene. Only the spectator sees that and can therefore connect this scene directly with an earlier sequence in which the same former mistress announced with satisfaction to Robert: "There are two officers here to see you too." At this point one possible interpretation is being reinforced: Robert Klein is being set up by his jealous former mistress.

Through such details, the spectator is given a little more information than the main character on his own fate. This increases the dramatic force of the film as the spectator knows Robert Klein is irremediably trapped while he is desperately fighting for his life. Until the very end, Robert tries regularly to deny that there is no escape possible for him. Similarly, the audience is regularly shown the police preparing for a major roundup. Robert Klein cannot see this and the spectator is being told at the same time that a trap is slowly but surely closing itself and that the main character cannot do anything about it.

First for the audience and next for Robert, it soon becomes obvious that there will be no escape possible for the victims of this "something inevitable" that is being prepared. Then, the audience, like Robert himself, wants to understand the reasons why one can be targeted as a victim. There will be no answer to this question as the extermination of the Jews will remain a perfectly organized and absurd machine of death. For this reason, all the ambiguities of the film will remain and serve perfectly the purpose of the film, insisting on the horror, the absurdity and the blindness of the persecutions. There will not be and there cannot be any "reason" that could "justify" or even explain why one becomes the victim of such an atrocity and such a well-ordered madness. The film only shows "how" it happened.

In consequence, various possible explanations for Robert Klein's persecution can be sustained during the film and they all remain at least partly possible in the end. Here are some of them to which different spectators could probably add a few more. First, Robert could really be a Jew coming forward to try to deny his real identity. This is the interpretation of the "préfecture de police." He could be set up by his former mistress as she is extremely jealous of his new girlfriend, Jeanine. He could be set up by the husband of his former mistress, his lawyer Pierre, as Pierre also seems to be the one who is profiting the most from the fact that Robert will have to sell his business and change his identity. Pierre is also the one who denounces Robert Klein to the police in the end. He could be set up by the friends and former girlfriends of Mr. Klein. Finally, he could be set up by the hiding Mr. Klein himself who would force a transfer of identity because he knows Robert, the art dealer, has the financial means to escape from the police whose attention would at the same time be confused and diverted by another man. In the meantime, Mr. Klein could disappear and "hibernate" until the end of the war. However this probable interpretation does not refute the others that remain simultaneously possible throughout the film.

Thus, *Mr. Klein* centers on the psychological evolution of one man, while offering a minute analysis of the various degrees of corruption of an individual as well as of a complete society. At the beginning of the film, Robert Klein is presented as a cold and totally insensitive business man who does not care a bit about the distress of his "customers," just for the sake of making a good deal. The film is even more powerful as the main character is never presented as a convinced anti-Semite. When he goes to talk to the publisher of *Information Juive*, Robert insists that no one could be "playing a prank like that on (him)!" When the publisher asks him if he thinks that what is happening to the Jews is a funny joke, Robert is embarrassed and he apologizes. When, with his girlfriend Jeanine, he sees an anti-Semitic show in a cabaret, he does not think it is funny and even if, in the end, he starts applauding, they both leave the place terrified.

Such scenes give a lot of power to the film as Robert Klein is described as a man who plays a very active role in the persecution of the Jews without identifying himself as an anti-Semite. In this way, Losey's film extends its criticism to all the French who during the Occupation did not see themselves as anti-Semites but who, through continuing their "business as usual," made the persecution of the Jews possible. As he slowly realizes what is happening to the Jews, Robert feels more compassionate. He does not want merely to get rid of his "new identity" but he wants first of all to understand what is going on. When he realizes that Mr. Klein is indeed a man extremely similar to himself trying to escape a blind and absurd persecution, he starts feeling a great deal of solidarity with him and he starts to identify with him. For this reason, he does not want to call the police when he finally knows where Mr. Klein is. He wants to meet with him in order to decide what should be done.

In the end of this long process of progressive identification, Robert shares the destiny of Mr. Klein as if something in himself was telling him unconsciously that it is the only thing to do. At the same time, he knows he can prove that he is not a Jew. As he is pushed to the train, he screams to his lawyer Pierre "Wait for me, I will be right back!" but it is clear to him that he can no longer ignore or be indifferent to what happens to Mr. Robert Klein the Jew. In consequence, the final identification/differentiation of the two Robert Kleins ends up with a final recurrence of remorse. As Robert is being taken away with thousands of Jews in a death train, his first "customer" of the film is behind him in the very same wagon while Robert remembers their "deal" and starts really understanding what happened to him and how he became a victim of his very own indifference.

The criticism of French society in this film is just as detailed and complex as is the evolution of Robert Klein's compassion. For this reason, Losey's film concentrates on people that are passively anti-Semitic. Only brief allusions are made for example to the Légion des Volontaires Français. One at the beginning of the film when Jeanine turns on the radio, one closer to the end of the film when we see a battalion of the LVF on the platform of a train station while Robert waits for his train to go south.

Here again, the film concentrates on the criticism of indirect and unrecognized anti-Semitism.

There are at least seven different aspects of this criminal indifference. First comes the criticism of the opportunism of professionals continuing "business as usual" like Robert, Pierre and all their friends. The opportunism of those always looking for a good deal is also denounced through the same characters and particularly through Pierre taking advantage "in spite of himself" of Robert Klein's problems. The police are also shown as doing their job as usual, looking for the security found in discipline at all costs, even obeying criminal orders. While repossessing Robert's belongings, the police commissioner says that he does not like what he is doing but such is the law. The film also violently criticizes the Kafkaesque organization of the French administration making it clear that there is no escape possible for its victims. Parisian high society is also shown as seeking oblivion in pleasure and the proliferation of Parisian cabarets. Through Jeanine abandoning Robert Klein and a man at the morgue declaring about dead Résistants "I would have done the same if I were younger and if I had more courage," the film criticizes the lack of courage and the paralysis by fear of a whole population. Finally, when Robert Klein's father violently rejects any link of his family with Jewish origins, Losey openly attacks the rampant traditional anti-Semitism in French society.

In conclusion, Joseph Losey's *Mr. Klein* can be characterized as the best fiction film made about the opportunism and the criminal indifference of individuals confronted with the persecution of the Jews. As a victim himself of institutionalized bigotry (McCarthyism) in the United States, Losey was able to stress in his film the political numbness of a population that in the end enabled intolerance and racism to turn into institutionalized murder. In the context of the mid-seventies, it also constitutes a violent criticism of anyone who pretends that everyday life, business and politics are not related.

9.   Claude Lanzmann's *Shoah*

Since it first came out in 1985, Claude Lanzmann's *Shoah* has been widely praised as a masterpiece, and very often as "the" cinematographic masterpiece on the extermination of the European Jews during World War II. Its immediate and enormous success both in Europe and in the United States was put in question only in Poland where Lanzmann was accused of being extremely biased by showing only anti-Semitic Poles, by not mentioning those who saved between thirty thousand and forty thousand Jews and finally by not describing the death threat that was put upon the Polish families who would try to hide and save some Jews. This controversy was later developed as many scholars have even recently criticized Lanzmann's film for reflecting more Lanzmann's personal obsessions rather than perfect historical accuracy. There have been mostly two kinds of reproach made to Lanzmann's film. First, historical criticism, as indicated above; second the director is rebuked for not treating his interviewees fairly and not respecting their personal feelings, for example, when he secretly films the Nazis, when he asks insidious questions to the Poles or when he forces survivors to speak.

Regarding historical points, Lanzmann is never accused of lying or distorting the truth but of offering only a very incomplete image of the times his film presents. Lanzmann often defended himself from such accusations by saying that the subject of his film is not a general presentation of Holocaust. His subject is the Shoah of the Jewish people (the annihilation in Hebrew), the extermination process itself and the people who directly witnessed it—i.e. a handful of Jewish survivors, the Nazis and the Poles. *Shoah* is a film about the uniqueness and the specificity of the systematic extermination of the Jews that took place in Poland. Because he decided to concentrate on such a topic, Lanzmann was not interested in the few Gentiles who helped some Jews in Poland nor was he interested in analyzing anti-Semitism in other countries like France.

This distinction is essential as it is at the origin of the most violent controversies surrounding the film. However, some critics would reject these explanations mostly for two reasons. First, as Tzvetan Todorov recently wrote, Lanzmann's goal in making *Shoah* was not to produce an historical documentary but to create a work of art that would transmit the suffering and the memory of the victims. However, Todorov adds: "It is art's rule that all that is not shown does not exist; consequently, Lanzmann's message is: all the Poles are anti-Semites")(Todorov, 250). In a recent essay, Wladyslaw T. Bartoszewski sees Lanzmann's fragmentary presentation as very dangerous because: "*Shoah* was a cinematographic masterpiece of great moral significance, but it was also intended to (and did) become a source of historical knowledge for a wider public" (Bartoszewski, 22). This lasting controversy forces us to examine Lanzmann's film under two simultaneous aspects: first as an historical work; second as a work of art.

Lanzmann himself never described his film as a purely historical work: "It is not an historical film" (Lanzmann, 1985: 22). It is most of all a "work of art." However, the director also indicated proudly that his film had taught many historians some facts they were not aware of. In a famous conference held in Oxford in 1985, he also presented himself, to an audience largely composed of professional historians, as "the leading specialist on the Holocaust" (Bartoszewski, 22). Bartoszewski alludes to some "small mistakes," denied by Lanzmann, and questions Rudolf Vrba's testimony stating that "he was *the first prisoner to escape* (from Auschwitz) bringing information to the outside world about life in the camps, including the mass extermination of Jews" (23). Lanzmann also rejected that criticism. Finally, according to Bartoszewski, "the greatest of Lanzmann's sins are those of omission" (23). Here we fall into a vicious circle as we already know Lanzmann's reply to this reproach.

Claude Lanzmann also indicated on many occasions that he prepared himself for the making of the film by reading an enormous quantity of books about the Holocaust: "I started by reading, for a year, all the history books that I could find on the subject, everything I found by searching through archives (written archives, no pictures)" (Lanzmann, 1985: 18). Raul Hilberg's monumental work *The Extermination of the European Jews* soon became his main reference. It is a book Lanzmann read many times and prides himself on knowing by heart. This first step was indispensable for as the director:

> One must know and see, and one must see and know. Indissolubly. If you go to Auschwitz without knowing anything about Auschwitz and the history of this camp, you see nothing, you understand nothing. In a similar way, if you know without ever going there, you do not understand anything either. Therefore I needed a conjunction of both (Lanzmann, 1985: 18).

Consequently, beyond its historical research and accuracy, *Shoah* defines itself as a work of art through its powerful conjunction of knowledge and image through the transmission of the testimonies of direct witnesses of the Shoah itself.

In this regard, the film became for others an indispensable complement for the work of the historian. In becoming an "incarnation" or a "resurrection" (in Deguy, 66) of an historical period, an art work can communicate information inaccessible to a purely scientific historical study. According to the historian Pierre Vidal-Naquet:

> Between the time lost and the time found again there is the work of art, and the challenge to which *Shoah* submits the historian is this obligation to be both a scholar and an artist, or else he loses, forever, a fraction of the truth he is searching for (in Deguy, 208).

Following this point of view, *Shoah* is *more* than a historical study precisely because it is a work of art that "incarnates" the truth. Consequently, we must now examine what aspects characterize *Shoah* as a "work of art"; that is to say, how this film "incarnates the truth" through the editing of various interviews and a constant and minute weaving of oral testimonies with images, sounds and music.

Beyond historical criticism, Tzvetan Todorov recently criticized *Shoah* as a work of art based on hatred. Todorov first recalls that this film is above all a work of art. That is to say that Lanzmann's ultimate goal is not to communicate a certain knowledge nor to be accurate but rather to create a powerful impact on the audience. Lanzmann himself often indicated that his goal was not to "communicate" information but rather to "transmit" an experience and a violent emotion:

> The film is not made from memories, I saw that right away. Memories horrify me: memories are weak. The film is the abolition of all distances between past and present; I have relived the whole story in the present. We see memories every day on television: guys with their tie on behind their desk, telling things. Nothing is more annoying (Lanzmann, 1985: 21).

(Consequently, Lanzmann's golden rule in selecting the witnesses for his interviews was to chose only those who were able not only to talk about their past but to "relive" it in the present, to reenact the past in front of the camera.) For this reason, he rejected not only the testimonies that did not deal directly with his subject (the testimony of Marek Edelman and parts of Jan Karski's interview), but also those who, according to his judgment, were only "reciting" an old story (Lanzmann mentioned Wladyslaw Bartoszewski), and those who were too overwhelmed by their experience to be able to present a coherent discourse ("Some are crazy and unable to transmit anything" Lanzmann, 1985: 18). Consequently, (Todorov reproaches Lanzmann with choosing his witnesses and segments of the testimonies in a partial manner rejecting everything that does not fit with his ultimate goal.)

Finally, Todorov criticizes Lanzmann for not taking into account the personal will of each witness. If he sees no problem with playing tricks on the Nazis who were lying to the Jews in order to murder them, Todorov does not accept the fact that Lanzmann insists only on the anti-Semitic aspects of the testimonies of the Poles and on the fact that the director forces the survivors to testify even when they beg him to stop filming.

In doing so, according to Todorov, Lanzmann creates an extremely powerful impact on his audience but he also denies any personal will to the witnesses and submits all the individuals involved to his own obsessions. Pushed to the extreme, Todorov's reproaches imply that Lanzmann denies any individuality and personal will to his witnesses in order to serve his ultimate obsessive goal—to create a powerful "transmission" of the Shoah. In doing so, the director's morality would become partly comparable to those of the Nazis even if it serves an opposite objective. This point becomes more explicit at the end of Todorov's study.

Insisting on the absolute need to create a most powerful film, Lanzmann often opposed the need to understand the Holocaust to the necessity to remember and share the absolute abandonment and despair of the victims. He went as far as writing that, regarding the Shoah, "there is an absolute obscenity in the project of understanding" (in Deguy, 279), or "there is something that is for me an intellectual scandal: the attempt to understand, historically, as if there were some sort of a genesis of death" (in Deguy, 289).

Because of this systematic rejection of understanding, according to Todorov, Lanzmann imprisons himself and his film in a logic of hatred that is not only unable to prevent the Holocaust from happening again but also makes it easier to recur. With such an outlook, Lanzmann makes his advice the advice of an SS to Primo Lévi: "Here, there is no 'why'," "*Hier ist kein warum*" (in Deguy, 279). According to Todorov: "Lévi spent forty years, after Auschwitz, trying to understand why, in order to fight the rule of Auschwitz; Lanzmann, on his side, prefers the morality of an SS" (Todorov, 254). Then, it is not surprising to Todorov that the same director wanted to kill the SS Suchomel by filming him with his camera, thus perpetuating a never ending chain of hatred:

> One evening, I almost had a fight with one of my cameramen, after the interview of the Nazi from Treblinka. The father of the cameraman had died in Auschwitz and he did not understand me being so nice

with this Nazi, inviting him for lunch, paying for his good meal. He would have wanted to kill him. Me, I did not want to kill him like this... (in Deguy, 287).

It is to be noticed however that Lanzmann does not reject understanding all together but a form of understanding that would lead to causes, reasons and some kind of excuses for the murder of the Jews. Coming up with such a logical explanation would indeed end up excusing many murderers as it would make of them irresponsible victims of historical, political and sociological circumstances. As it has been shown in Ophüls' *The Memory of Justice*, many Nazis indeed tried to present themselves as victims of circumstances. Lanzmann explained himself very clearly on this point: "Sometimes I would tell myself that these historians were becoming crazy while trying to understand. Sometimes, to understand is pure madness. All these presuppositions, all these conditions that they enumerate are true; but there is an abyss: to pass to the act, to kill. Any idea of a procreation of death is an absurd dream of the non-violent" (in Deguy, 289).

Except concerning this point, Lanzmann often insisted on his own need to understand how the extermination process—"the machine"—worked precisely: "I started with accumulating an enormous abstract and theoretical knowledge" (Lanzmann, 1985: 18). He needed to understand how the testimonies he kept on hearing could fit with the historical knowledge he had acquired previously: "There was an absolute gap between abstract knowledge and what people were telling me" (Lanzmann, 1985: 18). Finally, he expressed the need to understand how his own film transmits the horror of the Shoah: "One must understand how and why this horror is transmitted (in *Shoah*)" (in Deguy, 293). These three levels of comprehension play indeed a fundamental role in the "transmission" *Shoah* insures as a work of art.

Following key advice given to him by Raul Hilberg, Lanzmann does not ask big or general questions that would only lead him to small answers. On the contrary he constantly asks for more factual explanations, more precise details, more descriptions. In doing so he forces himself, the witness and the spectator to visualize in imagination what cannot be represented. In forcing this imaginary visualization helped by the return to the locations where the Shoah took place, the director forces the witnesses to make *present* in their minds the actual scenes of the past which they are evoking. Through this process, the witnesses are no longer conveying a purely historical knowledge. One detail recalling another, they are actually reliving in their imagination a precise scene of their own past as it has been engraved in their memory, with all its violence.

Lanzmann calls this process an "incarnation" of the truth "in the present" (Lanzmann, 1985: 20). It is on this fundamental process that Lanzmann bases the characterization of his film on the specificity of the murder of the Jews as a powerful, unique and irreplaceable work of art. It is this process that ultimately gives value to the understanding of how "the machine" worked, how abstract knowledge fits with the human experiences of the witnesses, and how the film itself becomes so powerful. Thanks to this process, only a work of art can save the memory of human experience and people's history. This point however raises many other key questions as one wonders under what conditions such an effect on the witnesses and the audience are obtained? What is exactly being transmitted? And at what cost?

What is being transmitted is the horror of the Shoah itself; that is to say, the absolute violence and irrationality of a systematic genocide that no human words can describe nor explain—the Unspeakable: "I precisely started with the impossibility to tell this story. I put this impossibility at the very beginning" (Lanzmann, 1985: 19). At the end of the film, the Shoah remains unspeakable and unnamed. The film however "evokes" it. It allows us to imagine and feel a minute fraction of this horror through facing us with the "incarnation" of the truth by the witnesses.

Then, understanding precisely what this "incarnation in the present" is and how it reveals an otherwise unattainable truth can only be done through a detailed analysis of how precise segments of the film actually work. Only such an analysis can help us understand how these powerful incarnations were obtained, at what cost and how *Shoah* can save a capital, accurate and authoritative memory of the Holocaust for future generations.

a. This Is the Place

Whereas there are three kinds of witnesses in *Shoah*, the survivors, the bystanders and the Nazis, Lanzmann's narration is always based on the point of view of the victims, going as far as trying to reconstruct with the movements of the camera the scene a witness is describing. This is the case, for example, when Filip Müller is asked to describe the first time he went to work in a crematorium. Very often in the film, the camera will try to bring the audience to visualize a testimony by reproducing a similar movement in what is left today of the places where the extermination of the Jews took place. In such cases, the camera itself becomes the eye of the survivor looking for any trace of the past in the same site.

It is also to be noticed that, for ethical reasons, Lanzmann never uses this process with Nazi interviews. One could easily imagine the same "story" being told from the point of view of the bystanders and, thanks to his characteristic sense of irony, Marcel Ophüls was able in *Hotel Terminus* to tell part of Klaus Barbie's life from the point of view of the murderer himself. As opposed to what happens in Ophüls' films, Lanzmann's work contains no humor. Ophüls himself indicated that such a difference is mostly due to the subject Lanzmann is dealing with:

> Lanzmann never winks at his spectators, and he does not try to seduce or please them. And this difference between the two of us might come from the fact that his intellectual formation comes from Jean-Paul Sartre while I have been conceived and raised by a man of cinema and theatre. However I am not even sure this is the real reason: Lanzmann, in my opinion, knows perfectly well all the seducing capabilities offered by cinema and the audiovisual media, and if he chose to

restrain from winking at the audience, it is because of
the unique character of his enterprise... (in Deguy, 182).
In previous interviews however, Ophüls had been a little more
distant with the director of *Shoah*, particularly concerning
Lanzmann's polemical approach:

> My film (*Hotel Terminus*) is *not* on the Holocaust, as
> *Shoah* is (...) Lanzmann felt that his camera should act
> as a substitute for a gun or a court of law; he put
> himself in the role of judge and jury. That's his own
> privilege... He's an ideologue, I concentrate on the
> revelation of character. Here's the major difference
> between us: Lanzmann's Sunday school teacher was
> Jean-Paul Sartre, whereas mine was Frank Capra (Du
> Plessix-Gray, 46).

Consequently, Ophüls could be considered as a genuine
"man of cinema" whereas Lanzmann would be above all an
ideologue who later turned to cinema. Indeed, Ophüls' film
precisely presents many complex characters with all their
hesitations, their justifications and their ambiguities. Unlike
Ophüls, all the testimonies gathered by Lanzmann go beyond the
individuals and reduce their experiences and testimonies only to
the subject of the film, the evocation of the annihilation process
itself. This goal is the very first rule of Lanzmann's editing
process. In regard to this extreme event, according to Lanzmann's
film, there are only victims and murderers. At this point, Ophüls'
mild remarks lead us very closely to other critics who reproached
Lanzmann with offering a simplistic and dangerously Manichean
vision of his subject (Todorov, 251).

Ophüls' remarks also recognize an extremely important point
that might justify all the controversial techniques used by the
director: Lanzmann's film is about the Shoah itself. As its title
indicates Lanzmann's work is entirely structured around one
word "Shoah" —annihilation—and the impossibility of telling a
story that, however, must be told and remembered. It is precisely
because the Nazis wanted the Shoah to be impossible to tell and
because they almost succeeded in this process that it is imperative
to find a way to pass on the testimonies of the few that had the

miraculous chance to survive. For this reason the main goal of *Shoah* is to continue to "re-present" the Holocaust from the point of view of the victims that were the closest to the end of the death chain. As indicated by the first half hour of the film, this process is extremely difficult for at least six major reasons: the disappearance of most traces of the Shoah and of most of its witnesses; the difficulty to locate survivors that worked at the doors of the gas chambers; the extreme difficulty experienced by these very few men when asked to tell what they lived through; the skills of the Nazis in hiding the Final Solution; the refusal of torturers to testify; and, last but not least, the personal risks one still has to take in order to obtain such testimonies.

In a constant struggle with all these obstacles, the general structure of the film describes first the progressive implementation of the extermination process, from life in the Polish *shtetlehs* to the deportations, the first selections, the arrival, the discovery of the camps and of the Final Solution; the systematic process from the implementation of the first exterminations to the annihilation of a complete people; the discovery that no escape or survival is possible and the importance of saving at least one Jew that could testify and in doing so would defeat the Nazi plan of total annihilation. For this reason, the general progression of the film can be described as following at the same a victim's, Lanzmann's or a given spectator's progressive awareness not only of what exactly the Shoah is but also of the capital importance of protecting its memory at all cost.

Shoah starts directly with the evocation of the horror of the extermination. As indicated by the film as well as Lanzmann's cutting of its published text, the progression of the film can be summarized as follows:

> *Introduction*: The horror of the Shoah. Difficulties in remembering and presentation of the key elements constituting the film

I   *From the shtetleh to the extermination camp*
- before the deportations
  (Pietyra; Filipowicz; Falborski)
- the roundups (Bomba; Borowi)
- deportations and waiting to enter the camp (Polish armers; Borowi; railroad employees; Bomba)
- arrivals (Gawkowski; Bomba; Glazar; Borowi; Gawkowski; Piwonski)
- entrance into the camp (Vrba; Bomba; Glazar)
- the first day in the camp (Bomba; Glazar)

II   *Implementation of the extermination*
- the deportations of the last German Jews (Deutschkron)
- the functioning of a "death factory" (Suchomel; Müller)
- the clogging of the "machine" (Müller; Suchomel; Oberhauser)
- improvements of the "machine" (Spiess; Piwonski)
- the Final Solution (Piwonski; Müller)
- its heritage and its innovations (Hilberg)

III *The mechanism of the first exterminations*
- the first systematic exterminations (Schalling)
- Chelmno and the vans (Podlechbnik; Michelson)
- Grabow Jews and the Polish population (Poles)
- Bystanders in Chelmno (Poles; Michelson; Srebnik)
- exterminations and the disappearance of the corpses (Fallorski; Srebnik)
- improvements of the vans (recommendations from the Geheime Reichssache)

Part II

IV *The extermination on a very large scale*
- From the camp to the gas chambers (Suchomel)
- At the gas chamber doors (Bomba)
- Treblinka's "infirmary" (Glazar)
- victims from the ramp to the gas chambers (Vrba; Müller)
- every European Jew is a victim (Mordo; Corfou Jews)
- organization of the trains throughout Europe (Stier; Hilberg)

V *No escape possible: the role of memory*
- work for death; a fake survival (Müller; Suchomel)
- murder by starvation and first plans of revolt (Glazar; Müller; Vrba)
- impossible dreams of survival; Jews from Theresienstadt (Elias; Vrba; Müller)
- revolt and testimony (Vrba)

VI *To see and to tell*
- Jan Karski's mission (Karski)
- Czerniakow's last days and diary (Grassler; Hilberg; Schneider)

Conclusion: The last Jew (Zuckermann; Rottem)

As Lanzmann himself indicated about the long and tedious editing of the film: "After having built the first half hour, the shape was here and was indicating the rest as a mold ('le reste en creux')" (Lanzmann, 1985: 22). It is therefore in a detailed analysis of the beginning of the film that I will look for its main components and structural lines.

Shoah starts with complete silence and a text written by Lanzmann but not read aloud. Before any image is shown, the director insists on a minimum knowledge one should have before watching his film or any testimony of the Holocaust, just like he started his film by reading many books on the Holocaust ("One must know and see, and one must see and know. Indissolubly. If you go to Auschwitz without knowing anything about Auschwitz and the history of this camp, you see nothing, you understand nothing either"). As a technique also used by Pierre Sauvage at the beginning of *Weapons of the Spirit* (1988), the written text captures the attention of all the audience and imposes silence and concentration in the theater. This silence imposed throughout the film is capital as it insists at the same time on the emptiness of the places visited, on the impossibility to describe the Shoah, on the disappearance of the millions of victims and of traces of the Shoah while inviting the spectators to rebuild in imagination what cannot be said and what cannot be shown by any film. The totality of the film will develop around this vacuum and this silence that constitute the major challenge to any film made on the Holocaust.

"The story begins in the present at Chelmno on the Narew River, in Poland." In the original French text written by Lanzmann, the first word of the film is not "story" but "action" ("L'action commence de nos jours à Chelmno-sur-Ner, Pologne"). The word "action" insists on the fact that this is a film, not a documentary. With this very first sentence *Shoah* starts like dozens of fiction films, novels or plays based on a precise historical description of the evolution of a given place or of a particular hero at a specific time.

As in fiction films, the witnesses—Lanzmann often calls them the "characters" of his film—were chosen according to certain roles they will play in Lanzmann's production. Their testimonies are carefully edited in order to produce a specific effect on the audience. The director will therefore stage certain scenes and search for some particular kind of "re-enacting" from his interviewees (All these remarks raise very important questions on the role of the director. I will consider them at the end of this study). Lanzmann himself commented on these first words of *Shoah* in an interview with the renowned *Cahiers du cinéma*:

Cahiers:	The first (written) sentence of the film is: "The action begins..." and, further, a subtitle designates one of the witnesses as the "first character," therefore in terms of a fiction.
C. Lanzmann:	Of a fiction yes, or of theater. It is like saying: "by order of appearance on stage."
Cahiers:	Yes but, at the same time you reject any type of fiction similar to *Holocaust*, you designate a person that is here, in front of us, who survived certain events, as a character.
C. Lanzmann:	They are the protagonists of the film.
Cahiers:	The protagonists of History?
C. Lanzmann:	Yes, not the characters of a reconstitution, because the film is not a reconstitution, but in a certain way, I had to turn these people into actors (Lanzmann, 1985: 21).

Consequently, *Shoah* would be a certain kind of "fiction" that would "incarnate" the truth better than any historical work because it forces the witnesses not only to testify but to "re-enact" scenes of their past in order to "relive" and "transmit" their experiences. All these points raise once again dozens of key questions that I will analyze.

The introductory text written by Lanzmann indicates clearly that this "story" is not a fiction in the traditional sense of the word. Everything that is shown or told in *Shoah* is real. The entire film is made in the present, on a real historical site, out of interviews of individuals that are asked to describe precisely their own experiences. Moreover, *Shoah* is not merely about the past. Every scene is filmed "in the present," ("*aujourd'hui*" in the French text), most often on location, in Poland. Indeed, as Lanzmann wrote: "The worst crime, both moral and artistic, one can commit while creating a work on the Holocaust, is to consider it as *past*" (in Deguy, 316).

As Hervé le Roux wrote: "*Shoah* is a film of Poland. Its subject is Poland" (Lanzmann, 1985: 17). The subject is indeed Poland, but only in part, because it is the country where the extermination camps where located. It is the land that *knew*, *saw*, and *remembers* everything and still *tells* stories about it. From this basic orientation of the film—Poland presented rightfully but only as a key element in the extermination process—originated the most violent controversies surrounding *Shoah*. Consequently, four verbs will be at the heart of the film, like four moral commands that will also summarize Jan Karski's mission after his visit to the Warsaw Ghetto: know, see, remember, and testify.

The introductory text gives at the same time general historical indications and very precise biographical data on its first two "characters," Mordechaï Podchelbnik and Simon Srebnik, the only two survivors of Chelmno. If this film is some kind of a fiction, it is not because of its basic material that is made out of very precise facts, very real places and witnesses. According to Lanzmann's wishes, this film has to be some kind of a fiction because its purpose is not one of a documentary that would be about past events as such. Its main goal is to bring to the present and to the imagination the series of memories, words, images and finally feelings (an extreme suffering) related to the events precisely described. Lanzmann borrows from the techniques of fiction that enable his witnesses and his film to "transmit" at least partially the incommunicable. This "transmission" can be best characterized as an extremely incomplete but violent sharing of feelings, suffering, and experiences taking place between the witnesses and the spectators thanks to the power of a work of art, both fictitious and real, acting as a medium between two poles that otherwise could not communicate in the same manner. For this reason I will study in detail the exact meaning of Lanzmann's expression characterizing his film as a "fiction of reality" (Lanzmann, 1985: 21).

Finally, Lanzmann's introductory text ends with this sentence: "I found him (Srebnik) in Israel and persuaded that one-time boy singer to return with me to Chelmno. He was forty-seven" ("C'est en Israel que je l'ai découvert. J'ai convaincu l'enfant chanteur de revenir avec moi à Chelmno. Il avait quarante-sept ans"). This sentence illustrates another key process of the film consisting in superimposing the various testimonies with images of the places they are mentioning filmed in the present. It is this "presence" of the place that Lanzmann uses as a basis for communicating to the audience the powerful evocation of horror in his film.

It is to be noticed that the English translation "one-time boy singer" loses an important connotation of the French "l'enfant chanteur." The English "one-time" suggests a clear separation between the past and the present that does not exist in Lanzmann's original text. In the French text, Srebnik, even at the age of forty-seven, comes back as the "boy singer" he was and still is, just as Mme. Lagrange said in *Hotel Terminus* that she had "stopped growing up" in Auschwitz. The basic movement of the film is to put in parallel words of the past said in the present with images of the same places filmed in the present. In this process, Lanzmann's goal is to bring to the present and to communicate a "story" that, according to Nazi plans, was never supposed to be told or believed. The testimonies gathered by the film should then enable us first to know and then to see what happened.

It is also to be noticed that this sentence introducing the film itself insists clearly on Lanzmann's work before he could even make this film. The director indeed already explains clearly that he first had to find Srebnik and then to convince him to go back to Poland so the film could be made (*"Je l'ai découvert..."*, *"J'ai convaincu..."*). Lanzmann does so not only during certain interviews, as may be expected, but in the film itself. *Shoah* very often insists on the preparatory work and the technical tricks that were necessary in order to produce the images shown. Moreover, as the opening credits insist on the fact that *Shoah* was produced by a rather large and changing team of close collaborators, it seems relevant to notice here that Lanzmann, himself, takes on the responsibility for the final result as well as for finding, persuading and interviewing Simon Srebnik.

After the silent reading of these long words of introduction written by the director, the film gets started. The fact that Lanzmann himself wrote this instead of having Srebnik tell it directly as a part of the film indicates again that the director had to play a key role in ordering the testimonies according to his final goal. From the very beginning, *Shoah* appears to be a film on the annihilation of the European Jews by the Nazis but it is also very clearly Claude Lanzmann's film, made according to his personal obsessions. This raises many important questions, sometimes very controversial ones which I will analyze in the last part of this study.

As Lanzmann indicated and as we just saw in a brief analysis of the first few minutes, the first half hour or so of the film contains indeed all the key points that will be developed throughout the film. This introductory segment ends with the interview, in Cincinnati, of Mrs. Paula Biren, a survivor of Auschwitz. A closer study of this first half hour will then enable us to present a general study of this nine and a half hour film.

To start with, many key moments of *Shoah* are introduced with a sentence which Lanzmann's montage insists on and develops in a particular way. As the film is first based on what one should "know" in order to understand what one "sees," words pronounced by the witnesses are of prime importance and are used as different sparks that give *Shoah* its first movements as the "re-presentation" of the Holocaust that it wants to be. It is therefore the method I will also use to conclude this analysis of the first thirty minutes of the film.

1) "*I truly relived what happened*" (a Polish farmer in Chelmno).

These words are pronounced by a Polish farmer we do not see while the screen shows a close-up of Simon Srebnik. They are heard as the conclusion of the very first images of the film in which Simon Srebnik was shown sitting and singing in a barge on a river, appearing progressively between tree trunks. This sequence depicts the trees that the Nazis planted in order to hide all traces of the murder of the Jews. In between these trees, images of the past become present and alive thanks to the voice of one survivor that agreed not only to testify but also to reenact partially a scene of his own experience. As a consequence of this partial reenacting, the witnesses of the film, like this un-named Polish farmer, will be able to "relive what happened" and to do so in front of the camera.

Such a process often used in the film remains highly controversial as it is extremely difficult to define what this key word
"re-live" really means. It also raises the problem of the moral
position of a film director asking a survivor to "relive" a chapter
of the Holocaust that is part of his or her personal experience,
even for the purpose of an historical film or a work of art.

2) *"Yes, this is the place"* (Simon Srebnik).
This expression indicates clearly the importance in the film
of conjugating the testimonies with images of what remains, in
the present, of the places where they occurred. Places and oral
testimonies are the two key elements from which the film
develops. It is important here to notice that Srebnik expresses
himself in the present and soon, talking about the past, he will
enable us to understand and to imagine what he says while
searching for the very few elements that have remained the same:
"It was silent. Peaceful. Just like now." The importance of such
a sentence explains also why Lanzmann often compared his film
to the work of a land surveyor or that of an archeological dig
successively bringing various layers of the past to the surface of
the present.

Following these words, the image switches from a medium
shot on Srebnik to a slow and silent panning of the site of the
camp. In this segment, the camera does not film an interview. It
shows the shock of a survivor's first encounter with a place he
thought he would never leave alive and then thought he would
not see again. The violent clash produced by this astonishing
encounter is precisely what Lanzmann felt during his first trip to
Poland and what he counts on in order to tell the "story" that is
in itself impossible to narrate.

In this sequence, as it will often happen throughout the film,
the panning of the camera reproduces the movements of the
survivor's eyes discovering the site today, searching for some
remaining traces and trying to imagine, to "re-present" to his
imagination what happened here. The encounter and the discovery of the place in the present become necessary media

towards understanding both the personal testimonies of the survivors and the totality of the film itself.

3) *"One cannot tell that. No one can imagine what took place here. Impossible. And nobody can understand this. And myself today..."* (Srebnik).

These sentences introduce clearly the challenge of the film: to tell a story that is incommunicable, to name the unspeakable. However, as soon as he is done with these first statements, Srebnik tries to explain; he starts saying how he feels: "And myself today..." In adding these few words the survivor indirectly expresses his need to try to communicate, to tell this "impossible" story. This segment shows exactly how the film will proceed with interviews. The director is above all looking for minute descriptions of personal experiences ("myself") and for feelings expressed in the present of the making of the film ("today").

After this, Lanzmann's work is once again that of an archeologist digging through different layers of memory, always trying to push the limits of the incommunicable a little further. At this point, the camera walks along with Srebnik in the camp, accompanying him in his effort to restructure his memory. It then switches to images of what remains of the foundations of the camp in Chelmno.

Srebnik's sentences are also echoed in this introduction by the refusal of another survivor to testify (Mordechaï Podchlebnik). Podchlebnik does not want to tell what he went through not only because no one could understand or because there are no words to describe such an experience. His reason is that it is "not good" for him: "It is not good, for me it is not good." This remark indicates clearly that Podchlebnik is trying to avoid the resurgence of images and memories he still suffers from because they are so present and so violent that he knows he might not be able to face them consciously again.

What follows is extremely relevant to Lanzmann's interviewing technique. As the survivor cannot talk directly about his personal experience, Lanzmann asks him a precise historical question: "At that time, they did not burn corpses, they were simply buried?" The survivor can then answer this as an historical witness, without directly mentioning a particular episode of his own life. However, a few minutes later, we see Podchlebnik again, in tears, telling how, one day, he had to transport the corpses of his wife and children from a gas van to a ditch. This progression in an interview will characterize the interviews of all the survivors that were not directly involved in resistance organizations or projects: difficulty or impossibility to talk, precise historical questions, the director's relentless insistence on an historical answer, personal testimony, violent suffering and tears sometimes threatening the continuation of the testimony.

After that, the montage uses the most common techniques of the film, switching directly from a close-up of a witness to a panning or a tracking shot, in the present, of the place just evoked by the testimony which we continue to hear in juxtaposition. In some other cases, silent images will show a place in the present and only a few seconds later, a voice will start a testimony related to the images we see and just saw. In both cases, redundance, repetition and superimposition, play a key role as they do throughout the film.

There is a third setting for the interview of survivors that is also introduced in the first half hour of the film; it is the double interview of Motke Zaïdl in the presence of his friend, Itzhak Dugin, and partly in the presence of Zaïdl's daughter, Hanna. In this case, the survivor's testimony can be made possible through the conjugated insistence of Lanzmann and of a loved one (Hanna), as well as through the description of the obsessive memory of a place. The difficulty is introduced by the confrontation of the daughter's need to know with her father's silence. Later on, in what is one of the most beautiful shots of the film, we see the two witnesses sitting next to each other with Hanna listening carefully behind and above them, as a quiet, attentive and very respectful protector and defender of their memory. All three of them are facing Lanzmann, the camera and the audience, insisting on the fundamental transmission the film is trying to achieve.

Once again, Lanzmann obtained these testimonies thanks to the detailed evocation of a place. However, as Motke Zaïdl compares Israel's to Ponari's forest that are, according to him, very similar, the audience discovers progressively that in reality, the Israeli forest shown on the screen has nothing to do with Lithuania's: "There, there were no stones... the forests were more dense... trees were taller and bigger...." What Lanzmann's interview reveals here once again is the obsessive character of some images of the past that never left the survivors, even if they never talked about it. Since the war, for this survivor, there is only one forest. All the forests Motke Zaïdl sees remind him of Ponari's, no matter how different they are.

Testimonies can also be made possible through the presence of a friend who knows and understands because he is himself a survivor. Like in the last minutes of *Shoah*, the camera insists on many occasions on the reactions of one survivor listening to another completing his testimony (Itzhak Zuckermann and Simha Rottem). While we hear Itzhak Dugin describe his work digging up corpses to burn them, the camera zooms to offer a close-up of Motke Zaïdl's face as he listens peacefully with, however, a very agitated blink of the eyelids. The conclusion of this sequence is that not only the images but also the terror and the pain expressed throughout the film are very present, just like the hatred or the anti-Semitism expressed in other testimonies.

4) *"When the family gets together, they talk about it, around the table. Because it was public, next to the street, everybody knew"* (Polish farmers).

These remarks characterize the film's second kind of witness, the bystanders. It does so through assigning them a very definite place in space both in the present and in the past (right next to the extermination sites), a definite knowledge ("everybody knew"), and a definite discourse, in the present, that is directly linked to what they saw and what they knew (they never stopped talking about the Holocaust). Unlike the survivors, the bystanders still talk a lot about the exterminations:

> (...) the Polish land, its rivers, the Polish forests, towns, villages, men and women in Poland *talk* about the Holocaust, revive it, restitute it in some sort of a timeless actuality that often abolishes any distance between present and past (Lanzmann; in Deguy, 212).

While Motke Zaïdl was unable to tell his own daughter what he saw, the Holocaust seems to be a favorite conversation subject for Polish family gatherings. Some Poles shown in the film take great pride or even some pleasure in telling their own version of what they saw, especially when they are interviewed as a group, throughout the first part of the film.

However, the first group is not interviewed as such. While we hear these sentences, the camera shows Simon Srebnik from far away, with a rower, sitting in a little boat crossing once again the river of death by singing the song he used to sing for the SS. A few seconds earlier, we saw, in the background, the tower of the Chelmno church where many exterminations started and where a key interview of a group of Poles will take place later in the film. At this point, the film is already superimposing different layers of the past in the present of its representation and announcing future segments: the discourse of the bystanders as a group, the "same" peaceful landscape, the "same" song sung by the "same" man and the church where "everything" took place and that will later offer a dominant segment to the film. Various presentations of the "same" places are also used as transition points throughout the film. After the segment showing the obsessive aspects forests have for two survivors in Israel, we see Jan Piworski, a Polish railroad worker, walking in the forest of Sobibor.

In this sequence the Polish man's testimony contrasts violently with Simon Srebnik's. A few minutes earlier in the film, we heard Srebnik declare, at Chelmno's site, that even when Germans were burning two thousand Jews per day: "It was always as quiet here, always." Now, Jan Piworski asserts that in Sobibor: "this silence did not always reign here. There was a time when, exactly where we stand, it was filled with screams, gun shots, barking."

A logical explanation would be that Srebnik and Piworski are not talking about the same place nor the same period (the burning of corpses in Chelmno vs. the camp of Sobibor during the exterminations). However, Piworski insisted previously on "the charm of our forests, this silence, this beauty." Throughout the film Lanzmann will oppose the extreme violence of the exterminations to the ageless "beauty" and "silence" of the Polish forests. Survivors like Richard Glazar, in the introduction, will also insist on the silence of the world and of God himself while the annihilation of six million Jews was taking place.

Therefore, the confrontation at a few minutes interval of Srebnik's and Piworski's testimonies already underlines a key theme of the film: the violent contrast between the well-known brutality of the Shoah, the eagerness of many Poles to get rid of the Jews, and the silence of the world. Srebnik remembers very vividly the perfect silence surrounding the Holocaust while the Polish man remembers both the screams he heard and the "beauty" of the world covering the massacres with an ocean of silence. Piworski will confirm later in the film that during the exterminations, there were days "as beautiful and even more beautiful than today."

In contrast, the end of this introductory segment will show beautiful images of the Narew river where the ashes and the crushed bones of the Jews used to be thrown. Mounted on a boat, the camera follows the fast stream. While the part of the sky we can directly see is grey and white, its reflection shows a burning sunset in the back of the camera as a reminder of the murders and of the fires meant to destroy all traces of the Holocaust. Accompanying the theme of the river, we hear once again Simon Srebnik's song. Like all places in the film, Polish rivers have kept bits and pieces of the memory of the Shoah the film is slowly gathering and offering to its audience.

From now on, the long periods of silence used in *Shoah* will play a central role as it is through this very silence recreated by the film that the audience will have to hear the cries nobody would hear less than half a century ago. Lanzmann himself insisted on the importance of this aspect of the role played by silence in his film: "Indeed, someone remarkably wrote to me: 'It is the first time that I heard the scream of a child in a gas chamber.'" He concluded that "this is the total power of the evocation and the oral expression" (Lanzmann, 1985: 20). This power however would not be nearly as strong without the totally silent periods that follow, precede or cut many testimonies.

The introductory segment contains indeed all the major themes to be developed in detail in the film. The role and the extreme cruelty of the Nazis whose interviews are not used in the introduction is of course implied all along. However, this first half hour does not directly open the film on an avalanche of testimonies. On the contrary it concludes itself and begins the film on the need to remember but also on the constant and extreme difficulties survivors always have facing their memories, precisely because they represent much more than an episode of their past.

> *Lanzmann*:   Did you ever return to Poland?
> *Paula Biren*:   No. I often wanted to. But what would I see? How could I face that?

The introduction (the first half hour of the film) ends on the evocation of the death of Paula Biren's grand-parents in the Lodz ghetto. It is linked to the very beginning of the film by a long silence during which we see contemporary images of one of the very few graves remaining in the Jewish cemetery of Lodz. From this close up, the camera moves back and then pans to reveal that all traces of Jewish lives and even deaths before and during the war have been almost completely erased. We are once again at the very beginning of the film, facing one more time the same problems. Starting with images of the places where the Holocaust took place, the purpose of the film will then be to turn this silence of death and oblivion into the silence of listening, contemplation and remembrance.

b. To Know and to See

"One must know and see, and one must see and know." The structure of this sentence itself insists on the importance of illustration, corroboration, superimposition, reenactment, redundancy and other sorts of repetitions throughout the film. The key articulation of Lanzmann's remark is indeed the conjunction of coordination, "and." In order to understand *Shoah* fully, one first must "know" *and* "see" in order to grasp the full meaning of what is being said and repeated. Progressively however, recurrent images will be backed up with enough knowledge so the audience can fill their silence and understand directly what the remaining traces represent, without needing a commentary explaining images being shown again and again.

Like Ophüls' films, *Shoah* is based on the power of repetition and corroboration as well as on an analysis of distortions and disjunctions. However, in Ophüls' work the first pair of techniques serves the latter to represent various characters minutely. On the contrary, in Lanzmann's film, the distortions and the disjunctions only reveal various degrees of repetition of the same truths that increase the intensity of the survivor's testimonies and the effect produced by the film on its audience. While Ophüls multiplies various portraits of characters, Lanzmann always directs his testimonies towards his final goal.

As *Shoah* reveals different layers of memory, repetition allows both the director and the audience to dig progressively deeper and push further the limits of this incommunicable testimony. Throughout the film and also after the viewing, the spectator will put together hundreds of recurring elements of both the soundtrack and the image in order to understand the reality, the importance and the specificity of the Shoah.

The film indeed repeats itself on many occasions. However, each repetition unveils a new part of the truth and pushes the film forward towards a progressively better representation of the Shoah's specificity. Poles repeat the same gestures again and again. Other witnesses repeat similar reactions to Lanzmann's questions. Many expressions are repeated, sometimes distorted.

Lanzmann's most obsessive questions are being asked again and again to the same or to different witnesses. Dates, episodes and anecdotes are repeated sometimes in an unexpected order that can lead to some confusion. Recurring topics are analyzed with different angles at different moments of the film. Images often try to repeat in the present the distance or the route a witness is describing in a simultaneous oral testimony. The same movements of the camera are used again and again.

Last but not least, some witnesses become acting "characters" in the film in agreement with a specific French sense of the word *répétition* (rehearsal). These men and women, very spontaneously or under the directions of Lanzmann, reenact an episode of their past like professional actors would. Then their past feelings reveal their actuality and enable us to draw many different lessons from our own reactions and future reflections on *Shoah*. In conclusion, these various kinds of repetitions show that all the elements that led to the Shoah are not dead. Many of them are still very present and it is essential to recognize and analyze them in order to prevent the always threatening repetition of the Holocaust itself.

In order to conduct this study, one can, however, isolate at least three main kinds of shots in *Shoah* that use various kinds of repetitions and relationships between the soundtrack and the image. Indeed, the film constantly combines these techniques and I will momentarily separate them only for a clearer progression of this analysis. In the first category, I include interviews in a setting that is familiar to the witnesses but not directly related to the extermination process. Such interviews are usually conducted in a room with one, two or three participants. Medium shots and close-ups play a key role in these segments.

Second, many segments of the film show interviews on location. In these cases, the background, the places or the objects shown play an extremely important role in the evocation created by the film. These segments give us the setting for interviews of various individuals, groups or even small crowds. I include in this category, interviews that required from Lanzmann a very elaborate staging as the place and the setting in such cases play a key role in the understanding of a given testimony.

Finally, many parts of the film show a site, a Polish landscape or what remains of an extermination camp, without showing the image of a witness. Many of these shots are also shown without any commentary, explanation or testimony accompanying them. In such cases, silence, but not the absence of soundtrack, becomes an essential part of the film. Such segments are used very differently and they progressively take on different values as the film continues. It is however to be remembered that repetition plays a very complex role at the same time in the soundtrack, in the image series, in the relationship of both and in the combined use of the three main kinds of shots I have just described. It is this complex network of repetition that I will now have to analyze more closely.

The most common example of interviews conducted in a familiar setting, not directly related to the places where the Shoah occurred, gathers sequences with witnesses that, for different reasons, Lanzmann could not or did not want to bring back to Poland. According to their different treatments, I will organize them in three groups differentiating between interviews with Filip Müller, Rudolf Vrba, Gertrude Schneider and her mother, Richard Glazar, Jan Karski; interviews of all the Nazis; and finally interviews of Abraham Bomba, and of some Polish bystanders.

Interviews of Filip Müller were all conducted in the same very bright room, in his home in Israel. At the beginning of this first and long interview, we do not see his face right away but instead we are shown a long sequence filmed in Auschwitz beginning with a reverse tracking shot starting on a close up of an execution wall. After this the film recreates his first walk from these barracks to the crematorium. As in one of the introductory shots with Srebnik in Chelmno, the camera becomes the eyes of the survivor and shows us a contemporary simulacrum of what he sees or saw. It offers a precise re-presentation of the images evoked. It is only after this long description of the discovery of the crematorium that we see Müller's face for the first time as he starts describing: "Suddenly an Unterscharführer ran toward me and said to me: 'Get out of here, go stir the corpses!'"

The beginning of this interview showing images of Auschwitz also indicates Lanzmann's answer to a precise problem of ethics. This interview was indeed immediately preceded by an interview of Treblinka's guard, Franz Suchomel. However, according to Lanzmann's own words:

> The elaboration (of the film) was also dictated by questions of morality. It was impossible to have Nazis meet Jews: not that I would have had them meet physically but that the montage could have had them meet. They are not war veterans gathering forty years after on TV for a virile handshake (Lanzmann, 1985: 23).

The long reproduction of Müller's first discovery of the gas chambers serves also as a separation from Suchomel's and Müller's testimonies. Thanks to this long and slow transition, the two are never competing and Müller's testimony is never "compared" to Suchomel's. Their testimonies represent two parallel and totally non-communicating experiences and descriptions of the same universe. In the film also, there is no possible debate between the victims and the executioners. Their experiences can never be put on an equal level for argumentation. The film is very conscious of this basic rule of ethics for any representation of the Holocaust.

As Filip Müller's first interview goes on, his testimony shifts from the description of the crematoria to the description of the work he had to do there. At that precise point ("We had already undressed some corpses when the order was given to feed the ovens"), the image shows a medium shot of Müller followed after a zoom by a close-up when Müller says that an SS told him: "Do as I do or I will kill you." This reinforcement of the violence and intensity of the testimony continues until the witness indicates that the duct connecting the crematorium to the chimney ended up clogging because of the intense heat that broke its bricks. At that point the camera shows the same chimney today and after that, Lanzmann's editing becomes much more inventive.

As Müller describes precisely his "work" on the same evening, the camera pans the countryside around Auschwitz, stops when the famous gate to the camp appears far away in the background, and the shot ends with a zoom towards this gate. When Müller mentions that this work had to stop at night, we see a beautiful dark blue night in or around Auschwitz with a full red moon. After this, Müller starts describing his work on the following day while the camera pans the camp covered with snow. As soon as the description and the tone of the voice become very emotional, the image goes back to a medium shot of Müller: "We had to go down this muddy pit in order to pile the corpses/(switch to a medium shot of Müller)/But they were slimy... For example, when I wanted to take a women, her hands...."

This long interview ends with another panning shot of Auschwitz covered with snow and a zoom on a sign that reads "Birkenau." During this, the voice of Filip Müller explains that more crematoria were successively added to Auschwitz's camps. His testimony ends with these words: "... up to three thousand people could be gassed at the same time."

This first interview of Filip Müller enables us to characterize key techniques used by Lanzmann in this kind of segment. These techniques can be listed as follows: First, this segment is separated from the interview of the SS by a long silence and a slow movement of the camera starting from an image at first difficult to identify. This creates a clear rupture between the two sequences, forcing the audience to concentrate on the upcoming segment.

Second, the camera reproduces in the present movements described in the past by the witness. The audience then is invited to imagine the episode described from what is left today of the same place.

Third, the first time we see the witness, he is describing an episode of his life for history's sake, as an example of what was going on in the camp. This is filmed with a medium shot giving a face to the words heard.

Fourth, as soon as the testimony brings violent emotions back to the present or leads the witness to reenact the past in a very personal manner, the camera stays put or offers a close-up of the person speaking.

Fifth, when the testimony becomes very long, it is cut with various images filmed on site reminding the audience that the events described took place in a very real and identifiable setting. As Lanzmann thinks a long interview of a "talking head" (an expression often used by Ophüls) is boring, this kind of editing serves two purposes. It makes it easier to concentrate on a long film or on a long interview and, most of all, it links the testimony to a real place. Not only some people but places and objects—a landscape, a camp site, a house, wagons, old trains, a street, etc.— that are part of our very own world were the very same when the Holocaust was being perpetrated. Through their presence today they can help us get a very incomplete but vivid and "real" image of the terror experienced by the victims.

In this regard, Lanzmann's search in *Shoah* often reminds us of these sentences written by Proust in *A la recherche du temps perdu*: "Each hour of our life, as soon as it dies, embodies itself in some material object (...). The object in which it is hiding—or the sensation—we may very well never encounter" (Marcel Proust, *Les Jeunes filles en fleur*). Part of Lanzmann's work then consists in making sure that this encounter takes place even before these places and these objects disappear.

Sixth, these images of camp sites or of countryside give the audience a personal experience of a key element of the Holocaust's horror: the silence of the world; the coldness of the snow; the indifferent beauty and peace of nature; the absence of any human feeling; the slow, regular and threatening movement of time always about to bring a terrifying event or image; and finally the omnipresence of the camp and of death, the impossibility of escape. Like all the survivors' testimonies, all the movements of the camera in the exterior—zooms, panning or tracking shots—invariably lead to a death camp, to a gas chamber, to a crematorium, to an image of death.

Filip Müller's last long interview narrates the extermination of the Czech families from Theresienstadt. This whole segment is filmed with an uninterrupted close-up as at this point, it is totally impossible for the witness to even try to separate his violent personal emotions from his historical testimony. After this very moving sequence in the middle of which Müller bursts out in tears, a silent segment slowly shows a model reconstitution in plaster of the gas chambers whose cold, black and white images can be conjugated with the memory of the words just heard.

All the indoor interviews conducted in "neutral" settings (not related even symbolically to the places where the Holocaust took place) use different combinations of the techniques just described. The other most important example is the long interview (forty minutes) of Jan Karski, conducted in his home in Washington, D.C. As is the case with Müller's interview, the image punctuates the testimony and its intensity with successions of medium shots, close-ups and extreme close-ups. Jan Karski's mission was to tell the Allied leaders in London and in the U.S. what he had seen in Warsaw's Ghetto and in the extermination camps in order to obtain an official denunciation of the atrocities being committed, the promise of a trial for the executioners as well as immediate actions to stop the exterminations. This mission is illustrated with images of American democracy's landmarks in Washington, D.C.

The middle of this interview however uses a technique that is very rarely used in the film. While Karski explains his mission narrating one of his two meetings with a Zionist and a Bundist leader before he was taken to see the Warsaw Ghetto, the screen shows contemporary images of the Rhur and then, images of thousands of personal belongings of the victims left and piled in Auschwitz. This is surprising because unlike what happens in the rest of the film, the images here have no direct link with the testimony heard at the same time (the request for arms for the Ghetto and the request for support from international Jewish leaders).

This dichotomy between the soundtrack and the image series insists symbolically on the importance and on the urgency of Karski's mission. The image suggests, in the present, that while

Karski's mission was launched, the extermination was already underway on an "industrial" scale; instead of images of an empty camp site, we are shown present images of a very active industrial plant in the Rhur with its enormous smoking chimneys and its gigantic and terrifying flames. These are directly followed by images of thousands of personal objects belonging to the victims, now piled in Auschwitz.

Such a sequence is characteristic of Lanzmann's insistence on sticking to the subject of the process of the extermination. It can also be considered as another expression of Lanzmann's strong belief in German collective complicity and guilt: "The extermination of the Jews did not result from the actions of a handful of mad men. Concerning Germany, the destruction process could be accomplished only on the basis of a general consensus of the German nation" (in Deguy, 311). Moreover, according to this segment superimposing Karski's testimony and contemporary images of the Rhur, even Germany's contemporary industrial wealth recalls, at least symbolically, the systematic and "industrialized" extermination of the European Jews by the Nazis. At this level, it seems that in Germany like in Poland, very little has changed since the war. As the last images of the first part of *Shoah* will indicate, even the truck company Saurer, who made the first gas vans, was still prospering forty years after the war.

Jan Karski's interview lasted indeed eight hours and was completed in two days. Of these eight hours, only forty minutes were used, insisting on Karski's painful process of recollection, on his reasons to testify, most of all, and on what he saw in the Warsaw Ghetto. Nothing is shown of what Karski said about other Poles that tried to help Jews, about what he saw in Belzec nor about the reasons his mission failed in London and in Washington. For Karksi "*Shoah* is unquestionably the greatest movie about the tragedy of the Jews that appeared after the war." However, referring to the segments of his interview that have not been mentioned in the film he adds:

> Including this material into the movie as well as
> general information about those who attempted to help
> the Jews, would have presented the Holocaust in a

historically more accurate perspective (Karski, 1986:
45).

The treatment of the segment of Karski's interview about the
three points of his mission (request for international
condemnation and retaliation, for arms and for action from
Jewish leaders) is clearly linked not to the analysis of the mission
itself but to its desperate aspect confronted with the extreme
violence of the Final Solution. Consequently, Jan Karski wrote
about *Shoah* that:

> The uncompromising restriction of the topic (of *Shoah*)
> creates an impression that the Jews were abandoned by
> all mankind, that all mankind was insensitive to their
> fate. This is however, untrue and disheartening,
> particularly for postwar and future generations of Jews.
> The Jews were abandoned by governments, by those
> who had the physical or spiritual power. They were not
> abandoned by mankind. After all, several hundred
> thousand Jews were saved in Europe. In Poland tens of
> thousands survived. The penalty for harboring a Jew in
> Poland was death. In Western Europe. although the
> punishment was not as extreme, helping and harboring
> Jews exposed people to great dangers. Nevertheless
> millions of peasants, workers, intellectuals, priests,
> nuns, endangering themselves and their relatives,
> provided aid to Jews in each country of Europe. How
> many of them perished? God only knows (Karski,
> 1986: 44).

Interviews of Raul Hilberg in his own house use the same
kind of editing. In many ways, their use and value in the film are
very similar to Pierre Mendès-France's interviews in Ophüls' *The
Sorrow and the Pity*. It is clear that Lanzmann has great
admiration for Hilberg's work and thought which are at the basis
of the historical research conducted for the making of *Shoah*. As
is the case with Mendès-France's interviews in *The Sorrow and
the Pity*, Hilberg's interviews always situate the film in a very
precise historical chronology and framework. They give all the
words heard their exact place and value within the general history

of the Holocaust. Used in the final sections of each part of the film, they gather the disseminated testimonies heard in one general and clear historical interpretation.

The last category of this type of indoor interview gathers testimonies of Nazis or SS. Many of them are filmed in black and white, without the witness knowing it, while others are done openly. These segments use similar combinations of medium shots, close-ups and images illustrating the testimony in the present that we characterized with the other witness. One new element here is the use of Treblinka's map with Suchomel reinforcing the excellent "technical" and "professional" knowledge the SS had of what he calls the "death factory." In this case we are always clearly shown Lanzmann's strategy through images showing the van where the technicians are hiding. As the SS conducted the mass murder of the Jews through various well-organized successions of tricks and lies, the way Lanzmann films them by lying to them in order to get their testimony is not shocking and is totally justified.

The use of Treblinka's song, sung by the SS Suchomel, at the very beginning of the second part of the film introduces another problem. In many occurrences, Lanzmann asks a witness to repeat what he just said, to explain something again or directly, to reenact a scene. When Suchomel sings for the second time the "Song of Treblinka," Lanzmann has disappeared from the screen. This time, the former guard does not sing the song just to let his interviewer hear the melody and the words, as he pretends. The second time, he sings with much more inspiration, in the present, with "all his heart." Ruth Angress writes about the conclusion of this scene: "Suchomel presumably means to say that he is having a good time remembering and that he feels a little bad about it" (Angress, 256).

In another example, Lanzmann and an interpreter are interviewing on site a Polish man who lived next to the railroad track in Treblinka. We first see the three of them on the screen. When the Polish man shows how, with a movement of the hand across his throat, he used to tell the Jews they were about to die, Lanzmann understands very well what the man is doing and saying. However, he asks him to start his explanation all over again and, at the same time, he and the interpreter disappear from the focus of the camera. The audience is left alone with the image of this smiling Polish man starting a very theatrical explanation of what he used to do and why he was doing it.

> When I interrogated the farmers in Treblinka, I asked the fat guy—this one was a swine—if he remembered the first convoy of Jews coming from Warsaw on July 22, 1942. He said that he remembers very well and immediately, he forgot that we were talking about the first time and he placed himself in the routine of the extermination and of the convoys that he saw arriving everyday (Lanzmann, 1985: 22).

This example takes us to the analysis of one other very famous "on site" segment revealing a deep-rooted collective anti-Semitism. In this scene, as people are entering and leaving mass at a church in Chelmno, a group of Poles is gathered around the survivor, Simon Srebnik. Women stand the closest to him, men a little farther behind or around him. Here again, Lanzmann starts the discussion by asking questions. These questions work only as a technique to push the group to start its own debate or individuals to start talking by themselves. Here again, Lanzmann progressively disappears as an actor and an author to leave us alone with the images of a past being reenacted in the present.

The most important event happens when these people do not answer questions anymore but begin volunteering testimonies. Many Poles, and one man in particular, the organist, walk to the center of the shot and testify unconsciously about the deep anti-Semitism installed in some of their myths and their traditional beliefs: "All this happened to the Jews because, they were the richest," or in this very revealing passage:

| *Lanzmann*: | Therefore, he thinks (Mr. Kantarowski, the church's organist) that Jews expiated Christ's death? |
| *The Organist*: | (standing in the middle of the group, addressing L. directly): He (voice of the translator talking for Mr. Kantarowski the |

334   Part II

organist)... He does not believe, and even he does not think that Christ desired *revenge*. No, it is not his opinion. The Rabbi said it!

Lanzmann: Ah! The Rabbi said it!

A Woman (stepping in the middle and staring at L.): *It was God's will, that's all* (The emphasis is mine).

During this complete segment, we see, in the background, the open doors of Chelmno church from which thousands of Jews climbed into gas vans to be exterminated and driven to the mass graves in the nearby forest. Christians on a celebration day are now being shown entering and leaving the same church. In the middle, the interview stops to show a procession of young girls throwing flower petals on the path of a statue of the Virgin Mary. At the end of the procession comes the local priest, his face completely hidden by the corpus christi he is carrying as a reminder of Christ's suffering and death.

This image, was used in the final editing to announce the following anti-Semitic remarks on Christ's passion and crucifixion. According to Lanzmann, this sequence has at least two purposes:

This scene is double. There is the first part: they see him (Srebnik), they find him again. They talk about him, an old woman says that she asked the Germans to let this child go. He exists. And suddenly the scene is interrupted by the procession leaving the church. After the procession, it is completely different. He does not exist anymore. He is in the middle of them, but they have forgotten him. The procession has reactivated the old anti-Semitic stereotypes, the death of Christ, etc. And he no longer exists. They do not find him again. And he is absent to himself (in Deguy, 283-284).

In this scene also, the past is reenacted in front of our eyes. The traditional Catholic anti-Semitism of these Polish farmers becomes very present both to Lanzmann, Srebnik, and to us. We are then the only judges of the scene and it is up to us to make up our mind. At this point we become joint authors and commentators of *Shoah* as the screen turns into a window on what happened and could still happen. These examples are also variations, indoor and on site, of Lanzmann's same technique of repetition in order to have the witnesses reenact the past and make it present in front of our very own eyes. In other segments, Lanzmann goes as far as completely staging an interview in order to recreate the surroundings or the gestures of the past in the present. In these cases, the setting is not "neutral" anymore. It plays a very active, decisive and also controversial role that will introduce to us the precise analysis of the director's role in the filming, the staging and the editing of the interviews.

At least on two occasions, Lanzmann organized a complete and complex staging for interviews. The first one was made for the sequences showing Henrik Gakowski driving a locomotive. In order to film this segment, Lanzmann rented a train, had part of the railroad track reopened and asked this retired Polish man to reenact the scene which he filmed from the tender attached to the back of the locomotive. It is while filming this sequence that Lanzmann saw for the first time the supposedly "warning" gesture across the throat made by the Poles:

> When I came back to film and I saw the locomotive, I told him: 'You are going to get in it and we will film an arrival in Treblinka.' I told him nothing more. We arrive at the station, he is here, bending over, and, by himself, he does this incredible gesture across his throat looking at the imaginary wagons (behind this locomotive of course, there was no wagon). In comparison to this image, historical footage becomes insufferable. This image itself became the truth. Further on, when I filmed the farmers, they all started doing the same gesture that they pretend is a warning, but it is a sadistic gesture (Lanzmann, 1985: 21).

There is indeed no doubt about the sadistic nature of this gesture. The Poles knew that most Jews would not or could not understand what it meant and in that case they were making fun of their ignorance. Other Poles also knew that some of them might understand and they felt happy letting the victims know that the

Nazis would soon get rid of the Jews. As the horrible laugh of Czeslaw Borowi shows when he sees Lanzmann himself trying to imitate the gesture, Poles, in both cases, were not "warning" the victims but enjoying the event.

However, Lanzmann himself offered two different interpretations of this gesture and it is perhaps the only case where he explicitly shows some sympathy for one of the Polish bystanders:

> I have no doubt: it is a gesture of pure sadism, of hatred. Take for example the locomotive driver, the first who makes this gesture in the film. I like him, he is different from the others, I feel some sympathy for him because I think he carries a true open wound that will not cure. Among all the Polish farmers in Treblinka, he is the only one who had human behavior (in Deguy, 282).

For this reason the segments showing Henrik Gawkowski (the locomotive driver), and other Poles repeating the same movement of the hand across the throat are not put together in the film. They do not have exactly the same implications. As Lanzmann explained: "The fat man placed himself in the logic of a routine while the other, by his silence, had suddenly realized that he had witnessed an unaccountable (*inoui*) event" (Lanzmann, 1985: 22).

This gesture is important because it reveals an important part of the truth about anti-Semitism and, cinematographically, because it provokes a spontaneous partial reenactment made possible by Lanzmann's direct intervention asking questions or setting interviews in the original places where the Holocaust took place. The director's strategy seems fully justified in order to trick old Nazis or to reveal deep-rooted anti-Semitism among bystanders. It poses however other problems when it is used to obtain very painful and personal testimonies from survivors. This is the case, for example, of the other most famous staged interview in *Shoah*: Abraham Bomba's testimony in a rented hair salon.

Abraham Bomba, a Jewish survivor, was retired when Lanzmann first went to see him. In order to film this sequence, Lanzmann rented a salon and asked Bomba to pretend he was cutting the hair of a customer while he was being filmed. At the beginning, the filming is difficult. As Bomba often turns his back to the camera and to Lanzmann, the camera films his face in the mirrors also showing other hairdressers at work. At the beginning, Bomba speaks very loudly, for history's sake, so that everybody can hear him. Such a tone of voice also reminds us of a child that would start talking very loudly because he is terrified by silence or the dark. At the same time, Abraham Bomba very rarely looks at Lanzmann, in order to avoid any eye to eye or emotional contact. On five instances, he also looks at the door as unknown men want to enter the pretend salon in order to get a real haircut. In doing so, they disturb the scene by making Bomba loose his concentration and putting in jeopardy Lanzmann's strategy. The director has to intervene at least once in order to keep the outsiders away.

Up to this point, however, Lanzmann noted that Bomba "only transmits a certain knowledge" (Lanzmann, 1985: 20). The director then asks him to reenact the way he was cutting the victims' hair just before they would enter the gas chamber. Abraham Bomba shows and explains. A few minutes later (in film time), Lanzmann pushes his questions further, on a more personal level: "But I asked you: 'What did you feel when you saw for the first time these naked women with the children. What did you feel?' You did not answer."

(Only after this, Bomba decides to tell a very personal episode of what he saw. As he says "I am going to tell you something," the camera drops the medium shot filmed in the mirror in order to film the complete end of the sequence with a continuous close-up, an extreme close-up, that will never stop, even when Bomba cannot talk anymore and starts crying.)It is at this point, and not as Lanzmann pretends when he is asked to show how he cut the hair, that "the truth incarnates itself and that he (Bomba) relives the scene for the next twenty minutes" (Lanzmann, 1985: 20).

After watching this scene, many spectators have had strong negative reactions to Lanzmann's techniques, many wondering if the director's insistence was really necessary in situations like this one. Other parts of the film are also controversial not because of their content that always reveals a certain truth about the Holocaust, but because of the director's direct choices and interventions that they required. Such a debate is extremely important as it touches the heart of the problem of the Holocaust's "representation" in Claude Lanzmann's very personal film. It also requires a closer analysis of this staged interview of Abraham Bomba.

All the images of *Shoah* also reveal Lanzmann's obsessions that surface in certain questions he always asks:

> The circularity of the film comes from the obsessional characteristics of my questions. It comes from my own questions: the cold, the terror of the East (the West for me is human, the East terrifies me) (Lanzmann, 1985: 21).

Many recurring questions as well as slow images of the same concentration camps or of a train station under the snow will remind us of the obsessive circularity of the film. This circularity is also marked by the general structure of *Shoah* starting and ending with the testimony of men surviving by an unbelievable chance as "the last Jew" after millions of their people have been assassinated.

The first part of the film also ends with an image of a Saurer truck running on a road in Germany just as the gas vans have been precisely described. The second part ends with images of a train running by the camera. The continuous, incomplete motion of these images reminds us that there is no end to *Shoah*. There is no moment after which the audience could reject as the past the images it just saw. There is no final, finished image after which one could think that he or she now knows enough about this "event of the past" and can feel free to forget about the Shoah.

The various but always obsessive uses of repetition make of *Shoah* a very powerful but also very personal film. This remark raises once again the question of Lanzmann's ability to create an "objective," "fair," or "just" representation of the historical times and the events described in his film. As we have already seen, such questions are at the origin of the violent controversies that often surround *Shoah*. I must add that such critiques are often the result of comments written by people who encountered difficulties dealing with Lanzmann as a very strong minded and dedicated individual. It should be clear however that such problems cannot influence our reading of *Shoah* as this masterpiece must be analyzed independently from any controversy of that sort.

Marcel Ophüls' cautious approach to *Shoah* allows us to summarize some of the reluctance some spectators might have had in seeing Lanzmann's film for the first time:

> I distrust very much all the reasons sometimes used to declare that documentaries are superior to fiction films, their pretention to monopolize the market of the truth, this incredible bourgeois respectability status they have and that they do not deserve. And, above all, I cannot stand that the greatest of popular arts, cinema, be committed by force to serve a cause, whatever this cause might be. All this is to say that I entered with mixed feelings the cinema where Lanzmann's film was being shown (in Deguy, 177).

Ophüls' distrust can therefore be summarized with two questions: Is *Shoah* a traditional historical documentary, and, is this film "committed by force to serve a cause"? From what precedes in this chapter we can confirm that the answer to the first question is "no." The answer to the second question requires further consideration.

Indeed, *Shoah* is a film committed to serving a cause, this cause being the transmission of the uniqueness and the horror of the Shoah so that the audience will remember it and testify for it in order to prevent it from happening again. Therefore, the most important question one can ask based on Ophüls' remark consists in wondering if *Shoah* is committed "by force" to serve this cause. In other words, this question raises one last time the problem of the relationship between the "work" the director had to provide and as a result, the final representation of the Shoah his film offers us.

As we have seen, because *Shoah* is a work of art, something "more than" a purely historical study, it required very active involvement from its director. Lanzmann's very first concern, however, was to create an historically accurate film and he succeeded with this goal in spite of some very minor imprecisions that he has been reproached with, mostly by some Polish historians (Bartoszewski, 22-23). For Lanzmann however: "Historically, the film is absolutely rigorous" (Lanzmann, 1985: 23). Consequently, the most serious accusations about *Shoah* consist in saying that the film presents an incomplete representation of the Holocaust (Bartoszewski, 24-30). Lanzmann has already answered such questions in 1985:

> One could tell me: 'But you did not treat this or that.' I know that. But no one can say I am wrong. There are a thousand things I treated and filmed but that I did not edit. There are others I did not treat for the simple reason that, in some cases, the destruction succeeded and for entire episodes there is no one, not one witness, nothing. But it was an important question: What does the public know? What does it not know? Up to what point can we keep the mystery? In the end, I told myself that I did not have to say everything, that people had to ask questions to themselves. The film was also made so that people can continue to work (...) I had to keep some mystery, make the imagination work: I did not have to say everything (Lanzmann, 1985: 23).

There are indeed three simultaneous answers to this problem: first, *Shoah* is not a general historical documentary about the Holocaust; second, it is the only film about the unique and systematic extermination of the European Jews, its horror, where and how it happened; third, *Shoah* is a work of art transmitting in the present the powerful memory of the most unthinkable and unique mass murder of human history—i.e. the systematically planned and realized annihilation of the whole European Jewish people. These remarks leave us only with one question to answer:

how Claude Lanzmann's work as such was able to "transmit" and
protect the memory of the victims of the Shoah?

Marcel Ophüls himself characterized best the construction of
Shoah: "This constant effort to abolish the passage of time and
to recreate a sort of lived continuity is, to my judgement, the
basic principle of construction of the whole film" (in Deguy,
178). This remark explains how this film is fundamentally
different from any historical study and how, according to Pierre
Vidal-Naquet, it makes Lanzmann both an historian and an artist
(in Deguy, 208). Reaching such a goal requires a total and
absolute commitment of the author's art and personality acting as
necessary media between two major groups: the witnesses and the
audience.

In this regard, the strangest sequence in *Shoah* is probably
the scene during which we see an old German couple dancing in
a cabaret. Just before, we had seen contemporary images of the
streets of Berlin at night with Inge Deutschkron's voice telling
how the Jews from Berlin were rounded up and gathered in a
cabaret called the "Klu," waiting for their deportation "to the
East." In the following sequence, we see an old German couple
waltzing alone in the center of the dance floor of an empty
cabaret. The woman is so made-up that her make-up shines. Both
of them are dressed up for a very fancy party. Their stiff and
shiny appearance makes them look like two empty China dolls.
Through this terrifying sequence accompanied with a loud
popular German waltz, the spectator is given an extremely
powerful image of the disappearance of thousands of Berlin Jews
(the empty cabaret) and of the morbid pleasure and indifference
of the rest of the German bourgeoisie enjoying night-life during
and after the Holocaust (the dancing couple). In this scene, the
popular German waltz becomes a sinister dance of death.

Claude Lanzmann's point of departure is that in order to
start communicating what the Shoah represents in the history of
humanity one cannot limit oneself to a necessary but purely
abstract knowledge. In order to start "realizing" what the Shoah
is, he had to go himself to Poland in order to see the very sites
where the extermination took place. According to Lanzmann's

own word, this encounter was "explosive" (in Deguy, 212). (Until then, Poland had been for him "the place of the imaginary par excellence." However, his first reaction when he arrived was to notice that "nothing had changed: there is no need in Poland to reconstruct the Holocaust or to force your imagination; the Holocaust presents itself to your eyes through the permanency of the places.) Why would it be otherwise if one knows that a trip to Poland is first of all a trip in time" (in Deguy, 213).

The violence of this encounter created an extremely powerful effect on the director, some sort of an hallucinatory effect in which he was able to "relive" in the present part of the events of the Holocaust: "I was hallucinating when I made this film" (in Deguy, 287). For this reason, Lanzmann also wrote that he was "the first man to return to the site of the crime" (in Deguy, 285). Because the shock of the encounter allowed him to identify with the victims and made him feel like he was suffering with them, the obsessive and repetitive aspects of the film also allow the audience to feel the suffering of the director's horrified "sympathy" (in the literal sense of the word) for the victims and to feel an infinitely small but essential part of the victim's suffering of the Shoah:

> I did not live this! I needed to go through a certain mental experience, that has nothing to do with what was experienced there, however... I needed to suffer while making this film, a suffering that does not consist in filming in Auschwitz in minus twenty-five degrees Celsius weather. A suffering... (I had the feeling that by suffering myself, a compassion would be communicated by the film, maybe allowing the spectators themselves to go through some sort of suffering (in Deguy, 291).)

For this reason, the camera films an entrance in the gas chambers and often repeats the movements indicated by oral testimony. At the same time Lanzmann knows, as does everybody that it is impossible to literally "relive" what the Jews or other victims experienced in the concentration camps; "with *Shoah* we come closer than we did and ever will to the question of 'what it was like': going further would be like becoming blind by staring at the sun" (Neal Ascherson, in Deguy, 230).

In order to reach this point, Lanzmann had to ask the Nazis, the bystanders and the survivors to "reenact" precisely some chapters of their past. The Nazis and the Polish farmers do so without difficulty and sometimes with much pleasure. The situation is entirely different with the survivors. As we have seen, all the survivors, and Jan Karski, all reach a point in their testimonies when it becomes too hard for them to continue talking. They burst out in tears and ask Lanzmann to stop filming. It is however at that point that Lanzmann reaches "the border of the unspeakable" and that he asks more personal and more precise questions. Many spectators are often violently shocked by Lanzmann's attitude in such situations and question the success of the whole film based on the fact that in these cases Lanzmann does not respect the feelings and the will of the people being interviewed.

It is however only through such segments that the spectator can realize how present the Shoah still is in the very soul of each survivor. By "forcing" some witnesses to go beyond the limits of what their emotions allow them to express, the director creates a fundamental rupture in the testimony. It is this rupture that brings the witness to the borderline between the unbearable and the unspeakable. By pushing this limit a little further Lanzmann forces the witness to directly "transmit" feelings and images to the audience, to talk about a personal experience that no "concept" can "communicate." Only these sequences make us clearly understand and feel that these men and women are not merely talking about events of the past. Moreover, all the survivors I could recently talk to recognized the necessity to go beyond such extremely painful moments in order to testify for the future or even to slightly lighten the terrible weight of unspeakable memories. These people, including Jan Karski, admit that Lanzmann's role is demanding, sometimes harsh, but it is also necessary and fully justifiable. Lanzmann's personal and absolute commitment to his film is a controversial but necessary condition to the success of *Shoah* as a unique and most powerful work of art.

10.   Pierre Sauvage's *Weapons of the Spirit*

Pierre Sauvage's documentary *Weapons of the Spirit* presents itself as a very personal investigation about a rather disorienting mystery. Pierre Sauvage's work is a deliberate attempt to understand why an entire population rescued thousands of Jews so "naturally," with so much "simplicity" while the whole world appeared to have turned its back on their persecution by the Nazis and the Collaborators. The entire film tries to understand not only how the Christians of the village of Le Chambon-sur-Lignon saved the lives of at least five thousand Jews but also why it appeared so obvious to them that "it was the only thing to do." Pierre Sauvage's own parents found refuge in Le Chambon where the director himself was born on March 25, 1944. Consequently, the most apparent characteristic of this film is that it presents, in a very personal manner, a whole community of rescuers, as very solid, independent, religious and simple people who acted without agonizing rather than agonizing without acting.[78]

Thematically, three main leitmotives will reappear throughout the film, explaining in part why Le Chambon was such an exception in occupied France. First, Sauvage and the villagers themselves recognize that the community was able to learn from its past as a population of Huguenots that had been persecuted for their religious beliefs since the seventeenth century. Even at a more individual level, Pastor Trocmé and his wife Magda had been able to see with their own eyes and to tell the people of Le Chambon what had happened to the Jews during the thirties in Mussolini's Italy (Magda Trocmé) and in Hitler's Germany (Magda and André Trocmé).

Second, their own historical awareness combined itself with a unpretentious and solid faith that always refused to separate its actions from values. When the director asks Pastor Edouard Theis to summarize his faith, his answer is:

345

E. *Theis*:	You shall love your God with all your heart, your soul, your mind, *and your neighbor as yourself* (E. Theis' emphasis).
P. *Sauvage*:	That's the summary?
E. *Theis*:	Yes. (pause) Of course.

In any other context, this answer could have sounded like pure rhetoric and somewhat pretentious. However, the history, the reserve, the simplicity, the directness and the conviction of the people of Le Chambon make of this unadorned definition a very powerful and convincing statement. Consequently, as we will see in the following pages, the very first quality of Pierre Sauvage's film is its perfect respect and rendering of the "spirit" of the people of Le Chambon.

Third, the people of Le Chambon are presented from the very beginning of the film as totally opposed to Marshal Pétain's armistice and politics of Collaboration with Germany. As Edouard Theis put it: "We considered Vichy as nothing." It was indeed the very day after the signature of the armistice that André Trocmé made his most influential sermon:

> The duty of the Christians is to resist the violence imposed on their conscience with *the weapons of the spirit*. We shall resist when our adversaries will demand that we submit to orders contrary to the ones of the Gospel. We shall do it without fear, but also without pride and without hatred (my emphasis) (Quoted by Pierre Fayol, 38).

The Chambonnais had made up their minds since they had heard the speech of the *Préfet* André Philipp explaining one of Pétain's first decisions was to return the German refugees to the Nazis. Throughout the documentary, dozens of crossed references will repeat these three important themes. They characterize the Chambonnais as an actively religious and simple people that is both historically and politically aware of their time.

Beyond the attempt to understand what happened in Le Chambon, Pierre Sauvage's film is thematically unified by a more general question. As the film constantly recalls that the entire community took part in the rescue effort, it also analyzes the influence the attitude of the Chambonnais had on the local authorities and on some German soldiers as well. The film suggests clearly that what took place in Le Chambon for five years was also possible because the *Préfet* Robert Bach, some members of the Vichy police, some Vichy officials, some German soldiers and even a German officer (Major Julius Schmähling) never really reported to higher authorities what was going on in the village.

For Pierre Sauvage, the Chambonnais also succeeded because they had involuntarily started a "conspiracy of goodness." *Weapons of the Spirit* analyzes ultimately how such a "conspiracy" worked and what it could teach us for our own future facing anti-Semitism, bigotry, and intolerance in general. This point raises the question of Pierre Sauvage's still on-going interpretation of what happened in Le Chambon. On one hand, one can wonder, for example, if this film does not exaggerate the power of active "goodness" when directly faced with mass murderers. On the other hand, Sauvage never fails to recall that Le Chambon is geographically isolated and that it constitutes an exception. Only a more detailed study of the film itself can provide us with the beginning of an answer to the various problems it raises about the limits of this "conspiracy of goodness."

In many respects Pierre Sauvage appears to be obsessed with his unending attempt to understand this "conspiracy of goodness." In a similar manner Claude Lanzmann was obsessed with the impossibility to represent the unspeakable horror of the Shoah. Like Lanzmann, Pierre Sauvage keeps on repeating similar questions to different people and each time he gets a slightly different answer. He also needed to meet the people of Le Chambon, to film their faces and their emotions, to ask them precise questions, to draw a map of the region, to understand who was doing what and when. In the end the mystery is not solved however the memory of a people is saved while the film raises many key questions that directly concern our future.

Consequently, *Weapons of the Spirit* develops according to two parallel axes. The first one is a very personal search and study of the "spirit" of an exceptional community; the second is a presentation of the history of the same community within the general framework of the history of persecution of the European Jews during World War II. The two combine in the general analysis of the implications of what happened in Le Chambon for our own future ethics of action.

Weapons of the Spirit is first of all Pierre Sauvage's quest for understanding of what happened in Le Chambon. Combining the three themes of historical awareness, active values, and political commitment, the documentary chronologically develops as follows:

Introduction:
- The director returns to Le Chambon to find out why he was saved while "the spiritual plague" that produced the Holocaust had exterminated most of his mother's family.
- Arrival and first encounter with Le Chambon; thankful rescuees and simplicity of the rescuers. A picture of M. and Mme. Héritier during the war with the opening credits.

Part I: (1940-1941)
- Historical summary of the first months of the war, the defeat, the invasion, the Occupation, the Collaboration, Pétain and the anti-Semitic campaigns of the Vichy regime.
- General presentation of Le Chambon (geography, history), its people, what they did and why they did it ("They risked their lives"; "It happened quite simply").
- "The area found spiritual leaders it needed and deserved"; André Trocmé, Edouard Theis, Magda Trocmé ("a dishonorable armistice," "love one another," "resist with the weapons of the spirit," "We just had a difficult past").

Part II: (1942)
- Heydrich in France, the systematic persecution and deportation of the Jews in France (drawings, names and photographs of the victims).

- The Jewish children in Le Chambon; Peter Feigl returns; finding a home for the children (Mme. Dreyfus); taking some children out of the French concentration camps; international help organizations (Swiss and American); organizing school for the children; a perfect integration; the underground railroad to Switzerland ("If we'd had an organization we would have failed"; "It was a general consensus," Magda Trocmé).
- The total respect for Jewish religion ("For us they were the people of God," Marie Brottes).
- Non-violent resistance to Lamirand and the Vichy Government; Lamirand in Le Chambon; a Vichy police raid in Le Chambon.

Part III: (1943-1944)
- December of 1942—Invasion of the "free zone" by the Germans; organization of the armed resistance; the Germans in Le Chambon.
- A center for the making of false identifications (Oskar Rosowsky, alias Jean-Claude Plunne); a Vichy policeman in Le Chambon ("I'm just about the only Jew in Le Chambon," Emile Sèches; "We were very scared," Ginette Weil).
- An orthodox Jew in Le Chambon (Marguerite Kohn). All her family was murdered in extermination camps.
- Christian apathy and responsibility in the Holocaust (Christian anti-Semitism and Pétain going to mass).
- What kind of Christians were the people of Le Chambon? ("It was a very solid faith that was put to the test and was not found wanting," Lesley Maber).
- Albert Camus in Le Chambon ("He was writing a book I think, and he was going for walks," Emile Grand).
- The "plague" arrives in Le Chambon. Arrest, beating and deportation of twenty four by the Gestapo. Daniel Trocmé's choice and death. The birth of the director. The murder of the doctor who had brought him to life (Roger le Forestier).
- Final contrast between Pétain's popularity and Le Chambon's freedom until the very last days of the war.

Conclusion:
- Did the Jews forget about their rescuers?
- The director's own story.
- What can be learned from the people of Le Chambon?

As this schematic summary shows, each major section of the documentary is introduced by historical footage. In this manner, the story of Le Chambon is always presented as an exception in its time. It also allows the director to indicate how the community reacted progressively to every new situation. It is Magda Trocmé who says in the film that if the village really had had an organization, the enterprise would have failed. Consequently the evolution of the film itself stresses the different ways of resisting the community created as it had to face constantly and rapidly changing historical situations.

Consequently, the ultimate repercussions of what happened in Le Chambon reach far beyond Pierre Sauvage's film itself. The director indicated ten directions for future research on who exactly were the Righteous Gentiles.

1) Just how Christian were these rescuers?
2) What sort of Christianity did they practice?
3) Can we learn something about non-violent resistance from the rescuers?
4) Do conventional male values limit our own perspective on resistance to the Holocaust?
5) How determinant was the sense of being socially marginal to the sense of active empathy for the plight of the Jews?
6) If self-esteem was characteristic of the rescuers, then how did they succeed in developing it in themselves and from their upbringing?
7) How do we learn to view the rescuers as ordinary people whom we can emulate rather than as inimitable saints?
8) How important is historical memory in the genesis of righteous conduct?
9) How does one recognize leaders in a time of moral decay and what form does their leadership take?

10)   Did communal rescue efforts result because people placed their trust in the beneficence of collective responsibility or from understanding that collective responsibility can only occur when there is individual responsibility? (Sauvage, 1986: 252)

Weapons of the Spirit already suggests many partial answers to these questions. There is however one question I would like to add based on the documentary's final chapter.

The story of the people of Le Chambon deserves undoubtedly our deepest respect and our most profound reflection. However, as the end of the film requires, one must also consider what the exact limits of a "conspiracy of goodness" are. In its final chapter, however, *Weapons of the Spirit* recalls that the community of Le Chambon had been also very lucky. In spite of all the precautions taken, nothing could be done to prevent the arrest, the deportation and the murder of some of its people. If the village had long created and benefitted from a "conspiracy of goodness" that had extended to some Vichy officials, to the Préfet Bach and even to the German soldiers and officers in convalescence in Le Chambon, all of these efforts were powerless when directly faced with some of the most violent murderers the Third Reich produced, i.e. the Gestapo and men like Klaus Barbie.

One cannot simply deduce from this film that, for example, if the Polish farmers had acted like the people of Le Chambon it would have meant the end of the "Final Solution." On one hand, as *Shoah* recalls, the deeply rooted Christian anti-Semitism of the Polish farmers facilitated greatly the extermination of six millions Jews. On the other hand, *Weapons of the Spirit* testifies that the active goodness and the faith of five thousand Christians living in the geographically isolated Le Chambon was able to save at least five thousand Jews. But one cannot forget that when it is already too late to change the people itself, when directly faced with the SS, the Gestapo, war criminals and men like Klaus Barbie, saving lives requires strategies and actions that are entirely different from the ones mostly shown in the film. Consequently, a quite different but complementary film could also be made on the Jewish armed resistance as it is briefly shown in Pierre Sauvage's masterpiece.

In many respects, Pierre Sauvage's *Weapons of the Spirit* can be considered as a "little brother," a very modest but essential supplement to *Shoah*. Pierre Sauvage did not see *Shoah* until after he completed his own documentary. However, both films reveal striking similarities in the ways they deal with their very different and specific subjects. While Lanzmann's work is a monumental presentation of the uniqueness of the Shoah that excludes France and insists on the systematic extermination of the European Jews in Poland; Sauvage's modest documentary analyzes the exception of a small French village of five thousand inhabitants that saved the lives of five thousand Jews against all odds. Moreover, Lanzmann's and Sauvage's works can be often characterized by the same fundamental qualities: the urgency they felt to return to the sites where the events they describe took place; their need to meet the "actors" of these events on the same sites; the image and the interviews they selected in order to respect and render the specificity of their respective subjects, i.e. the unspeakable horror of the Shoah for Lanzmann, and the "extraordinary simplicity" of the rescuers of Le Chambon for Sauvage.

While Lanzmann's most exceptional work confronts us once and for all with the fact that no European Jew, not even the children, were to be spared by the Nazis and their accomplices, Sauvage's work concentrates on one exceptional village which saved thousands of Jewish children. Only quick generalizations and a misunderstanding of the specificity of these two films could justify opposing them to each other. They both deal with different subjects and serve different purposes. However, they both participate in the same necessary preservation of the memory of the Holocaust for future generations.

Unfortunately, the differences between Lanzmann's and Sauvage's works are sometimes presented as being opposed and irreconcilable. In the United States, Michael Berenbaum rightfully insisted on the fact that: "the Holocaust is primarily about defeat not about victory, about tragedy and not triumph, about failure not success."[79] Pierre Sauvage is very well aware of that fact and has never put it in question. However, Berenbaum went so far as to characterize the Holocaust as the "mysterium tremendum," "the awesome mystery—which cannot be penetrated," because "the Holocaust defies meaning and negates hope. The scope of victimization reduces even survival to a nullity. The reality of Auschwitz should silence the optimists."[80]

Berenbaum's extreme interpretation could in part illustrate Lanzmann's focus in the making of *Shoah* insisting on the heart of the systematic extermination of the Jews. Indeed for Lanzmann, as we have seen in the preceding chapter, "understanding" why the Jews were massacred would provide a logical genesis of death, and ultimately, an excuse for the executioners as victims of their times. For this reason, in Berenbaum's words, the Shoah will always "defy meaning." However, it is also to be remembered that, as Lanzmann wrote: "the purpose of the theory of the aberration (of the Holocaust) is today to sweep away the idea of *historical responsibility*, the responsibility of Germany and that of the nations" (in Deguy, 310-311). Then, in parallel with everything he wrote against the "understanding" of the mass murder itself, Lanzmann concludes that: "we must hold strongly both ends of the chain: *the Holocaust is unique but not aberrant*" (in Deguy, 311).

What is "aberrant" is what Lanzmann called: "to pass to the act; to kill" (in Deguy, 289). Understanding or comprehending a historical period is not synonymous with making logical or forgiving the atrocities that have been committed in these times. Collective and historical situations never free anybody from individual choices and individual responsibilities; they just make it easier to find false justifications to personal actions. For this reason, it is essential to *understand* the historical and collective contexts that allowed many individuals to make many personal choices and commit *aberrant* crimes under the cover of historical pressure. It is also to be recalled that, for similar reasons, Marcel Ophüls refuses to believe in collective guilt.

Consequently, Berenbaum's conclusion, with its total rejection of hope, does not derive directly from its premises and it mixes up various issues that are not synonymous as his argument pretends. What is missing in order to articulate the two aspects of Lanzmann's thought—"it is impossible to 'understand' the Shoah" and "the Holocaust is not aberrant"—is a detailed reflection on the relationship between *collective* and *individual* responsibility. Indeed, the Shoah itself defies meaning because the murder of six million Jews serves no purpose whatsoever. However, this does not systematically imply that it negates hope. In equating the hopeful with the optimist, Berenbaum ironically assimilates hope with dull and blind optimism. The Shoah generates no hope. However the people who tried to fight it do. The kind of hope they inspire has not been created by Auschwitz but has survived in spite of Auschwitz. The people of Le Chambon acted the same before, during and after the war. They are exceptional people precisely because their self esteem, their life style and their values were strong enough so that they did not vanish when their faith was put on trial.

Consequently, Pierre Sauvage's film does not derive hope *from* the Shoah but from *an extraordinary exception* making it clear that each individual is always entirely responsible for his/her "illogical" actions of love or of hatred. Regarding another reproach indicating that he paid too much attention to an exceptional situation, the director himself answered:

> *"There were so few of them."* As if moral or spiritual significance is a matter of numbers. As if we even knew the numbers in this largely uncharted chapter of our past. As if we did not believe, we Jews especially, that even tiny minorities may own important, perhaps even divine, truths (Sauvage, 1983: 31).

Pierre Sauvage's *Weapons of the Spirit* constantly recalls that the villagers of Le Chambon represented an almost unique exception. His film allows no one to forget about widespread anti-Semitism nor about the most horrifying reality of the Holocaust. It simply recalls that for a very few ordinary people, it was indeed possible and quite "natural" to save the Jews. Such a statement does not give any "meaning" to the Holocaust nor does it let us forget that the Shoah was perpetrated by Christian anti-Semites. It simply and realistically teaches us that the Holocaust was not part of an unavoidable fate and that the attitude of some rare and isolated men and women can teach us how to prevent it from happening again. As many American critics did, Laurence Jarvik noted that for Sauvage, "Le Chambon is an indictment of every other community that could have done what Le Chambon did."[81]

For this reason Pierre Sauvage's hopefulness is vital to many precisely because it has nothing to do with a blind "optimism." Next to Lanzmann's gigantic masterpiece about the extermination of the European Jews, *Weapons of the Spirit* remains a modest but fundamental film, a dim and extremely fragile light in an ocean of darkness. After seeing *Shoah* the spectator experiences an infinite part of the despair of a man that has spent ten years of his life "licking the poisonous heart of humanity," while *Weapons of the Spirit* is a tribute to the few anonymous Gentiles who risked their lives to save some Jews including the director himself and his family.

The film starts in a small, bright and totally opened mountain train. This convoy contrasts with the deportation trains that run throughout *Shoah*. Instead of bringing to their deaths thousands of anonymous victims, this train saved three very precise individuals: Pierre Sauvage, his mother and his father. Like *Shoah*, the film also insists on a very specific place and still living bystanders. These are directly opposed to the concentration camps and the anti-Semites shown in Lanzmann's film. Finally, while there is no music in *Shoah* except to evoke the anguish, the despair and the suffering of the Jews, the music used in *Weapons of the Spirit* is very reassuring, light hearted, never ironic and never anguishing.

Considering the specificity of its symmetrically opposite subject (the rule/one exception; the horror of an unspeakable crime/the simplicity of goodness; a monumental work/a modest tribute), Sauvage's film reveals some of the key reactions of the director confronted with his subject that are also found in *Shoah*. As Lanzmann did, Sauvage felt the need to *return* to the places where "the event" took place (Poland/Le Chambon). This first encounter provoked a violent shock that completely changed both Lanzmann's and Sauvage's lives because they realized that the same people were living in the present in the same places with the same values (the Polish anti-Semitism/the simple goodness of the people of Le Chambon).

Finally, both films are based on a unsolvable mystery. For Lanzmann, there is no "understanding" possible of the horror of the Shoah. The goal of the film is precisely to "transmit" the memory of this most unspeakable event as such. For Pierre Sauvage, the exact reason why it was so "natural" to the people of Le Chambon to decide to "pass to the act" of saving Jews will always have a part of mystery. It is however essential to try to understand in what historical, geographical, moral and religious contexts their action was possible, even if none of this will ever absolutely explain what they did nor totally protect us from the resurgence of hatred. The individual remains at all times responsible for his choices and actions. For all these reasons, I consider the success of the modest *Weapons of the Spirit* as being in part comparable to the best achievements of the monumental and irreplaceable *Shoah*.

Like *Shoah*, *Weapons of the Spirit* starts with a long silence allowing the audience to read a text on a dark screen. This text is the following quote from Albert Camus' *The Plague*:

> There always comes a time in history when the person who dares to say that two plus two equals four is punished with death. And the issue is not what reward or what punishment will be the outcome of that reasoning. The issue is simply whether or not two plus two equals four.

We will learn later on in the film that Camus wrote part of *The Plague* in Le Chambon and that his stay in the community had a strong influence on his composition of this literary masterpiece. While imposing silence on the spectator before entering the community of Le Chambon, this text reminds us that in critical situations like during World War II, the simple fact of standing up for basic truths and human values can be punished by death. In such a context, real heroism does not consist in making great self-justifying speeches but in acting according to some very simple but fundamental truths.

Historians have rightfully emphasized the fact that the people who rescued Jews during the war were very often farmers, workers, people of popular origins with little formal education. Unlike some members of the Résistance or official party members, these people neither gained nor asked for official glorification after the war. As their deeds did not influence major war time turning points but represented an everyday life total commitment, historians of the Second World War have largely forgotten to study them. As their religious convictions and basic moral principles often underlined the inefficiency of modern ideologies when faced with crimes against humanity, idealogues have also forgotten to analyze what appears to be the only beliefs that directly lead to an unquestioned action for the rescue of victims of the Nazis' mass murders.

For this reason, the very first quality of Pierre Sauvage's film is its absolute success in rendering the simplicity of the total commitment of the Chambonnais. When asked why they hid Jews at the risk of their lives, the people of Le Chambon give answers such as: "We never asked for explanations. Nobody asked anything. When people came, if we could be of help..." (M. Héritier), "We were used to it" (Mme. Héritier), "It all happened very simply. We did not ask ourselves why we were doing it. It was the human thing to do or something like that... that's all" (M. Darcissac).

The camera never fails to show the uneasiness these men and women feel at being made some sort of local heroes. They look at the interviewer to see if he has any other question and then they look at their feet because there is nothing else to say. They "just" did what had to be done and there is nothing else to say about it. As Mme. Barraud put it "It happened so naturally, we cannot understand the fuss. It happened simply (....) I helped because they needed help." While Sauvage's film has been some-times criticized for its "simplicity," one has to underline the fact that the same "simplicity" characterizes best the people of Le Chambon. Consequently it is the only "style" Sauvage could use in his film without betraying the essence of the community he wanted to portray. Moreover it is this "simplicity" that saved at least five thousand lives including thousands of Jewish children. For this very reason it deserves no irony and it demands our most dedicated attention.

What is most disturbing for a "modern" audience, as Jean Hatzfeld underlined in the *Cahiers du cinéma*, is the fact that "no one in this film plays the role of the hero, the traitor, the victim as we find them in classical drama" (Hatzfeld, 9). This explains in part the limited success this film had in France, a country in which largely elitist intellectual life is still very much oriented by belief in the leading role idealogues should play based on their prior education in highly selective government controlled schools. Albert Camus himself can be considered as a victim of such an exclusive conception of the formation of an intellectual. On the other end, Sauvage's film was a much greater success in the United States, and in California in particular, where one's immediate community life plays a much more important role in determining individual commitments.

There was indeed no "hero" in Le Chambon, no "theory" and no "heroic" leader either. As Laurence Jarvik put it, this film is about a community who was "actively doing good instead of rationalizing doing nothing." Even Pastor André Trocmé who gave most of the cohesion to the community is presented as nothing but the leader that this community deserved. He and his wife were militant pacifists who always stood up for their beliefs even when, in 1939, all the villagers disagreed with them. André Trocmé could play the major role he did in Le Chambon only because the whole community accepted and recognized his authority based on his active values and sincere faith. In this simple but fundamental manner, *Weapons of the Spirit* establishes a very clear relationship between individual responsibility, collective responsibility and leadership. By contrast, at the end of the film, Marshal Philippe Pétain will also be characterized by Sauvage as "the leader (France) deserved" at that time.

Following the quotation of Camus, the first words of the film are pronounced by the director himself: "I am a Jew." While

Shoah reveals nothing directly about the identity of its director, *Weapons of the Spirit* appears from the very beginning as a personal film based on a clear personal motivation. From this point on, Sauvage's film also becomes a quest towards one's origins and the understanding of why what had been possible and so "natural" in the village of Le Chambon remained an exception in France and throughout Europe where the apathy and the bigotry described in *Shoah* dominated.

Sauvage's film is constantly linked to the personal experience and personality of its director. It is a film Pierre Sauvage made for three parallel purposes: so he could himself understand "the mystery" of Le Chambon; so he could pay tribute to the memory of the people who saved his family; so he could try to learn what moral lessons we can drawn from this community's actions for future generation and especially for the director's own son, David. It is always presented as an exceptional, individual and ordinary tale. Consequently, Pierre Sauvage's work, like the actions of the Chambonnais, can be best characterized both by its personal and collective implications as the two cannot be separated from each other. In this sense we are here at the direct opposite of Ophüls' and Lanzmann's works which privileged individual or collective responsibilities respectively.

After spending the first four years of his life in France, Pierre Sauvage moved with his parents to New York City. He attended the Lycée Français in New York and then went back to France to pursue literary studies at the renowned Lycée Henri IV in Paris. He took some classes at the Sorbonne. After dropping out of school he started working at the Cinémathèque Française under the direction of the famous Henri Langlois. From that date he became a dedicated man of cinema. His parents, journalist and writer Léo Sauvage and Barbara Sauvage née Suchowolski, did not tell him he was Jewish until he turned eighteen. Pierre Sauvage grew up as a non-religious man. They did not want him to live in the past and they did not tell their son about Le Chambon either. As a result they did not support the project of making the film. It is mostly after he met his wife, Barbara M.

Rubin, and had a son that Pierre Sauvage felt a strong need to
learn about his past and his Jewish heritage: "Without the birth
of my son and my wife's prodding, *Weapons of the Spirit* would
not have been made. For me, making the film was a growing
experience" (Johnson, 12).

In this regard, the project of making this documentary fits
perfectly with the teaching of the people of Le Chambon as it
always refuses to separate one's values and ideological commitments from one's actions and concern for one's immediate
surroundings and vice versa. If this film was to make sense for
thousands of anonymous spectators worldwide it first had to
make sense for the director's own son:

> This is why, as I tell David of these things, as he learns
> that there is in all of us a capacity for evil and an even
> greater and more insidious capacity for apathy, I want
> him to learn that the stories of the righteous are not
> footnotes to the past but cornerstones to the future. I
> owe my life to the good people of Le Chambon. I owe
> even more than that to my son (Sauvage, 1983: 36).

Here again, individual commitments are inseparable from
collective or more universal responsibilities. It is because this
film was made from a personal, sincere and profound need of its
director that it was ultimately able to convey the complex
simplicity of the people of Le Chambon without reducing its
mystery to a purely "objective" reasoning or to the point of view
of a specialist. As Sauvage himself indicated, the people of Le
Chambon were "very reluctant" when he told them he wanted to
film them: "They were very wary. They believe that to appear to
trumpet your deeds is to devalue them" (Bernstein, 36). A
villager of Le Chambon confirmed the same statement:

> An attempt was made by a American team to make a
> film about Le Chambon as a harbour for refugees and
> a center for active Résistance to the Occupation. For
> that reason, at his request, I had a very pleasant
> meeting with M. Carl Foreman who was supposed to
> write the scenario of the film. He was famous for

having worked on films such as *The Bridge on the River Kwai* and *The Guns of Navarone*.

We feared, Dr. Rosowsky (Jean-Claude Plunne) and myself, that a large audience film would be forced to respect the commercial requirements and that it would be unable to limit itself to the strict reality of the facts. For that reason, we rejected his offer.

On the contrary, we had a great interest in Pierre Sauvage's project because of his attachment to Le Chambon where he was born in 1944 and because he decided to base his film only on interviews of the witnesses, without any intrigue. This seemed to guarantee his sincerity (Pierre Fayol, 22).

Like the director of *Shoah*, but dealing with an opposite subject, the director of *Weapons of the Spirit* felt a powerful personal need to tell his "story" in a manner that would respect entirely the complexity and the mystery of its subject, even if in this case the subject is the "simplicity" of a rural protestant community.

Consequently, *Weapons of the Spirit* is best characterized, at the same time, by its clarity, its coherence and the complexity of its structure and of the questions its raises. The director combines international and local events, various studies of characters and personal history with outstanding mastery. The film is never confusing in spite of its alluding to dozens of different and most often unknown individuals, including thirty four villagers of Le Chambon. If the main "story" is a very personal search for the understanding of an exceptional community, the backbone of the narration follows the chronology of the war and that of the persecution of the Jews in occupied France. The film does not forget one key aspect of the history of this community and always situates it within the more general frame of French history. At the same time it is able to present a most faithful and vivid analysis of the people involved with the events described. Because it was able to successfully achieve all these goals at the same time, the apparent "simplicity" of Pierre Sauvage's film is certainly its most complex achievement.

As the work of a man of cinema about Occupied France, *Weapons of the Spirit* often recalls some of the best sequences of Marcel Ophüls' *The Sorrow and the Pity*. Like Ophüls' masterpiece, Pierre Sauvage's work intertwines historical footage and black and white pictures with contemporary interviews while following the chronology of the events. Sauvage's film is also a very successful attempt to make visible the personality, the emotions and the deep motivations of the witnesses he interviews. In this regard, the director never fails to include an expression, a gesture or glance from the witnesses that reveals more about these people than any word could. The camera also includes all the elements of the setting that can bring more information about the witness being interviewed.

In this respect, the second interview of Pastor Edouard Theis is extremely revealing of the best cinematographic qualities of Sauvage's film. The sequence starts with a vertical panning showing a picture of Martin Luther King and a picture of Gandhi posted on Theis' bulletin board in his study. In the same movement, the camera encounters drawings made by children, a photograph of a woman holding a child in her arms, a copy of the *Old Testament*, other books and then pauses briefly on Theis' hands while Sauvage asks the Pastor to summarize his faith in a few words. After this, the camera films Theis' face, looking at the director while he gives his answer: "You shall love the Lord your God with all your heart, your soul, your mind, and your neighbor as yourself." In the middle of this answer, we see Theis' hands opening up and raising up in order to reinforce the idea that this answer is so obvious that the question itself seems a little dull. While finishing his answer, Theis lightly raises his shoulders and looks Sauvage straight in the eyes. Sauvage asks him: "That's it? It just had to be applied?", Theis firmly replies: "Yes! Of course!" and then he lowers his eyes simply because there is nothing else to say until the next question comes.

In such a sequence, the cameraman included all the elements of the natural setting that could reveal the personality of the interviewee. This is extremely important as the people of Le Chambon are very softspoken and uncomfortable at being made the stars of a film. Pierre Sauvage's interviewing technique always respects the personality of these people and his editing of the film reveals in a powerful manner everything that Theis' simplicity does not allow him to put in words, i.e. Theis' pacifism and non-violent activism (King's and Gandhi's pictures), his dedication to children and his community (the photograph with a woman holding a child), his faith (the *Old Testament*), his rugged life in a mountain village (his hands and face), the strength of his faith (the movements of his opening hands and his straight forward look at the interviewer) and his sincere unwillingness to become some sort of a local hero (his looking down at his hands after he is done answering the question). All this is expressed in the same and continuous movement of the camera that insists on the fact that all these elements are part of Theis himself. The editing had to bring no exterior element or tricks in order to reveal the personality of this man.

In contrast with this sequence is the interview of Lamirand, the former Youth Minister of Vichy. Lamirand is filmed sitting in a heavy armchair that holds his body perfectly, limiting uncontrolled gestures to the strict minimum. At first he looks the director straight in the eye, bending slightly his head on his left shoulder in order to show that he has nothing to hide and that he is doing his best to understand and answer the questions.

Lamirand's first answers about his visit in Le Chambon are obviously well prepared. However, when he is being asked about his personal responsibilities in the deportation of seventy five thousand Jews from France, his eyelids reveal a very nervous and uncontrollable agitation. The camera then shows him joining his hands as he justifies himself by explaining that, at that time, he did not know anything about the deportations of the Jews. The interview ends with a short segment in which Lamirand explains that he has "many Jewish friends." Therefore, he had nothing to do with the persecution of the Jews.

Lamirand's conclusion represents one of the very few touches of irony in Sauvage's film. Sauvage borrowed many interviewing and editing techniques from Ophüls but, because of his subject, he almost never used Ophüls' characteristic irony. By contrast, the villagers are often very humorous especially when describing the various subterfuges the village put together to hide the identity of the refugees. In order to respect and render the "spirit" and the goodness of the people of Le Chambon, Sauvage could not use sarcasm nor too much irony while they represented perfect tools for Ophüls' subject and witnesses.

Finally, like Ophüls, Sauvage uses much historical footage or newsreels in order to reinforce the chronology of the film and to put the testimonies in contrast with national and international events. However, Sauvage's use of old photographs is very characteristic of the director's personal style. Prior to making his film, Sauvage gathered literally thousands of pictures of Le Chambon. These pictures are included in the film with three main purposes.

First, many pictures disclose what it was like to live in Le Chambon. That's what happens for instance with the many group pictures showing children studying or at play or people doing farm work. In this case, pictures allow us to visualize the various testimonies heard in the present and to see some of the children refugees. They take us back from the nineteen eighties to the nineteen forties. Second, other pictures show places that no longer exist like the terrace of the *Coteau Fleuri*. They also take us from the present to the past while allowing us to imagine everyday life in Le Chambon.

The last use of pictures by Sauvage is most crucial and characteristic of his film. It consists in showing old portraits of the people involved, in putting them in parallel with the faces of the same people in the present or in superimposing old pictures of the same people at different ages in order to indicate their growing up. By using the first technique, the audience is constantly being reminded that the children of Le Chambon looked just like today's children. This is a story that could be ours. These people cannot be reduced to names or statistics in a history book.

Second, by putting in parallel old pictures and contemporary faces of the same people, Sauvage insists on the fact that the Chambonnais, like Henri and Emma Héritier, have not changed since the war. Of course they became older but their expressions, their lifestyle and their values remained the same. Consequently, the story of Le Chambon belongs to our own present. Even today it is possible to think, live or act like the Chambonnais did almost fifty years ago.

Third, the superimposing of portraits of the same people at different ages underlines the fact that throughout their lives these men and women, at least in spirit, belonged to the same community and that the moral strength and simplicity shown on their faces was not just an attitude put on for the time of a picture taking. For this reason, the openness and calm shown on the pictures of Daniel Trocmé and Roger Le Forestier contrast violently with the commentary's evocation of their violent deaths as they were both assassinated by the Nazis. By using these three different ways to include old photographs in his documentary, the director once more characterizes his film as a work dedicated to saving the memory of a community of individuals that always claimed responsibility for each one of its actions, even when facing the utmost danger.

Pierre Sauvage's *Weapons of the Spirit* is a personal and modest masterpiece that nonetheless can be compared to the best achievements of the monumental *Shoah* and *The Sorrow and the Pity*. It represents unfortunately a tiny event and an extraordinary exception in the history of the extermination of the European Jews during World War II. However, what happened in Le Chambon raises many fundamental questions for our own future. Because Pierre Sauvage's film renders the "spirit" of the Chambonnais with outstanding faithfulness and integrity, it can and must play a key role in our necessary reflection on the best strategies to be adopted in order to fight bigotry, intolerance and ultimately hate crimes.

CONCLUSION

It is now possible, at the end of this study, to have a clearer idea of the general evolution of the representation of the Holocaust in French cinema. First, no French film was entirely and specifically dedicated to the presentation of the persecution or the extermination of the Jews until Frédéric Rossif made his *film de montage Le Temps du Ghetto* (*Witnesses*), in 1961. Until then, French films about World War II either totally omitted the Holocaust or mentioned it only within more general representations of the deportations, the concentration camps, the occupation of France or the history of the war.

In 1965, Philippe Arthuys' *La Cage de verre*, was the first French fiction film completely centered around the trial of a Nazi judged for his responsibility in the Final Solution. Arthuys' film was also the first one, in France, to closely analyze the survivors' painful process of recollection as well as the key role the memory of the Holocaust plays in the foundation and existence of Israel. In 1973, Claude Lanzmann's *Pourquoi Israel?* began and ended at Yad Vashem, also indicating that Israel exists primarily as a haven for all the persecuted Jews, in order to guarantee that the Holocaust will never happen again.

Marcel Hanoun's fiction film *L'Authentique procès de Carl Emmanuel Jung* (1967) can be characterized as the first French film that clearly put in parallel the memory of the Holocaust and the search for new cinematographic techniques that would offer a more powerful representation of the challenges one faces when evoking the necessity to remember the persecution of the Jews. Similar formal experimentations already played an important role in Arthuys' film. They also characterize, for example, the films of Michel Drach, Frank Cassenti or Edgardo Cozarinsky.

Claude Berri's *Le Vieil homme et l'enfant* (1967) was the first French film entirely structured around the memories of a Jewish child in hiding in France during the Occupation. This film

uncovers most of the crucial themes that will be developed
during the seventies. It introduces the extremely controversial
issues of Marshal Pétain's wide popularity, French anti-Semitism,
Catholic anti-Semitism, the politics of Collaboration, the
persecution of the Jews and Jewish children in France, the
Résistants "of the last hour," the purges of the Libération.

In the following years, Jacques Doillon, Jacques Rouffio and
Louis Malle also made feature films based on the memories of a
child. Only one film however, Simone Boruchowicz's *1942*
(1975), was based on the memories of a Jewish girl remembering
her family's life in France until the deportation and death of both
of her parents. Besides some very rare exceptions (Simone
Boruchowicz, Clarissa Henry and Diane Kurys), French films
dealing with the Holocaust were made by male directors and
focus on male experiences. Women are presented from the point
of view of a son, a husband, a lover, a friend, a male director or
a male commentator. Very little if anything at all is said in these
films about persecuted women, women in the concentration
camps or in French internment camps.

In 1971, Marcel Ophüls' *The Sorrow and the Pity* was the
first French documentary to analyze in depth the various attitudes
of the French population during the Occupation. It is not a film
about the Holocaust but it represents an indispensable and irreplaceable step toward the analysis of French responsibilities in
the persecution of the European Jews. This kind of study will be
developed in French cinema throughout the seventies and in the
early eighties. The success and the repercussions of Ophüls'
masterpiece must be considered in parallel with the publication
in France of Robert O. Paxton's *La France de Vichy* (1973).

The scandal created by Louis Malle's *Lacombe Lucien*
(1973) is in great part due to the fact that this work represents
the first French feature film describing the Occupation and the
persecution of the Jews from the point of view of a character
who is a Collaborator. Several Collaborators played a central role
in other French films—before *Lacombe Lucien*—for example, in
Jean Cayrol's *Le Coup de grâce*. However Malle's work is the
first one that presents a Collaborator as caught in a series of

circumstances that make his repulsive and irrational behavior almost logical considering the man's total lack of education. For this reason, it remains a very ambiguous film.

On the other hand, Michel Mitrani's *Les Guichets du Louvre* (*Black Thursday*, 1974) demonstrates clearly that the arrest and the deportation of the Jews was conducted by responsible French officials. This film also shows for the first time in French cinema different reactions of the Jews to the sudden roundups. Finally the film timidly introduces the problem of what should and could have been done by the French population in order to save more Jews. This important theme will be developed in French cinema mostly in the late eighties and early nineties.

Frank Cassenti's *L'Affiche rouge* (1976) can be considered as the first French film largely based on the key role played by Jews in the French Résistance and in the worldwide struggle against totalitarianism. Cassenti's work develops clearly a theme that had been approached by Dumoulin in 1970 (*Nous n'irons plus au bois*) and by Costa-Gavras in 1975 (*Section Spéciale*). Cassenti's 1987 film *Le Testament d'un poète juif assassiné* will present another aspect of the Jewish fight against fascism and totalitarianism in several European countries before, during and after World War II.

Claude Lanzmann's *Shoah* (1985) is the first film to describe minutely the Nazi's systematic process of extermination of the European Jews from the cities and villages where they lived to the gas chambers. Because the extermination took place in Poland, the subject of the film itself never brings Lanzmann to mention France or even French anti-Semitism. The goal of the film is to "transmit in the present" the unspeakable horror of the annihilation of a whole people. *Shoah* is a gigantic masterpiece that allows us to understand precisely the specificity of the Jewish Holocaust. However, it is also a film that must be seen in parallel with many other masterpieces in order to get a comprehensive and adequate overview of the persecution of the European Jews between 1933 and 1945.

Marcel Ophüls' *The Memory of Justice* (1976) and *Hotel Terminus* (1987) can be considered as the first films that analyze closely the international complicities that allow crimes against humanity to take place as well as the inability of justice to punish those crimes. Ophüls' films are always of great consequence for our conception of individual responsibility and for our sense of justice. Ophüls is a man of cinema whose art can be characterized as an ironic investigation of our sense of justice and individual responsibility. For that reason, he has produced cinema's most important masterpieces on the various individual and collective attitudes that are directly responsible for the Holocaust. The excellence and relevance of his complete work make Ophüls one of the predominant film directors of the twentieth century.

Finally, since the late eighties, with films like Louis Malle's *Goodbye Children* (1987) and Pierre Sauvage's *Weapons of the Spirit* (1988), several films have been centered around a few individuals who stood up for the Jews or around the description of rare communities who organized themselves in order to save a few Jews. Such films never forget the horror of the systematic murder of six million Jews by the Nazis. They act as an indictment against other communities by showing that it was not impossible to act differently. They are also directly oriented towards our future by reminding us that we are individually responsible for the rise of anti-Semitism at anyplace or time in history as well as for what happens to the people living in our own communities. Because they deal with rare exceptions, such films can only offer a very fragmentary and incomplete representations of how individuals reacted to the Holocaust throughout Europe. However, they raise fundamental questions that we cannot afford to neglect.

This general evolution also allows us to identify several different representations of the Jews, bystanders and executioners during World War II in French cinema. First of all, Jews are most often and very accurately represented as disoriented and powerless victims abandoned by the rest of the world. They can only rely on themselves and on the support they can give each other if they want to have a chance to survive (Rossif's *Le Temps du Ghetto*). In Arthuys', Berri's, Drach's, Mitrani's, Doillon's,

Boruchowicz's, Losey's, Malle's and even Sauvage's films, being a Jew is first associated with being the victim of persecution and hatred. Many Jewish children in these films acknowledge that they do not know what a Jew is except that they know they are being persecuted because they are Jewish (Arthuys, Doillon, Drach, Mitrani). For them, being a Jew first meant being rejected, insulted and beaten up by their schoolmates.

Jews shown in these films are seldom presented as being religious. Only a few allusions are made to their faith or even their traditions. Jewish Résistance is also very seldom represented. When it is, it is most often presented either as a part of the Communist Résistance (Dumoulin, Costa-Gavras, Cassenti) or as an ultimate and desperate reaction facing a specific extermination or deportation (Rossif, Mitrani, Lanzmann). In spite of the importance of these subjects for the history of the war, there is no French film dealing specifically with Jewish Résistance or the faith of the Jews faced with the persecutions.

Still missing is also a film studying or representing the reactions, or the lack of reactions, of the Résistance faced specifically with the persecution and the deportation of the Jews in France. It is a subject that a former member of the French Communist Résistance like Claude Lanzmann must know very well but, to the best of my knowledge, never commented on in film. Very little has also been said, in film, about the actions of international Jewish and non-Jewish organizations who succeeded in rescuing some European Jews. Pierre Sauvage's *Weapons of the Spirit* is the only one that mentions several of them. Otherwise, Jewish organizations—like the Union Générale des Israelites de France (UGIF) or the Judenrat of the Warsaw Ghetto—are presented either as collaborating with the executioners (*Le Temps du Ghetto* and *Les Guichets du Louvre*) or as attempting the impossible to enable more people to survive (*Shoah*).

Many films also concentrate on the story of a Jewish child or of a group of Jewish children (Berri, Drach, Mitrani, Doillon, Malle, etc.). The vast majority of these works tell the story of young boys. Only Simone Boruchowicz's *1942* is based on the testimonies of a little girl. Mitrani's *Les Guichets du Louvre*, Drach's *Les Violons du bal* and Malle's *Lacombe Lucien* present clearly the story of young Jewish women. One survives because she is beautiful and becomes a model (Mitrani), another can escape also because she is pretty and a Collaborator falls in love with her (Malle), and the last one has an opportunity to escape after a French university student falls in love with her (Drach). All these young female characters have a chance to survive in great part because they are stereotyped as sexually attractive Jewish women.

Drach's *Les Violons du bal* and Doillon's *Un Sac de billes* present two very similar images of young Jewish mothers. The stories are narrated from the exterior point of view of their sons. They are characterized as responsible for the unity and the survival of the family but they are not specifically presented as women nor from their own point of view. In Malle's *Lacombe Lucien*, the old Jewish mother is presented as the distant and mysterious guardian of the family's heritage threatened by men like Lacombe. By comparison, the fathers of the same children are either absent, in hiding, or soon to be deported to their death. Men are always the ones to revolt (Rossif, Lanzmann), friends (Mitrani), fathers (Enrico) or older brothers (Drach). Nothing is said about women and the Résistance or women's struggles to protect their families or to resist the persecutions. Only Ophüls' and Lanzmann's "documentaries" (*Hotel Terminus* and *Shoah*) allow a few women to testify from their own points of view on persecuted, deported or tortured Jewish women. Consequently there is, to this date, no French film focusing specifically on Jewish women and the Holocaust.

All the films dealing with the persecution of the Jews in France denounce clearly, however with various degrees, the responsibilities of French authorities in the Holocaust. Several films attack in a powerful way the rampant anti-Semitism that was so helpful to Vichy and German officials in carrying out the persecution of the Jews in France. Several films clearly show how some individuals took advantage of the persecution of the Jews while pretending "to help them," by stealing their belongings, or buying them for nothing, or by taking charge of their businesses. The fear, the selfishness, the indifference or the blindness of large parts of the population serves as a background to all the films representing the persecution of the Jews.

Considering the above mentioned themes, then, 1961 and 1967/1968 and 1985 could be regarded as turning points in the representation of the Holocaust in French cinema. It is only since the early sixties and Eichmann's trial in Israel that French films have clearly focused on the persecution of the Jews by the Nazis as such (starting with *Le Temps du Ghetto*, 1961). Until the late sixties, early seventies, the films that allude to the persecution of the Jews in France present it as a crime among many others committed by the Germans or by some mad and isolated Collaborator, by an "enemy of France." It was to be understood that, since the total defeat of 1940, only the Résistance represented the French spirit and that the vast majority of the population supported its struggle while "managing" to survive waiting for the Liberation.

It is only since the late sixties and the early seventies that French cinema has conclusively represented and analyzed French anti-Semitism, the enormous popularity of Marshal Pétain and French responsibilities in the Holocaust (starting with Berri's *Le Vieil homme et l'enfant* in 1967; and Marcel Ophüls who started working on *The Sorrow and the Pity* in 1968). In 1985, Claude Lanzmann's *Shoah* represents the major masterpiece that exclusively focuses on the specificity and absolute horror of the systematic extermination of the European Jews. *Shoah* concentrates on the extermination process itself. However, as Jan Karski put it:

> The movie *Shoah* through its greatness of talent, determination and fierce truth, but also its self-limitation, has created the need for the next movie, equally truthful—a movie which will present a second reality of the Holocaust (...) Not in order to contradict that which *Shoah* shows but to complement it (Karski, 45).

In spite of this tardiness in coming to terms with the most dreadful chapter of modern French history, one must recognize that several French directors have finally succeeded in producing major masterpieces offering highly dependable representations of extremely complex and distressing events. As the preceding remarks suggest there are still many aspects of these times and events that cinema has not yet represented. However the massive demonstrations and the many official condemnations that took place in France after recent anti-Semitic incidents prove that considerable numbers of the French population are now very much aware of the dangers and the consequences of recurring waves of anti-Semitism and hatred.

The evolution of the representation of the Holocaust in French cinema since 1967 certainly played a major role in the increase of this public awareness. As everywhere else in the world, including the United States, there are still politicians in France that try to use anti-Semitism and politics of hatred for the benefit of their personal influence. However, their propaganda is also opposed by a better preserved memory of the truth. By its continuing struggle to offer an always more complete and truthful memory of the Holocaust and of the persecution of the Jews, several masterpieces of French cinema can be considered as exceptional media to fight anti-Semitism and bigotry in France or anywhere else.

Appendix:
An Interview with Pierre Sauvage

A: What are the different circumstances that brought you to make *Weapons of the Spirit*?

P: To begin with, I could not have made it earlier, as I was not interested enough in the subject or psychologically equipped to deal with it. I also was not professionally in a position to make such a film. The film really happened precisely when it needed to happen. And since my parents initially did not want me to make the film, it was also something that I had to undertake at a time when I was able to negotiate with them.

A: Your wife also played an important role?

P: My wife played a very important role in telling me that being Jewish was important. I cannot overstate how inconceivable it is that the film could have been made another time considering what it is saying: that a sense of rootedness and identity is important; that religion can be a source of good. These are things that I did not believe *at all* a few years before making the film.

A: There was also a great curiosity on your part at the outset?

P: I think there was. At the point where I decided to make it, I was already quite interested in the Holocaust, and had begun attempting to understand it and figure out what its importance is to me personally. I had also begun realizing that one legacy that my father had tried to give me was a very dangerous one: that one can simply discard the past; that it is not important. Then I went back to Le Chambon on

375

a visit and was just stunned by the people there. I felt that there was something special about them, something special about their faces. But even when I started shooting I had no idea what the film was going to end up being.

A: You had no script.

P: No, I have never done a documentary with a script.

A: How did people react in Le Chambon when you told them you wanted to make a film about them?

P: They were wary. They were certainly not excited about the idea. They are very modest people, and the last thing they would want is for others to think that they are promoting themselves.

A: Did they put any restrictions on you in terms of making the film?

P: They really did not. Nobody refused anything. Even the old family photographs I asked to film. I think a certain trust set in. It started by filming people I knew and the word got around. I do not doubt for a second that the fact that I had been born there meant a lot. It was simply a sense that . . .

A: . . . they could trust you?

P: Yes. And that this was meant to be.

A: There had been other films made about their story.

P: Not really. There have been small attempts, little television programs. Marcel Ophüls told me afterwards that he had been thinking of doing it but had learned that I was about to do it. It didn't matter that *I* was doing it, but that someone was doing it.

A: You use a lot of faces in your film as well as pictures, old and more recent pictures. What is their precise role in your film?

P: I really think faces are important and I really like knowing what people look like. I have always been curious about what people look like at various stages of their life. Probably the boldest sequence along those lines in the film is actually when, in talking about Roger Le Forestier's death, I show pictures of him as a child and then as he gets older and older. I realize that it is sort of a strange sequence and I am still not sure if the viewers get it right away or if they think it's someone else. I guess they understand it eventually. But it was very meaningful to me. When a man is killed it is the person he was in all the previous years and the child that are killed too. This brings it home in a way.

A: Concerning the filming of the faces and the people... did you give any instructions to the cameramen?

P: Nothing important. I had a very good cameraman, Yves Dahan.

A: You worked with the same team all along?

P: Yes. They were very committed—just fantastic. They really got into it.

A: They did not understand what people were saying?

P: Oh no. This was a French crew and so they understood everything.

A: Did you give them any kind of instructions before filming?

P: Well, the main "battle" I would always have—and this is a traditional issue with cameramen for documentaries—is that the cameraman always wanted to set up the nicest shot he could and I was willing to let them do that but sometimes it's more important not to break the mood or not to tire your subjects.

A: And so, sometimes you had to ask the same question again to the same witness?

P: No, this would happen before the interviews. But sometimes you would have to set up the light and ask the person to sit so you can set it up. But I realized that older people can get tired. I remember one story which is sort of funny. When I first called Joseph Atlas on the phone. He is the Polish Jew that appears several times in the film.

A: He is also the first one you name in the film.

P: Yes. He is sort of my starting symbol in a way, the little boy of fourteen. He talks about his experience almost in fairy tale terms. I'd had an assistant who had talked to a number of people and had said "this one's good, this one's not so good," and I made up my mind who I was going to interview. I called Joseph Atlas and he started asking all these annoying questions about what my attitude was and what my approach was, and I said to myself "The guy is a pain in the neck." I did not cancel the interview but I told my cameraman "I don't care about the 'image.' Just set the cameras, we have to go quickly." And it turned out to be one of the most important interviews. The moment I asked my first question I realized "Oh, this is good." It does not look very pretty because I did not allow my poor cameraman to set up the lights properly. So you cannot predict these things.

A: When you were editing the film, what were the main problems you ran into?

P: There were so many. I would say the main problem was understanding the material, understanding what these people were saying. I do not mean that literally. I just mean that I knew nothing about religion. I knew nothing about Christians. I spent months just listening to the footage over and over and over again. And in fact a lot of the footage that is in the film is footage that I ignored the first forty or fifty times I heard it. It did not seem important. I thought something else was important. It took a long time for me to realize: "*No! That* was the important stuff."

A: There were also a few sequences that were important at first and you could not include them?

P: Yes. There were a number of sequences that I am extra-ordinarily surprised *now* that they are not in the film. They were passages that sometimes had things that were too explicit, in a way. At first I thought "This is perfect." And then I got bored with it. It did not really have the authenticity, the mystery too, but also the authenticity. In the first section—it is because it is the first that it is so important — when I use M. et Mme. Heritier. I say to her "But you kept them anyway. Why?" "*Oh, j'sais pas,*" "*J'sais pas*" "I don't know," is not something that right away I saw as important.

A: Now as opposed to some survivors who sometimes, in their interviews, are telling stories for the first time, the people of Le Chambon you interviewed had the opportunity to tell these stories before. Was that a problem?

P: It is a very interesting question actually because I think unlike films that include interviews with survivors who *have* told their stories over and over again, these people had *not* told their stories over and over again. These were stories they *did not* tell. The Jews who were in Le Chambon did *not* talk about it that much, and certainly the people of Le

Chambon did not. There were a few young Chambonnais
who sort of hung around and listened and they had never
heard these people talking about these things. And when
there was family, the family would listen with incredible
attention. No, I did not have that problem.

A: Sometimes in the film, one gets the impression that you
have been influenced by Ophüls and Lanzmann. Is that a
real influence? Did you do certain things on purpose? I am
thinking about two or three different things. In the interview
of Lamirand there is a close-up on his hands and Ophüls
does that a lot, showing people's hands as they hesitate or
when they are embarrassed. And of course the train that is
completely opposed to the train shown in Lanzmann's film,
and the village of the people that is completely opposed to
the Polish villages in *Shoah*. Did you think about these
parallels when you were making the film or did you realize
this after?

P: There are rather simple answers to these questions. First of
all in terms of *Shoah*, I had not seen *Shoah* when I finished
my film so *Shoah* had absolutely no influence on me. It has
since but it had no influence on me at that time. In fact,
when I saw *Shoah*, I was stunned because one of the
strongest impressions one gets from *Shoah* is that sense of
having been constantly on a train and there was my little
film with its little train, and it did look like it was a
deliberate counterpart. Ophüls, of course, I had seen his
films and I admire them.

A: What about that interview of Lamirand?

P: The interesting thing is that Lamirand comes out rather well
in *Le Chagrin et la pitié*. You know he is very charming
and dapper, and he comes across fine. In fact, I believe that
is one of the reasons that Lamirand agreed to be interviewed
by me. I will tell you that I do not like shots of hands. I do

not like cut-aways. It is an editing technique that one almost *has* to use. You are not like a writer: you cannot jump from one sentence to the next sentence. You have to get from point A to point B. If you have a jump cut you have to bridge it and it is going to be a painting on the wall... The biggest cliché in cut-aways is hands generally. So the last thing I would want to do is hands. There are only two real cut-aways like that in the whole film. And they are both hands. No, one is not a cut-away, one is deliberate. When you see Lamirand's hands, his hands are closed and the other hands are Pastor Theis' and his hands are open. It is very trivial metaphorically but I liked it. I needed a cut-away at that point.

A: But you did not think of Ophüls while doing this?

P: No, I really did not. I needed a cut-away. I was cutting something in what Lamirand said. I was not distorting him. I doubt that there is a filmmaker—this may sound like a terribly boastful thing to say—who is more cautious than I am in terms of representing fairly what the people say. You can make anybody look like anything. The power that we have when we edit these things is just so tremendous. No matter how I present somebody, I wanted them to say "this is what I was."

A: Did you choose the setting for the interviews? For example with the picture of Martin Luther King behind Pastor Theis... it just happened to be there?

P: That was the retirement place where Edouard Theis was living, and that was what was indeed on the wall behind his desk. That is the shot that actually ends with the hands. It was an irresistible shot. I did not put the picture there. In fact I would not do that. There was even in that shot, as it is panning down, the Bible. It is the *Ancien Testament*, the *Old Testament*. I did not put it there. It was there.

A: What kind of scenes did you have to prepare for? The train
     is not running anymore.

P: No that is right. The train, I rented.

A: Anything else?

P: I had to rent the services of the two railway engineers. It is
     their hobby. One, I think, is a chemist and I do not know
     what the other one does. They used to like doing that.
     Unfortunately they cannot do it anymore.

A: What is your answer to people or critics who say that your
     film is too optimistic?

P: I must tell you that people used to express that concern
     before they saw the film. They have not said that after
     seeing the film. I think that fear existed that, somehow,
     focusing on the good would create an alibi that would let
     the world off the hook. But people realize that is not what
     happens. In fact, the good makes you accountable because
     against the good you have to ask yourself, "What would I
     have done?" Those are tough questions. Next to the evil,
     you do not ask yourself these questions. You walk out
     feeling wonderful. "I am such a wonderful guy. I am not
     Hitler or Goebbels."

A: It makes people aware that it was possible to act differently.

P: It also underscores the fact that it was possible for people to
     act well. The survivors' community was traditionally very
     concerned that one might play up the righteous Gentiles in
     a way that would do exactly what you were quoting. I mean
     that it would take the edge off the experience. But not a
     single survivor who has seen the film has come away with
     that feeling. In fact, I have been criticized in exactly the
     opposite direction.

I have been criticized a few times for a line that some people think is much too tough, rather than the opposite, and that is the line on Christianity: "The Holocaust occurred in the heart of Christian Europe and would not have been possible without the apathy or complicity of most Christians, and without the virulent tradition of anti-Semitism that had long infested the very soul of Christianity." People have said to me: "This is like a slap in the face." But the good Christians that I have known are Christians who are ready and eager to face the extent of Christian responsibility. And the Christian responsibility is massive.

A: How do you situate your film in comparison to *Le Chagrin et la Pitié* and *Shoah*? I ask this because it is a documentary and it is one of the excellent documentaries made in French dealing with the Holocaust.

P: First of all, I am flattered by the question because those are both extraordinarily important films. But, at the same time, I would not even know how to answer that question. I think *Le Chagrin et la Pitié* is a remarkable film in many respects. It is also very much a film of its time. I doubt that Ophüls would have made the same film today. Probably, the most glaring omission is that the film conveys no real sense of the importance of the Jewish question in France at that time. You know, *that* was the test of France then. That was the moral test. And it talks about all sorts of things, but it does not talk about that.

A: It is not a film on the Holocaust.

P: No, but it is a film about French attitudes and French responsibility. There is a very brief interview with Claude Lévy which is very good actually. But it is very brief and there are I think one or two other references. But again, if I had made a film in 1968, I probably would cringe at what it would be because I have changed so completely since 1968.

A: The context is different. I mean at that time it was a necessary step also for the French to face their responsibilities.

P: Perhaps it was a necessary step. I do not know that anybody would have been capable of making a film that would have realized the importance of the Jewish question at that time. There are still people today who do not realize it so it would be the most unfair of criticisms to self-righteously make that point. However, having said that, that to me probably would be the main difference with *Le Chagrin et la Pitié*. My film, *Weapons of the Spirit*, puts the Jewish question at the very heart of any moral assessment of France. Even to the point of almost deliberately brushing aside things that other people consider important. For instance, I have very little on the Resistance because the Resistance simply did not interest me. I think anyway, that the Resistance is essentially a myth. I mean, there was a small Resistance, but what has been made of it is simply not historically accurate. Incidentally, the Resistance failed that test which people are still having great difficulty facing. The Resistance never realized the importance of helping the Jews. The Resistance did not stop a single train to Auschwitz.

A: What about *Shoah*?

P: I told Lanzmann that my fantasy was that my film would be considered a little bit like the little brother of *Shoah*. One deals with the magnitude of the evil...

A: ...the systematic extermination, while yours is about an exception.

P: *Weapons of the Spirit* is certainly about the exception.
    Obviously I believe that the exception is important. I believe
    that many people would go see *Shoah* after seeing *Weapons
    of the Spirit* who might not have gone otherwise because
    Weapons of the Spirit is an entry point for this material, for
    this history. *Shoah* is not an entry point. Nobody goes to see
    a nine hour film who already does not have a certain
    commitment. Also, it is very scary material. People need to
    be brought into this material.

A: How do you see the role of responsible leaders in all this?
    Trocmé was a leader but the people of Le Chambon were
    still doing the main work.

P: It is a very good question. I worked very, very hard to find
    the balance. I think that Trocmé is a strong presence in the
    film. At the same time I do not have this image that leaders
    create something out of nothing. I believe that leadership is
    overvalued, that leadership, at its best, reflects. I tried to
    suggest the extraordinary balance that occurred in Le
    Chambon. Trocmé was an extraordinary man, Pastor Theis
    was an extraordinary man. These were brilliant people who
    really understood what was called for.

A: You are a man of cinema. How do you think this influenced
    your representation of the Holocaust as it is, in comparison
    with the work of an historian or a philosopher. What is
    specific to your experience as a filmmaker? Did you learn
    something by making other films that helped you to make
    this film?

P: I am sure that of course is true. But I like history very
    much. I am fascinated by history. I was just having lunch
    today with Michael Marrus who is one of the greatest
    historians on the Holocaust. I am proud that I have such
    friends. I really admire Michael's brilliance. I said that as a
    prologue to say that historians place such a large emphasis

on the written word, on the document. And that is only a
pale reflection of the richness that is history. We filmmakers
have the opportunity of showing pictures, of showing faces,
of showing photographs and directing the eye on a
photograph where we think it's important. We have the
opportunity of playing music. I believe there's an almost
magical connection between things. I remember talking to an
historian once, a very important historian, about something
that I had discovered in a newsreel. He was quite surprised
because I realized he had never bothered to look at
newsreels. I think there is extraordinarily valuable
information that a film can provide.

A: Like information about everything that cannot be put in
     words.

P: And also things that can be put in words. Part of the
     tremendous danger of film is that you have to make things
     so simple. There are no foot-notes. It is hard to even get
     away with a parenthesis in a film. It has to have this clean,
     linear structure, and you're chopping away. There is a great
     danger in that and I am envious of what an historian can do.
     On the other hand, that very obligation to simplify can force
     you to really look for the most profound truths. In a way,
     historians can get away with: "on the one hand... on the
     other hand..." and you do not really know what anything is
     about. It gives you massive information but it does not cut
     down to the bone about what was going on. When I was
     editing the film, I was wondering how long the film was
     going to be and I did not want it to be long. I wanted it to
     be reasonably short. At one point I thought three hours was
     wonderful. And then I realized it cannot be three hours
     because it had to be modest in appearance, like its subject.
     The form had to match the subject. Which is also why I
     could not do any movie tricks. I could not do anything
     fancy. It had to be extraordinarily simple. It is hard to be
     simple. In order to shorten the film, in order to remind

myself of this need to trim, trim, trim, I wrote in big letters over my editing table a sentence I had stumbled on at that time in the writings of Jacques Maritain, the great Catholic thinker: *"Plus un artiste est grand, plus il élimine,"* "The greater the artist, the more he eliminates." In books you do not have to eliminate. You do not have that pressure to eliminate. With film, you have no choice.

A: And you have to pick the size that fits the subject.

P: That is true. Also, I truly believe that the more you understand something, the more you should be capable of explaining it to a smart ten-year-old. I truly believe that. With some exceptions of course, some things that are beyond a ten-year-old's emotional and psychological experience. But that is really the test: to say things simply. And that is a test for filmmakers. That challenge is tremendously energizing.

A: Were you thinking about the future when you were making the film. Was it a way for you to tell people "Well, if anything similar happens again this is a way to react"?

P: It was a way of telling myself that. It was a way of convincing myself that I can raise my children with a certain level of optimism that humanity is not irredeemably evil. I think humanity is pretty terrible but it is a cop-out to forget that the choice is ours. And that it is possible to resist evil at any time.

FILMOGRAPHY

The following list includes only the films I have analyzed or mentioned in this study for several reasons: because they represent an important date in the history of French cinema in relationship with the Occupation, because they contain anti-Semitic propaganda, because they allude to the Holocaust or because they clearly represent a specific chapter of the persecution of the Jews. For a general list of films dealing with France during the Occupation and the Second World War, see Henry Rousso's *Le Syndrome de Vichy* (Paris: Editions du Seuil, 1990), 376-380.

French Films with Anti-Semitic Propaganda

Les Corrupteurs, 1942, Pierre Ramelot (scenario by François Mazeline). Première with Henri Decoin's *Les Inconnus dans la maison*, based on the novel by Georges Simenon.

Français vous avez la mémoire courte, première on April 9, 1942, Jean Morel and Jacques Chavannes.

La Terre qui renaît, première in July 1942, Gérard Bennett.

Le Péril juif, première on July 6, 1942, Dr. Taubert, German-French film produced by the "Institut d'étude des questions juives." *Le Jeune hitlérien (Hitlerjunge Quex)*, 1933, Germany, Hans Steinhoff. Première in Paris on March 14, 1942. French versions of other German propaganda films: *Le Juif Süss* (1940); *La Libre Amérique*; *Victoire à l'Ouest*.

Forces occultes, première on March 10, 1943. Jean Mamy and Paul Riche (executed in 1946; scénario by Jean-Marquès-Rivière).

••••••••••••••••••••••••••••••••••

Other Analyzed Films

L'Assassinat du Père Noël, 1941, Christian Jacque.

L'Assassin habite au 21, 1942, Henri-Georges Clouzot.

Lumière d'été, 1942, Jean Grémillon.

Les Visiteurs du soir, 1942, Marcel Carné.

Pontcarral, colonel d'Empire, 1942, Jean Delannoy.

Le Ciel est à vous, 1943, Jean Grémillon.

Le Corbeau, 1943, Henri-Georges Clouzot.

La Libération de Paris, 1944, Collectif.

La France libérée, 1944, Soviet Union, Serge Youtkévitch, 1944.

Caméras sous la botte, 1945, Albert Mahuzier.

Les Camps de la mort, 1945, Actualités Françaises.

Le Six juin à l'aube, 1945, Jean Grémillon.

Le Massacre des innocents, 1946 (project, film never shot), Jean Grémillon. This film was to represent the Spanish Civil War, the Munich agreement, the concentration camps and the return of the prisoners in a completely destroyed Europe.

Au coeur de l'orage, 1946, Jean-Paul Le Chanois. Includes a fictitious sequence representing Jean Moulin's arrest.

La Bataille du rail, 1946, René Clément.

Nous continuons, 1946, M. Bahelfer, O. Fessler, A. Hamza, I. Holodenko, J. Weinfeld.

Offlag XVIIA, 1946, Maurice Reynaudet and Jean Faurez.

Patrie, 1946, Louis Daquin.

Le Père tranquille, 1946, René Clément.

Présence au combat, 1946, M. Cravenne.

Le Retour (Reunion), 1946, USA, Cartier-Bresson.

Les Maudits, 1947, René Clément.

Le Bal des pompiers, 1948, A. Berthomieu.

Manon, 1948, Henri Georges Clouzot.

Retour à la vie, 1949, Dréville, Cayatte, Clouzot, Lampin.

Le Silence de la mer, 1949, Jean-Pierre Melville, from the novel by Vercors.

Maître après Dieu, 1950, Louis Daquin.

Buchenwald, made before 1954, film presented by the *Amicale Francaise des Deportés Résistants Patriotes et Familles de Disparus*.

Nuit et Brouillard (Night and Fog), 1955, Alain Resnais, text by Jean Cayrol.

Un Condamné à mort s'est échappé (*A Man Escaped*), 1956, J.-J. Bresson.

La Traversée de Paris, 1956, Claude Autant-Lara.

Hiroshima mon amour, 1959, Alain Resnais, text by Marguerite Duras.

Marie-Octobre, 1959, Julien Duvivier.

Le Passage du Rhin, 1959, André Cayatte.

La Vache et le prisonnier, 1959, Henri Verneuil.

L'Enclos, 1961, France and Yugoslavia, Armand Gatti.

Léon Morin, prêtre, 1961, Jean-Pierre Melville.

Un Taxi pour Tobrouk, 1961, Denis de la Patellière.

Le Temps du Ghetto (*The Witnesses*), 1961, Frédéric Rossif.

Edith Stein, 1962, Dominique Delouche.

La Mémoire courte, 1962, Torrent and Prémysler.

Muriel, ou le temps d'un retour, 1963, Alain Resnais.

La Cage de verre, 1965, Philippe Arthuys.

Le Coup de grâce, 1965, Jean Cayrol and Claude Durand.

La Grande vadrouille, 1966, Gérard Oury.

La Ligne de démarcation, 1966, Claude Chabrol.

Paris brûle-t-il?, 1966, René Clément.

Le Vieil homme et l'enfant, 1967, Claude Berri.

L'Authentique procès de Carl Emmanuel Jung, 1967, Marcel Hanoun.

L'Armée des ombres, 1970, Jean-Pierre Melville.

Nous n'irons plus aux bois, 1970, Georges Dumoulin.

Le Chagrin et la pitié (*The Sorrow and the Pity*), 1971, Marcel Ophüls, Alain de Sédouy and André Harris.

Français si vous saviez, 1973, André Harris and Alain de Sédouy.

Lacombe Lucien, 1973, Louis Malle and Patrick Modiano.

Pourquoi Israël?, 1973, Claude Lanzmann.

Les Violons du bal, 1973, Michel Drach.

Au nom de la race (*Of Pure Blood*), 1974, Marc Hillel and Clarissa Henry.

Les Guichets du Louvre (*Black Thursday*), 1974, Michel Mitrani (based on the book by Roger Boussinot).

Toute une vie, 1974, Claude Lelouch.

1942, 1975, Simone Boruchowicz.

Section spéciale, 1975, Henri Costa-Gavras (based on the book by Hervé Villeré).

Un Sac de billes (*A Bag of Marbles*), 1975, Jacques Doillon (based on the novel by Joseph Joffo).

L'Affiche rouge, 1976, Frank Cassenti.

Chantons sous l'Occupation, 1976, A. Halimi.

La Mémoire de la justice (*The Memory of Justice*), 1976, USA,
Marcel Ophüls.

Monsieur Klein, 1976, Joseph Losey.

Le Dernier métro, 1980, François Truffaut.

Les Uns et les Autres (*Bolero*), 1980, Claude Lelouch.

La Guerre d'un seul homme (*One Man's War*), 1981, Edgardo
Cozarinsky, based on Ernst Jünger's *Journal parisien*.

La Passante du Sans-Souci, 1982, Jacques Rouffio, based on the
novel by Joseph Kessel.

Au nom de tous les miens, 1983, Robert Enrico, based on the
book by Martin Gray and Max Gallo.

Coup de foudre (*Entre Nous*), 1983, Diane Kurys.

Shoah, 1985, Claude Lanzmann.

Au revoir les enfants (*Goodbye Children*), 1987, Louis Malle.

Le Testament d'un poète juif assassiné, 1987, Frank Cassenti,
based on the novel by Elie Wiesel *The Testament*.

Les Armes de l'Esprit (*Weapons of the Spirit*), 1988, Pierre
Sauvage.

Hôtel Terminus, 1988, Marcel Ophüls.

De Nuremberg à Nuremberg, 1989, Frédéric Rossif.

Une Affaire de femmes (*A Story of Women*), 1989, Claude Chabrol.

Docteur Petiot, 1990, Christian de Chalonge.

Korczak, 1991, Andrzej Wajda.

Milena, 1991, Véra Belmont.

BIBLIOGRAPHY

Adler, Jacques. *The Jews of Paris and the Final Solution*. New York: Oxford University Press, 1987.

Angress, Ruth K. "Lanzmann's 'Shoah' and Its Audience." *Simon Wiesenthal Center Annual* 3 (1986).

Ansen, David. "A Village Conspiracy of Goodness." *Newsweek*. (September 18, 1989). On P. Sauvage.

Armes, Roy. *French Cinema Since 1946*. London: A. Zwemmer Ltd., 1966.

----------. *The Cinema of Alain Resnais*. New York: A.S. Barnes, 1968.

Arnold, Gary. "Filmmaker's 'merci' captures town's spirit." *The Washington Times* (January 19, 1990). On P. Sauvage.

August, Mary. "Reminders of Holocaust reverberate in France." *Sunday Patriot News* (February 24, 1991).

Aumont, Jacques. "Comment on écrit l'histoire." *Cahiers du cinéma* 238-239 (May-June 1972). About René Allio's film *Les Camisards*.

Avisar, Ilan. *Screening the Holocaust: Cinema's images of the unimaginable*. Bloomington: Indiana University Press, 1988.

Bartoszewski, Wladyslaw. *The Convent at Auschwitz*. New York: George Braziller, 1990.

Baudry, Pierre. "*Le Chagrin et la pitié.*" *Cahiers du cinéma* 231 (August-September 1971).

Bazin, André. *What Is Cinema?* Trans. Hugh Gray. Berkeley: University of California Press, 1967 and 1971.

Benayoun, Robert. *Alain Resnais arpenteur de l'imaginaire.* Paris: Stock, 1986.

Bernstein, Richard. "A Movie Maker Preserves Those Who Preserved Him." *The New York Times* (August 27, 1989). On P. Sauvage.

Blady-Szwajger, Adina. *Je ne me souviens de rien d'autre.* Paris: Calmann-Lévy, 1990.

Blatter, Janet, and Sybil Milton. *Art of the Holocaust.* New York: Routledge, 1981.

Bonitzer, Pascal. "Histoire de sparadrap." *Cahiers du cinéma.* 250 (May, 1974). About Louis Malle's film *Lacombe Lucien.*

Bouzet, Ange-Dominique. "Y a-t-il une affaire *Korczak?*" *Libération* (January 9, 1991).

Bower, Tom. *Klaus Barbie: The Butcher of Lyons.* New York: Pantheon Books, 1984.

Buache, Freddy. *Le cinéma français des années soixante.* Paris: Hatier, 1987.

Burguière, André. "Au nom de la vérité." *Le Nouvel Observateur* (January 17-23, 1991). About Wajda's film *Korczak.*

Burk, Joan Juliet. "Shame and Punishment." *Vogue* 177 (November, 1987).

Buss, Robin. *The French Through Their Films*. New York: Ungar, 1988.

Canby, Vincent. "Ophüls's Monumental Film on Barbie." *International Herald Tribune* (May 21, 1988).

Cargas, Harry. *Shadows of Auschwitz*. New York: Crossroad, 1990.

Carr, Jay. "*Weapons*: Luminous look at a 'conspiracy of goodness'." *The Boston Globe* (November 15, 1989). On P. Sauvage.

Cayrol, Jean. *Poèmes de la nuit et du brouillard*, followed by *Larmes publiques*. Paris: Editions Pierre Seghers, 1945.

----------. "Pour un romanesque Lazaréen" published in *Lazare parmi nous*. Paris: Editions Pierre Seghers, 1950.

----------. *Corps étrangers*. Paris: Union Générale d'Editions, 1964.

Cayrol, Jean, and Alain Resnais. *Night and Fog*. Trans. R. Hughes and Merle Worth, in Robert Hughes, ed. *Film: Book 2. Films of Peace and War*. New York: Grove Press, 1962.

Celle, Raymond "*Les Armes de l'esprit*: le choc des mots et des images pour le film de Pierre Sauvage." *Le Progrès* (October 16, 1990). On P. Sauvage.

Centerpoint: A Journal of Interdisciplinary Studies V 4:1 (Fall 1980). Special issue: "The Holocaust."

Champlin, Charles. "Film Maker Exposes a 'Conspiracy' of Good." *Los Angeles Times* (October 5, 1989). On P. Sauvage.

Chase, Chris. "A Village That Saved Its Jews." *The New York Times* (July 19, 1982). On P. Sauvage.

Chevassu, François. "Le Film en France de 1940 à 1945." *Image et son* 188 (November, 1965).

Chevrie, Marc. "Das ist das platz." *Cahiers du cinéma* 374 (July-August, 1985). On *Shoah*.

Chirat, Raymond. *Le Cinéma français des années de guerre.* Paris: Hatier, 1983.

Ciment, Michel. *Conversation with Joseph Losey.* London: Methuen, 1985.

Conan, Eric, and Caradec'h, Jean-Michel. "Il n'y aura pas de procès Leguay." *L'Express* (July 14, 1989).

Courtade, Francis. *Les Malédictions du cinéma français.* Paris: André Moreau, 1978.

Daney, Serge. "Anti-rétro." *Cahiers du cinéma* 252 and 253 (August-September and October-November, 1974).

Dawidowidcz, Lucy S. *The War Against the Jews.* New York: Bantam Books, 1976.

Decock, Jean. "Un Entretien avec Louis Malle: un cinéma du regard." Volume 63, Number 4 *The French Review* (March, 1990).

Deguy, Michel, ed. *Au Sujet de 'Shoah.'* Paris: Belin, 1990. A collection of essays and articles on *Shoah*. Includes texts by Claude Lanzmann, Marcel Ophüls, Pierre Vidal-Naquet, Michel Deguy, Bernard Cuau, Rachel Ertel, Soshana Felman, Elisabeth de Fontenay, Elisabeth Huppert, Gertrud Koch, Sami Naïr, Anny Dayan-Rosenman, Abraham

Brumberg, Neal Ascherson, Timothy Garton Ash, Jacek Kuron, Jean-Charles Szurek.

Deleuze, Gilles. *Proust et les signes.* Paris: Editions de Minuit, 1979.

----------. *L'Image-temps.* Paris: Editions de Minuit, 1985.

Delpech, François. "La persécution nazie et l'attitude de Vichy." *Historiens-Géographes* 273 (May-June, 1979). In reaction to the American series *Holocaust.*

Denby, David. "Lanzmann Meets His Audience." *New York Magazine* (November, 1985).

----------. "Criminal Elements." *New York Magazine* (October 17, 1988).

----------. "Weapons of the Spirit." *New York Magazine* (September 18, 1989). On P. Sauvage.

Desjardins, Aline. *Aline Desjardins s'entretient avec François Truffaut.* Paris: Ramsay, Ramsay Poche Cinema, 1987.

Des Pres, Terrence. *The Survivor. An Anatomy of Life in the Death Camps.* New York: Oxford University Press, 1976.

----------. "War Crimes." *Harper's* (January 1977).

Doneson, Judith E. *The Holocaust in American Film.* Philadelphia: Jewish Publication Society, 1987.

Doniol-Valcroze, Jacques. "Le Massacre des innocents." *Cahiers du cinéma* X: 59 (May, 1966).

Dreyfus, François-Georges. *Histoire de Vichy: vérités et légendes.* Paris: Perrin, 1991.

Du Plessix-Gray, Francine. "Bearing Witness." *The New York Times Magazine* (August 30, 1987).

Ehrlich, Evelyn. *Cinema of Paradox.* New York: Columbia University Press, 1985. French Cinema during the Occupation.

Erens, Patricia. *The Jews in American Cinema.* Bloomington: Indiana University Press, 1984.

Les Etudes Philosophiques (January-March, 1990). Special issue: "Le Mal."

Fayol, Pierre. *Le Chambon-sur-Lignon sous l'occupation.* Paris: L'Harmattan, 1990.

Felman, Shoshana. "A l'âge du témoignage: *Shoah.*" In Michel Deguy, ed. *Au Sujet de Shoah* Paris: Belin, 1990.

Ferro, Marc. "Cinéma et histoire." *Cahiers du cinéma* 257 (May-June, 1975).

----------. *Analyse de films, analyse de sociétés.* Paris: Hachette, 1975.

----------. *Cinéma et histoire.* Paris: Denoël Gonthier, 1977.

----------. *The Use and Abuse of History or How the Past Is Taught.* London: Routledge & Kegan Paul, 1984.

Finkielkraut, Alain. *Le Juif imaginaire.* Paris: Editions du Seuil, 1980.

Flamm, Matthew. "A Saving Grace." *New York Post* (September 2, 1989). On P. Sauvage.

Ford, Charles. *Histoire du cinéma français contemporain 1945-1977*. Paris: France-Empire, 1977.

Foucault, Michel. "Entretien." *Cahiers du cinéma* 251-252 (July-August, 1974).

----------. "Les meurtres qu'on raconte." *L'Avant-scène du cinéma* 183 (March, 1977).

Frappat, Bruno. "Le Choc de *Shoah*." *Le Monde* Radio/Télévision (July 5-6, 1987).

Friedlander, Judith. *Vilna on the Seine*. New Haven: Yale University Press, 1990.

Friedländer, Saul. *When Memory Comes*. Trans. Helen R. Lane. New York: Farrar, Straus, Giroux, 1979.

----------. *Reflections of Nazism*. Trans. Thomas Weir. New York: Harper & Row, 1984.

Friedman, Lester. *Hollywood's Image of the Jew*. New York: Frederick Ungar, 1982.

Frodon, Jean-Michel. "Le Courage et la fierté." *Le Monde* (October 12, 1990). On P. Sauvage.

Frois, Emmanuèle. "Des Gens bien tranquilles." *Le Progrès* (October 13, 1990). On P. Sauvage.

Gauthier, Guy. Interview with Alain Renais. *Image et Son* 196 (1966).

Gay, Pierre-Angel, and Véronique Mortaigne. "Programmation: la peur des mots." *Le Monde* (February 15, 1991).

Grassowski, Henryk. "*Shoah*, version polonaise, ne convainc personne." *Libération* (December 2, 1985).

Gray, Martin. *Au Nom de tous les miens*. Paris: Laffont, 1971.

Gruber-Ejnes. "Entre morts et vivants, *Shoah*." *Regards* 160 (April 24-May 7, 1986).

Haft, Cynthia. *The Theme of Nazi Concentration Camps in French Literature*. The Hague: Mouton, 1973.

Hallie, Philip. *Lest Innocent Blood Be Shed*. New York: Harper and Row, 1979. On Le Chambon-sur-Lignon.

Hamon, Hervé, and Patrick Rotman. *Génération* I and II. Paris: Editions du Seuil, 1987-1988.

Harris, André, and Alain de Sédouy. "A Propos d'une fresque." *L'Avant-scène du cinéma* 148 (1972).

Hatzfeld, Jean. "*Les Armes de l'esprit*: Résistance sans héros." *Cahiers du cinéma* 438 (December, 1990). On P. Sauvage.

Hayward, Susan, and Ginette Vincendeau, eds. *French Film. Texts and Contexts*. New York: Routledge, 1990.

H.C. "Les houles de la douleur." *Le Monde* Radio/Télévision (June 28-29, 1987). On *Shoah*.

Heymann, Danièle. "Un homme exemplaire." *Le Monde* (January 11, 1991). On *Korczak*.

Hilberg, Raul. *The Destruction of the European Jews*. Chicago: Quadrangle Books, 1961.

Hirsh, Foster. *Joseph Losey*. Boston: Twayne, 1980.

Hoffmann, Stanley. Introduction to the transcript of *The Sorrow and the Pity*. See Ophüls.

Hughes, Robert, ed. *Film: Book 2. Films of Peace and War*. New York: Grove Press, 1962. 234-256. Contains a translation of Jean Cayrol's script of *Night and Fog* with a description of the images that accompany the text.

Hunter, Stephen. "Film Documents: A Wartime Miracle of Faith." *The Sun* (February 26, 1990). On P. Sauvage.

Insdorf, Annette. *Indelible Shadows: Film and the Holocaust*. New York: Random House, Vintage Books, 1983.

Jarvie, I.C. *Movies as Social Criticism*. Metuchen: Scarecrow Press, 1978.

Jarvik, Laurence. "The Banality of Good." *Tikkun* (March-April, 1988). On P. Sauvage.

Joffo, Joseph. *Un Sac de billes*. Paris: Lattès, 1973.

Johnson, Mary. "A Filmmaker's Odyssey." *Facing History and Ourselves News* (Winter 1989-90). On P. Sauvage.

"Joseph Losey 1909-1984," *Positif* 293/294, Special Issue (July-August 1985), 2-62. Includes "Losey revisité" by Edgardo Cozarinsky.

Kael, Pauline. *Going Steady*. New York: Bantam, 1971.

----------. *Deeper into Movies*. Boston: Little, Brown, 1973.

----------. *Reeling*. Boston: Little, Brown, 1976.

----------. *When the Lights Go Down*. New York: Holt, Rinehart and Winston, 1980.

Kahn, Nicole "Télévision: *Shoah*, une fiction du réel." *Eaux Vives* 509 (December, 1987).

Karski, Jan. "*Shoah*." *Together* I: 2 (July, 1986).

----------. "Eyewitness to Holocaust Could Find No Help." *The Baltimore Sun* (October 15, 1989).

Kauffmann, Sylvie. "Les intentions pures de Wajda." *Le Monde* (January 11, 1991).

Kemp, Philip. "Childhood's end." *Sight and Sound* 4 (Autumn 1986).

Klarsfeld, Serge. *Memorial to the Jews deported from France.* New York: B. Klarsfeld Foundation, 1983. First published in France under the title *Le Mémorial de la déportation des Juifs de France.* Paris: Centre de Documentation Juive Contemporaine de Paris, 1979.

----------. *The Children of Izieu.* New York: H.N. Abrams, 1984.

Kogon, Eugen. *L'Etat SS.* Paris: Le Seuil, 1970.

Kracauer, Siegfried. *From Caligari to Hitler: A Psychological History of the German Film.* Princeton: Princeton University Press, 1947.

Kyrou, Ado. *Luis Buñuel.* Paris: Seghers, 1962.

Langer, Lawrence. *The Holocaust and the Literary Imagination.* New Haven: Yale University Press, 1975.

Lanzmann, Claude. "Le Lieu et la parole." *Cahiers du cinéma* 374 (July-August, 1985).

----------. "Enfin *Shoah!*" *Le Nouvel Observateur* (July 26-August 2, 1987). Entretien avec Catherine David.

----------. "Ce que je n'ai pas dit dans *Shoah.*" *VSD* (July 9-15, 1987). Interview with Jean-Pierre Chabrol.

----------. "*Shoah,* de Claude Lanzmann." *Le Monde* Radio/Télévision (June 28-29, 1987). Entretien avec Catherine Humblot.

----------. Preface to Henry Orenstein *I Shall Live*. New York: Touchstone, 1987.

----------. "L'infilmable." *Vertigo* 3 (1988).

----------. "Un cinéaste au-dessus de tout soupçon?" *Le Nouvel Observateur* (January 17-23, 1991): 95-96. About Wajda's film *Korczak.*

Lazare, Bernard. *L'Antisémitisme, son histoire et ses causes.* Paris: Editions 1900, 1990.

Léglise, Paul. *Histoire de la politique du cinéma français: 2 - entre deux républiques, 1940-1946.* Paris: Filméditions, Pierre Lherminier, 1970.

Lehrer, Natasha "*Shoah.*" *Windmill* 4 (Hilary Term 1987).

Leiser, Erwin. *Nazi Cinema.* Trans. G. Mander and David Wilson. New York: Collier Books, 1974.

Le Roux, Hervé. "Un Film de Pologne." *Cahiers du cinéma* 374 (July-August, 1985). On *Shoah.*

Lévi, Primo. *Si c'est un homme.* Paris: Julliard, 1987.

Lévy, Bernard-Henri, ed. *Archives d'un procès. Klaus Barbie.* Paris: Globe, 1986.

Lewin, Abraham. *Journal du ghetto de Varsovie: une coupe de larmes.* Paris: Plon, 1990.

Losey, Joseph. *Monsieur Klein.* Transcript of the film. *L'Avant-scène du cinéma* 175 (November 1, 1976).

MacBean, James R. *Film and Revolution.* Bloomington: Indiana University Press, 1975.

Malle, Louis. *Cinéma 62/63* (February 1962). Quoted by Prédal, 1989: 54. Interview on *Vie Privée.*

----------. *Positif* 320 (October 1987). Quoted by Prédal, 1989. Interview on *Goodby Children.*

Malle, Louis, and Patrick Modiano. *Lacombe Lucien.* Trans. Sabine Destree. New York: Viking Press, 1975.

Marienstras, Elise "*Shoah.*" *Positif* 293-294 (July-August, 1985).

Marrus, Michael. *The Holocaust in History.* Toronto: Lester & Orpen Dennys Limited, 1987.

Marrus, Michael, and Robert O. Paxton. *Vichy France and the Jews.* New York: Basic Books, 1981.

Martin, Marcel. *Le Cinéma français depuis la guerre.* Paris: Edilig, 1984.

Matis, David. "Films of the Holocaust." *Yiddish V* I (Summer 1982).

McCarthy, Todd. "*Spirit* Docu Is More Than Labor of Love for Sauvage." *Variety* (March 16, 1987). On P. Sauvage.

Meltzer, Milton. *Rescue: The Story of How Gentiles Saved Jews in the Holocaust.* New York: Harper and Row, 1988. On P. Sauvage.

Metz, Christian. *Esthétique et psychologie du cinéma.* Paris: Editions Universitaires, 1963, I.

----------. *Essai sur la signification au cinéma I* and *II.* Paris: Klincksieck, 1968 and 1972.

Michel, Henri, and Olga Wormser, eds. *La Tragédie de la déportation.* Paris: Hachette, 1954.

Mitry, Jean. *Esthétique et psychologie du cinéma.* Paris: Editions Universitaires, 1963.

----------. *La Sémiologie en question.* Paris: Editions du Cerf, 1987.

Modiano, Patrick. *La Place de l'étoile.* Paris: Gallimard, 1968.

Monaco, James. *Alain Resnais.* New York: Oxford University Press, 1978.

Morin, Edgard. *La Rumeur d'Orléans.* Paris: Editions du Seuil, 1969.

Moritz, Charles, ed. *Current Biography.* Bronx, New York: H.W. Wilson Company, 1977.

Muffs, Judith Herschlag. *The Holocaust in books and films.* New York: Center for Studies on the Holocaust, Anti-Defamation League of B'nai B'rith, 1982.

Nichols, Bill. *Ideology and the Image: Social Representation in the Cinema and Other Media.* Bloomington: Indiana University Press, 1981.

Oms, Marcel. *Alain Resnais*. Paris: Editions Rivages, 1988.

Ophüls, Marcel. "Regardez donc dans vos greniers." *L'Avant-scène du cinéma* (1972).

----------. *The Sorrow and the Pity*. Trans. Mireille Johnston. New York: Outerbridge and Lazard, 1972. With an introduction by Stanley Hoffmann.

----------. "In a Way, This Work Is a Curse." *The Progressive* (May, 1982). An interview with Claudia Dreifus.

Paxton, Robert O. *La France de Vichy: 1940-1944*. Paris: Editions du Seuil, 1972.

Peretz, Martin. "The French and the Jews." *The New Republic* (June 4, 1990).

Poliakov, Léon. *Auschwitz*. Paris: Gallimard-Julliard, 1964.

----------. *Le Bréviaire de la haine*. Paris: Calman-Lévy, 1979.

Prédal, René, et al. *Etudes Cinématographiques*. 64-68 (1968). Collection of essays on Alain Resnais.

----------. *La société française à travers le cinéma. 1914-1945*. Paris: Armand Colin, 1972.

----------. *Louis Malle*. Paris: Edilig, 1989.

R.A. "Cinq millions de Français ont regardé *Shoah*." *Le Monde* (July 2, 1987).

Resnais, Alain. *Image et Son* 196 (July, 1966).

Revue de l'Université de Bruxelles 1-2 (1987). Special issue: "Les juifs entre la mémoire et l'oubli." Includes articles by Emmanuel Lévinas and Alain Finkielkraut.

Rittner, Carol, and Sondra Myers, eds. *Courage to Care: Rescuers of Jews during the Holocaust.* New York: New York University Press, 1988. On P. Sauvage.

Rosenthal, Donna. "The Obsession of Marcel Ophüls." *The Washington Post* (March 15, 1987).

Rousset, David. *L'Univers concentrationnaire.* Paris: Editions de Minuit, 1965.

----------. *Les Jours de notre mort.* Paris: Ramsay, 1990.

Rousso, Henry. *Le Syndrome de Vichy.* Paris: Seuil, 1990.

Rubinstein, Leny. *"Hotel Terminus." Cineaste* XVII: 1 (1989).

Rutowsky, Adam. *La Luttte des Juifs en France à l'époque de l'occupation.* Paris: Centre de Documentation Juive contemporaine, 1975. Introduction by Georges Wellers.

Ryan, Allan A. Jr. *Klaus Barbie and the United States Government.* Frederick, MD: University Publishing Group, 1984.

Ryan, Desmond. "A Quiet Heroism in Town that Hid Jews." *The Philadelphia Enquirer* (December 6, 1989). On P. Sauvage.

Sadoul, Georges. *Histoire du cinéma mondial.* Paris: Flammarion, 1963.

Sarris, Andrew. *Cinema and Politics.* New York: Columbia University Press, 1978.

Sartre, Jean-Paul. "Une idée fondamentale de la Phénoménologie de Husserl: l'intentionnalité." *Situations I*. Paris: Gallimard, 1947.

----------. "Présentation des *Temps Modernes*." *Situations II*. Paris: Gallimard, 1948. First published in *Les Temps Modernes* 1 (October, 1945).

----------. *Réflexions sur la question juive*. Paris: Gallimard, 1954.

Sauvage, Pierre. "A Most Persistent Haven: Le Chambon-sur-Lignon." *Moment Magazine* (October, 1983).

----------. "Ten Things I Would Like to Know about Righteous Conduct in Le Chambon and Elsewhere During the Holocaust." *Humboldt Journal of Social Relations* XIII: 1-2 (1986).

----------. "*Weapons of the Spirit*: A Journey Home." *The Hollywood Reporter* (March 17, 1987).

----------. "Learning Hope from the Holocaust." Unpublished paper presented at the International Scholars' Conference at Oxford University, England, July 10-13, 1988.

----------. "The Persistence of a People." *MPT Magazine* (December, 1990).

Schwartz-Bart, André. *Le Dernier des Justes*. Paris: Seuil, 1959.

Sherman, Betsy. "Pierre Sauvage looks at courage in the Holocaust." *The Boston Globe* (November 23, 1989). On P. Sauvage.

Short, K.R.M., ed. *Feature Films as History*. Knoxville: University of Tennessee Press, 1981.

Siclier, Jacques. *La France de Pétain et son cinéma*. Paris: Henri Veyrier, 1982.

----------. "La Mort de Frédéric Rossif, l'homme des documentaires." *Le Monde* (April 20, 1990).

Sinaï, Ruth. *"Weapons of the Spirit*: l'héroïsme d'un village français sous l'Occupation." *France-Amérique* (February 1-7, 1990). On P. Sauvage.

Slama, Alain-Gérard. "Intelligence avec l'ennemi." *Le Point* (January 29, 1990).

Solinas, Franco. *Mr. Klein. L'Avant-scène cinéma* 175 (November, 1976). Includes the script of the film, an article by Robert Chazal, and a press review.

Sontag, Susan. *Under the Sign of Saturn*. New York: Farrar, Straus, Giroux, 1980.

Steiner, George. *Language and Silence: Essays in Language, Literature, and the Inhuman*. New York: Atheneum, 1967.

Stein-Schneider, H. "L'Antidote du *Chagrin et la pitié*." *France-Amérique* (February 1-7, 1990). On P. Sauvage.

Sullivan, Scott. "Europe Faces Its Nazi Past." *Newsweek* (April 20, 1987).

Sweets, John F. "Hold that Pendulum! Redefining Fascism, Collaborationism, and Resistance." *French Historical Studies* XV, 4 (Fall, 1988).

Szafran, Maurice. *Les Juifs dans la politique française de 1945 à nos jours*. Paris: Flammarion, 1990.

Taguieff, Pierre-André. "La Nouvelle judéophobie," *Les Temps Modernes* (November, 1989).

Thibaud, Paul. "La Culpabilité française." *Esprit* 168 (January, 1991).

Thomas, Sari. *Film/Culture*. Metuchen: Scarecrow Press, 1982.

Tillion, Germaine. *Ravensbrück*. Paris: Editions du Seuil, 1973.

Todorov, Tzvetan. *Face à l'extrême*. Paris: Seuil, 1991.

Toubiana, Serge. "Français si vous saviez..." *Cahiers du cinéma* 245-246 (April-May-June, 1973).

Trano, Stéphane. "Tonnerre de Lanzmann!" *Le Nouvel Observateur*. (August 14-20, 1987).

Van Biema, David H. "Filmmaker Claude Lanzmann Devotes 11 Years of His Life to a Biography of Death." *People Weekly* 25 (February 10, 1986).

Vaugeois, Christian. "Filmer la dialectique." *L'Avant-Scène du cinéma* 174 (October 1976).

Vittori, Jean-Pierre. "A Bâtons rompus avec Claude Lanzmann." *Le Patriote Résistant* (April, 1986).

Ward, John. *Alain Resnais or the Theme of Time*. Garden City, NY: Doubleday, 1968.

Wellers, Georges. *L'Etoile jaune à l'heure de Vichy*. Paris: Fayard, 1973.

----------. *Les Chambres à gaz ont existé*. Paris: Gallimard, Témoins, 1981.

Wiesel, Elie. *La Nuit*. Paris: Editions de Minuit, 1958.

----------. "A Survivor Remembers other Survivors of Shoah." *The New York Times* (November 3, 1985).

----------. *Silences et mémoire d'hommes*. Paris: Seuil, 1989.

----------. *The Testament: A Novel*. New York: Summit Books, 1990.

Willemen, Paul, ed. *Ophüls*. London: British Film Institute, 1978. On Max Ophüls.

Williams, Alan. *Republic of Images: A History of French Filmmaking*. Cambridge: Harvard University Press, 1992.

Williams, Christopher, ed. *Realism and the Cinema*. London: Routledge & Kegan Paul, 1980.

Wilmington, Michael. "Poignant, Powerful *Weapons of the Spirit*." *Los Angeles Times* (October 4, 1989). On P. Sauvage.

Winock, Michel. *Nationalisme, antisémitisme et fascisme en France*. Paris: Seuil, 1982.

Wormser-Migot, Olga. *Le Système concentrationnaire nazi, 1933-1945*. Paris: Press Universitaires de France, 1968.

Yakir, Dan. "In the Twilight Zone: *1000 Eyes* Talks to Alain Resnais." *1000 Eyes* (March, 1977).

Zimmer, Christian. "La Ligne de démarcation." *Les Temps Modernes* 298 (May, 1971).

NOTES

1. The script of this film was translated by Robert Hughes and Merle Worth, 234-255.

2. For a detailed analysis of this heritage, see Michel Winock *Nationalisme, antisémitisme et fascisme en France.*

3. On these points see the article "Programmation: la peur des mots." *Le Monde* (vendredi 15 février, 1991), 14.

4. Its members included famous names such as Georges Lefebvre, Henri Michel, Edouard Perroy, Pierre Caron, Gilberte Brossolette, Lucien Febvre, Pierre Renouvin. It was formed by the unification of the Commission d'Histoire de l'Occupation et de la Libération de la France (CHOLF) with the Comité d'Histoire de la Guerre. On the formation of the Comité, see Henry Rousso, 276-278.

5. Some of these early testimonies have been gathered and published again in Henri Michel and Olga Wormser's *Tragédie de la déportation.*

6. Among other crimes, Paul Touvier was judged for the execution of Victor Basch and his wife on January 10, 1944, a series of executions in Rillieux-la-Pape and a roundup in Montmélian. Condemned twice to the death penalty after the war (Lyon, December 10, 1945; Chambéry, March 4, 1947), Touvier is said to have escaped thanks to the help of Abbé Vautherin under the authority of Archbishop Charles Duquaire and Cardinal Pierre Marie Gerlier in exchange for the liberation of forty-two hostages to be executed in retaliation of various actions of the Résistance. Touvier's amnesty by President Georges Pompidou, on November 23 ,1971, was also obtained thanks to the constant

support of Bishop Duquaire. Paradoxically, it is the announcement of the amnesty that provoked public outrage and brought
for the first time in many years the *affaire Touvier* to the
limelight. The same year, the French government was asking the
extradition from Bolivia of Klaus Barbie for the first time.

7. Serge Klarsfeld, in B.-H. Lévy, 135.

8. Based on Georges Simenon's *Les Inconnus dans la maison* in
which the criminal already had a Jewish name. This film was
shown on French TV in June 1991. Very curiously, the press
made no allusion, at that time, to the anti-Semitic implications of
the film nor to its final speech.

9. Other propaganda films of that time include Jean Morel and
Jacques Chavannes' *Français vous avez la mémoire courte* (1942;
anti-Communist), Gérard Bennett's *La Terre qui renaît* (1942; in
support of Pétain's National Revolution, includes an anti-Semitic
sequence). René Prédal, *La Société française à travers le cinéma*,
286-292.

10. See, for example, Raymond Borde in his preface to Francis
Courtade, 1978: 13-15. In disagreement with critics such as
Martin, Chirat, Siclier or Courtade, Borde denies that any of
these films meant to criticize Vichy or the Germans. Borde
mentions seven other films that, according to him, illustrate a few
"moments of freedom" and a "spirit of revenge." These films are:
Christian-Jaque's *Voyage sans espoir*, Roland Tual's *Bonsoir
mesdames, bonsoir messieurs*, Pierre Prévert's *Adieu Léonard*,
Marcel L'Herbier's *La Nuit fantastique*, Henri Decoin *Les
Inconnus dans la maison*, Claude Autant-Lara's *Douce* and
Henri-Georges Clouzot's *Le Corbeau*.

11. Ado Kyrou, quoted by Prédal, 1972: 201-202.

12. *Les Malédictions du cinéma français*, 221-222. Quoted by M.
Martin, 15.

13. Jacques Siclier, *La France de Pétain et son cinéma*, 225. Quoted by M. Martin, 15.

14. This analysis is based on Marcel Martin's *Le Cinéma français depuis la guerre*, 8-10.

15. This is also the interpretation of Jacques Siclier in *La France de Pétain et son cinéma*, 459-460. Also quoted by Martin, 10.

16. Raymond Borde, preface to Francis Courtade's *Les Malédictions du cinéma français*, 17.

17. This line caused some violent controversy as it made it sound like the poor, in general, were scum for Autant-Lara.

18. Resnais declared to Robert Benayoun: "I would never characterize myself as politically committed ['engagé']." Benayoun, 239.

19. For many other examples concerning other countries, see Raul Hilberg, *The Destruction of the European Jews*, 704-715.

20. See also *Normandie-Niémen*, J. Dréville, 1960; *Le Passage du Rhin*, A. Cayatte, 1959; *Le Caporal épinglé*, J. Renoir, 1962; *Les Culottes rouges*, Alex Joffé, 1962.

21. Ilan Avisar wrote the following about these images filmed by the Nazis: "The existing footage of the Warsaw ghetto was taken by Nazi crews. These films were designed—at times literally, for some of the scenes were staged—to denigrate the victims and show that they were subhuman. Ironically, they are among the most forceful pieces of visual evidence of the Nazis' inhumanity, as they show the subhuman conditions imposed by the Germans on the Jews" (Avisar, Chapter I, note 63).

22. See also *La Dénonciation* J. Doniol-Valcroze, 1962.

23. See also *La Vie de château* J.-P. Rappeneau, 1966.

24. See Hervé Hamon, and Patrick Rotman, *Génération* I and II. See also Judith Friedlander, *Vilna on the Seine*.

25. Introduction to the transcript of *The Sorrow and the Pity* (see Ophüls).

26. On Max Ophüls' life see Paul Willemen, *Ophüls* (London: British Film Institute, 1978).

27. Introduction to the transcript of *The Sorrow and the Pity*, VII.

28. "Ah! Quelle grande époque pour le spectacle! Et, si vous me permettez l'expression, cette fois nous ferons 'fureur' car il s'agira d'une co-production franco-allemande."

29. Elie Wiesel *The Testament: A Novel* (New York: Summit Books, 1990). Originally published as *Le Testament d'un poète juif assassiné* (Paris: Editions du Seuil, 1980).

30. Introduction to the transcript of the film, Losey, 5.

31. On this point see Annette Insdorf, 106.

32. *Cahiers du cinéma* 354 (December 1983), 53.

33. Lanzmann, "Ce que je n'ai pas dit dans *Shoah*," 10-12.

34. On these three terrorist actions, see Judith Friedlander, 30-33.

35. "C'est vous qui avez produit cela. Je ne vous félicite pas," "Madame, vous ne savez pas à quel point c'est mal." Claude Lanzmann, 1991: 95.

36. On this subject see Alain Finkielkraut "'Sioniste': généalogie d'une accusation" *Le Juif imaginaire*, 179-198; and the excellent

essay by Pierre-André Taguieff "La Nouvelle judéophobie," *Les Temps Modernes*, 1-80.

37. "I would never characterize myself as a committed artist." Interview with Robert Benayoun, 239.

38. A. Resnais, *Esprit* 6 (June 1960). Quoted by Prédal 10.

39. On Resnais' irony, see Monaco, 4.

40. On the making of *The Triumph of the Will* and the organization of the Nuremberg Rally, see Susan Sontag "Fascinating Fascism," *The New York Review of Books* (February 6, 1975), reprinted in *Movies and Methods* edited by Bill Nichols (Berkeley: University of California Press, 1976). 36. Reprinted also in Susan Sontag, *Under the Sign of Saturn*, 72-105.

41. Elie Faure, *Mystique du cinéma*. Quoted by Oms, 32.

42. The key role of this "pure past" throughout Resnais' work was particularly studied in Gilles Deleuze's *L'Image-temps*, 137, 152-164, 268-272.

43. This is also the title of the 1956 Resnais' documentary about the French National Library.

44. On the influence of Cayrol's poetry on Resnais' work, see René Prédal, Jacques Belmans, Jacques Sternberg and Christian Zimmer, *Etudes Cinématographiques: Alain Resnais*. See in particular the chapter entitled "Personnages lazaréens et amours difficiles" (Prédal, 1968: 103-119).

45. This essay was published again in *Corps étrangers* (Paris: Union Générale d'Editions, 10/18, 1964).

46. Cayrol's exact expression is "Ne pas se livrer, tout est là." The verb "se livrer" in French implies at the same time "to

surrender," "to turn oneself in," and "to confide in someone." "Pour un romanesque lazaréen," quoted by Prédal, 106.

47. Roland Barthes "La rature." in Cayrol, 1964: 243.

48. This quote and the preceding are also used by Prédal et al., 1968: 115, 119.

49. Night and Fog Decree issued by Hitler on December 7, 1941.

50. On this point see Prédal, 1968: 26.

51. Resnais and Cayrol developed these technics in *Muriel* (1963), the second film they made together. On this point see Monaco, 11, 86.

52. On all of these points, see Christian Metz, *Essais sur la signification au cinéma*, 26-29.

53. In 1956, Jacques Doniol-Valcroze referred to it as a "funerary oratorio," a "great work of art," (Doniol-Valcroze, 37) and Truffaut called this documentary a "poem" (quoted by Insdorf, 43).

54. Interview with *Clarté* (February 1961). Quoted by Oms, 14.

55. Resnais and George Semprun used excerpts of Sartre's preface to Roger Stéphane's *Portrait de l'aventurier* as an epigraph for the published version of the script of *La guerre est finie* and for the writing of the script of *Stavisky*. These excerpts are quoted and analyzed by James Monaco in *Alain Resnais*, 112; 175.

56. Here Metz is using a concept defined by Jean Mitry in his *Esthétique et psychologie du cinéma*, 183.

57. As opposed to what happens with photography.

58. Alain Resnais, interview with Sylvain Roumette, *Clarté* (February 1961). Quoted by Oms, 20. On Resnais' relations with the surrealist movement see Prédal, 1968: 10-12; Oms, 45-51.

59. A. Resnais *Image et son* 148 (February 1962). Quoted by Prédal, 1968: 66.

60. About *Marienbad*, Alain Prédal wrote: "It remains however that this film is presented like a true psychoanalytic session". On this point see Prédal, 1968: 66-68.

61. Léon Grinberg, *Bulletin de Psychologie* 12-17 (July-August 1978). Quoted by Oms, 78.

62. This is the title of chapter V of Prédal's book ("Objets plus parlants que les êtres") analyzing mainly the central role of the statue in the garden of *Last Year in Marienbad*.

63. Also known as the Schleissheim Castle.

64. On a very different level, another spider web structure of Proust's work, with madness in its center, has also been studied in Gilles Deleuze's excellent book *Proust et les signes* See the conclusion of this book entitled "Présence et fonction de la folie: l'Araignée," 205-219.

65. *Les Jeunes filles en fleur* (Paris: Gallimard, la Pléiade, 1963), I, 579-581. Quoted and analyzed by Deleuze in *Proust et les signes*, 1964: 30.

66. The word "mannequin" in French is used both for a model and a dummy.

67. Introduction to the transcript of *The Sorrow and the Pity*, XXIV-XXV.

68. James R. MacBean, 1975: 255. Quoted by Avisar, 19.

69. Quoted by Tom Bower, 93-94.

70. Following his lawyer's advice, Klaus Barbie remained silent and refused to attend his own trial until, in agreement with the French law, he was forced to come to the court house of Lyon to hear his sentencing.

71. American TV crews left Lyon as soon as they realized Barbie would not attend his own trial.

72. In 1940 Jean Moulin was *préfet* of the *départment* of the Eure-et-Loire. He refused to sign a German declaration accusing colonial battalions of the French army of committing crimes against civilians in Chartres. While imprisoned, he tried to commit suicide. Accused of being a Freemason, he was revoked and then joined de Gaulle in London. Made head of the Résistance, he was parachuted into France with the mission of unifying and organizing the underground forces on the French territory itself. In 1943, he succeeded in having the Communist forces join the *Directoire de la Résistance*. He was betrayed, arrested and tortured in Lyon. According to French or German sources, he died either in Lyon, while he was being tortured by Barbie and his accomplices, or in the train that was deporting him to Germany. To this date, no one has been able to prove who betrayed Jean Moulin even if heavy suspicions have been put on René Hardy for several years by the French Résistance.

73. See for example, Tom Bower, *Klaus Barbie: The Butcher of Lyons*.

74. On this point, see the chapter entitled "Qu'est-ce que le classicisme?" in René Prédal's *Louis Malle*, 53-71.

75. Term used by Malle to characterize his adaptation to the screen of Queneau's novel *Zazie dans le métro*. (quoted by Prédal, 1989: 43).

76. Louis Malle, *Positif* 320, October 1987. Quoted by Prédal, 1989: 152.

77. Louis Malle, *Cinéma 62/63*, February 1962. Quoted by Prédal, 1989: 54.

78. "People who agonize don't act, people who act don't agonize." Pierre Sauvage. Interview with Bill Moyers, PBS.

79. Michael Berenbaum. Unpublished paper presented at the Association of Holocaust Organizations (U.S.) in Dallas, June 17, 1987. Quoted by Pierre Sauvage in his address to the International Scholars' Conference at Oxford University, England, July 10-13, 1988.

80. Michael Berenbaum "The Americanization of the Holocaust" *Tikkun* Vol. I, No. 2. Quoted by Laurence Jarvik.

81. Pierre Sauvage quoted by Laurence Jarvik. See also *New York Magazine* (September 18, 1989).

INDEX

ABOUT THE AUTHOR

ANDRE PIERRE COLOMBAT is an Assistant Professor of French at Loyola College in Baltimore. He was born and grew up in Roanne, France, near Lyon, the capital of the French Resistance, and Vichy, the capital of the French Collaboration during World War II. After the khâgne in Lyon, he received his Licence and Maîtrise in Modern Literature from the Université Lyon II, and his Ph.D. from Washington University in Saint Louis. In 1985 he attended the philosopher Gilles Deleuze's seminar on Michel Foucault in Paris. He taught for two years at the Universidad Nacional Autónoma de Honduras in Tegucigalpa. He has lectured and published various articles on French literature and civilization. His latest book is entitled *Deleuze et la littérature* (Peter Lang, 1991). He is currently working on the implications of Gilles Deleuze's seminal books on cinema for contemporary film studies.